FORGOTTEN HOME APOTHECARY

250
Powerful Remedies
at Your Fingertips

Nicole Apelian, Ph.D.

© 2024 Global Brother SRL
All rights reserved

This book is protected by copyright.
Subject to statutory exception and to the provision of relevant collective licensing agreements, no reproduction of any part may take place without the written permission of the publisher.

DISCLAIMER

The information contained in this book, including any reference to plants, herbs, fungi, remedies, herbal remedies, and other is strictly provided for informational, entertainment, and educational purposes only. It is not intended nor shall be intended as a replacement or substitute for professional medical advice, diagnosis, or treatment of any kind of health or wellness related matter whatsoever. Statements have not been evaluated by the Food and Drug Administration and are not intended to diagnose, treat, cure, or prevent any disease or medical condition. Use of the terms "disease" and "medical condition" are general statements about disease prevention and medical conditions that do not refer explicitly or implicitly to a specific disease, condition, class of diseases or condition, or to a specific product or ingredient. BY READING THIS BOOK, YOU HEREBY AGREE TO BE BOUND BY THIS DISCLAIMER, OR YOU MAY RETURN THIS BOOK WITHIN THE GUARANTEED TIME FOR A FULL REFUND.

Not a Substitute for Medical Treatment:

The plants, herbs, fungi, remedies and herbal remedies discussed in this book are not to be considered as alternatives or substitutes for professional medical treatment, illness or disease prevention, including but not limited to any diagnosis, cure, medications and treatments such as chemotherapy, radiation, or any other medical procedure, methods or therapies used to treat cancers or any other illness, disease, virus, infection or other medical conditions.

Consult Healthcare Professionals:

Always seek advice of a physician or other healthcare professional with any question you may have regarding any actual or potential disease, injury, symptoms, medical concerns or any other condition related to health and wellness. Do not disregard professional, medical advice, medical standards, or delay in seeking any treatment or advice based on anything in this book.

No Medical Claims:

This book does not and shall not be use or considered to be used as an authority on any diagnosis, treatment, cure, or prevention of any disease, virus, infection, or medical condition whatsoever. Information provided herein are ideas and information on ideas that are being provided based on some traditional, folklore, rumors, and/or old-fashioned uses of plants, herbs, and fungi and is for entertainment purposes only and should not be interpreted as an endorsement of usefulness, efficacy of anything reported or discussed.

Use with Caution:

While some plants, herbs, fungi or alternatives disclosed in the book may offer complementary benefits to overall well-being, any use should be approached with caution and under the guidance of a qualified healthcare professional, especially when being used with other medications and treatments. The contents herein shall not and shall never be used to replace professional medical advice.

Individual Reactions:

Everyone's health and response to foods, plants, fungi and treatments vary. Information provided in this book is general. It is not tailored to a specific health need of any individual nor does it consider any type of sensitivity, allergy, existing illness or conditions, or other possible side-effects one may have, including death. Therefore, it is crucial and necessary to consult with a healthcare professional before using any proposed treatment or remedy you chose as failure to do so may cause a counter reaction with other medicines, treatments or conditions, and may negatively affect tests, diagnoses, cures or treatments.

Liability Limitation:

The author and publisher of this book are not responsible for any adverse effects or consequences resulting from the use or appropriation of any suggestion, preparation, treatment or procedure discovered in the book. You acknowledge and agree that you are solely responsible for your health and well-being, and that you should consult with a healthcare professional before starting any treatment or therapy that relates to your life, health and wellness.

Medical Advice Disclaimer:

This book was created to provide a source of entertainment and information about natural medicines, proposed remedies or treatments, that people have alleged to have used or that could possibly have been used in the past. This information is made available with the understanding that the publisher, editor, and authors do not offer any legal or medical advice nor that any of the information contained herein is accurate or that any information is useful for any purpose. If you are not feeling well, are ill, have a medical condition, believe you may have a medical condition, illness or other, you should immediately consult a healthcare professional without delay.

Completeness Disclaimer:

This book does not contain nor claim to contain all information available on certain plants, herbs, fungi or remedies. While the authors, editor, and publisher have gone to great lengths to provide the most useful and accurate collection of information directed to healing plants and remedies in North America, the information is not verified, is folklore, it is outdated, it is erroneous, and contains typographical and content errors. This book must not and should not be used as a medical guide or reference.

Responsibility and Liability Disclaimer:

The authors, editor, and publisher shall incur no liability nor be held responsible to any person or entity regarding any loss of life or injury, alleged or otherwise, that happened directly or indirectly because of information in the book. It is you, the readers sole responsibility, to first consult with a physician or healthcare professional before attempting to make or use a potion, tincture, decoction, or other application from this book.

Compliance:

The information in the book has not been reviewed, tested, or approved by any official testing body, government, or agency and is intended for informational, entertainment, and educational purposes only.

No Guarantees:

The authors and editor of this book make no guarantees of any kind, expressed or implied, regarding the any result obtained by use of or applying information in this book. Making, using, consuming, modifying and/or distributing any of the products, elements, or remedies described herein are done at ones own risk.

Misuse and Misidentification Disclaimer:

The authors, editor, and publisher hold no responsibility for the use, misuse or misidentification of any plant, herb, treatment, or other because of any consequence to your health or health of others that may result therefrom.

Privacy Protection:

Some names and identifying details have been changed to protect the privacy of the authors and other individuals. By reading this book, you hereby agree to be bound by this disclaimer, or you may return this book within the guaranteed time for a full refund.

About the Author

Nicole Apelian, Ph.D.

Dr. Nicole Apelian is an herbalist, a mother, a survival skills instructor, an anthropologist, and a biologist. She graduated with a degree in Biology from McGill University in Canada and has her Master's degree in Ecology from the University of Oregon. She earned her Doctorate through Prescott College while working as an anthropologist and ethnobotanist in Botswana. She is also the author of "The Lost Book of Herbal Remedies: The Healing Power of Plant Medicine" Series (Books 1 and 2) "The Forager's Guide to Wild Foods: Edible Plants, Lichens, Mushrooms, and Seaweeds", "The Holistic Guide to Wellness: Herbal Protocols for Common Ailments", "Wilderness Long-Term Survival Guide: Forgotten Skills to Make the Wild Your Home", "A Reference Guide to Surviving Nature: Outdoor Preparation and Remedies", and her Online Herbal Academy (The Lost Skills Academy). For more about Nicole please visit www.nicoleapelian.com.

Nicole spent years living in nature with the San Bushmen of the Kalahari Desert, one of the last indigenous peoples who still live as hunter-gatherers. Developing strong relationships within the tribe helped Nicole learn many of the remedies and skills she practices and teaches today.

An unexpected diagnosis of multiple sclerosis in 2000 led Nicole to apply her research skills toward her own personal wellness. She focuses on a healthy living strategy, including deep nature connection and gratitude practices. Through changes in her lifestyle, recognizing profound mind-body linkages, and making and using her own remedies, Nicole went from bedridden to being fully alive and from surviving to thriving.

She believes that there are many more people suffering who need to find their own remedy. This became her life's mission and her primary reason for writing. She pours over 30 years of plant knowledge and her first-hand experiences of making her own poultices, tinctures, decoctions, salves, infused oils, and other herbal remedies. She has helped thousands of people treat themselves naturally by following her holistic wellness protocols and by using herbal remedies.

In 2015 she was among the first women ever selected for the History Channel's hit TV show "Alone". Despite having MS, she went on to survive solo for 57 days straight in a remote area of Vancouver Island with little more than her hunting knife and the wild foods and medicines she found there.

Dr. Nicole Apelian's knowledge was key to this recipe book. Many of the plants, lichens, and mushrooms you'll find here are ones that she's used with great results. She has selected some of the best for people wanting to utilize natural medicine. These remedies are part of a holistic philosophy of being self-reliant - of connecting your mind with your body and your body with nature.

Here's to thriving!

You've taken an amazing first step in learning about herbal remedies by purchasing this book. The next step is using your new knowledge. I want to help you by inviting you to join my Survive & Thrive community. Go to the link below to join my private email list and become part of the Survive & Thrive Crew.
Use this link: www.nicoleapelian.com to *join now!*

Forgotten Home Apothecary

Table of Contents

Disclaimer 2

Table of Contents 4

Introduction 13

Part 1: Setting Up Your Herbal Apothecary 14

Sourcing Quality Herbs and Ingredients............15

Choosing the Right Equipment and Supplies 17

Storage and Preservation.................18

Part 2: The Basics: Herbal Preparation and Use 20

Teas, Infusions, Decoctions, Sun brews..23

Tincture Making........26

Oil Infusions................29

Oxymels........................31

Syrups and Elixirs.......32

Lozenges, Gummies, and Capsules..............34

Balms, Salves, Creams, and Lotions..................36

Baths and Steams........39

Essential Oils and Hydrosols.....................42

Musculoskeletal Health 168

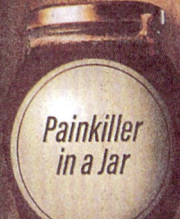 Painkiller in a Jar
169

 Amish Ibuprofen
170

 Cartilage Support Cream
171

 Comfrey and Lavender Herbal Oil for Joint Support
172

 "Better Than Collagen"
173

 Herbal Liniment for Sports Injuries and Strains
174

 Grandma's Hot Salve for Back Pain
175

 Mobility Maintenance Tincture for Arthritis
176

 Joint Pain Reliever
177

 Three Herb Poultice for Arthritis Pain
178

 Anti-Inflammatory Tincture for Joints
179

 DIY Relieving Balm
180

 Pineapple Painkilling Extract
181

 Backyard Calming Pills
182

 Magnesium Rub for Leg Cramps
183

 Fermented Red Clover (Can Help You Rebuild Bone Mass)
184

 Dandelion Salve for Sore Muscles and Joints
185

 Watercress Broth to Strengthen Your Joints and Bones
186

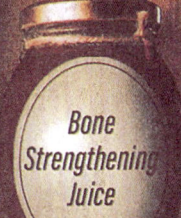 Bone Strengthening Juice
187

 Cabbage "Socks" for Inflammation and Joint Pain
188

Pine Needle Infused Oil (for Rheumatism and Arthritis Pain)
189

Willow Bark Bath Salts for Inflammation
190

Patches with Nature's "Ibuprofen"
191

Soothing Herbal Blend for Fibromyalgia Pain
192

Immune System 193

 Immune Boosting Elderberry Syrup
194

 Turmeric Golden Milk (Anti-Inflammatory)
195

"Penicilin" Soup
196

 Echinacea and Astragalus Tincture (for a Strong Immune System)
197

 Antiviral Herbal Honey
198

Immunity Mushroom Blend
199

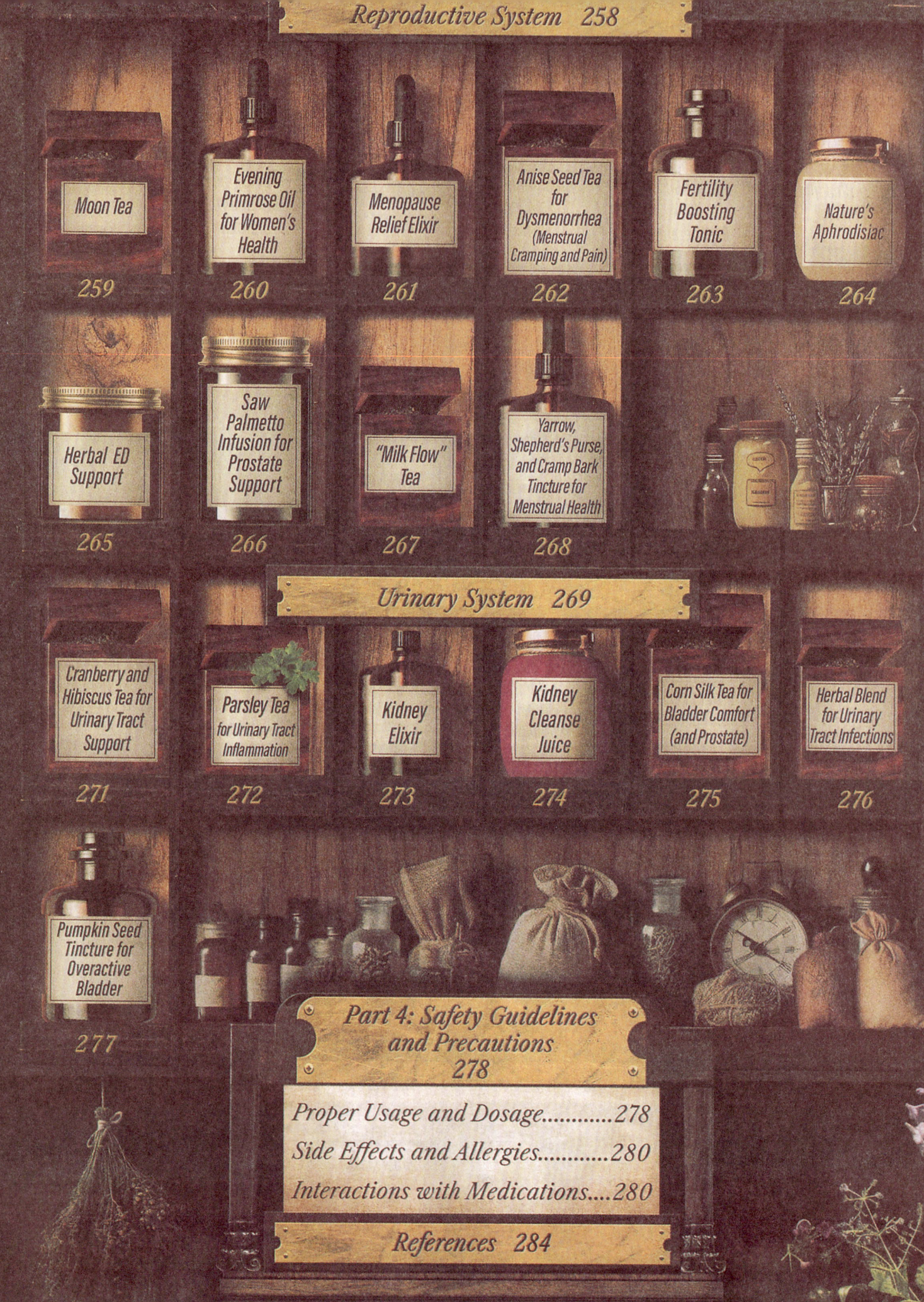

INTRODUCTION

Despite our fast-paced, disconnected modern lives and the constant barrage of synthetic medications and quick-fix remedies, the science and art of herbal healing has stood the test of time, offering us a bridge to nature's bounty.

This book stands as a testament to the remarkable synergy between nature and the human body, offering a wealth of recipes tailored to address your specific needs. Whether you're seeking relief for a troublesome tummy, a soothing balm for tired muscles, or a calming elixir to ease a restless mind, there's an herbal recipe within these pages to guide you on your quest for wellness.

Inside "The Forgotten Home Apothecary," you'll discover:

The principles of holistic wellness
that go beyond merely managing symptoms, seeking to restore balance to your entire being.

Insightful and fun guidance
on understanding how to set up your own home apothecary.

The tools to take charge of your well-being,
fostering a sense of self-empowerment in managing your wellness journey.

Practical tips
for sourcing, harvesting, and storing herbs to preserve their potency.

A diverse collection of over 200 herbal recipes,
meticulously crafted to address specific needs for each part of the body.

Step-by-step instructions and illustrative images
to ensure you can create herbal preparations with confidence.

Wisdom on blending herbs
to achieve synergistic effects, enhancing their individual virtues.

An exploration of the mind-body connection
and how herbal remedies can support emotional and mental well-being.

Essential guidance on using herbs safely,
particularly if you have allergies, medical conditions, or are taking medications.

Whether you are a novice herbalist or an experienced practitioner, it is our sincere hope that this book will be your trusted guide as you unlock the boundless potential of herbal remedies for a healthier, more vibrant life.

Setting Up Your
HERBAL APOTHECARY

SOURCING
Quality Herbs and Ingredients

Most herbal apothecaries require a few basic ingredients. Generally, this includes the herbs themselves plus solvents and other staples like honey or glycerin, vodka or brandy, apple cider vinegar, beeswax, Epsom salts, olive oil/other carrier oils, and glass jars/bottles.

There's a lot you can do with only herbs and water, but these other ingredients greatly expand your possibilities and shelf life. Those topics will be discussed in greater detail in Part 2. For now, let's focus on the herbs.

Whether you're an experienced herbalist or a beginner, knowing how to find and select quality herbs is key to creating potent herbal remedies.

Here are some steps and tips to help you find and select the best herbs:

UNDERSTAND THE IMPORTANCE OF QUALITY

In the world of herbal apothecaries, sourcing high-quality herbs and ingredients is essential to ensure the potency and effectiveness of your herbal preparations. High-quality herbs contain a higher concentration of active compounds, making them more potent and effective.

If you are going to put the time and energy into crafting your own home apothecary, you want to make sure that the spices and herbs you are sourcing are of the highest quality.

Whether you're shopping for herbs online, in your local natural foods co-op, herb shop, or farmers' market, it's important to assess various quality indicators to ensure the highest standards. These indicators include:

- *Appearance:* Inspect the herbs for fresh, vibrant colors, intact leaves, and no signs of mold or contamination. Plant material degrades when exposed to air, and a poorly sealed container may permit moisture to seep inside, allowing mold to grow or pantry pests to invade.
- *Aroma:* High-quality herbs have a strong, distinct aroma and scent that indicates freshness and potency. Dried plant matter tends to fade and become less aromatic as it ages.
- *Texture:* The texture of herbs should be crisp, not brittle or overly dry, indicating that they have been properly stored.

LOCAL AND SUSTAINABLE SOURCING

Opting for organic and sustainably sourced herbs and ingredients is not only beneficial for the environment but also for the quality of your herbal remedies. Organic herbs are grown without the use of synthetic pesticides or fertilizers, ensuring a purer and more potent end product. Additionally, choosing herbs that have been sustainably harvested helps support biodiversity and the long-term availability of these precious resources.

When it comes to buying bulk spices and herbs, it is always a good idea to first look at what you can purchase right within your own local community. Sourcing herbs and ingredients locally not only supports local farmers but also cultivates a deep connection between the apothecary and its surroundings.

So whenever possible, consider sourcing herbs locally or from sustainable farms (or growing your own). This supports local economies and reduces the carbon footprint associated with transportation. Look for suppliers who prioritize sustainable farming practices. By establishing relationships with them, you can gain firsthand knowledge about their cultivation practices and ensure the freshness and quality of the herbs you acquire. Visiting local farmers' markets or participating in community-supported agriculture programs can help you establish these connections.

There is no doubt that this isn't always possible for everyone, so if you are seeking a specific herb or plant that isn't available or cannot be grown in your area, you can, of course, take advantage of the wonders of our global food system by sourcing bulk herbs and spices online. But start local and expand from there.

RESEARCH RELIABLE SUPPLIERS

Remember that the quality of your ingredients is a critical factor in the success of your apothecary, so invest time and effort into finding the best suppliers.

To ensure consistent quality, it is essential to find reliable suppliers for your herbs and ingredients. Look for suppliers who have a good reputation, are transparent about their sourcing methods, and provide detailed information about the quality of their products. How were the herbs grown? Were they grown organically and with care for the land? Were they harvested at the right time of their growth cycle and in the right season?

Before placing a large order, consider doing a trial order or request samples to assess the quality of the herbs and ingredients, the shipping time, and the overall experience with the supplier. This allows you to assess the herbs firsthand before committing to a supplier. Online directories, industry networks, and recommendations from other herbalists are valuable resources in finding reputable suppliers. Depending on the products you want to create, consider working with suppliers that offer a wide variety of herbs and ingredients to meet your needs.

And don't forget to establish relationships. Building good relationships with your suppliers can lead to better deals, priority access to new or rare herbs, and a deeper understanding of their sourcing practices. Regular communication can help you stay informed about new arrivals, seasonal availability, and any potential issues.

REQUEST CERTIFICATES OF ANALYSIS

To have complete confidence in the quality of your herbs and ingredients, request certificates of analysis (COAs) from your suppliers. COAs provide detailed information about the botanical identity, purity, and potency of the herbs, ensuring transparency and accountability. It's advisable to work with suppliers who can provide these documents upon request.

Check if the suppliers have relevant certifications, such as organic, non-GMO, or Fair Trade. These certifications can indicate that the herbs and ingredients are produced under specific quality standards. A certified organic seal is also important, as organically grown herbs are highly preferable to those sprayed with chemicals.

CONSIDER GROWING YOUR OWN HERBS

For ultimate control over the quality of your ingredients, consider growing your own herbs. This allows you to ensure organic cultivation practices, harvest at the peak of potency, and provide the freshest herbs for your apothecary. Depending on your available space and resources, you can start with a small herb garden or even explore hydroponics or indoor gardening options.

WILD HARVESTING

While wild harvesting can be a sustainable and rewarding way to obtain resources, it's important to approach it with care and respect for the environment. Here are some key points to keep in mind when harvesting medicinal plants:

- *Identification:* Ensure you can accurately identify the plant you intend to harvest. Mistaking a similar-looking plant for the desired one can have serious consequences, as some plants are toxic and even life-threatening.
- *Sustainability:* Only harvest from abundant populations and follow ethical guidelines to prevent overharvesting. Some plants are endangered or at risk due to excessive harvesting, so it's important to research and understand the plant's status before collecting. Replant, if possible, tending the wild.
- *Legal Regulations:* Check local, state, and national regulations regarding the harvesting of medicinal plants. Some plants may be protected or require permits for collection.
- *Timing:* Harvest at the appropriate time to ensure maximum potency. This is an important step when you harvest your homegrown herbs as well. Different parts of the plant may need to be harvested at specific stages of growth:
  — *Leaves and Flowers:* Leaves are usually harvested right before a plant blooms, and flowers are best harvested the day they open. Collect them on dry mornings after the dew has evaporated.
  — *Roots:* Harvest roots in the plant's dormant season, usually in the fall after the leaves have died back. Carefully dig around the root to avoid damaging it.
  — *Bark:* Harvest bark in the spring when sap is rising or in the fall when the plant is preparing to go dormant.
- *Tools:* Use proper tools to minimize damage to the plant and its surrounding environment. Sharp, clean tools reduce stress on the plant and prevent the spread of diseases.
- *Quantity:* Only harvest what you need. Taking more than necessary can harm the plant population and ecosystem.
- *Habitat:* Be mindful of the plant's habitat. Choose natural sites, far away from traffic and dump sites. Car exhaust, herbicides sprayed to control weeds, and other pollutants can contaminate herbs grown along the roadside. Minimize disturbance to the surrounding environment, avoid trampling other plants, and leave no major trace of your presence.
- *Processing:* Process the harvested plant material promptly to maintain its medicinal properties. Proper drying, cleaning, and storing methods are crucial.
- *Ethical Considerations:* Respect the land and the communities that rely on these plants. Traditional knowledge and practices of indigenous peoples should be acknowledged and respected.
- *Record Keeping:* Maintain records of when, where, and how you harvested the plants. This information can be valuable for future reference.
- *Safety:* Wear appropriate clothing and protective gear to prevent allergies or skin irritations that some plants may cause.

Remember, proper harvesting practices are vital to maintaining the balance of ecosystems and ensuring the availability of medicinal plants for generations to come. If you're unsure about any aspect of harvesting, it's wise to seek guidance from experts, local botanists, or herbalists. Sourcing quality herbs is an ongoing process. Whether you choose to source from trusted suppliers or grow your own herbs, prioritizing quality will help you create exceptional products for you or your valued customers.

Choosing
the Right Equipment and Supplies

Setting up an herbal apothecary involves careful consideration of equipment and supplies to ensure you can efficiently and effectively prepare and store herbal remedies. However, your home apothecary can be as simple or elaborate as you like. The specific items you need will depend on the types of herbal preparations you plan to make, your space, and your budget.

It's also a good idea to start with the basics and gradually expand your collection as your skills and needs evolve, but don't forget to always prioritize quality and hygiene.

Here's a comprehensive list of items you might need:

Equipment and Supplies

- Dropper or regular-topped dark-colored glass bottles
- Glass jars with tight-fitting lids
- Kitchen scale
- Mixing bowls
- Mortar and pestle
- Spice grinder
- Funnels
- Cheesecloth, muslin bags, or nut milk bags for straining
- Saucepans
- Crockpot or double boiler
- Measuring cups and spoons
- Glass measuring cups
- Spatula
- Kitchen scissors
- Cutting boards
- Blender/ food processor

- Dehydrator for controlled and efficient drying or drying racks/ hanging lines for air-drying herbs
- Tea kettle/french press
- Tea canvas bags
- Teapots, tea infusers
- Salve or balm containers with lids
- Sharp knives
- Pocket knife
- Magnifying glass 10x for accurate plant identification
- Foraging bag
- Foraging scissors
- Labels and pens
- Notebooks and pens for documenting recipes, observations, and experiments
- Essential oil distiller (for those interested in making their own oils)

Forgotten Home Apothecary

Storage and Preservation

The active ingredients in herbs are volatile oils and other chemical constituents. As powerful as these constituents are, they are easily destroyed by light, air, and heat. To get and maintain the best quality of herbs, it's necessary to take care from the initial sourcing of the herb and how they are harvested, to how they are prepared, stored, and used.

Properly storing and preserving herbs is crucial to maintain their potency and effectiveness in creating herbal remedies.

DRYING HERBS

Drying is one of the most common methods for preserving herbs. Proper drying prevents mold and preserves the medicinal properties of the herbs:

The first and probably the most important step is to wash the herbs before drying. Dirt and bacteria will decay the herbs, making them unsuitable for storage or medicinal use. Wash them in cold running water to get rid of the dirt, shake out any excess water, and pat dry before attempting to dry them.

Here are some guidelines to help you store and preserve herbs:

- *Air Drying:* Tie a small bundle of herbs together with a string or rubber band. Hang them upside down in a warm, well-ventilated area out of direct sunlight. Make sure the bundles are not too thick to allow proper air circulation. This can take several days to a couple of weeks, depending on the herb and humidity levels. To air dry herbs successfully, the temperature needs to be above 85°F with humidity below 60%.
- *Drying Racks:* Use a mesh or wire rack to provide adequate air circulation around the herbs. Place the herbs on the rack in a single layer. This method is especially useful if you have limited hanging space. Drying takes about 1-2 weeks, but always check them for moisture before storing. Baskets also work well.
- *Brown Paper Bags:* Place herbs in a single layer inside a brown paper bag and loosely close the top. Hang the bag in a well-ventilated area.
- *Screen Drying:* Lay herbs on a clean, dry screen or mesh. Elevate the screen slightly to allow air to circulate beneath it. This method works well for delicate herbs like chamomile flowers.
- *Oven Drying:* Use the lowest possible oven temperature (usually around 100-110°F or 37-43°C) for a few hours with the oven door slightly ajar to allow moisture to escape. Place herbs on a baking sheet lined with parchment paper. Monitor closely to prevent over-drying.
- *Microwave:* Place herbs between paper towels and microwave them in short bursts (10-20 seconds at a time) on a low setting. Be cautious, as herbs can easily burn in the microwave. This is not a method I personally use.
- *Dehydrator:* Follow the manufacturer's instructions for herb drying settings. Dehydrators provide controlled temperature and air circulation, making them a convenient option. Herbs are dried within 1-4 hours, depending on the type of herb. Keep checking the trays and take out any herbs that are ready. This works especially well for roots, mushrooms, and berries (always slice your roots and mushrooms before drying).

Different herbs have varying moisture content and optimal drying methods, so it's a good idea to research the specific herbs you're working with. Properly dried herbs can provide a burst of flavor and fragrance to your culinary creations or potent medicinal benefits to your herbal remedies.

REMOVING MOISTURE

Ensure that the herbs are completely dry before storage. Herbs with residual moisture are prone to mold and spoilage. You can check the dryness by crushing a leaf or stem – it should easily crumble.

STORAGE CONTAINERS

Once the herbs are completely dry, store them in airtight containers. Ensure the jars are clean and completely dry before adding herbs in order to prevent mold growth. Avoid plastic, as it can trap moisture and degrade the herbs.

Choose jars that are appropriately sized for the quantity of herbs you're storing, leaving minimal air space.

LABELING

Label each container with the herb's name, the date of harvest or drying, and any other relevant information, such as the part of the plant used (leaves, flowers, roots). This helps you keep track of freshness and potency.

DARKNESS

Store your herb containers away from direct sunlight. Store them in a cool, dark place, such as a cupboard or pantry. Light can degrade the quality of the herbs over time.

TEMPERATURE AND HUMIDITY

Herbs should be stored in a place with consistent temperature and humidity levels. Avoid storing herbs near stoves, ovens, or other sources of heat and moisture, as well as in areas prone to temperature fluctuations. High temperatures and exposure to humidity can cause herbs to deteriorate and lose their flavor and medicinal properties.

GRINDING AND PROCESSING

Grind herbs into powder or smaller pieces only when you're ready to use them. This helps retain their freshness and potency. You can use a mortar and pestle or an electric herb grinder.

FREEZING

Some herbs may be frozen to preserve their freshness. This method is particularly useful for herbs that you intend to use in culinary dishes. Wash and dry the herbs, chop them if needed, and place them in airtight containers or freezer bags. Label and date the containers.

CHECKING FOR FRESHNESS

Regularly check stored herbs for any signs of mold, off odors, or discoloration. If you notice any of these, discard the herbs. If properly stored, there should be no color change or bad smells.

> Remember that different herbs may have slightly different storage requirements due to variations in moisture content, volatile compounds, and other factors. By following these guidelines and paying attention to the unique characteristics of each herb, you can ensure that your stored herbs remain potent and effective for your herbal remedies.

Forgotten Home Apothecary

The Basics:
HERBAL PREPARATION AND USE

There are a wide variety of natural remedies available, each derived from different plants, herbs, minerals, and other natural sources. These remedies have been used for centuries in traditional medicine systems and are still used today for various health and wellness purposes.

Although herbs may be taken whole, preparing them with a solvent, such as water, alcohol, vinegar, or glycerin, helps to extract the constituents from fibrous plant material that may otherwise pass through the body.

SOLVENTS/MENSTRUUM

Solvents are substances used to extract beneficial compounds from herbs, plants, or other natural sources in the process of creating various natural remedies. Different solvents are chosen based on the specific compounds being extracted and the intended use of the remedy.

Here are some common solvents used in natural remedies:

- *Water:* Water is one of the most common solvents used in creating herbal infusions and decoctions. It's especially effective for extracting water-soluble compounds such as vitamins, minerals, and certain plant constituents.
- *Alcohol:* Alcohol is commonly used to make tinctures, which are concentrated liquid extracts of herbs. Alcohol can extract components, such as resins and alkaloids, that are not water-soluble. Alcohol is particularly effective at preserving the extracted compounds and has a long shelf life.
- *Glycerin:* Glycerin is often used as an alternative to alcohol for creating glycerites. Glycerites are suitable for people who want to avoid alcohol or have alcohol sensitivities. Glycerin is a good solvent for extracting some plant constituents, but it may not extract all compounds as effectively as alcohol. It has a shorter shelf-life as well.
- *Vinegar:* Vinegar is used to make herbal vinegars, which are mild acidic extracts. It is effective at extracting minerals and some alkaloids, making it a suitable solvent for certain herbs.
- *Oil:* Oils like olive oil, coconut oil, and other carrier oils are used for making herbal infused oils. This method is particularly useful for extracting fat-soluble compounds, essential oils, and aromatic compounds from herbs.
- *Honey:* Honey can be used as a solvent to create honey-based herbal remedies. While not as commonly used as other solvents, honey can extract some water-soluble compounds and has health benefits of its own.
- *Milk:* In some traditional remedies, milk is used as a solvent to extract specific compounds. This is less common and may be culturally specific.

The choice of solvent depends on several factors, including the type of compounds you want to extract, the intended use of the remedy, personal preferences such as avoiding alcohol, and the traditions or methods you follow. It's important to research and understand the specific properties of each solvent and how they interact with the compounds in the herbs you're working with to create effective and safe natural remedies.

FRESH HERBS VS. DRIED HERBS

The decision to use medicinal herbs, dried or fresh, depends on the specific herbs and the compounds you are looking to extract for their therapeutic benefits. Keep in mind that some herbs can be used both dried and fresh, but the choice may affect the concentration and potency of their active compounds. It's important to research each herb's characteristics, traditional uses, and methods of preparation to determine whether using it dried or fresh is more appropriate for your intended purposes.

Forgotten Home Apothecary

Let's explore the differences between the two:

FRESH HERBS:

- *Potency:* Fresh herbs contain higher water content and volatile oils, which can result in more potent and aromatic medicinal properties. These properties can be beneficial when seeking immediate relief or intense flavors in teas, tinctures, or poultices. As a general rule, double or triple the amount of herbs if using fresh herbs for tea instead of dry.
- *Nutritional Value:* Fresh herbs generally retain more of their nutritional content, including vitamins and minerals, due to their minimal processing.
- *Visual Appeal:* Fresh herbs are visually appealing and can add a vibrant touch to dishes, remedies, or displays.
- *Availability:* Depending on the region and season, fresh herbs may or may not be available year-round. Some herbs are more sensitive to weather conditions and may be harder to find during certain times of the year.
- *Short Shelf Life:* Fresh herbs have a limited shelf life and can spoil quickly if not used promptly. Proper storage techniques, such as refrigeration or growing them at home, can help extend their usability.

DRIED HERBS:

- *Concentration:* Drying herbs removes water, concentrating the active compounds responsible for their medicinal effects. This can make dried herbs more suitable for longer-term use and for creating potent extracts or capsules. Always check safety information to determine whether your herb is safe to consume fresh, as some plants are toxic unless dried or cooked.
- *Longevity:* Dried herbs have a much longer shelf life compared to fresh herbs. They can be stored for months to years without losing their potency, provided they are kept in a cool, dark, and dry place. This can be valuable for maintaining a well-stocked apothecary and ensuring the availability of herbs year-round.
- *Convenience:* Dried herbs are readily available year-round and can be used at any time, regardless of the herb's growing season.
- *Ease of Storage and Transport:* Dried herbs are lightweight, compact, and easy to store, making them convenient for creating herbal blends, tinctures, and teas in advance.
- *Flavor Evolution:* While drying concentrates flavors, it can also cause some subtle changes in flavor profiles as certain volatile compounds may be altered during the drying process.

In an apothecary, it's common to have a combination of both fresh and dried herbs. The choice will depend on the specific remedies, products, or applications you're working with and the qualities you're looking to achieve.

Teas, Infusions, Decoctions, Sun Brews

In the captivating world of herbal concoctions, a diverse range of methods bring herbs to life, each offering its own unique flavors, aromas, and health benefits. Here's a breakdown of the key differences between herbal teas, infusions, decoctions, and sun brews and how to prepare them:

Herbal Teas

Herbal teas, also known as tisanes, are perhaps the most well-known form of herbal concoctions. For beginning herbalists, creating herbal tea blends is a simple and accessible way to become more comfortable working with herbs and plants. They offer a delightful and simple way to enjoy the flavors and benefits of various herbs.

Be aware that while it's acceptable to refer to all herbs brewed in water as "tea," true tea is made from leaves of the tea plant *Camellia sinensis*. Black, green, white, oolong, matcha, and all other true teas are made from this plant and have simply been processed in different ways. Tisanes are teas that don't contain leaves of *Camellia sinensis*. Instead, they are infusions made from the flowers, leaves, roots, or berries of other plants. By nature, herbal teas are caffeine-free, unlike black, green, white, and oolong teas derived from *Camellia sinensis*, which are naturally caffeinated.

Herbal blends often have medicinal properties and can be used to manage everything from sore throats to upset stomachs. So whether you're seeking relaxation, a boost in immunity, or simply a comforting drink, making herbal tea is an easy and rewarding process.

Here's a step-by-step guide to help you prepare a delicious cup of herbal tea:

KEY FEATURES:

- Quick and simple preparation.
- Delicate herbs like chamomile, peppermint, and lavender are commonly used.
- Brewed with hot water, usually at or near boiling point.
- Steeping time is generally 5-10 minutes.
- Offers a soothing and aromatic experience, often enjoyed for relaxation.

INGREDIENTS:

- Fresh or dried herbs of your choice: about 1 teaspoon for dried herbs or 2 teaspoons for fresh herbs per 8-ounce cup of boiling water.

INSTRUCTIONS:

1 | **Choose Your Herbs:** Select the herbs you'd like to use based on your desired flavor and benefits. Crush the herbs in your hand or with a mortar and pestle to help weaken the plant's cell walls.

2 | **Boil Water:** Boil fresh, filtered water. The temperature will depend on the type of herb you're using. Generally, use boiling water for hardy herbs like peppermint and ginger and slightly cooler water (around 190°F or 90°C) for delicate herbs like chamomile.

3 | **Prepare the Herbs:** If using loose herbs, place the desired amount into a tea infuser or strainer. If you're using teabags, simply place the teabag in your cup or teapot.

4 | **Infuse the Herbs:** Pour the hot water over the herbs in the teapot or cup. Cover the teapot to trap the aromatic compounds and essential oils within.

Forgotten Home Apothecary

5 | Steep the Tea: Steeping time varies depending on the herb and factors such as desired flavor and strength. Let the herbs steep in the hot water for the recommended time:
- Delicate herbs like chamomile and lavender: 3-5 minutes.
- Hardy herbs like peppermint and ginger: 5-7 minutes. Steeping time can also vary based on personal preference, so you can adjust it to achieve the desired strength of flavor and potency.

6 | Strain and Enjoy: Once the tea has steeped, remove the infuser or strain the tea to separate the herbs from the liquid. Take a moment to inhale the wonderful aroma before taking your first sip.

7 | Optional Additions: Feel free to enhance your herbal tea with additional flavorings:
- Sweeteners: Raw honey, maple syrup, or stevia for a touch of sweetness.
- Citrus: A slice of lemon, lime, or orange can add a zesty twist.
- Spices: A dash of cinnamon, cardamom, or cloves can introduce warming notes.

8 | Relax and Savor: Find a cozy spot, take a deep breath, and enjoy your freshly brewed herbal tea. Let its flavors and soothing effects wash over you, offering a moment of tranquility in your day.

By following these simple steps, you'll be able to prepare a delightful cup of herbal tea tailored to your preferences and needs. Experiment with different herbs and combinations to discover your favorite flavors and the potential health benefits they can provide.

Infusions

Infusions are a gentle form of extraction, allowing herbs to steep in hot water for an extended period, often several hours or overnight. An herbal infusion is made with a larger quantity of herbs. They are steeped in hot water for longer than when making an herbal tea. This produces a stronger-tasting and more potent drink.

KEY FEATURES:

- More prolonged steeping time, usually 4 hours to overnight.
- Use a larger quantity of herbs, making them stronger and more potent.
- Ideal for more delicate herbs like hibiscus, lemon balm, and elderflower.
- It is best used for aerial parts of a plant (flowers, leaves, buds, and berries)
- Yields a more potent flavor and stronger herbal essence.
- Beneficial compounds are gently extracted, resulting in a mild yet effective infusion.

INSTRUCTIONS:

1 | Place the herbs in a heatproof container (*e.g.* a glass jar).
2 | Pour boiling water over the herbs and cover the container with a lid or cloth to trap all the beneficial elements.
3 | Let steep for at least 4 hours or overnight for a stronger infusion.
4 | Strain the herbs. After leaving the herbal infusion to cool down, you can store it in the refrigerator for up to 2 days.

INGREDIENTS:

- 1 ounce (about 30 grams) of dried herbs per quart (950 ml) of boiling water.

Decoctions

Decoctions involve simmering tougher/woody plant parts like roots, bark, and seeds in water to extract their medicinal properties. Of course, for every rule there are exceptions. There are some dense plant materials that can be prepared as infusions with excellent results, such as licorice root, cinnamon bark, and valerian root.

NOTE:
Roots can be decocted several times before being composted or discarded.

KEY FEATURES:

- Involves simmering herbs in water for around 20-40 minutes.
- Best suited for robust plant materials like burdock root, dandelion root, and white willow bark.
- Extracts the deeper and hardier constituents of plants.
- Produces a rich and hearty brew with concentrated flavors and benefits.

INGREDIENTS:

- 1 ounce (about 30 grams) of dried herbs or 2 ounces of fresh herbs per quart (950 ml) of water.

INSTRUCTIONS:

1 | Place the herbs in a pot and add cold water.
2 | Slowly bring the mixture to a simmer and let it gently boil for 20-40 minutes.
3 | Strain the herbs and enjoy. You can also use the decoction as a base for other preparations, like syrups.

Sun Brews (Solar Infusions)

Sun brews, also called solar infusions, use the sun's warmth to gently extract flavors and properties from herbs over several hours.

KEY FEATURES:

- Utilizes the sun's energy to infuse herbs into water.
- Herbs are placed in a glass container with water and left in the sun for 4-6 hours.
- Ideal for delicate herbs and flowers like chamomile, rose petals, and lemon verbena.
- Offers a gentle infusion process, resulting in a subtle and refreshing taste.

INGREDIENTS:

- A handful of fresh or dried herbs per quart (950 ml) of cold water.

INSTRUCTIONS:

1 | Place the herbs in a clean glass jar.
2 | Fill the jar with cold water and cover it with a lid or cloth.
3 | Set the jar in direct sunlight for about 4-6 hours, allowing the herbs to infuse.
4 | Strain the herbs and refrigerate the sun brew for freshness. Drink within a day or two.

In summary, each method—herbal tea, infusion, decoction, and sun brew—offers a unique approach to extracting herbs. The choice of method depends on the type of herbs you're using, the specific compounds you're aiming to extract, and the flavor profile you desire. Experiment with different herbs and preparation methods to discover the flavors and benefits that suit your preferences and needs.

NOTE:
No matter the method used, you should try to use straight away. As water is the base and there is no preservative present, mold may form. They can be kept for 24-48 hours in the fridge.

Tincture Making

Tinctures extract a wider range of constituents than water-based infusions and can last for many years if stored properly. They are generally more concentrated than water infusions and are absorbed into the bloodstream more quickly. This is due to the alcohol base, which starts absorbing through the stomach wall and even through the mouth upon taking the tincture. Rather than being digested, like other things that are eaten and drunk, the herbs are absorbed directly into the bloodstream.

Water, alcohol, glycerin, or vinegar? What solvent should you use? Technically, all tinctures are extracts, but not all extracts are tinctures! To obtain a tincture, alcohol must be the solvent used to extract the herbal properties. You can, of course, use apple cider vinegar or food-grade vegetable glycerin. Essentially still a tincture, yet technically called an extract as it lacks alcohol. These often don't work as well for many herbs, and they don't last as long.

Here's everything you need to know about herbal tincture making:

INGREDIENTS AND MATERIALS:

- **Herbs:** Choose high-quality dried or fresh herbs. Different parts of the plant, such as leaves, flowers, roots, or bark, can be used, depending on the plant and its medicinal properties. Another factor to consider when choosing herbs is solubility. Alcohol can extract properties like alkaloids, sugars, enzymes, essential oils, minerals, and vitamins but precipitates the healing mucilage you may be trying to extract in herbs like marshmallow root (cold water infusion is the preferred method for marshmallow root).
- **Alcohol:** High-proof alcohol, typically vodka, brandy, or grain alcohol (at least 40% alcohol by volume = 80 proof), is used as a solvent to extract the active compounds from most dried and fresh herbs. You can use a higher percentage - 70% alcohol by volume - if you want to extract the most volatile aromatic properties. Good for fresh, high-moisture herbs like lemon balm, berries, and aromatic roots.
- **Glass Jar:** Use a clean glass jar with a tight-fitting lid. Dark-colored glass jars, such as amber or cobalt blue, help protect the tincture from light.
- **Labels:** Properly label your tincture jars with the herb's name, date of preparation, and alcohol used. This information is crucial for tracking and dosing.

Tincture Making Process:

SINGLE EXTRACTION TINCTURE

A single extraction tincture is a straightforward method of creating a tincture using a single solvent - alcohol. Here's how the process generally works:

1. **Selecting the Herb:** Choose the plant material (such as herbs, roots, berries, or other botanicals) that you want to extract.
2. **Preparation:** Chop, grind or crumble the plant material to increase its surface area and aid in the extraction process.
3. **Ratio:** The general rule of thumb is to use a 1:5 or 1:2 herb-to-alcohol ratio. For example, 1 part herb to 5 parts alcohol means 100 grams of herbs would require 500 milliliters of alcohol. However, the amount you put into the jar will depend on the type of plant material you are using:
   - Dried leaves and flowers: Fill around half of the jar.
   - Fresh leaves and flowers: Fill around three-quarters of the jar.
   - Dried roots, berries, bark: Fill around a quarter of the jar.
   - Fresh roots, berries, bar: Fill around half of the jar.
4. **Alcohol Soaking:** Pour the alcohol over the herbs, ensuring they are completely submerged. The alcohol should cover the herbs by an inch or more. If the herbs absorb the alcohol and expand, top off the jar. Leave ¼ to ½ inch of headspace at the top.

Forgotten Home Apothecary

5. **Maceration:** Seal the jar tightly and place it in a cool, dark place. Tinctures can take anywhere from 4 weeks up to 6 months to fully extract, depending on the herbs you are using. 2 months works well for most herbs. Shake the jar gently every day, if possible, or a few times a week to facilitate the extraction process. This is especially important when using powdered herbs.
6. **Straining:** After the maceration period, strain the liquid through a fine mesh strainer, cheesecloth, or muslin cloth into another clean glass container. Squeeze the herbs to extract as much liquid as possible.
7. **Bottling:** Transfer the strained liquid (now your herbal tincture) into amber or dark-colored glass dropper bottles. Label the bottles with the herb's name, date, and other relevant information.
8. **Storage:** Store your tinctures in a cool, dark place. Properly stored tinctures can last for several years.

DOUBLE EXTRACTION TINCTURE

A double extraction tincture (dual-extraction) involves a two-step process using both water and alcohol as solvents to extract a wider range of active compounds from the plant material. This method is often used when working with medicinal mushrooms and lichens. If only a water-based decoction is used with Reishi Mushroom, for example, it extracts the beneficial polysaccharides (including the betaglucans) and the glycoproteins but not the triterpenes (like ganoderic acid in Reishi), as they are not soluble in water. Both water and alcohol are needed to extract all of the medicinal compounds.

Method #1

Starting with the alcohol extraction

Feel free to scale down this recipe. You'll need 8 ounces (224g) or more of dried mushroom or lichen, 24 ounces (750ml) of 80 to 100 proof alcohol (40 to 50% alcohol), and 16 ounces (500ml) distilled water.

1. Fill a quart-sized (1 liter) canning jar half-full with diced dried mushrooms, then fill it to about 1/2 inch (1.25 cm) of the top with alcohol. Stir and cap it, shaking it every day for 2 months. Then strain out the alcohol and set it aside for later.
2. Make the water decoction. Put 16 ounces (500ml) of water into a ceramic or glass pot with a lid and put the mushrooms into it (you may use the same mushrooms you just strained). Cover and simmer the mixture until half of the water has boiled off. This will take a few hours. If the water level drops too quickly, add more so that you can continue simmering your mushrooms. The end result should be 8 ounces (250ml) of your decoction.
3. Allow the water to cool, and then strain out the mushrooms. Mix the water and alcohol (you should have about 24 oz (710ml) of alcohol tincture – thus your final ratio is 3:1 of alcoholic tincture to your decoction) together to create the finished double-extraction. It has a high enough alcohol content (~30%) that it should be shelf-stable for many years, as long as it is stored in a sealed container.

Method #2

Starting with the water extraction

You can use a crockpot for this recipe or place the herbs and water into a jar, which is then covered and placed into a crockpot of water on low or a pot of water on low on the stove. Feel free to scale down this recipe. You'll need 8 ounces (230g) or more of dried mushroom or lichen, 24 ounces (710ml) of 80 to 100-proof alcohol, and 16 ounces (500ml) of distilled water.

1. Cut up the herbs into very small pieces. Place the distilled water and the dried herbs into the crock-pot and stir well. Cover and cook on the lowest possible setting for 3 days. It will cook down to about 8 oz (250ml) of medicinal decoction (water).
2. Allow the herb and water mixture to cool slightly, and pour it into a large glass jar. Add the alcohol while the mixture is still quite warm but not hot. Make sure the jar is large enough that you are adding 24 ounces (710ml) of alcohol, or split everything evenly between 2 jars.
3. Cap the jar tightly, label and date the jar, and allow it to macerate for 6 to 8 weeks, shaking the jar daily.
4. Strain out the herb (cheesecloth works well for this) or carefully decant the tincture off. Store it in a tightly capped glass jar. Label and date.

Both single and double extraction tinctures have their uses in herbal medicine and natural remedies. The choice between the two methods depends on the specific properties of the herbal material and the desired therapeutic effects. It's important to note that making tinctures requires a good understanding of the plants being used, proper preparation techniques, and safety precautions to ensure the final product is safe and effective for use.

DOSAGE AND USAGE:

Dosages vary depending on the herb and the purpose of use. ½ to 1 teaspoon is a normal dose for adults. However, it's recommended to consult a qualified herbalist or healthcare professional for specific dosing instructions. In general, tinctures can be taken straight by the dropper (just under the tongue) or diluted in tea or water.

Similar to alcohol-based tinctures, liquid extracts can also be made using vinegar or glycerin as a solvent for a tastier option or for those who prefer not to use or are sensitive to alcohol. Herbal vinegars and glycerites are typically less potent than alcohol tinctures as they do not extract as many active constituents, and while they are more shelf-stable than infusions and decoctions, they have a shorter shelf life than tinctures.

Glycerites

Glycerites, or herbal glycerin extracts, are liquid herbal preparations that use glycerin as the solvent instead of alcohol. Vegetable glycerin is a clear, odorless liquid produced from vegetable oils such as palm, soy, or coconut. While glycerin has a sweet taste, it is not metabolized by the body like sugar and will not spike blood sugar levels. These "tinctures" are a great alternative for those who want to avoid alcohol or for situations where alcohol consumption is not suitable, such as for children, individuals with alcohol sensitivities, or those in recovery.

Here's how to make a non-alcoholic glycerite:

INGREDIENTS:

- Dried or fresh herbs
- Vegetable glycerin
- Water

INSTRUCTIONS:

1. **Preparation:** Choose the herbs you want to use for your glycerite. Dried herbs are generally preferred to prevent microbial growth in the glycerin. If using fresh herbs, wilt them slightly to reduce moisture content.
2. **Herb Preparation:** If using dried herbs, chop or grind them to increase their surface area. This helps with the extraction process. If using fresh herbs, chop them finely.
3. **Mixing Glycerin and Water:** The glycerin used for making glycerites is typically vegetable glycerin, which is sweet and acts as a natural preservative. For the solvent mixture, a common ratio is a 3:1 ratio = 75% glycerin and 25% water. This helps create a balanced extract that both extracts the herbal constituents and prevents spoilage.
4. **Extraction:** Fill the jar with clean, chopped fresh plant material or half-full of ground dried plant material and cover them with the glycerin-water mixture. Stir to ensure the herbs are fully saturated.
5. **Maceration:** Seal the jar and place it in a cool, dark location for about 4 to 6 weeks. Shake the jar gently every day or so to aid in the extraction process.
6. **Straining and Bottling:** After the maceration period, strain the liquid to remove the plant material. Squeeze out as much liquid from the herbs as possible. Transfer the glycerite to dark glass bottles for storage.

It's important to note that glycerites have a different consistency and shelf life compared to alcohol-based tinctures. Glycerites tend to be sweeter and have a thicker texture. They also have a shorter shelf life than alcohol-based tinctures, usually around 1 to 2 years.

Vinegar "Tinctures"

Vinegar "tinctures", also known as herbal vinegars, are liquid herbal preparations that use vinegar as the solvent to extract the active compounds from plant materials. They are a versatile and easy-to-make alternative to alcohol-based tinctures, and they are particularly well-suited for extracting minerals and water-soluble compounds from herbs. Herbal vinegars can be used in culinary, therapeutic, and cosmetic applications.

Here's how to make an herbal vinegar tincture:

INGREDIENTS:

- Dried or fresh herbs
- Apple cider vinegar or another type of vinegar
- Glass jars with lids

INSTRUCTIONS:

1. **Choose Herbs:** Select the herbs you want to use for your vinegar tincture. Either fresh or dried ingredients may be used, however if you do use fresh plants, be sure to store in a cool place or even better, the refrigerator. Vinegar is ideal for extracting minerals from mineral-rich plants such as dandelion leaf, horsetail leaf and stem, and red clover aerial parts. It is also used to extract alkaloids from herbs.
2. **Prepare Herbs:** If using fresh herbs, chop them finely to increase the surface area. If using dried herbs, crush or grind them slightly to enhance extraction.
3. **Fill the Jar:** Place the prepared herbs into a glass jar. Fill the jar loosely, about halfway, with the herbal material.
4. **Add Vinegar:** Pour the vinegar over the herbs until they are fully covered and there's about an inch of extra liquid above the herbs. Apple cider vinegar is a popular choice due to its mild flavor and health benefits, but other types of vinegar like white vinegar or red wine vinegar may also be used.
5. **Seal and Shake:** Seal the jar with a tight-fitting lid. Shake the jar gently to ensure the herbs are well-saturated by the vinegar.
6. **Steeping Period:** Place the sealed jar in a cool, dark location for about 2 to 6 weeks.
7. Shake the jar gently every day to facilitate the extraction process.
8. **Straining:** After the steeping period, strain the liquid to remove the herb material. You can use a fine mesh strainer or cheesecloth for this.
9. **Bottling:** Transfer the strained vinegar tincture into dark glass bottles for storage. Label the bottles with the herb's name, date of preparation, and other relevant information.

Keep in mind that herbal vinegars are primarily water-based and may have a milder extraction of certain compounds compared to alcohol-based tinctures. Herbal vinegars will remain shelf-stable for approximately six months and can last longer if refrigerated.

Herbal tincture making can be a rewarding way to harness the medicinal properties of plants, mushrooms, and lichens. However, it's crucial to gather accurate information, exercise caution, and seek guidance from professionals to ensure you create safe and effective tinctures.

Oil Infusions

Herbal oil infusions are a process of extracting the beneficial compounds from herbs using oils as a solvent. These infusions are commonly used in aromatherapy, skincare, and culinary applications. The resulting herbal oil can be used for massage, skincare products, hair care, cooking, and more.

Here's how to create herbal oil infusions:

INGREDIENTS AND SUPPLIES:

1. **Herbs:** Choose dried herbs that are free from moisture to prevent spoilage. It's okay to use fresh herbs in an infusion that you use up fairly quickly, but you don't want moisture in something you're going to store. Common herbs used for infusions include lavender, chamomile, rosemary, calendula, and arnica.
2. **Oil:** A carrier oil is needed for the infusion. There are several carrier oils that can be used for herbal infusions, each with its own unique properties and benefits. The choice of carrier oil can impact the final product's texture, aroma, and therapeutic qualities. Here are some common carrier oils used for herbal infusions and their benefits. Use organic products.

- Olive Oil is rich in antioxidants and healthy monounsaturated fats. It's deeply moisturizing and suitable for most skin types. It has anti-inflammatory properties and can help soothe dry, irritated skin.
- Coconut Oil is well-known for its moisturizing and nourishing properties. It's solid at room temperature but melts upon contact with the skin. It's especially beneficial for dry and damaged hair, and it has antimicrobial properties that can help with various skin conditions.
- Jojoba Oil closely resembles the skin's natural sebum, making it a fantastic moisturizer for all skin types. It's lightweight and non-greasy, making it suitable for facial and body use. It can help regulate oil production and is often used in skincare products for acne-prone skin.
- Sweet Almond Oil is rich in vitamins and minerals, making it nourishing for the skin. It's easily absorbed and helps soothe dry and sensitive skin. It can also promote a healthy complexion and improve the appearance of scars.
- Grapeseed Oil is a lightweight oil that absorbs quickly. It's high in linoleic acid, which can be beneficial for oily and acne-prone skin. It's also rich in antioxidants and can help tighten and tone the skin.
- Sunflower Oil is high in vitamin E, which is known for its antioxidant properties. It's moisturizing and can help maintain the skin's natural barrier function. It's suitable for all skin types, including sensitive skin.
- Apricot Kernel Oil is rich in essential fatty acids and vitamins. It's moisturizing, soothing, and helps improve the skin's elasticity. It's often used in massage oils and skincare products for its light texture.

Forgotten Home Apothecary

- Avocado Oil is deeply moisturizing and rich in vitamins A, D, and E. It's suitable for dry and mature skin, as well as hair care. It can help improve skin texture and promote a healthy scalp.
- Argan Oil is known for its nourishing and hydrating properties. It's rich in essential fatty acids and vitamin E, making it beneficial for skin and hair health. It can help improve skin elasticity and promote shine in hair.

When choosing a carrier oil for herbal infusions, consider the intended use of the infused oil (*e.g.*, skincare, hair care, culinary), the properties of the herbs being infused, and your personal preferences. Always use high-quality organic carrier oils and herbs to ensure the best results.

1 | **Glass Jar:** Use a clean, dry, and airtight glass jar to hold the herbs and oil.
2 | **Strainer or Cheesecloth:** You'll need a strainer or cheesecloth to separate the infused oil from the plant material.
3 | **Dark Bottle:** After straining, store the infused oil in a dark glass bottle to protect it from light.

INSTRUCTIONS:

1 | **Preparation:** Make sure the herbs are completely dry to prevent mold growth. Crush or bruise the herbs slightly to release their essential oils and enhance the infusion process.
2 | **Choosing a Method:**
- Cold Infusion (Folk Method): In this method, herbs are placed in a jar and covered with oil. The jar is then sealed and left to sit for 4-8 weeks, allowing the oil to gradually extract the herbal properties. Give the jar a gentle shake from time to time. This method is gentler and better for delicate herbs.
- Heat Infusion: Heat speeds up the infusion process. Combine herbs and oil in a heatproof container and gently warm the mixture using a double boiler or a low-heat setting. Be cautious not to overheat or burn the herbs. It's important to keep everything at 110F or below to avoid degrading the quality of the oil and herbs.

3 | **Infusion Time:** The infusion process can take anywhere from a few days to a few weeks, depending on the method used and the herbs chosen. For a heat infusion, allow the oil and herbs to simmer together for at least 30 minutes, up to several hours for a more potent infusion. Some medicinal herb oil recipes call for 12 to 24 hours in a slow cooker.
Cold infusions require more time for the oil to extract the herbal properties fully (usually 4-8 weeks).
4 | **Straining:** Once the desired infusion time has passed, strain the oil to remove the plant material. Use a fine mesh strainer or cheesecloth to ensure that no plant particles remain in the infused oil.
5 | **Storage:** Transfer the strained herbal oil into a dark glass bottle. Dark glass helps protect the oil from light exposure, which can degrade the oil and reduce its shelf life.
6 | **Shelf-life:** Infused oils keep for a long period of time, usually 1-2 years.
7 | **Labeling:** Clearly label the bottle with the name of the infused oil and the date it was made.

USAGE:

- Massage: Use the herbal oil as a massage oil to help relax and soothe muscles.
- Skincare: Incorporate infused oils into your skincare routine for moisturizing, aromatherapy, or as a base for homemade skincare products (Balms, creams, salves, etc.).
- Hair Care: Apply herbal oil to your hair and scalp for conditioning, promoting hair growth, and addressing specific hair concerns.
- Cooking: Some herbal oils, like rosemary or basil-infused oils, can be used in cooking to add flavor to dishes.
- Salves: Herbal oils are the base for salve-making. More on this in Section 2.7.

> Be aware that herbal oil infusions are not suitable for all herbs. Some herbs may cause allergic reactions or skin sensitivities, so it's essential to research the properties of the herbs you're using and perform a patch test before applying them to larger areas of the skin.

Forgotten Home Apothecary

Oxymels

Oxymels are herbal preparations made by combining vinegar and honey, creating a tangy and sweet mixture infused with the properties of herbs. These preparations are used for their health benefits and are both flavorful and versatile.

Oxymels can offer digestive support, immune-boosting effects, respiratory relief, anti-inflammatory properties, and antioxidants, depending on the herbs used. They can be taken by the spoonful, diluted in water, or used in culinary applications.

INGREDIENTS AND SUPPLIES:

- **Vinegar:** Choose apple cider vinegar, white wine vinegar, or any other mild vinegar.
- **Honey:** Use raw, unprocessed honey for its health benefits and flavor.
- **Herbs:** Select dried or fresh herbs with medicinal or culinary properties.
- **Glass Jar:** A glass jar with an airtight lid for the infusion.

INSTRUCTIONS:

1 | **Herb Selection:** Choose herbs based on your desired health benefits or flavor profile. For example, thyme and sage may be used for respiratory health, while rose petals and elderflowers offer a delicate floral taste.
2 | **Preparation:** Chop or crush the herbs slightly to release their flavors and properties.
3 | **Infusion:** Fill your glass jar a quarter of the way full with your chosen chopped herbs (if you are using fresh herbs, instead, fill the jar three-quarters of the way full) and pour vinegar until the jar is three-quarters full, topping the rest of the jar with raw honey. Seal the jar and let it sit in a cool, dark place for about 2 weeks, shaking daily.
4 | **Straining:** After the infusion period, strain out the herbs using a fine mesh strainer or cheesecloth.
5 | **Bottling:** Pour the oxymel into a clean glass bottle, seal it, and store it in the refrigerator. It will last for several months.

Oxymels can be taken by the spoonful for health benefits, added to sparkling water for a refreshing drink, or used in salad dressings and marinades.

Syrups and Elixirs

Herbal Syrups

Herbal syrups are typically made by infusing herbs or botanicals in a mixture of water and sweeteners, such as honey or sugar. The herbs are steeped in the liquid to extract their beneficial compounds, and the resulting syrup is often used to manage coughs, sore throats, and other respiratory issues.

Examples of herbs commonly used in herbal syrups include:

- Elderberry: Demonstrated to have immune-boosting properties and often used to alleviate cold and flu symptoms.
- Marshmallow Root: Used for its soothing and demulcent properties, often found in cough, throat, and gut syrups.
- Thyme: Known for its antibacterial properties and used to address respiratory issues.

INGREDIENTS:

- Dried or fresh herbs of your choice
- Water
- Sweetener (raw honey, sugar, maple syrup, etc.)

INSTRUCTIONS:

1 | **Choose Your Herbs:** Select the herbs you want to use in your syrup. Consider the potential health benefits and flavors of the herbs.

2 | **Prepare the Herbal Infusion:** In a pot, combine water and your chosen herbs. The ratio of herbs to water can vary, but a common starting point is around 1 ounce (28 grams) of dried herbs to 1 quart (about 950 ml) of water. You can adjust this based on your preferences and the potency of the herbs.

3 | **Simmer:** Gently heat the mixture over low to medium heat. Avoid boiling, as this could degrade some of the beneficial compounds. Let the herbs steep in the water for about 20-30 minutes.

4 | **Strain:** After steeping, strain the herbal infusion to remove the plant material using a fine mesh strainer or cheesecloth.

5 | **Add Sweetener:** Return the strained liquid to the pot and gently warm it. Add your chosen sweetener (such as raw honey or sugar) while stirring until it's fully dissolved. The amount of sweetener varies based on taste preferences. Some people like a sweeter syrup, using a 1:1 ratio of honey to decoction, while others use a 1:2 ratio, using less honey. The 1:1 ratio will store longer, as honey doesn't spoil easily.

6 | **Cool and Store:** Allow the syrup to cool before transferring it to clean, sterilized glass bottles or jars. Typically, these syrups will last about six months in the refrigerator if you use a 1:2 ratio.

7 | Store the syrup in the refrigerator to extend its shelf life.

Herbal Elixirs

Herbal elixirs are more concentrated herbal preparations, often created by steeping herbs in alcohol or another solvent. The alcohol helps to extract the active compounds from the herbs and acts as a preservative.

INGREDIENTS:

- Dried or fresh herbs of your choice
- Alcohol (such as vodka, brandy, or rum)
- Opional: Sweetener (raw honey, sugar, maple syrup, etc.)

INSTRUCTIONS:

1. **Select Herbs:** Choose the herbs you want to use in your elixir, considering their potential benefits and compatibility with alcohol.
2. **Prepare the Herbal Extraction:** Place the herbs in a glass jar and cover them with alcohol. The ratio of herbs to alcohol can vary, but a common starting point is around 1-part herbs to 4 parts alcohol by volume. Ensure that the herbs are fully submerged.
3. **Seal and Steep:** Seal the jar tightly and place it in a cool, dark place. Allow the herbs to steep in the alcohol for about 4 to 6 weeks, shaking the jar gently every few days to encourage extraction.
4. **Strain:** After the steeping period, strain the liquid to remove the plant material. Use a fine mesh strainer or cheesecloth.
5. **Optional:** Add Sweetener: If desired, you can add a sweetener like honey or syrup to the strained elixir. Mix well until the sweetener is fully dissolved.
6. **Bottle and Store:** Transfer the strained elixir to dark glass bottles with airtight caps. Store the elixir in a cool, dark place to preserve its potency.

Remember that the potency and effectiveness of herbal syrups and elixirs will vary based on factors such as the quality of herbs used, the extraction method, and individual preferences. It's also important to research each herb's potential interactions with medications and possible side effects before preparing and using these preparations. If you're unsure, consult with a healthcare professional or experienced herbalist for guidance.

Lozenges, Gummies, and Capsules

Lozenges, gummies, and capsules are popular dosage forms used in apothecaries and herbal medicine. Each form has its advantages and considerations when it comes to preparing and using herbal remedies.

Here's an overview of each:

Herbal Losenges

Herbal lozenges are solid, candy-like preparations that dissolve slowly in the mouth, allowing the active herbal compounds to be absorbed through the mucous membranes. They are often used for soothing sore throats and coughs. They can be formulated to taste pleasant, making them suitable for children and those who have difficulty swallowing pills.

INGREDIENTS:

- ½ cup herbal infusion or tincture
- ¼ cup natural sweeteners (such as honey or maple syrup)
- 2 tablespoons binder (vegetable glycerin)
- Powdered sugar (optional for coating)

INSTRUCTIONS:

1| Prepare an herbal infusion or tincture using the desired herbs. You can make a strong infusion by steeping about ¼ cup of dried herbs in ½ cup of hot water for about 15-20 minutes. For a tincture, use ½ cup of alcohol (such as vodka) and approximately 2 tablespoons of dried herbs. Let the tincture sit for several weeks, shaking it daily.

2| Mix the herbal infusion or tincture with ¼ cup of your chosen natural sweetener (like honey or maple syrup) and 2 tablespoons of vegetable glycerin. Adjust the sweetener to taste if needed.

3| Heat the mixture gently in a double boiler (preferable) or microwave until it's well combined and forms a thick, smooth consistency. If using a double boiler, heat it over low heat, stirring constantly until it thickens.

4| Drop small spoonfuls of the mixture onto a silicone mat or parchment paper. Optionally, roll the drops in powdered sugar to prevent sticking.

5| Allow the drops to cool and harden. Once firm, store them in a dry, airtight container.

Herbal Gummies

Herbal gummies are chewy, gelatin or agar-based treats infused with herbal extracts. They are a fun and flavorful way to consume herbs, especially for those who prefer a sweeter taste. Gummies can be formulated for immune support, digestive health, as a sleep aid, and more, depending on the chosen herbs.

INGREDIENTS:

- 1 cup of herbal infusion or tincture
- 3 tablespoons of gelatin or vegetarian/vegan alternative (such as agar-agar or carrageenan)
- ¼ cup of sweeteners (*e.g.*, honey, fruit juice)

INSTRUCTIONS:

1 | Prepare an herbal infusion or tincture using your chosen herbs.
2 | In a saucepan, combine the herbal infusion or tincture with the sweetener.
3 | Gradually sprinkle and whisk in the 3 tablespoons of gelatin (or alternative) until it's fully dissolved and the mixture becomes smooth.
4 | Heat the mixture over low heat, stirring constantly, until it's warm, but avoid boiling.
5 | Carefully pour the mixture into silicone molds or an ice cube tray.
6 | Allow the gummies to cool and set in the refrigerator for approximately 2-3 hours.
7 | Once set, remove the gummies from the molds and store them in an airtight container in the refrigerator.

Remember that the exact quantities and choice of herbs for gummies or lozenges may vary depending on your personal preferences and the specific herbs you're using for the infusion or tincture. Adjust the sweetness and consistency to your liking.

Herbal Capsules

Herbal capsules are a convenient way to take herbal supplements in a precise and measured dosage.

INGREDIENTS:

- Herbal powders or finely ground herbs

INSTRUCTIONS:

1 | Obtain or prepare herbal powders by grinding dried herbs into a fine consistency using a mortar and pestle or a grinder (a coffee grinder works well).
2 | Use empty vegetable-based or gelatin capsules. You can purchase these from health food stores or online. Capsules come in three sizes; "0," "00" and "000."
3 | Carefully open the capsules and fill them with the desired amount of herbal powder using a small funnel or a capsule-filling machine.
4 | Once filled, reassemble the capsules by pressing the two halves together.
5 | Store the filled capsules in a cool, dry place in an airtight container.

Remember to research the herbs you plan to use and their appropriate dosages before creating any herbal remedies. If you are going to make any sort of herbal mix, you'll need a scale to measure out your various herbs. Be sure to mix powdered herbs well, so that your capsules all have the same herbal concentration.

When creating herbal lozenges, gummies, or capsules, it's crucial to ensure the quality of the herbs used, accurate dosing, and proper sanitation during the preparation process. Keep in mind that individual dosages and formulations may vary based on the specific herbs, desired effects, and individual health considerations.

Balms, Salves, Creams, and Lotions

Balms, salves, creams, and lotions are popular topical applications in herbal apothecaries. They allow for the external use of herbal remedies to address various skin concerns and provide localized relief. Each has a different texture and consistency, making them suitable for different applications.

Balms

Balms are semi-solid mixtures that typically include herbal-infused oils or extracts combined with beeswax or another solidifying agent. They have a thicker texture and provide a protective barrier on the skin. Balms are great for providing moisturization, soothing dry or irritated skin, and delivering herbal benefits directly to the skin's surface. While balms may feel greasier than lotion, those oils are doing their job at nourishing your skin. They are particularly suitable for areas that need a concentrated and longer-lasting application.

INGREDIENTS:

- 1 cup herbal-infused oil
- ¼ cup beeswax or plant-based wax (*e.g.*, candelilla or carnauba wax)
- 10-15 drops essential oils (optional for fragrance and added benefits)

INSTRUCTIONS:

1 | Prepare the herbal-infused oil by infusing 1 cup of dried herbs in a carrier oil of your choice. You can use the double boiler method or a slow cooker for this step (see Part 2.3).
2 | Strain the herbs from the infused oil and measure out 1 cup for your recipe.
3 | In a double boiler, melt ¼ cup of beeswax or plant-based wax.
4 | Once the wax is completely melted, add the 1 cup of herbal-infused oil and mix thoroughly.
5 | If desired, add 10-15 drops of essential oils for fragrance and additional benefits. Adjust the quantity based on your preference for scent.
6 | Pour the mixture into clean and sterilized containers, such as tins or jars. Before pouring the entire batch, test the consistency by dropping a small amount onto a surface. To achieve a harder consistency (*e.g.*, for lip balm), simply add more beeswax. For salves, use a 4:1 ratio of infused oil to beeswax. For harder-consistency balms, add slightly more beeswax as needed.
7 | Allow the balm to cool and solidify in the containers before sealing them securely.

Salves

Herbal salves are similar to balms but usually contain less beeswax than balms and utilize more herbs. They typically have a smoother, lighter consistency than balms and are usually used medicinally.

INGREDIENTS:

- 1 part beeswax to 4 parts infused oil mixture, and common usage is ¼ cup to ⅓ cup per cup of oil. For 8 oz (250ml) of oil, I usually use 2 oz (48g) of beeswax.
- 15 to 20 drops or more of each of your essential oils for every 8 oz (250ml) of infused oil. Vitamin E may be added to help rancidity: ½ tsp for 16 oz (250ml) oil.

INSTRUCTIONS:

1 | Follow the same steps for preparing an herbal-infused oil, as mentioned earlier.
2 | In a double boiler, melt the measured beeswax or plant-based wax.
3 | Once the wax is melted, add the herbal-infused oil and mix thoroughly.
4 | Optionally, add a few drops of essential oils for fragrance and benefits.
5 | Pour the mixture into clean, sterilized containers. Before you pour into your containers (jars/tins) to set, add a few drops to your container to test the consistency. If it's too hard, add more oil, and if it's too soft, add more beeswax to your mixture. Then complete pouring, label, and date.
6 | Allow the salve to cool and solidify before sealing the containers.

Creams

Herbal creams are water-based formulations that often combine herbal-infused oils or extracts with water or hydrosols. They have a lighter texture than balms and are more easily absorbed by the skin. Creams are versatile for providing hydration, supporting skin health, and delivering herbal properties. They are suitable for both face and body and can be customized for different skin types. They can be used for daily moisturizing, soothing sensitive skin, and addressing various skin issues like eczema or irritation.

INGREDIENTS:

- ¼ cup herbal-infused oil
- ½ cup aqueous phase (distilled water, hydrosols, or aloe vera gel)
- 2 tablespoons emulsifying wax
- ¼ teaspoon preservative (if using water-based ingredients)
- 10-15 drops essential oils (optional for fragrance and benefits)

INSTRUCTIONS:

1 | Prepare an herbal-infused oil as described earlier.
2 | In a double boiler, melt the emulsifying wax in the herbal-infused oil.
3 | In a separate container, gently warm the aqueous phase (water, hydrosols, etc.).
4 | Slowly add the warmed aqueous phase to the oil and wax mixture while stirring continuously.
5 | Continue stirring until the mixture forms a stable emulsion.
6 | If desired, add essential oils for fragrance and added benefits.
7 | Once the mixture has cooled down, add the preservative if you're using water-based ingredients to prevent microbial growth.
8 | Transfer the cream into clean and sterilized containers.

Lotions

Herbal lotions are similar to creams but have a higher water content, making them even lighter and more hydrating.

INGREDIENTS:

- Herbal-infused oil
- Aqueous phase (distilled water, hydrosols, or aloe vera gel)
- Emulsifying wax
- Preservative
- Essential oils (optional for fragrance and benefits)

INSTRUCTIONS:

1 | Follow the same steps as for making an herbal cream, but adjust the ratios of the aqueous phase and the oil phase to create a lighter consistency.
2 | Make sure to use an appropriate emulsifying wax to ensure the lotion forms a stable emulsion.
3 | Use a reliable preservative to ensure the lotion remains safe to use over time.

Forgotten Home Apothecary

LABELING AND STORAGE:

Label your balms, creams, and lotions with the ingredients used, date of preparation, and intended purpose. Store your products in a cool, dry place away from direct sunlight to preserve their quality.

Shelf life: Creams and lotions are water-based so they need to be stored in the fridge in order to prevent spoilage.

USAGE:

Apply a small amount of the balm, cream, or lotion to the desired area and gently massage it in.

Use as needed, following the recommendations for the specific herbs and intended purpose. Before using or selling any herbal skincare products, consider conducting patch tests to ensure they are well-tolerated by different skin types. Additionally, consulting with a qualified herbalist or skincare professional can provide further guidance on formulation and usage.

If you're looking for alternatives to beeswax in creating salves, balms, and creams, there are several options available, especially for those who prefer vegan alternatives. Here are some alternatives you can consider:

1 | **Candelilla Wax:** Candelilla wax is derived from the leaves of the candelilla shrub. It has a similar consistency to beeswax and is often used as a vegan alternative in cosmetic and skincare products.
2 | **Carnauba Wax:** Carnauba wax comes from the leaves of the carnauba palm. It's a hard wax that can be used to increase the firmness of balms and salves. It's commonly used in many cosmetic products and is also vegan-friendly.
3 | **Soy Wax:** Soy wax is derived from soybean oil. It's commonly used in candle making, but it can also be used in skincare products. Keep in mind that soy wax can be softer than beeswax, so you might need to adjust your recipe accordingly.
4 | **Shea Butter:** Shea butter is a popular natural fat extracted from the nut of the shea tree. It's rich and creamy, making it a great base for salves and creams. It's also known for its moisturizing properties.
5 | **Cocoa Butter:** Cocoa butter is derived from cocoa beans and has a pleasant chocolate scent. It's a solid fat at room temperature and is often used in skincare products due to its moisturizing and nourishing properties.
6 | **Mango Butter:** Mango butter is obtained from the kernels of the mango fruit. It's similar in texture to shea and cocoa butters and can be used as a base for various skincare products.
7 | **Jojoba Wax:** Jojoba wax is technically a liquid wax rather than a true wax. It's derived from the seeds of the jojoba plant and closely resembles the natural sebum produced by our skin. It can be a great addition to balms and creams.
8 | **Plant Oils:** Depending on the desired consistency and benefits of your product, you can also consider using various plant oils like coconut oil, almond oil, olive oil, and more as a base. These oils can provide excellent moisturization and nourishment.

When substituting beeswax with any of these alternatives, keep in mind that each wax or butter has different properties, melting points, and textures. You might need to experiment and adjust your recipes to achieve the desired consistency and performance. Always perform a small-scale test before making larger batches to ensure that the final product meets your expectations.

Creating medicinal balms, creams, and lotions is a rewarding process that allows you to harness the benefits of herbs for topical use. It's essential to practice proper sanitation, use high-quality ingredients, and be mindful of individual sensitivities when crafting these products. If you're new to herbal formulation, consulting with experienced herbalists or skincare professionals can provide valuable insights.

Forgotten Home Apothecary

Baths and Steams

Herbal baths and steams are soothing and therapeutic practices that involve using herbs to enhance relaxation, promote well-being, and address various physical and mental concerns.

Here's a guide to creating and enjoying herbal baths and steams:

Herbal Baths

Herbal baths involve adding herbal infusions or preparations to your bathwater for a relaxing and rejuvenating experience.

INGREDIENTS AND SUPPLIES:

- **Dried Herbs:** Choose herbs based on your desired effects. Lavender, chamomile, rose petals, calendula, and mint are popular choices.
- **Muslin Bag or Tea Ball:** To contain the herbs and prevent debris in the bathwater.
- **Bathtub:** Use a clean bathtub with warm water.
- **Optional Additions:** Epsom salts, Himalayan salt, oatmeal, or essential oils for additional benefits.

INSTRUCTIONS:

1 | **Herb Preparation:** Place the desired herbs in a muslin bag or tea ball. This prevents the herbs from floating in the bathwater and makes cleanup easier.
2 | **Bathwater Preparation:** Run warm water in the bathtub and add the herbal bag to the bathwater.
3 | **Steeping:** Allow the herbs to steep in the bathwater as you soak. The warm water will help release the herbal properties into the water.
4 | **Relaxation:** Immerse yourself in the herbal-infused bathwater and relax for 15-30 minutes. Breathe deeply and enjoy the aroma.
5 | **Cleanup:** After your bath, remove the herbal bag and drain the water.

Herbal Steams

Herbal steams involve inhaling the steam of infused herbs, which can help open up the respiratory system, relax the mind, and soothe the skin.

INGREDIENTS AND SUPPLIES:

- **Dried Herbs:** Choose herbs with respiratory benefits, such as eucalyptus, thyme, rosemary, or peppermint.
- **Large Heatproof Bowl:** For containing the hot water and herbs.
- **Towel or Blanket:** To create a steam tent and trap the steam.
- **Optional Additions:** Essential oils or citrus peels for enhanced aroma.

INSTRUCTIONS:

1. **Herb Preparation:** Place a handful of dried herbs in the bottom of a large heatproof bowl.
2. **Boil Water:** Boil water and pour it over the herbs in the bowl.
3. **Steam Tent:** Sit comfortably with your face over the bowl, creating a steam tent by draping a towel or blanket over your head and the bowl.
4. **Inhale Steam:** Inhale deeply, allowing the steam and herbal aroma to reach your respiratory system. Close your eyes and relax.
5. **Duration:** Enjoy the steam for about 10-15 minutes. If the steam becomes too hot, you can lift the towel slightly to release excess heat.
6. **Skin Soothing:** For a facial steam, position your face further away from the steam to avoid overheating sensitive skin.

SAFETY CONSIDERATIONS:

1. Be cautious with hot water and steam to avoid burns.
2. Perform a patch test with the chosen herbs to check for allergies or sensitivities.
3. Consult a healthcare professional if you have respiratory issues, skin conditions, or other health concerns before using herbal baths or steams.
4. Stay hydrated during and after your bath or steam session.

Both herbal baths and steams offer wonderful ways to relax, unwind, and experience the benefits of herbs through aromatherapy and skin absorption. Customize your experience by selecting herbs that align with your wellness goals and preferences.

Poultices, Compresses, and Washes

Poultices, compresses, and washes are topical applications of herbal remedies that offer targeted relief for various skin and muscle issues. These applications involve direct contact with the affected area to deliver the benefits of herbs externally.

Here's a guide to creating and using poultices, compresses, and washes:

Poultices

A poultice is a soft, moist mixture of herbs that is applied directly to the skin to address localized issues like inflammation, wounds, venom, or swelling.

INGREDIENTS AND SUPPLIES:

- **Fresh or Dried Herbs:** Choose herbs with properties suited to your purpose, such as soothing herbs for inflammation or wound-healing herbs for cuts.
- **Water or Herbal Infusion:** Use water to moisten the herbs and create a paste-like consistency.
- **Cloth or Gauze:** To hold the herbal mixture and prevent direct skin contact.
- **Optional:** Olive oil, flaxseed oil, or other carrier oils to enhance the poultice's texture.

INSTRUCTIONS:

1 | **Herb Selection:** Choose herbs based on their properties and the specific issue you want to address.
2 | **Preparation:** Crush, chop, or blend the herbs to release their juices or oils.
3 | **Creating the Poultice:** Mix the crushed herbs with enough water or herbal infusion to form a paste. Optionally, you can add a bit of carrier oil.
4 | **Application:** Spread the herbal paste onto a clean cloth or gauze.
5 | **Applying the Poultice:** Place the poultice directly onto the affected area.
6 | **Securing:** Wrap the area with a bandage or cloth to hold the poultice in place.
7 | **Duration:** Leave the poultice on for about 15-30 minutes.
8 | **Removing:** Gently remove the poultice and clean the area.

Forgotten Home Apothecary

Compresses

A compress involves soaking a cloth in an herbal infusion and applying it to the skin to address various issues such as muscle pain, inflammation, or bruising.

INGREDIENTS AND SUPPLIES:

- **Dried Herbs:** Choose herbs that suit your purpose, such as anti-inflammatory herbs or those that promote circulation.
- **Hot Water:** For creating the herbal infusion.
- **Clean Cloth:** Cotton or muslin cloth for soaking in the herbal infusion.
- **Optional:** Cold water or ice packs for cold compresses.

INSTRUCTIONS:

1 | **Herb Selection:** Choose herbs based on their properties and the issue you want to address.
2 | **Herbal Infusion:** Prepare a strong herbal infusion by steeping the herbs in hot water.
3 | **Soaking the Cloth:** Dip the clean cloth in the herbal infusion, ensuring it's wet but not dripping.
4 | **Application:** Apply the cloth directly to the affected area.
5 | **Securing:** Use a bandage or wrap to hold the cloth in place.
6 | **Duration:** Leave the compress on for about 15-30 minutes.
7 | **Cold Compresses:** For cold compresses, use cold water or place the soaked cloth in the refrigerator for a while before applying.

Washes

Herbal washes involve using herbal infusions or decoctions to cleanse and soothe the skin. They can be used for various skin issues, including rashes, irritations, and infections.

INGREDIENTS AND SUPPLIES:

- **Dried Herbs:** Select herbs that match your purpose, such as chamomile for soothing or calendula for healing.
- **Boiling Water:** For creating the herbal infusion or decoction.
- **Clean Cloth or Cotton Balls:** To apply the herbal wash.

INSTRUCTIONS:

1 | **Herb Selection:** Choose herbs based on their properties and the issue you want to address.
2 | **Herbal Infusion/Decoction:** Prepare an herbal infusion by steeping the herbs in hot water or create a decoction by simmering the herbs.
3 | **Cooling:** Allow the infusion or decoction to cool to a comfortable temperature.
4 | **Application:** Dip a clean cloth or cotton ball into the herbal infusion.
5 | **Gentle Application:** Gently apply the infused cloth or cotton ball to the affected area, patting or pressing lightly.
6 | **Repetition:** You can repeat the process several times a day, depending on the severity of the issue.

! SAFETY CONSIDERATIONS:
Proper wound care is essential to promote healing and prevent infections.

1 | Gently clean the wound with mild soap and warm water. Avoid using harsh antiseptics, as they can delay healing.
2 | Perform a patch test before using herbal applications on larger areas of the skin to check for sensitivities or allergies.
3 | Keep the applications clean and follow proper hygiene practices.
4 | **Protect the Wound:** Apply an appropriate dressing to cover the wound and keep it clean. Choose dressings that are non-stick and breathable to allow for proper airflow.
5 | Choose herbs based on their properties and your specific needs.
6 | **Know When to Seek Medical Attention:** If the wound is deep, large, or doesn't stop bleeding after applying pressure, seek medical help. Watch for signs of infection, such as increased redness, swelling, warmth, pus, or fever.

Poultices, compresses, and washes are effective ways to harness the benefits of herbs for external use. They can provide localized relief and are often used in traditional herbal practices to support skin and muscle health.

Essential Oils and Hydrosols

Herbal essential oils and hydrosols are potent and aromatic extracts obtained from plants through various methods. They are widely used in aromatherapy, skincare, and natural health practices to harness the therapeutic properties of plants.

Here's an overview of herbal essential oils and hydrosols:

Herbal Essential Oils

EXTRACTION METHOD

Distillation is a process used for extracting essential oils from herbs or other plants. Not all plants provide essential oils; but for those that do, this is one of the best methods of extracting the essential oils. There are three basic types of distillation, requiring minor differences in the still:

- *Water distillation* – The herbs are immersed in water, and the water is boiled. This works best for herbs that don't break down easily.
- *Water and Steam distillation* – The only difference in the equipment for this and water distillation is the insertion of a rack inside the still, which holds the herbs up out of the water and only allows the steam to have contact with it. This method produces essential oils much more quickly than water distillation.
- *Direct Steam Distillation* – A different sort of still is needed for this method so that the steam can be created in a separate chamber. The steam is then injected into the retort/still that is holding the herbs below a rack holding the herbs. This allows a lower temperature to be used, reducing the potential for heat damage to the essential oil. This is the most common method used commercially, especially for essential oils like rosemary and lavender.

CONCENTRATION

Essential oils are highly concentrated extracts containing the volatile compounds that give plants their characteristic aromas and therapeutic properties.

USAGE

Essential oils can be used in aromatherapy, diluted in carrier oils for topical use, added to bathwater, or used to create natural cleaning products and perfumes.

BENEFITS

Different essential oils have diverse benefits, such as promoting relaxation, improving mood, supporting respiratory health, relieving muscle tension, and addressing skin issues. Examples: Lavender, tea tree, eucalyptus, peppermint, and chamomile are commonly used herbal essential oils.

Forgotten Home Apothecary

Hydrosols (Hydrolats or Floral Waters)

EXTRACTION METHOD

Hydrosols are co-products of the essential oil distillation process. They are the water-based byproducts that remain after the essential oil is separated. Simply bottle this by-product and store it in your refrigerator.

CONCENTRATION

Hydrosols are milder than essential oils and contain trace amounts of essential oil components, making them safer for direct skin application.

USAGE

Hydrosols can be used as facial toners, body sprays, room fresheners, and in skincare products.

BENEFITS

Hydrosols offer gentle and hydrating effects, along with subtle aromatic benefits. They are suitable for sensitive skin and can have astringent, soothing, or cooling properties.

EXAMPLES

Rose hydrosol, lavender hydrosol, and chamomile hydrosol are popular choices.

USAGE TIPS:

- **Dilution:** Essential oils must be diluted before applying to the skin. A common dilution ratio is 1-3% essential oil in a carrier oil.
- **Patch Test:** Perform a patch test before using any essential oil on your skin to ensure you don't have sensitivities or allergies.
- **Quality Matters:** If purchasing, choose high-quality, pure essential oils and hydrosols from reputable sources to ensure safety and efficacy.
- **Caution:** Some essential oils can be skin sensitizers or have contraindications, especially during pregnancy or if you have certain medical conditions. Research thoroughly or consult a professional before using.
- **Storage:** Store essential oils and hydrosols in dark glass bottles away from direct sunlight to maintain their potency and prevent deterioration.

When working with herbal essential oils and hydrosols, it's important to have a good understanding of the specific properties of each oil, as well as proper usage and safety guidelines. Consulting with a certified aromatherapist or herbalist can provide you with more detailed information tailored to your needs and preferences.

Herbal Remedies and Recipes
FOR COMMON AILMENTS

Maintaining a healthy body and mind involves a holistic approach that encompasses various aspects of your well-being. Before we dive into herbal recipes, here are tips to support overall health:

BALANCED DIET:
Consume a diverse and balanced diet rich in fruits, vegetables, whole grains, lean proteins, and healthy fats.

STAY HYDRATED:
Drink plenty of water throughout the day to stay hydrated, which is essential for overall health.

REGULAR EXERCISE:
Engage in regular physical activity, such as walking, jogging, yoga, or any exercise you enjoy.

STRESS MANAGEMENT:
Practice stress-reduction techniques like meditation, deep breathing, or mindfulness to support mental well-being.

ADEQUATE SLEEP:
Ensure you get enough restorative sleep each night, typically 7-9 hours for adults.

ROUTINE CHECK-UPS:
Regularly visit your healthcare provider for check-ups and screenings to catch and address any health issues early.

SOCIAL CONNECTIONS:
Maintain healthy social connections and engage in activities that bring joy and fulfillment.

LIMIT TOXINS:
Minimize exposure to environmental toxins and pollutants whenever possible.

MODERATION:
Practice moderation in all aspects of life, including food, alcohol, and caffeine consumption.

HYGIENE AND SAFETY:
- Practice good hygiene to prevent illness and infections.
- Follow safety guidelines to prevent accidents and injuries.

Remember that holistic health involves a balance of physical, mental, and emotional well-being. These tips are general guidelines, and individual needs may vary. It's essential to consult with a healthcare professional, such as doctors, naturopaths, dietitians, and mental health experts, to create a personalized plan that supports your specific health goals and needs.

Now, let's get to the recipes. Throughout this chapter, we explore the many ways herbs can benefit you - from aromatic culinary delights to soothing balms. Each recipe is carefully crafted with detailed instructions, making the process an enjoyable and intuitive experience. Whether you're an aspiring herbalist or simply someone seeking a more natural approach to wellness, I hope that you'll find these recipes accessible and gratifying.

As you embark on this journey of natural remedies, it's essential to be fluent in the language of measurements. You might notice that recipes come in a lot of different forms. Most of the time, recipes are listed with specific units of measure. Other times, recipes are given in ratios, listing each component as a part or a percentage.

In the end, the standard of measurement is up to you and will depend on how much of the recipe you would like to make. For example, if you wanted enough for 1 cup of tea, you might choose 1 teaspoon for your "part." Thus, you may use 1 teaspoon chamomile, 2 teaspoons peppermint, and 1 teaspoon lavender. If you choose to fill a jar with enough dried tea blend to store for future use, you might make your "part" 1 cup. Thus, you would use 1 cup chamomile, 2 cups peppermint, and 1 cup lavender.

Here's a conversion chart to help you seamlessly transition between various units, ensuring your concoctions and elixirs turn out as envisioned:

U.S. AND METRIC EQUIVALENTS

Weight	Liquid Capacity	U.S. Liquid Capacity	Volume	Length	Temperature
1 oz=28.35 gr	1 fl oz=29.57 ml	1 c =8 oz	1 oz=30 cc	1 inch = 25.4 mm	250°F=130°C
8 oz=227 gr	8 fl oz=236.6 ml	1 pt=16 oz	8 oz=237 cc	2 inch = 50.8 mm	300°F =150°C
16 oz=454 gr	16 fl oz=473.2 ml	1 qt=32 oz	16 oz= 473 cc		350°F =177°C
32 oz=908 gr	32 fl oz=946.4 ml	½ gal=64 oz	32 oz= 946 cc		400°F =200°C
35 oz (2.2 lbs) = 1 kg	1 U.S. gallon =3.78 l				450°F =230°C

ABBREVIATIONS

tsp, t = teaspoon	oz = ounce	pt = pint	cc = cubic centimeter	Lb. = pound
Tbsp, T = tablespoon	c = cup	qt = quart	gr = gram	°F = Fahrenheit
Fl.= fluid	gal = gallon	ml = milliliter	L = liter	C = Celsius

HERBAL SUPPORT
for the Cardiovascular System

The cardiovascular system serves as the body's transportation and communication network, providing oxygen, nutrients, and essential components to all cells while removing waste products. It plays a pivotal role in maintaining homeostasis, supporting organ function, and responding to various physiological needs. Its proper functioning is crucial for overall health and well-being.

Tips to Maintain a Healthy Cardiovascular System:

HEART-HEALTHY DIET:

- Choose sources of omega-3 fatty acids, such as fatty fish (salmon, mackerel, sardines), flaxseeds, and walnuts
- Reduce consumption of highly processed foods, as they often contain unhealthy fats, sugars, and excessive salt.
- Reduce sodium intake by avoiding processed foods and using herbs and spices for flavor.
- Minimize added sugars in your diet, as excessive sugar consumption can contribute to obesity and heart disease.
- Include herbs like hawthorn, garlic, turmeric, and ginger in your diet. These herbs have been shown to have cardiovascular benefits. You can add them to your meals, use them in cooking, or consume them as herbal teas or tinctures.
- Consider using olive leaf extract as a supplement or adding it to your diet. Olive leaf is thought to have antioxidant properties that may benefit heart health.

PHYSICAL ACTIVITY:

- Engage in at least 150 minutes of moderate-intensity aerobic exercise or 75 minutes of vigorous-intensity aerobic exercise weekly to improve cardiovascular fitness.
- Incorporate strength training exercises to build muscle and improve metabolism.

QUIT SMOKING:

Smoking is a major risk factor for heart disease. Seek support and resources to quit smoking if you are a smoker.

LIMIT ALCOHOL:

If you consume alcohol, do so in moderation. For most people, this means up to one drink per day for women and up to two drinks per day for men.

HERBAL SUPPORT

Hawthorn (*Crataegus*)
Hawthorn is known for its potential to support heart health by improving blood flow, reducing blood pressure, and strengthening the heart muscle.

Garlic (*Allium sativum*)
Garlic has been traditionally used to support cardiovascular health, with a focus on managing blood pressure and cholesterol levels.

Ginger (*Zingiber officinale*)
Ginger may help lower blood pressure and improve circulation, potentially reducing the risk of cardiovascular issues.

Turmeric (*Curcuma longa*)
Turmeric contains curcumin, which has anti-inflammatory and antioxidant properties that may benefit heart health by reducing inflammation and oxidative stress.

Ginkgo (*Ginkgo biloba*)
Ginkgo is believed to improve circulation and protect against heart-related conditions by enhancing blood flow and reducing blood clotting.

Green Tea (*Camellia sinensis*)
Green tea contains catechins, which have been associated with lower cholesterol levels and improved heart health.

Cayenne (*Capsicum annuum*)
Cayenne pepper contains capsaicin, which may help improve circulation and reduce blood pressure.

Cinnamon (*Cinnamomum* spp.)
Cinnamon may aid in regulating blood sugar levels, reducing LDL (bad) cholesterol, and promoting better blood flow, all of which contribute to cardiovascular health.

Motherwort (*Leonurus cardiaca*)
Motherwort is traditionally used to support heart health by regulating heart rhythm and reducing palpitations.

Cinnamon Infusion
for Blood Pressure

Cinnamon tea contains lots of antioxidants, compounds recognized for their health benefits. Cinnamon is traditionally used to help ease inflammation and support cardiovascular health. Components like cinnamaldehyde and cinnamophilin in cinnamon are known in herbal practices for their roles in maintaining healthy blood pressure levels and supporting vascular health.

INGREDIENTS:

- 1 cinnamon stick (or 1 tsp of ground cinnamon, (*Cinnamomum verum*)
- 1 cup of water
- Honey or lemon (optional, for flavor)

NOTES:

While cinnamon can be beneficial, excessive consumption may have adverse effects.

Cinnamon contains a chemical called coumarin.

Eating too much can cause liver damage, cancer, low blood sugar, or breathing problems.

INSTRUCTIONS:

1 | **Boil the Water:** Start by bringing 1 cup of water to a boil.
2 | **Add Cinnamon:** If you're using a cinnamon stick, break it into a few smaller pieces and add it to the boiling water. If you're using ground cinnamon, you can add it directly to the water.
3 | **Simmer:** Reduce the heat to low and let the cinnamon simmer in the water for about 10-15 minutes. This will help infuse the flavor of cinnamon into the water.
4 | **Strain:** After simmering, remove the pot from the heat and strain the tea to remove any cinnamon pieces or ground cinnamon.
5 | **Serve:** Pour the cinnamon tea into a cup. If desired, add a teaspoon of raw honey or a squeeze of lemon juice for extra flavor. Both honey and lemon have potential health benefits.
6 | **Enjoy:** Sip the cinnamon tea while it's still warm. Remember that individual sensitivities can vary, so start with a small amount of cinnamon and monitor your body's response. You can also lower your blood pressure by simply adding half a teaspoon of ground cinnamon to your morning coffee, smoothie, oats. etc.

DOSAGE:

Adults shouldn't have more than one teaspoon of cinnamon per day.

Heart Harmony Elixir
with Hawthorn Berry
(Happy Heart Elixir)

This herbal elixir is crafted with the goodness of hawthorn berries, traditionally known for their heart-boosting properties. Hawthorn berries have been used for centuries to support cardiovascular health, and this recipe combines them with other heart-healthy herbs and ingredients to create a delicious and nourishing elixir for a healthy and happy heart. Feel free to customize this tea with other heart-healthy herbs like lavender or lemon balm for added flavor and benefits.

INGREDIENTS:

- 1 tablespoon dried hawthorn berries (*Crataegus monogyna*)
- 1 teaspoon dried rose hips (*Rosa canina* and/or *Rosa* spp.)
- 2 cups filtered water
- Honey or maple syrup (optional, for sweetness)
- Fresh lemon slices (for garnish, optional)

NOTES:

Rose hips are rich in vitamin C and antioxidants, which can be beneficial for overall health. However, excessive consumption may lead to digestive discomfort in some individuals. Consult with a healthcare professional, especially if you have any underlying health conditions or are taking medications, to determine the appropriate dosage for your specific needs.

INSTRUCTIONS:

1. **Boil the Water:** In a pot, bring 2 cups of filtered water to a boil.
2. **Add the Herbs:** Once the water is boiling, add the dried hawthorn berries and dried rose hips.
3. **Simmer:** Reduce the heat to low, cover the pot, and let the herbs simmer for about 10-15 minutes. This will allow the flavors and beneficial compounds to infuse into the water.
4. **Strain:** After simmering, use a fine mesh strainer or a tea infuser to strain the tea into a cup or teapot. Press down on the herbs to extract all the liquid.
5. **Sweeten (Optional):** If desired, add honey or maple syrup to taste for a touch of sweetness. Start with a small amount and adjust to your preference. Excessive sugar intake can have adverse effects on heart health.
6. **Garnish and Serve:** Optionally, garnish with a fresh lemon slice for added flavor and aroma.
7. **Enjoy:** Sip on this heart-healthy hawthorn berry tea and savor its natural benefits for heart health.

DOSAGE:

It is recommended to drink 1 to 2 cups of this tea per day for heart health support.

Forgotten Home Apothecary

Garlic and Lemon Tonic
for Cholesterol Management

This garlic and lemon tonic is a natural remedy that combines the cholesterol-lowering properties of garlic and the antioxidant-rich benefits of lemon. Garlic contains compounds like allicin, which have been shown to help lower LDL (bad) cholesterol levels in the body. It can also support overall heart health. Lemons are rich in antioxidants, particularly vitamin C, which can help protect blood vessels from damage caused by free radicals.

INGREDIENTS:

- 4-5 cloves of fresh garlic (*Allium sativum*)
- 1 organic lemon
- 1 tablespoon raw honey (optional)
- 1 cup of filtered water

NOTES:

Be aware that individual responses may vary, so it's crucial to monitor your cholesterol levels over time with the guidance of a healthcare provider.

Garlic can cause digestive discomfort or heartburn in some individuals. If you experience such issues, reduce the garlic content in your tonic or discontinue use if the discomfort persists. If you're on blood-thinning medications or have a bleeding disorder, consult your doctor before consuming garlic in large amounts.

INSTRUCTIONS:

1 | **Prepare the Garlic:** Start by peeling and crushing 4-5 cloves of fresh garlic. Crushing the garlic helps release its active compounds, which are beneficial for cholesterol management.

2 | **Prepare the Lemon:** Wash and scrub the organic lemon thoroughly to remove any pesticides or residue. You'll be using both the juice and the zest, so make sure to grate the lemon zest before juicing it.

3 | **Boil the Water:** In a small saucepan, bring 1 cup of filtered water to a boil. Once it reaches a rolling boil, remove it from the heat and let it cool for a couple of minutes.

4 | **Combine the Ingredients:** In a heat-resistant glass or mug, add the crushed garlic and lemon zest. Pour the hot water over them.

5 | **Squeeze Lemon Juice:** Cut the now-zested lemon in half and squeeze the juice into the glass. Lemon juice is not only a flavorful addition but also helps with cholesterol management.

6 | **Optional Sweetener:** If you find the tonic too strong, add 1 tablespoon of raw honey to make the tonic more palatable.

7 | **Mix Well:** Stir the mixture thoroughly to ensure that all the ingredients are well combined. Let it steep for about 5-10 minutes. This allows the flavors to meld together and infuse into the water.

8 | **Strain and Serve:** After steeping, strain the tonic to remove the garlic and lemon zest. You can use a fine mesh strainer or a piece of cheesecloth to do this. Discard the solids.

DOSAGE:

Consume this tonic once a day, ideally in the morning on an empty stomach for better absorption.

Forgotten Home Apothecary

Hibiscus Tea
for Cardiovascular Support

Hibiscus tea is traditionally consumed for its potential to support cardiovascular health. It is known for its antihypertensive properties, which may help manage high blood pressure, a factor in reducing risks associated with heart disease and stroke. The tea is also rich in antioxidants, including anthocyanins and vitamin C, which are traditionally used to help combat oxidative stress and inflammation, both of which can contribute to heart disease.

INGREDIENTS:

- 2 tablespoons of dried hibiscus petals (*Hibiscus rosa-sinensis*)
- 2 cups of water
- Optional: Honey or lemon for added flavor (to taste)

NOTES:

If you are already taking medications for hypertension, consult your healthcare provider before incorporating hibiscus tea into your routine. They can help you adjust your medication if necessary.

Hibiscus tea may interact with certain medications, including antihypertensive drugs and diuretics. Always inform your healthcare provider about any herbal remedies or supplements you are using.

INSTRUCTIONS:

1 | **Boil the Water:** Start by boiling 2 cups of water in a kettle or a saucepan.
2 | **Rinse Hibiscus Petals:** While the water is heating, rinse the dried hibiscus petals under cold running water to remove any dust or impurities.
3 | **Add Hibiscus Petals:** Place the rinsed hibiscus petals into a teapot or heatproof pitcher.
4 | **Pour Boiling Water:** Once the water reaches a rolling boil, pour it over the hibiscus petals in the teapot or pitcher.
5 | **Steep:** Cover the teapot or pitcher and let the hibiscus petals steep in the hot water for about 5-10 minutes. The longer you steep, the stronger the flavor will be. Adjust the steeping time to your taste preference.
6 | **Strain:** After steeping, strain the tea into cups or mugs to remove the hibiscus petals. You can use a fine mesh strainer or a tea infuser.
7 | **Add Optional Flavorings:** If desired, add a touch of honey or a squeeze of fresh lemon to your tea for added flavor. Adjust the amount to suit your taste.
8 | **Serve and Enjoy:** Your hibiscus tea for cardiovascular support is ready to be enjoyed. Serve it hot or allow it to cool and serve it over ice for a refreshing iced tea option.

DOSAGE:

You can enjoy hibiscus tea daily as part of your beverage routine.

Beetroot and Aronia Juice
for Circulatory Health

Beets are rich in folate (vitamin B9), which plays a crucial role in supporting blood vessel health. They are also high in nitrates, which are converted into nitric oxide in the body. This process may help relax and widen blood vessels. Similarly, aronia is traditionally recognized for its potential to support heart health by helping to manage plaque formation in arteries. Both aronia and bilberry extracts are used for their traditional role in promoting tissue relaxation and improving blood flow, which can be beneficial in maintaining flexible arteries and supporting blood pressure management.

INGREDIENTS:

- 1 medium-sized beetroot, peeled and chopped (*Beta vulgaris*)
- ½ cup of fresh or frozen aronia berries (*Aronia melanocarpa*)
- ½ cup of water
- Optional: 1-2 tablespoons of honey for sweetness (adjust to taste)

NOTES:

Remember that individual dietary needs and preferences vary; adjust the serving size and sweetness to suit your taste and health goals.

The vibrant color of this juice can stain surfaces and clothing, so be cautious when handling it, and clean up any spills promptly.

INSTRUCTIONS:

1. **Prepare the Beetroot:** Start by washing, peeling, and chopping the beetroot into small, manageable pieces. This will make it easier to blend.
2. **Blend the Ingredients:** Place the chopped beetroot, aronia berries, and water in a blender.
3. **Blend Until Smooth:** Blend the mixture until you achieve a smooth and well-incorporated consistency. The vibrant color of the beetroot will give the juice a rich, deep hue.
4. **Sweeten to Taste (Optional):** Taste the juice. If you prefer a sweeter flavor, you can add 1-2 tablespoons of honey. Blend the juice again briefly to ensure the honey is well mixed. Adjust the honey quantity to your taste preference.
5. **Strain the Juice:** To remove any solids and achieve a smoother texture, strain the juice through a fine-mesh strainer or a piece of cheesecloth into a glass or pitcher.
6. **Serve Immediately or Refrigerate:** Your beetroot and aronia juice is ready to be enjoyed. Serve it immediately for the freshest taste, or refrigerate it for later use. Fresh juice is best, but it can be stored in the refrigerator for up to 2-3 days.
7. **Enjoy:** Sip and savor this nutritious juice, knowing it's contributing to your circulatory health.

DOSAGE:

½ to 1 cup (120-240 ml) of this juice per serving for circulatory health benefits.

Blood Vessel Care
with Butcher's Broom

Butcher's broom is a traditional herbal remedy known for its potential benefits in supporting blood vessel health and circulation. It contains compounds called ruscogenins that may help strengthen blood vessels and reduce symptoms associated with poor circulation, such as varicose veins and swollen legs.

INGREDIENTS:

- 1-2 teaspoons of dried butcher's broom root (*Ruscus aculeatus*)
- 1 cup of boiling water

NOTES:

You can adjust the amount based on your preference and tolerance. It's important to be mindful of your body's response and consult with a healthcare professional if you have any concerns or experience any adverse effects.

Butcher's broom tea has a slightly bitter taste, so sweetening it is optional but makes it more palatable. You can also add a pinch of black pepper for extra strength. It is known for its ability to stimulate circulation.

INSTRUCTIONS:

1. **Boil the Water:** Start by boiling 1 cup of water in a kettle or a saucepan.
2. **Prepare the Butcher's Broom:** While the water is heating, measure out 1-2 teaspoons of dried butcher's broom root and/or leaves. You can adjust the amount based on your preference and tolerance.
3. **Place the Herbs in a Cup:** Put the dried butcher's broom root and/or leaves into a heatproof cup or mug.
4. **Pour Boiling Water:** Once the water has reached a rolling boil, carefully pour it over the butcher's broom in the cup.
5. **Steep:** Cover the cup with a saucer or small plate to trap the steam and let the tea steep for about 10-15 minutes. This allows the butcher's broom to infuse its beneficial compounds into the water.
6. **Strain:** After steeping, strain the tea to remove the butcher's broom root or leaves. You can use a fine-mesh strainer or a tea infuser for this step.
7. **Optional Sweetener:** If you find the tea too bitter, add a touch of honey or another natural sweetener to taste. Stir well to dissolve.
8. **Serve and Enjoy:** Your butcher's broom tea for blood vessel care is ready to be enjoyed.

DOSAGE:

Enjoy this tea as part of your daily routine in the morning or evening for blood vessel support. Start with 1 teaspoon and increase to 2 teaspoons if desired.

Bilberry
Heart-Drops

Bilberries are small, dark berries closely related to blueberries and are known for their potential heart-health benefits. Bilberry tincture is a convenient way to harness these benefits.

INGREDIENTS:

- 1 cup fresh bilberries (*Vaccinium myrtillus*) or frozen, if fresh are not available
- 1 cup high-proof vodka or brandy (at least 80 proof)

NOTES:

While the recipe mentions using fresh bilberries, you can also experiment with other bilberry varieties like European bilberries or huckleberries if they are available in your region.

Each variety has slightly different flavors and potential health benefits.

INSTRUCTIONS:

1 | **Prepare the Bilberries:** Rinse the fresh bilberries thoroughly and allow them to air dry. If using frozen bilberries, make sure they are fully thawed.
2 | **Mash the Bilberries:** Place the bilberries in a clean, glass jar and gently mash them with a spoon or a muddler. This will help release their juices and active compounds.
3 | **Add Alcohol:** Pour the high-proof vodka or brandy over the mashed bilberries, ensuring they are completely submerged. The alcohol will extract the beneficial compounds from the berries.
4 | **Seal the Jar:** Seal the jar tightly with its lid.
5 | **Shake and Store:** Give the jar a good shake to mix the contents. Store it in a cool, dark place for at least 4-6 weeks. During this time, shake the jar gently every few days to agitate the mixture.
6 | **Strain the Tincture:** After the steeping period (4-6 weeks), strain the tincture through a fine-mesh strainer or cheesecloth into a clean, glass bottle. Squeeze the solids to extract as much liquid as possible.
7 | **Label and Store:** Label the bottle with the contents and date. Store the bilberry tincture in a cool, dark place. When stored properly, it can last for several years.

DOSAGE:

1-2 dropperfuls (about 20-40 drops) of bilberry tincture daily.

Horse Chestnut Cooling Gel
for Varicose Veins

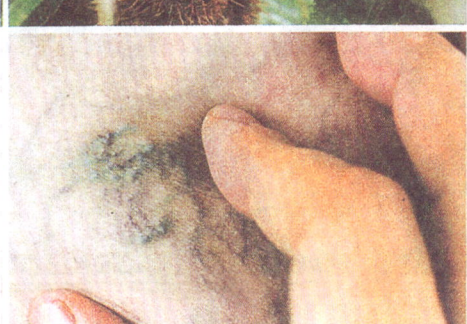

The main active component in horse chestnut is aescin, typically comprising 16-20% of the extract. Aescin is traditionally used for its potential to reduce inflammation and support circulation, particularly in the legs, and is often used in the management of varicose veins. Witch hazel, known for its astringent and anti-inflammatory properties, alongside aloe vera, valued for its soothing and moisturizing effects, are commonly combined in traditional practices to support the management of vein-related concerns like varicose veins.

INGREDIENTS:

- ¼ cup of dried horse chestnut seeds or ½ cup of fresh horse chestnuts (*Aesculus hippocastanum*)
- 1 cup of witch hazel extract (*Hamamelis virginiana*)
- ¼ cup of aloe vera gel
- 10-15 drops of lavender essential oil (optional)

NOTES:

Be careful not to confuse the horse chestnut (*Aesculus hippocastanum*) with California buckeye (*Aesculus californica*) or Ohio buckeye (*Aesculus glabra*). They are different plants with different effects. You can also take approx. 300 mg of horse chestnut seed extract that has esculin, a poisonous chemical, removed to reduce some symptoms of poor blood circulation.

INSTRUCTIONS:

1 | **Prepare the Horse Chestnut Powder:** If you're using fresh horse chestnuts, peel and finely chop them. If you're using dried horse chestnut seeds, grind them into a fine powder using a coffee grinder or a mortar and pestle.

2 | **Create the Infusion:** Place the horse chestnut powder or chopped chestnuts into a glass jar. Pour the witch hazel extract over the chestnuts until they are fully submerged. Seal the jar with a lid and shake it well to mix the ingredients. Store the jar in a cool, dark place for at least two weeks. Shake the jar gently every day to ensure a thorough infusion.

3 | **Strain the Infusion:** After two weeks, strain the infused witch hazel through cheesecloth or a fine strainer to remove any solid particles. You should be left with a clear liquid.

4 | **Combine with Aloe Vera Gel and Essential Oil:** In a clean bowl, mix the strained horse chestnut-infused witch hazel with the aloe vera gel. If desired, add 10-15 drops of lavender essential oil for its soothing properties and pleasant scent. Stir well to combine all the ingredients thoroughly.

5 | **Transfer to a Container:** Pour the mixture into a clean glass jar or container with a secure lid for storage.

6 | **Storage:** Store your homemade gel in a cool, dry place. Refrigeration is not necessary but can provide an extra cooling effect when applied.

DOSAGE:

Apply the horse chestnut cooling gel to your varicose veins by gently massaging it into the affected areas. Use it as needed for relief, but avoid excessive use.

Forgotten Home Apothecary

"Young Heart" Elixir
(The Vital Heart Blend)

This homemade tonic blend elixir combines the heart-protective properties of hawthorn berries (*Crataegus*) with the anti-inflammatory and antioxidant effects of turmeric (*Curcuma longa*), ginger (*Zingiber officinale*), and the potential blood pressure regulation benefits of garlic (*Allium sativum*). The addition of lemon juice provides vitamin C and a refreshing flavor, while the optional cayenne pepper helps aid circulation.

INGREDIENTS:

- 1 tbsp of dried hawthorn berries
- 1 small piece of fresh turmeric (about 1 inch) or ½ tsp of dried turmeric powder
- 1 small piece of fresh ginger (about 1 inch) or ½ tsp of dried ginger powder
- 1-2 cloves of fresh garlic
- Juice of half a lemon
- A pinch of cayenne pepper (optional)
- 1-2 teaspoons of honey (optional, adjust to taste)
- 1 cup water

NOTES:

If you plan to use this elixir for an extended period, consider periodic breaks to assess its continued effectiveness and any changes in your health. Start with a small serving and then gradually increase the amount if you tolerate it well and do not experience any adverse effects.

Each variety has slightly different flavors and potential health benefits.

INSTRUCTIONS:

1 | **Prepare the Herbs:** If you're using fresh turmeric and ginger, peel and thinly slice them.
2 | **Boil the Water:** Bring 1 cup of water to a boil.
3 | **Infuse the Herbs:** Add the hawthorn berries, fresh or dried turmeric, fresh or dried ginger, and fresh garlic cloves to the boiling water.
4 | **Simmer:** Reduce the heat to low, cover the pot, and let the mixture simmer for about 15-20 minutes. This will allow the herbs to release their beneficial compounds into the water.
5 | **Strain:** After simmering, strain the mixture into a cup or mug to remove the solid ingredients.
6 | **Add Lemon Juice:** Squeeze the juice of half a lemon into the herbal infusion and stir.
7 | **Add Cayenne Pepper (Optional):** If you like a bit of heat, add a pinch of cayenne pepper to the elixir. Adjust to your taste.
8 | **Sweeten (Optional):** If you prefer a sweeter taste, you can add raw honey to the elixir. Start with 1-2 teaspoons and adjust to your taste.
9 | **Stir and Serve:** Mix the elixir well and enjoy it while it's warm. You can have this tonic in the morning or throughout the day, but it's often consumed in the morning to kickstart the day.
10 | **Storage:** If you have any leftover elixir, you can store it in the refrigerator for a day or two.

DOSAGE:

Consume this amount once a day, preferably in the morning on an empty stomach.

Forgotten Home Apothecary

Warming Turmeric and Cayenne Balm
to Promote Circulation

By harnessing the natural properties of these ingredients, this balm offers potential benefits such as increased blood flow through the capsaicin in cayenne pepper (*Capsicum annuum*), anti-inflammatory effects from turmeric (*Curcuma longa*), a warming sensation aided by black pepper (*Piper nigrum*), skin hydration via coconut oil, and protective barrier support from beeswax. Together, these elements are traditionally used to support circulation, alleviate discomfort, and provide a holistic solution for improved blood flow and localized pain relief.

INGREDIENTS:

- ½ teaspoon of finely ground turmeric
- ½ teaspoon of finely ground cayenne pepper
- ¼ teaspoon of finely ground black pepper
- 3 tablespoons coconut oil
- 0.2 oz (6 g) of beeswax

NOTES:

Do not apply this warming pain-relief balm to any open wounds or cuts since it will cause a sharp stinging sensation. Avoid contact with your eyes or mucous membranes, as the cayenne pepper can cause irritation.

This balm will stain the skin due to the turmeric and cayenne pepper, but since these stains are more soluble in oil, to remove them, massage some oil into your skin and then wash off with soapy water afterward.

INSTRUCTIONS:

1 | **Create/Use a Double Boiler:** Fill a saucepan with about an inch of water and bring it to a simmer over low to medium heat. Place a heat-safe glass or metal bowl on top of the saucepan, creating a double boiler. Make sure the bottom of the bowl doesn't touch the simmering water.

2 | **Combine Coconut Oil and Beeswax:** In the double boiler, add the coconut oil and the grated beeswax to the bowl. Gently heat the mixture until the beeswax is completely melted into the coconut oil, stirring occasionally with a wooden or silicone utensil. This should take about 5 minutes.

3 | **Add the Spices:** Carefully add the ground turmeric, cayenne pepper, and black pepper to the melted oil and beeswax mixture. Stir well to combine. Continue to heat for an additional 2-3 minutes. Once you are happy with the consistency, remove the bowl from the pot of water and allow it to cool slowly to infuse the oil with the spices, stirring constantly.

4 | **Transfer to a Container:** Carefully pour the hot balm mixture into your clean glass jar or container. Use a silicone spatula or a funnel for ease. Allow the balm to cool and solidify. This may take a few hours.

5 | **Storage:** Once the balm has solidified, seal the jar with a tight-fitting lid.

DOSAGE:

Whenever needed, scoop a small amount of the balm and massage it onto sore or stiff areas of your body, such as muscles or joints, to promote circulation and alleviate discomfort.

Forgotten Home Apothecary

Arterial
De-Clogger

This recipe features a blend of ingredients traditionally known for supporting cardiovascular health. Garlic (*Allium sativum*) and ginger (*Zingiber officinale*) are valued for their potential to assist in managing cholesterol levels and improving circulation. Cinnamon (*Cinnamomum verum*) is traditionally used to support blood pressure and cholesterol management. Lemon not only adds a refreshing flavor but also provides vitamin C, which is recognized for its role in supporting heart health. This combination of potent ingredients is used traditionally to support the cardiovascular system.

INGREDIENTS:

- 2 cloves of garlic (*Allium sativum*)
- 2 inches of ginger root (*Zingiber officinale*)
- 1 x 2-inch cinnamon stick (*Cinnamomum verum*)
- ½ lemon, cut into wedges
- 1.5 cups of water
- Honey, to sweeten (optional)

NOTES:

Garlic can thin the blood, so individuals on blood-thinning medications should use caution and consult a healthcare provider before consuming large amounts.

Ginger may interact with certain medications, such as blood thinners and diabetes medications, so use caution if you are taking these medications.

INSTRUCTIONS:

1 | **Prepare the Ingredients:** Peel and crush the garlic cloves to release their juice and set them aside for 10 minutes. Chop the ginger into small pieces. Use fresh, organic ingredients for the best flavor and health benefits.
2 | **Boil the Water:** Boil 1.5 cups of water over medium heat in a pot.
3 | **Infuse Ingredients:** Add the chopped ginger, crushed garlic, and cinnamon stick to the boiling water. Continue boiling until the water reduces to about a cup, ensuring the flavors are infused into the water.
4 | **Add Lemon:** Add the lemon wedges to the pot and then turn off the heat.
5 | **Steep Mixture:** Cover the pot and let the mixture steep for 5 minutes to allow the flavors to meld.
6 | **Strain Liquid:** After steeping, strain the mixture to remove any solid particles.
7 | **Sweeten:** Sweeten the tea with honey if desired, stirring until dissolved.

DOSAGE:

Take one cup of this tea on an empty stomach daily for 7 days for arterial health benefits.

HERBAL SUPPORT
for the Digestive System

The digestive system plays a crucial role in maintaining our overall health and well-being. It is responsible for breaking down the food we consume into essential nutrients, which our body can then absorb and use for energy, growth, and repair.

Tips to Maintain a Healthy Digestive System:

HEALTHY DIET:
- Consume plenty of fiber from whole grains, fruits, vegetables, and legumes to support digestive health.
- Avoid excessive processed foods, sugary snacks, and large meals before bedtime.
- Eat in moderation - not overloading your stomach can prevent discomfort and aid digestion.
- Include probiotic-rich foods like yogurt, kefir, sauerkraut, kimchi, and kombucha to promote a healthy gut flora.
- Identify and avoid foods that trigger digestive discomfort, such as spicy foods, high-fat foods, and foods you're intolerant to.

CHEW FOOD THOROUGHLY:
Take your time to chew food properly. Chewing initiates the digestive process in the mouth and eases the workload on the stomach.

MANAGE PORTION SIZES:
Avoid overeating. Eating smaller, balanced meals can prevent discomfort and bloating.

LIMIT ALCOHOL AND CAFFEINE:
Excessive alcohol and caffeine intake can irritate the digestive tract. Consume them in moderation.

AVOID SMOKING:
Smoking can contribute to digestive issues, including acid reflux. Quitting smoking can improve digestive health.

STAY ACTIVE AFTER MEALS:
Take a short walk or engage in light activity after meals to aid digestion.

HYDRATION:
Drink enough water to aid digestion and prevent constipation.

HERBAL SUPPORT

Peppermint *(Mentha piperita)*
Traditionally used to calm digestive spasms, ease gas, and soothe indigestion. Peppermint tea and essential oil capsules are commonly used.

Ginger *(Zingiber officinale)*
Known for reducing nausea, supporting digestion, and its anti-inflammatory properties. Ginger can be enjoyed as tea or used fresh in cooking.

Chamomile *(Matricaria chamomilla)*
Often used to soothe an upset stomach, relieve indigestion, and promote relaxation. Typically consumed as tea.

Fennel *(Foeniculum vulgare)*
Traditionally used to relieve bloating and gas and to support digestion. Fennel seeds may be chewed or brewed as tea.

Turmeric *(Curcuma longa)*
Contains curcumin, which is recognized for its anti-inflammatory properties and digestive health support. Turmeric may be used in cooking or taken as an oral supplement or tincture.

Dandelion *(Taraxacum officinale)*
Used to support liver health, which indirectly benefits digestion. Available as root tea or in supplement or tincture form.

Licorice *(Glycyrrhiza glabra)*
Traditionally used to soothe the stomach lining, aid digestion, and support overall digestive health. It's advised to use licorice root tea or supplements cautiously.

Marshmallow Root *(Althaea officinalis)* and Slippery Elm Bark *(Ulmus rubra)*
Known to aid digestion, coat the digestive tract with mucilage, and provide anti-inflammatory benefits, which support gut health.

3-Ingredient
Digestive Tonic

Fennel seeds are traditionally known for their carminative properties, which may help relieve bloating and gas. Angelica root is valued for its anti-inflammatory qualities that may soothe digestive discomfort. Agrimony, with its astringent nature, is often used as an aid in alleviating minor digestive issues. Whether you've overindulged in a meal or just want to promote healthy digestion, this homemade tonic can offer a gentle and effective solution.

INGREDIENTS:

- 1 tbsp dried fennel seeds (*Foeniculum vulgare*)
- 1 tbsp dried angelica root (*Angelica archangelica*)
- 1 tbsp dried agrimony (*Agrimonia eupatoria*)
- 2 cups boiling water
- 1-2 tablespoons of honey or maple syrup
- Fresh lemon juice (from 1 lemon)
- Fresh mint leaves for garnish

NOTES:

As with any plant-based product, some individuals may be allergic to certain herbs. Exercise caution. Agrimony may interfere with blood-thinning and blood glucose medications. If you are on these medications or have diabetes, consult a healthcare provider before using agrimony. You may also replace agrimony with mint.

INSTRUCTIONS:

1 | **Gather Your Ingredients:** You'll need dried fennel seeds, dried angelica root, dried agrimony, water, and honey (if desired).
2 | **Measure the Herbs:** Use about 1 tablespoon of each herb per cup of water. You can adjust the quantities based on how much tonic you want to make.
3 | **Boil the Water:** In a pot, bring the desired amount of water to a boil.
4 | **Add the Herbs:** Once the water is boiling, add the fennel seeds, angelica root, and agrimony to the pot.
5 | **Simmer:** Reduce the heat to low and let the herbs simmer for about 10-15 minutes. This allows the herbs to infuse into the water.
6 | **Strain:** After simmering, strain the mixture to remove the herbs. You can use a fine-mesh strainer or a piece of cheesecloth.
7 | **Sweeten (Optional):** If desired, add honey to the strained liquid while it's still warm to sweeten the tonic. Start with a teaspoon of honey and adjust to taste.
8 | **Cool:** Allow the tonic to cool to room temperature.
9 | **Store:** Transfer the tonic to a clean glass container with a lid, and store it in the refrigerator. It can be kept for several days.

DOSAGE:

Take a small amount of the tonic (¼ to ½ cup) before or after meals to help support digestion. You can also drink it as a soothing herbal tea if you experience digestive discomfort.

Chamomile and Lemon Balm
Calming Infusion

Chamomile is traditionally celebrated for its soothing effects, anti-inflammatory properties, and ability to provide relief from gas, bloating, and indigestion. Lemon balm is known for its calming effects, acting as an antispasmodic, reducing nausea, and providing mild laxative support. When combined in a tea, these herbs form a harmonious blend that can alleviate various digestive discomforts and promote overall digestive well-being. Additionally, this remedy is commonly used to help with anxiety and hay fever, making it a versatile option for supporting general health.

INGREDIENTS:

- 1 tablespoon of dried chamomile flowers (*Matricaria chamomilla*)
- 1 tablespoon of dried lemon balm leaves (*Melissa officinalis*)
- 1 cup of boiling water
- Optional: Honey or fresh lemon for added flavor

NOTES:

This infusion has a mild and pleasant flavor, making it suitable for most palates.

The honey or lemon is optional and can be added to enhance the taste.

If you have known allergies to chamomile, lemon balm, or related plants, avoid this infusion.

INSTRUCTIONS:

1 | **Boil the Water:** Start by boiling 1 cup of water using a kettle or saucepan.
2 | **Prepare Chamomile and Lemon Balm:** Place 1 tablespoon of dried chamomile flowers and 1 tablespoon of dried lemon balm leaves in a teapot or a large heatproof cup.
3 | **Pour Boiling Water:** Carefully pour the boiling water over the dried herbs in the teapot or cup.
4 | **Steep the Infusion:** Cover the teapot or cup with a saucer or small plate to trap the steam, and let the herbs steep in the hot water for about 5-10 minutes. This will allow the flavors and beneficial compounds to infuse into the water.
5 | **Strain the Infusion:** After steeping, strain the infusion through a fine-mesh strainer or a tea infuser to remove the dried herbs.
6 | **Optional Flavorings:** If desired, add a touch of honey or a squeeze of fresh lemon to your infusion for added flavor. Adjust the amount to your taste.
7 | **Serve and Enjoy:** Your chamomile and lemon balm infusion with dried herbs is ready to be enjoyed. Sip it slowly while it's still warm, especially when you have an upset stomach.

DOSAGE:

1 cup of chamomile and lemon balm infusion as needed

Forgotten Home Apothecary

Soothing Syrup
for an Upset Stomach

Gingerol, a key component in ginger, is traditionally recognized for its influence on gastrointestinal motility (the rate of digestion). This homemade stomach-soothing syrup combines the natural properties of ginger with optional spices that add warmth and comfort. It's a gentle remedy commonly used for soothing an upset stomach or relieving nausea. This blend harnesses the well-regarded benefits of ginger to provide a natural option for digestive discomfort.

INGREDIENTS:

- 1 cup fresh ginger root (*Zingiber officinale*), thinly sliced
- 2 cups water
- 1 cup raw honey
- Optional flavors: cinnamon stick, whole cloves, star anise, cardamom pods

NOTES:

For the best results, use fresh ginger root (rather than dried). The peel of ginger has some vital nutrients. If you can find an organic option, you can keep the peel on. If conventional ginger is your only option, it's better to remove the peel.

Even if you don't feel sick, taking a serving after dinner will improve digestion. For a peppy pick-me-up, stir a spoonful into some bubbly water for a DIY ginger ale.

INSTRUCTIONS:

1| **Prepare the Ginger:** Wash and peel the ginger root. Cut into thin slices or small pieces. The thinner the slices, the more flavor will infuse into your syrup.
2| **Create the Infusion:** In a medium saucepan, combine the sliced ginger and 2 cups of water. If you'd like to add optional flavors like cinnamon stick, whole cloves, star anise, or cardamom pods for extra soothing effects, this is the time to include them. Place the saucepan over medium heat and bring the mixture to a boil. Once boiling, reduce the heat to a simmer, cover the pot, and let simmer for about 30-45 minutes. This will infuse the water with the ginger's beneficial properties and flavors.
3| **Strain:** After simmering, remove the saucepan from the heat and let it cool for a few minutes. Strain the ginger-infused liquid into a bowl or another saucepan, using a fine-mesh strainer or cheesecloth. Make sure to press the ginger slices to extract as much liquid as possible.
4| **Sweeten:** Return the ginger-infused liquid to the saucepan and place it back on the stove over low heat. Add 1 cup of honey to the ginger-infused liquid. Stir continuously until the sweetener is completely dissolved. You can use less or more depending on how sweet you want the syrup to be.
5| **Store:** Once the honey is fully dissolved, remove the saucepan from heat and let it cool to room temperature. Pour your syrup into a clean, airtight glass bottle or jar. Store it in the refrigerator for up to two weeks.

DOSAGE:

Take 1-2 tablespoons of the syrup as needed. You can consume it as is or dilute it with warm water for a milder flavor.

Lemon and Ginger
Nausea Lollipops

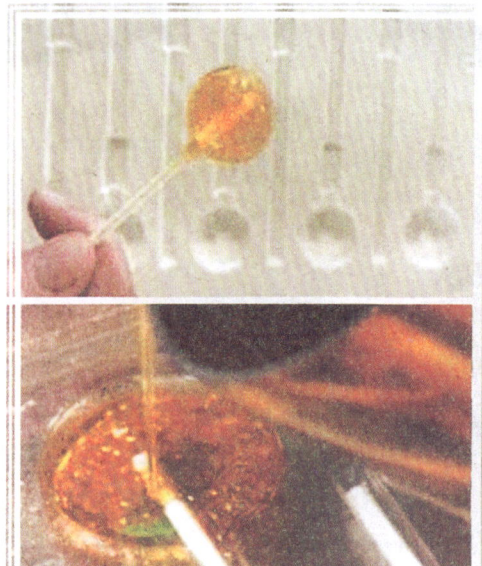

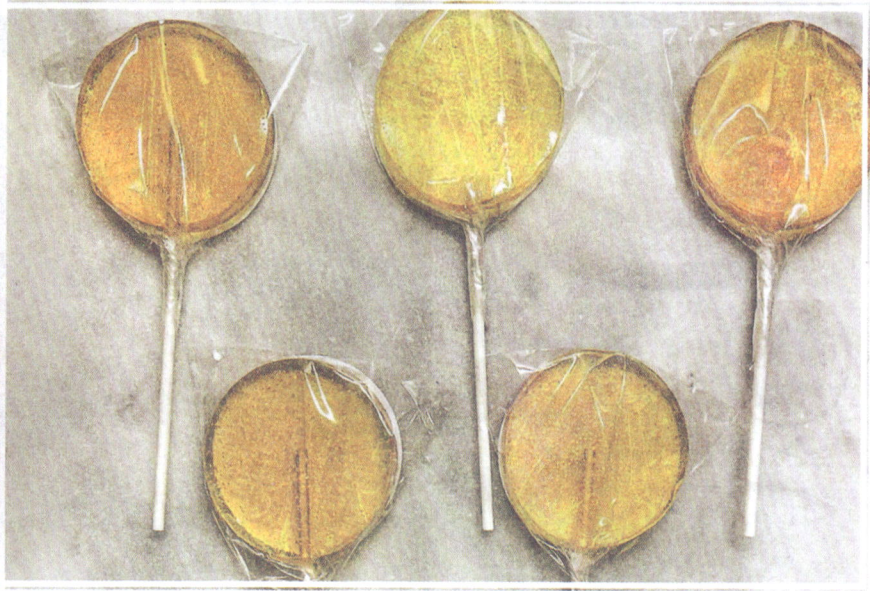

These homemade lemon and ginger nausea lollipops are a delicious and natural way to ease nausea. Ginger is traditionally known for its anti-nausea properties, and when combined with lemon, it creates a soothing and refreshing flavor. These lollipops are a convenient and enjoyable option for managing nausea naturally.

INGREDIENTS AND MATERIALS:

- 1 cup fresh lemon juice (about 4-5 lemons)
- 2 tablespoons grated fresh ginger (*Zingiber officinale*)
- 1 cup granulated sugar
- ¼ cup honey
- Lollipop sticks
- Candy thermometer
- Lollipop molds

NOTES:

Be cautious with hot sugar. The sugar mixture will be extremely hot, so use caution when pouring it into molds and handling the lollipops afterward.

You might want to use oven mitts or gloves. Silicone lollipop molds work well for this recipe, but you can also use metal lollipop molds or simply metal spoons or shape the lollipops on parchment paper.

INSTRUCTIONS:

1 | **Prepare Your Equipment:** Insert lollipop sticks into the molds. Make sure they are securely in place. Have a candy thermometer ready.
2 | **Combine Ingredients:** In a medium saucepan, combine the fresh lemon juice, grated ginger, granulated sugar, and honey.
3 | **Heat and Stir:** Heat the mixture over medium heat, stirring constantly until the sugar has completely dissolved.
4 | **Boil and Cook:** Once the sugar has dissolved, insert the candy thermometer into the mixture. Continue to cook without stirring until the temperature reaches 300°F (hard crack stage). This should take about 15-20 minutes.
5 | **Remove from Heat:** Once the mixture reaches 300°F, immediately remove it from the heat.
6 | **Pour into Molds:** Carefully pour the hot mixture into your lollipop molds, filling each cavity.
7 | **Cool and Set:** Allow the lollipops to cool and harden. This usually takes about 20-30 minutes.
8 | **Remove from Molds:** Once the lollipops are completely cool and solidified, gently remove them from the molds. Be careful not to break them.
9 | **Store:** Wrap each lollipop individually in plastic wrap or place them in an airtight container to prevent moisture from softening them. Store them in a cool, dry place.

DOSAGE:

Enjoy one whenever you need relief from nausea.

Restorative
Liver Tea

This herbal tea is traditionally used to support liver health and overall wellness. Dandelion and milk thistle have been valued in herbal practices for their potential benefits. Dandelion root is commonly known to help with digestion and is believed to support liver function. Milk thistle has been traditionally used to promote liver health. This simple and natural tea may offer a gentle way to incorporate these herbs into your daily routine.

INGREDIENTS:

- 2 tablespoons of fresh milk thistle root, chopped (*Silybum marianum*)
- 2 tablespoons of fresh dandelion root, chopped (*Taraxacum officinale*)
- 4 cups of water

NOTES:

You can grind these herbs into a powder and put it into capsules for people who find the flavor disagreeable or need an easy way to take it.

In some cases, milk thistle is used in clinical settings for individuals exposed to certain toxins. For example, it has been used in cases of poisoning from Amanita mushrooms, which can be harmful to the liver. It is important to note that such treatments should only be administered by healthcare professionals.

INSTRUCTIONS:

1 | **Gather and Prepare the Roots:** Collect fresh dandelion and milk thistle roots. Wash the roots thoroughly under running water to remove any dirt and impurities. Use a knife to chop the roots into small, uniform pieces. This will help to release their beneficial properties during the simmering process.

2 | **Simmer:** Place the chopped dandelion and milk thistle roots in a medium-sized pot. Add 4 cups of water to the pot, ensuring the roots are fully submerged. Bring the water to a gentle boil over medium heat. Once boiling, reduce the heat to low and let the mixture simmer for about 20 minutes. This allows the roots to infuse the water with their natural compounds.

3 | **Steep the Tea:** After simmering, remove the pot from heat. Cover the pot with a lid and let the mixture steep for an additional 10-15 minutes. This helps to extract the maximum benefits from the roots.

4 | **Strain and Serve:** Use a fine mesh strainer or cheesecloth to strain the tea, removing the root pieces. Pour the tea into a cup or teapot. You may add a natural sweetener like honey or a slice of lemon if desired.

DOSAGE:

It is generally recommended to drink 1-2 cups of this restorative tea daily.

Forgotten Home Apothecary

Fatty Liver
Tincture

Fatty liver, medically termed hepatic steatosis, is a condition characterized by the accumulation of excess fat in the liver, which can lead to inflammation and potential liver issues over time. While conventional medical treatments and lifestyle modifications are essential for managing fatty liver disease, incorporating supportive herbal remedies may offer additional benefits.

This herbal blend features three herbs traditionally used for their liver-supportive properties: schisandra, licorice root, and ginger. Each herb in this blend contributes unique compounds that are believed to promote liver health by supporting traditional practices aimed at reducing inflammation, aiding detoxification processes, and protecting liver cells.

INGREDIENTS:

- 2 parts dried schisandra berries (*Schisandra chinensis*)
- 1 part dried licorice root (*Glycyrrhiza glabra*)
- 1 part grated ginger (*Zingiber officinale*)
- High-proof alcohol (such as vodka) or vegetable glycerin (for an alcohol-free option)

NOTES:

Consult with your healthcare provider before, especially if you have a medical condition or are taking medications.

Pregnant and breastfeeding women should consult their healthcare provider before using this tincture. Consider reducing alcohol consumption and avoiding processed foods high in unhealthy fats to further support liver health.

INSTRUCTIONS:

1. **Preparation:** Measure the dried herbs using the parts method (*e.g.,* if using tablespoons, 2 tablespoons of schisandra berries, 1 tablespoon of licorice root, and 1 tablespoon of grated ginger). Place the measured herbs into a clean glass jar.
2. **Infusion:** Pour the high-proof alcohol or vegetable glycerin over the herbs, ensuring they are fully submerged. Leave about ½ - inch of space at the top of the jar. Seal the jar tightly with a lid.
3. **Steep:** Store the jar in a cool, dark place for 4-6 weeks, shaking it gently every few days to help the infusion process.
4. **Strain:** After 4-6 weeks, strain the liquid through a fine mesh strainer or cheesecloth into a clean glass bottle, discarding the herbs.
5. **Storage:** Store the tincture in a dark glass bottle to protect it from light. Label the bottle with the date and ingredients.

DOSAGE:

The general dosage for a tincture is 1-2 droppers full (approximately 20-40 drops) in water or juice, taken 1-2 times daily. Start with a lower dose and consult with a healthcare provider to find the dosage that works best for you.

Forgotten Home Apothecary

Moringa Powder
for Liver Detox

Moringa powder is believed to offer potential benefits for liver health due to its antioxidant, anti-inflammatory, and hepatoprotective properties. It may help protect the liver from damage, reduce inflammation, and support detoxification.

INGREDIENTS:

- Fresh moringa leaves (*Moringa oleifera*)

NOTES:

Remember that while moringa is considered safe for most people, excessive consumption of moringa powder may have laxative effects due to its high fiber content. If you experience any adverse effects, reduce the dosage or discontinue use. Consult a healthcare professional before significant dietary changes, especially if you have liver issues. It should complement a holistic approach to liver health, including a balanced diet and lifestyle choices. If you suspect liver problems, consult a healthcare provider for proper evaluation and treatment.

INSTRUCTIONS:

1 | **Harvest:** If you have moringa trees in your backyard, simply harvest a bunch of stalks. You may also purchase them. Always opt for the mature, rich green leaves.

2 | **Wash the Leaves:** Thoroughly wash the leaves to remove any dirt or contaminants. Use clean, cold water for this step.

3 | **Air Dry:** Shake the excess water off the leaves, tie the ends of the stalks together, and hang them upside down in an enclosed place that doesn't get direct sunlight, to preserve the nutrients. Leave the leaves hanging for three to four days till they are brittle to the touch.

4 | **Remove the Stems:** Separate the leaves from the stalks and stems. The fewer stems there are, the smoother the powder will be.

5 | **Grind into Powder:** Place the dried moringa leaves in a blender or a spice/coffee grinder. Grind them into a fine powder. You may need to do this in batches, depending on the quantity of leaves.

6 | **Store:** Keep the moringa powder in an airtight container to preserve the nutrients, and store it in a cool, dry place. Keep the container closed to keep moisture out and to preserve a longer shelf life. The powder will last up to six months without preservatives.

DOSAGE:

1-2 teaspoons. To incorporate moringa powder into your diet for potential liver health benefits, you can add it to smoothies, soups, salads, or use it as a seasoning in your cooking.

IBS Relief
Peppermint Oil

Peppermint oil is often used as a natural remedy for irritable bowel syndrome (IBS) symptoms such as abdominal pain, bloating, and gas. The active ingredient in peppermint oil, menthol, has been shown to relax the muscles of the gastrointestinal tract and reduce spasms, which can help alleviate some of the discomfort associated with IBS.

INGREDIENTS:

- 1 cup fresh peppermint leaves (*Mentha piperita*) -packed
- 1 cup carrier oil (*e.g.*, olive oil, almond oil, or coconut oil)

NOTES:

Enteric-coated peppermint oil appears to be safe to take internally at safe doses. However, healthcare professionals do not recommend ingesting essential oils. Pure essential oils are highly concentrated and can be toxic. Here we use an infused oil (versus an essential oil).

Menthol can cause serious side effects in children, so parents and caregivers should not apply peppermint essential oil to a child's skin or allow them to inhale or ingest it.

INSTRUCTIONS:

1. **Harvest and Prepare the Peppermint Leaves:** Pick approximately 1 cup of fresh peppermint leaves from your garden or a trusted source. Wash the leaves to remove any dirt or debris. Make sure the leaves are air-dried for a few days prior to using.
2. **Crush or Bruise the Leaves:** Gently crush or bruise the peppermint leaves with a mortar and pestle to release the essential oils and aroma.
3. **Prepare the Infusion:** Place the crushed peppermint leaves in a glass jar. Pour exactly 1 cup of your chosen carrier oil over the leaves to fully cover them. Ensure that the leaves are completely submerged in the oil.
4. **Seal and Steep:** Seal the glass jar with a tight-fitting lid. Store it in a cool, dark place for about two to three weeks. This allows the peppermint leaves to infuse their flavor and beneficial compounds into the oil.
5. **Shake Daily:** Shake the jar gently once a day to help with the infusion process and distribute the peppermint.
6. **Strain the Oil:** After the steeping period, strain the oil through a cheesecloth or fine mesh strainer into a clean bowl or container. Squeeze the cheesecloth to extract as much oil as possible.
7. **Transfer to a Storage Bottle:** Pour the strained peppermint-infused oil into a small, dark glass bottle with a dropper or cap for easy dispensing and storage.
8. **Store Properly:** Store the peppermint oil in a cool, dark place away from direct sunlight. Properly stored, it can last for several months.

DOSAGE:

0.5 ml (~½ a dropperful) for adults taken 3 times a day. It's best to take it about 1 hour before meals.

Forgotten Home Apothecary

Dandelion and Gentian Bitter Tonic
for Indigestion

This homemade dandelion and gentian bitter tonic is a natural remedy for indigestion.

Dandelion root is traditionally used to stimulate the production of digestive juices, helping with indigestion and bloating, while gentian root is known for its traditional use as a digestive aid, believed to stimulate digestive enzymes and improve appetite. It is particularly valued for supporting those with weak digestion.

INGREDIENTS:

- 2 tablespoons of dried and chopped dandelion root (*Taraxacum officinale*)
- 1 tablespoon of dried and chopped gentian root (*Gentiana lutea*)
- 2 cups of water
- 1-2 tablespoons of honey or maple syrup (optional for sweetness, adjust to taste)

NOTES:

Start with a small dosage, as the bitterness can be intense, and adjust to your preference. Shake the bottle before each use, as the herbs may settle at the bottom.

If you have known allergies to dandelion or gentian, avoid using this tonic.

INSTRUCTIONS:

1 | **Prepare Your Ingredients:** Measure 2 tablespoons of dried and chopped dandelion root and 1 tablespoon of dried and chopped gentian root. Pour 2 cups of water into a saucepan.
2 | **Boil the Water:** Place the saucepan on the stove and set it to medium-high heat. Wait until the water comes to a rolling boil.
3 | **Infuse the Roots:** Add the dried dandelion and gentian roots to the boiling water. Reduce the heat to low.
4 | **Simmer the Mixture:** Allow the mixture to simmer for about 15-20 minutes. This step lets the roots infuse their bitterness into the water, creating the tonic.
5 | **Cool the Tonic:** Remove the saucepan from the heat source. Let the mixture cool naturally to room temperature.
6 | **Strain:** Strain the liquid into a glass container or bottle.
7 | **Sweeten (Optional):** If you prefer a sweeter taste, add 1-2 tablespoons of honey or maple syrup to the tonic. Stir.
8 | **Store Your Tonic:** Transfer the finished tonic to a glass bottle or jar with a lid.

DOSAGE:

Take 1-2 tablespoons of this bitter tonic before meals to aid digestion.

Ginger and ACV
for Bloating and Gas Relief

This homemade remedy combines the soothing properties of ginger and the digestive benefits of apple cider vinegar (ACV) to provide relief from bloating and gas. It's a simple and natural way to ease discomfort after a heavy meal.

INGREDIENTS:

- 1-2 inches of fresh ginger root (*Zingiber officinale*), peeled and thinly sliced (or 1-2 tsp of ginger powder)
- 1 tablespoon of raw, unfiltered apple cider vinegar
- 1 cup of warm water
- Optional: Honey or maple syrup for sweetness
- Optional: A slice of lemon for added flavor

NOTES:

The honey or maple syrup is optional and can be adjusted to your taste preference.

Some people find the drink palatable without sweeteners due to the natural sweetness of ginger.

INSTRUCTIONS:

1 | **Prepare the Ginger:** If you're using fresh ginger, peel the ginger root and thinly slice it. You can also grate it for a more intense ginger flavor.
2 | **Heat Water:** Heat 1 cup of water to a warm, not boiling, temperature. You can use a kettle or a saucepan.
3 | **Combine Ingredients:** Place the sliced or grated ginger in a heatproof cup or mug. Add 1 tablespoon of raw, unfiltered apple cider vinegar to the cup.
4 | **Pour Warm Water:** Carefully pour the warm water over the ginger and ACV in the cup.
5 | **Optional Sweetener and Lemon:** If desired, add a teaspoon of honey or maple syrup to sweeten the drink. You may also squeeze in a slice of lemon for added flavor.
6 | **Stir Well:** Stir the mixture thoroughly to ensure the ginger and ACV infuse well.
7 | **Steep and Infuse:** Allow the drink to steep and infuse for about 5 minutes; longer if you prefer a stronger ginger flavor.
8 | **Remove Ginger Slices:** If you used fresh ginger slices, you can remove them from the cup before drinking, or leave them in for added flavor and benefits.
9 | **Serve and Enjoy:** Your drink is ready to be enjoyed. Sip it slowly, especially after meals or when you're experiencing bloating or gas discomfort.

DOSAGE:

Consume this drink as needed, especially when you experience bloating or gas discomfort after meals. Start with a small amount, such as half a cup, and gradually increase the quantity if needed.

Forgotten Home Apothecary

Dandelion Lemonade
for Gallbladder Health

This refreshing dandelion lemonade not only quenches your thirst but also incorporates the traditional benefits of dandelion, which is used to support gallbladder health. Lemons are known for their cleansing properties and high content of B and C vitamins, which also help balance the bitterness of dandelion. Both dandelion and lemon are traditionally used to support the reduction of oxidative stress and maintain healthy cellular metabolism, making them an ideal combination.

INGREDIENTS:

- 2-3 fresh dandelion leaves and root (*Taraxacum officinalis*) or 1 tsp of dried dandelion leaves and root
- 1 cup of boiling water
- 1-2 tablespoons of fresh lemon juice (adjust to taste)
- 1-2 teaspoons of honey or maple syrup (optional, for sweetness)
- Ice cubes (optional)
- Lemon slices and fresh dandelion flowers for garnish (optional)

NOTES:

If you have known allergies to dandelions or related plants, avoid this recipe. While dandelion is generally safe in moderate amounts, excessive consumption may lead to stomach upset in some individuals. Start with a small serving. It can be kept in the refrigerator in a sealed container for up to a week, or frozen for two to three months.

INSTRUCTIONS:

1. **Harvest or Prepare Dandelion:** If you have access to fresh dandelion leaves and roots, harvest a young tender plant. Rinse it thoroughly and chop it all into small pieces. If you don't have fresh dandelion, you can use 1 teaspoon of dried dandelion leaves and root instead.
2. **Boil the Water:** Bring 1 cup of water to a boil using a kettle or a saucepan.
3. **Prepare Infusion:** Place the fresh or dried dandelion in a heatproof cup or teapot. Pour the boiling water over the leaves.
4. **Steep the Infusion:** Cover the cup or teapot and let the dandelion steep for about 5-10 minutes. This allows the dandelion's beneficial compounds to infuse into the water.
5. **Strain the Infusion:** After steeping, strain the dandelion infusion to remove the leaves and root. You can use a fine-mesh strainer or a tea infuser.
6. **Add Lemon Juice:** Stir in 1-2 tablespoons of fresh lemon juice, adjusting the amount to your taste preference.
7. **Sweeten (Optional):** If desired, add 1-2 teaspoons of honey or maple syrup to the lemonade for sweetness. Stir well.
8. **Chill and Serve:** Allow the dandelion lemonade to cool to room temperature, then refrigerate it until it's cold. You can add ice cubes for quicker cooling.
9. **Garnish (Optional):** When serving, garnish your dandelion lemonade with lemon slices and a few fresh dandelion flowers for a lovely touch.

DOSAGE:

Drink 1 glass of lemonade first thing in the morning to support your body's natural cleansing processes.

Rejuvelac
for Leaky Gut

Rejuvelac is a fermented beverage, traditionally valued for its probiotic content. It is often consumed to support digestion, enhance nutrient absorption, and contribute to overall gut health.

INGREDIENTS AND MATERIALS:

- ½ cup of gluten-free whole grains (such as quinoa, buckwheat, or millet)
- Filtered water
- A large glass jar or a sprouting jar

NOTES:

If you're not enjoying the natural tangy flavor, you can add some honey to make it taste better. Another great way to get your daily Rejuvelac is to use it as a base for smoothies. This tends to mask the flavor completely, and seriously boosts its nutritional value.

Other ways to get creative is to use it in your homemade salad dressings. Rejuvelac is also used as a base to create vegan cheese, because it adds a cheesy fermented flavor.

INSTRUCTIONS:

1. **Rinse the Grains:** Begin by rinsing the gluten-free grains thoroughly under cold running water. Make sure to remove any debris or impurities.
2. **Soak the Grains:** Place the rinsed grains in a glass or sprouting jar and add enough filtered water to cover it. Use a breathable lid, like a piece of cheesecloth or a clean kitchen towel, secured with a rubber band or string. Let the grains soak for 6-8 hours or overnight.
3. **Drain and Rinse:** After soaking, drain the grains and rinse them well under running water. Drain thoroughly to remove excess water.
4. **Sprout the Grains:** Cover the jar with cheesecloth and leave it in a dark place at room temperature for 24-48 hours, rinsing and draining the grains every 8-12 hours. You should see small sprouts emerging.
5. **Fermentation:** Once the grains have sprouted, add 2 cups of filtered water to the jar. Re-cover with the breathable lid. Allow the grains to ferment at room temperature for 1-3 days. During this time, the water will become cloudy, and bubbles may form. This is a sign of fermentation.
6. **Strain the Liquid:** Once the fermentation process is complete, strain the liquid into a clean glass container. This liquid is your rejuvelac. You can discard the grains or feed them to the birds.
7. **Refrigeration:** Rejuvelac should be stored in an airtight container in the refrigerator to maintain freshness and prevent spoilage. Properly stored rejuvelac can last for up to two weeks in the fridge. If you notice any signs of spoilage, such as a foul odor or mold, discard the rejuvelac and make a new batch.

DOSAGE:

Start with ¼ cup of rejuvelac daily. Gradually increase the amount as your body adjusts, up to 1 cup per day.

Gut Health
Morning Shots

Morning gut health shots are a simple way to support your digestive health and overall well-being. These shots are a concentrated blend of ingredients traditionally used to aid digestion. They may help reduce bloating, support nutrient absorption, promote a healthy gut biome, and assist in managing blood sugar levels. With a variety of ingredients to choose from, you can customize your gut health shot to fit your needs and preferences. Here's a recipe to start you off, but feel free to tweak to your own liking.

INGREDIENTS:

- 1 cup water
- 1 lemon
- ½ orange
- ¼ cup apple cider vinegar (with the mother)
- 1 tbsp fresh turmeric (*Curcuma longa*)
- A pinch of pepper (*Piper nigrum*)
- 1 tbsp fresh ginger (*Zingiber officinale*)
- 1 tsp honey (for sweetness)
- 1 tbsp chia seed

NOTES:

Turmeric can stain, so be careful when handling it. There are so many different takes on a morning health shot.

Here are a few other ingredients that work well: cayenne pepper, beetroot, greens, psyllium husk, papaya, aloe vera juice.

INSTRUCTIONS:

1 | **Prep Ingredients:** Measure out one cup of water, then juice in the lemon and half the orange. *The high acidity in the citrus and vinegar can be harsh on the system. In fact, the high acidity can damage your teeth and throat. Always water down your gut booster shots when they have such highly acidic ingredients.

2 | **Grate the Turmeric and Ginger:** Using a zester, grate the fresh turmeric and ginger roots. Both these roots are high in fiber and have highly nutritious peels. If you can find organic options, then leave the peel on. Otherwise, it's best practice to peel your roots before adding them to your gut health shots.

3 | **Mix It All Up:** Add the grated roots, the pepper, the apple cider vinegar, the honey, and the chia seeds to a jar.

4 | **Stir or Blend:** You have two options. Either stir the mixture thoroughly to ensure all ingredients are well combined or blend the ingredients to make a more homogenous mixture.

5 | **Allow Chia Seeds to Swell:** Let the mixture sit for a few minutes to allow the chia seeds to absorb liquid and swell.

6 | **Enjoy and Store:** Pour yourself a 1.5-ounce serving and enjoy the fiery, tangy boost to your morning. Store in a sealed container for a week.

DOSAGE:

Take one shot daily for improved gut health. Consume it first thing in the morning on an empty stomach for the best results.

Herbal
Acid Reflux Reliever

There are many natural options for supporting relief from acid reflux, and this recipe is a staple. Carrot juice provides a vitamin-rich and low-acidity base, combining its soothing properties with those of aloe juice. Aloe juice, known for its antioxidant and anti-inflammatory properties, is traditionally used to help relieve symptoms of GERD. Ginger, a natural digestive aid, is a key ingredient in this anti-acid reflux juice. Powdered cinnamon and turmeric, both used for centuries to support digestive health, add to the effectiveness of this blend. Mix it all together to create a soothing and delicious drink to help manage acid reflux.

INGREDIENTS:

- 1 carrot
- 1-inch piece of ginger (*Zingiber officinale*)
- 1 cup aloe vera juice
- ¼ tsp cinnamon (*Cinnamomum verum*)
- ¼ tsp turmeric (*Curcuma longa*)

NOTES:
Aloe vera juice is known for its soothing properties, but some people may be sensitive to it. If you're new to aloe vera consumption, start with a small amount to check for any adverse reactions. Turmeric and cinnamon are anti-inflammatory spices that can help with digestion, but they should be used in moderation.

INSTRUCTIONS:

1 | **Prepare Ingredients:** Wash the carrot and ginger pieces, then roughly chop them into about ½ inch chunks.
2 | **Combine Ingredients:** Add the carrot and ginger into your blender, then pour in the aloe juice.
3 | **Sprinkle the Cinnamon and Turmeric on Top:** Blend ingredients until pulverized.
4 | **Strain Out the Pulp:** Place a small sieve over a glass and slowly pour the contents of the blender through the sieve. Use a spoon at the end to press the juice out of the carrot pulp.

You don't have to strain the juice if you want to take advantage of the fiber from the carrot and ginger but this way is easier to digest and will provide the quickest relief for acid reflux. If you have a juicer, feel free to juice the carrots and ginger then mix in the aloe and spices.

DOSAGE:

Consume this anti-acid reflux juice about 30 minutes before a meal or whenever you experience acid reflux symptoms. Start with a small amount (around ⅛-¼ cup) to see how your body reacts, and you can gradually increase the dosage if needed. Do not exceed one cup per day.

Forgotten Home Apothecary

Gastritis, Colitis, and Ulcer
Tea Blend

Herbal teas have long been cherished for their soothing and healing properties, and in this recipe, we'll explore a blend of botanical ingredients carefully chosen to promote digestive wellness and reduce inflammation. Each herb has a unique set of benefits that, when combined, create a harmonious blend to provide relief and support for those grappling with gastrointestinal discomfort.

INGREDIENTS:

- 1 tablespoon dried chamomile flowers (*Matricaria chamomilla*)
- 1 tablespoon dried marshmallow root (*Althaea officinalis*)
- 1 tablespoon dried licorice root (*Glycyrrhiza glabra*)
- 1 tablespoon dried calendula flowers (*Calendula officinalis*)
- 1 teaspoon dried meadowsweet leaves (*Filipendula ulmaria*)
- 1 teaspoon dried slippery elm bark (*Ulmus rubra*)
- 4 cups of water

NOTES:

Licorice root should be used with caution and for short periods, as it may raise blood pressure in some individuals. If you have high blood pressure, consult a healthcare professional before using this tea.

- **Marshmallow Root:** Forms a protective layer in the stomach and intestines, reducing irritation.
- **Chamomile:** Soothes inflammation and eases digestive discomfort.
- **Licorice root:** Offers gastrointestinal relief and can help with healing.
- **Calendula:** Known for its anti-inflammatory properties, it can aid in soothing digestive issues.
- **Meadowsweet:** Helps with reducing acidity and inflammation in the stomach.
- **Slippery Elm:** Forms a soothing coating in the digestive tract, alleviating discomfort.

INSTRUCTIONS:

1. **Boil the Water:** In a medium-sized pot, bring 4 cups of water to a boil.
2. **Add the Herbs and Roots:** Once the water is boiling, reduce the heat to low and add 1 tbsp each of the dried herbs.
3. **Simmer:** Simmer the herbal mixture gently for about 10-15 minutes. Be sure it doesn't come to a rolling boil.
4. **Steep:** After simmering, remove the pot from heat. Let the herbal mixture steep for an additional 10 minutes with the lid on.
5. **Strain:** Strain the tea into a teapot or cup, discarding the used herbs.
6. **Sweeten (Optional):** If desired, add a touch of honey for sweetness.

DOSAGE:

Drink 1 cup of this herbal tea blend 2-3 times a day, ideally 30 minutes before meals.

Forgotten Home Apothecary

Bowel-Balance
Elixir

Berberine is a compound found in various plants, such as goldenseal and barberry, both of which are traditionally recognized for their potential digestive benefits. It possesses antimicrobial and anti-inflammatory properties that may support the regulation of bowel movements. Additionally, berberine is known for its potential to balance gut microbiota and promote a healthy digestive environment. It may also help with the management of certain digestive issues by reducing harmful bacteria and inflammation in the gastrointestinal tract. For those seeking natural support for digestive health, berberine-containing plants can be a valuable addition to their regimen.

INGREDIENTS:

- Dried goldenseal root (*Hydrastis canadensis*) or barberry root bark (*Berberis vulgaris*)
- 80-proof vodka or alcohol of your choice

NOTES:

If diarrhea persists for more than 48 hours or worsens despite using berberine tincture, it is crucial to seek medical attention promptly.

While berberine tincture may provide temporary relief, it is not a substitute for proper medical care when diarrhea becomes severe or prolonged.

Many people with autoimmune conditions cannot use goldenseal, as it's too immunostimulatory. Replace with Oregon grape root or use barberry.

INSTRUCTIONS:

1 | **Prepare the Ingredients:** Begin by gathering the dried goldenseal root or barberry root bark.
2 | **Chop or Crush the Ingredients:** If the herb is not already in a fine form, chop or crush it to increase its surface area. This will aid in the extraction process.
3 | **Mix with Alcohol:** Place the chopped or crushed herb into a clean glass jar. Pour enough 80-proof vodka or your chosen alcohol to completely cover the herb. Ensure that the jar has a tight-fitting lid.
4 | **Steep:** Seal the glass jar tightly. Store the jar in a cool, dark place for a minimum of 4-6 weeks. During this time, gently shake the jar every day to mix the contents.
5 | **Strain:** After the steeping period is complete, strain the liquid through a cheesecloth or fine strainer into a clean container. This step separates the liquid tincture from the solid plant material.
6 | **Store:** Transfer the strained tincture into amber or dark glass bottles for storage. This helps protect the tincture from light, which can degrade its potency.

DOSAGE:

Start with a small dose, around 10-20 drops. It can be taken up to three times a day whenever necessary. If the tincture is too bitter, you may dilute the tincture in a small amount of water or juice.

Anti-Parasitic
Black Walnut Drops

Historically, black walnut hull tincture has been valued for its potent antioxidant, anti-fungal, anti-viral, anti-bacterial, and anti-parasitic properties. It also specifically acts against helminths (parasitic worms), which cause diseases such as schistosomiasis (bilharzia), one of the world's leading health concerns. It has also been used as a cytotoxic agent and to reduce excessive sweating, aid digestion, and alleviate heavy menstrual bleeding. Additionally, it may support heart health and help improve various skin conditions, especially those of a fungal nature. Its anti-parasitic properties primarily stem from its high juglone (5-hydroxy-1,4-naphthalenedione) content. Juglone has been shown to significantly reduce parasite load.

INGREDIENTS:

- 7 whole green walnuts (*Juglans nigra*). *For the best results, use the freshest black walnuts available, ideally when they are still very green. You will be using the walnut hulls.
- 100-proof vodka

NOTES:

Wear gloves while processing to avoid staining (the hulls are also used as a sustainable dye).

Pregnant or breastfeeding women, as well as those with certain medical conditions, should consult a healthcare professional before use.

Prolonged or excessive use may lead to gastrointestinal discomfort or other adverse effects. Not for long-term internal use.

INSTRUCTIONS:

1 | **Add the Walnut Hulls:** Cut or smash (a hammer works well) the walnut hulls into small pieces and place them in a glass quart canning jar.
2 | **Prepare the Jar:** Fill the jar full of vodka, ensuring the hulls are submerged, leaving about ¼ inch of headspace at the top of the jar.
3 | **Seal and Store:** Cap the jar. Label and date.
4 | **Steep:** Allow the tincture to steep for 4-8 weeks. The longer it steeps, the more potent it will become. The freshness of the black walnuts also influences the tincture's strength.
5 | **Strain:** Once the tincture is ready, strain the mixture using cheesecloth to remove the walnut hulls and any debris.
6 | **Store:** Pour the strained liquid into small, dark-colored bottles with droppers for ease of use. Label.

DOSAGE:

Typically, 20 drops of the tincture three times a day is suitable for most adults.

Nature's Laxative
Blend

Together, these herbs work synergistically to offer a gentle and natural solution for occasional constipation.

Senna leaves, known for their natural laxative properties, help stimulate the colon to promote regular bowel movements, providing short-term relief from constipation. Dandelion root supports overall digestive health and liver function, aiding in the alleviation of digestive discomfort. Psyllium husk adds soluble fiber, increasing stool bulk and facilitating healthy bowel movements. Fennel seeds not only contribute to digestive well-being but also enhance the tea's flavor.

INGREDIENTS:

- 1 teaspoon of dried senna leaves (*Senna alexandrina*)
- 1 teaspoon of dried dandelion root (*Taraxacum officinale*)
- ½ teaspoon of psyllium husk (*Plantago ovata*)
- ½ teaspoon of dried fennel seeds (*Foeniculum vulgare*)
- 1 cup hot water

NOTES:

Senna should not be used for extended periods as it may lead to dependence on laxatives.

Several other herbs can serve as alternatives or additions: Cascara sagrada (*Rhamnus purshiana*), buckthorn bark (*Rhamnus frangula*), slippery elm bark (*Ulmus rubra*), meadowsweet (*Filipendula ulmaria*), triphala: an Ayurvedic herbal blend consisting of amalaki (*Emblica officinalis*), bibhitaki (*Terminalia bellirica*), and haritaki (*Terminalia chebula*).

INSTRUCTIONS:

1. **Combine the Herbs:** Combine all the dried herbs and seeds (except the psyllium husk) in a clean, dry bowl.
2. **Boil the Water:** In a pot, bring 1 cup (8 oz) of water to a rolling boil.
3. **Add the Herbs:** Remove the pot from the heat source and carefully add the herbal blend to the hot water.
4. **Infusion:** Place a lid on the pot and let the herbs infuse in the hot water for an extended period, ideally for 30-45 min. This longer infusion allows for a more thorough extraction of the herbal properties.
5. **Strain:** After the infusion time has passed, strain the tea into a cup using a fine mesh strainer or tea infuser.
6. **Add Psyllium Husk:** Be aware that the psyllium husk will absorb some water and create a thick, mucilaginous consistency. This thick consistency adds bulk to the stool and helps facilitate healthy bowel movements. Drink plenty of water throughout the day when using laxative herbs to prevent dehydration.

DOSAGE:

Start with a small amount, around ½ cup (4 oz), and drink it before bedtime. If needed, gradually increase the amount.

Homemade
Colon Detox Shot

In making a colon detox shot, each ingredient is chosen for its traditional role in supporting digestive health.

Apple cider vinegar is used to stimulate digestion and balance pH levels, while lemon juice, rich in vitamin C, is believed to cleanse the body and aid liver function. Ground ginger is known for easing stomach discomfort and promoting efficient digestion. Turmeric, with its anti-inflammatory properties, is often used to support gut health. Finally, cayenne pepper is thought to boost metabolism and enhance the production of digestive enzymes. These ingredients should complement a balanced diet and healthy lifestyle, and always consult with a healthcare provider before starting any new dietary regimen.

INGREDIENTS:

- 1 tablespoon apple cider vinegar
- 1 teaspoon lemon juice
- ½ teaspoon ground ginger
- ¼ teaspoon turmeric powder
- A pinch of cayenne pepper
- 1 cup warm water

NOTES:

If the taste is too strong, you can add a teaspoon of honey to sweeten it slightly. Keep in mind that adding sweeteners might affect the intended benefits of the detox shot.

Always check with a healthcare provider before starting any new dietary regimen, especially if you have existing health conditions or are pregnant.

INSTRUCTIONS:

1 | **Prepare the Mixture:** In a glass, combine the apple cider vinegar, lemon juice, ground ginger, turmeric powder, and cayenne pepper.
2 | **Add Water:** Pour the warm water into the glass with the other ingredients. Stir well to ensure everything is fully dissolved and mixed.
3 | **Serve:** Drink the shot on an empty stomach, ideally in the morning, to maximize its potential benefits on digestion.

DOSAGE:

You can take this shot once a day. However, it's best to start with a few times a week to see how your body responds.

Black Milk

Activated charcoal is known for its adsorptive properties, traditionally used to bind with certain substances.

This beverage combines the soothing qualities of nondairy milk with the intriguing properties of activated charcoal. This drink is not only visually striking but has been used traditionally to support digestive comfort. It is a comforting choice for those familiar with occasional bloating and stomach discomfort, offering a potential supportive remedy to start the day. Enjoy the rich, creamy texture complemented by the vanilla's sweetness and nutmeg's warm spice.

INGREDIENTS:

- 3 cups nondairy milk of your choice (such as almond, oat, or coconut milk)
- 1 tsp of activated charcoal (approximately three capsules, emptied)
- 2 tsp of vanilla extract or powder
- 3 tsp of honey (or adjust to taste)
- A sprinkle of nutmeg (for garnish and taste)

NOTES:

Black milk and activated charcoal can interfere with medication and nutrient absorption; consume them separately. Activated charcoal may not suit those with digestive issues and is not recommended for pregnant or breastfeeding women. Excessive consumption can cause gastrointestinal problems. Consult your healthcare provider with any concerns.

INSTRUCTIONS:

1 | **Warm the Milk:** Pour the nondairy milk into a saucepan and gently bring it to a simmer over medium heat.
2 | **Mix the Charcoal and Vanilla:** In a small bowl, blend the activated charcoal and vanilla extract or powder until well combined.
3 | **Combine Ingredients:** Once the milk is just bubbling, remove it from the heat. If you have a blender, pour the milk in and add the charcoal-vanilla mixture along with the honey. Blend until smooth and fully integrated. Alternatively, use a frother directly in the pan to mix everything together (my preference for ease).
4 | **Froth and Serve:** Set aside most of the milk mixture in a cup. Froth the remaining milk in the pan using a frother until you achieve a light foam. Gently spoon this foam over the milk in the cup.
5 | **Garnish:** Lightly sprinkle nutmeg on top for a touch of spice and an aromatic finish.

DOSAGE:

It is best to have your black milk drink on an empty stomach and at least two hours prior to taking any medications or vitamins. First thing in the morning is ideal.

Forgotten Home Apothecary

Intestinal Relief
Infusion

This gut-healing homemade tea combines a variety of herbs known for their digestive benefits.

Peppermint leaves help alleviate indigestion and bloating; Chamomile flowers are recognized for their anti-inflammatory properties, aiding various digestive issues; Marshmallow root, rich in mucilage, soothes and protects the digestive tract; Slippery elm bark is soothing and provides protective effects on the digestive system; Licorice root assists with indigestion and supports a healthy mucosal lining; Cinnamon bark, aside from adding flavor, helps regulate blood sugar levels; and Ginger is renowned for its digestive effects, including nausea relief and overall gut health support.

INGREDIENTS:

- 8 ounces of scalding hot water
- ½ tsp of dried peppermint leaves (*Mentha piperita*)
- ½ tsp of chamomile flowers (*Matricaria chamomilla*)
- ¼ tsp of marshmallow root (*Althaea officinalis*)
- 1 pinch of slippery elm bark (*Ulmus rubra*)
- ¼ tsp of licorice root (*Glycyrrhiza glabra*)
- ¼ tsp of cinnamon bark (*Cinnamomum verum*) or tsp of ground cinnamon
- ¼ teaspoon of ginger (*Zingiber officinale*)
- Sweetener to taste (honey, stevia, monk fruit; optional)

NOTES:

This tea is intended to support digestive health but should not be used as a replacement for medical treatment if you have a serious digestive condition.

INSTRUCTIONS:

1 | **Boil the Water:** Start by boiling 8 ounces of water. Once it reaches a scalding hot temperature, remove it from the heat source.
2 | **Prepare Herbs:** In a teapot or tea infuser, combine the dried herbs.
3 | **Pour Hot Water:** Pour the scalding hot water over the herbs.
4 | **Steep:** Cover and let the mixture steep for about 5-7 minutes. Steeping time varies depending on your personal preference for tea strength.
5 | **Strain and Serve:** After steeping, strain the tea into your cup, removing all the herbs.
6 | **Sweeten (Optional):** Optionally, add sweetener to taste. Honey, stevia, or monk fruit are excellent choices. You can skip sweeteners if you prefer your tea unsweetened.
7 | **Enjoy:** Sit back, relax, and enjoy your gut healing homemade tea for its soothing and digestive benefits.

DOSAGE:

You can enjoy this gut-healing tea up to three times a day, depending on your digestive needs. It can be particularly soothing when consumed after meals or when you're experiencing digestive discomfort.

Forgotten Home Apothecary

Herbal Parasite
Flush

Papaya seeds have long been used in traditional herbal practices for their potential benefits in supporting digestive health.

If you've ever grabbed a doorknob, played with your pet, or walked barefoot in the grass, there's a good chance you may have parasites inside you! These parasites could be contributing to your health issues.

This "Herbal Parasite Flush" is a simple way to use papaya seeds to help address these concerns.

INGREDIENTS:

- 1 whole papaya
- Honey
- Glass of water
- Knife
- Small bowl

INSTRUCTIONS:

1 | **Prepare the Papaya Seeds:** First, slice the papaya in half lengthwise and scoop out the seeds with a spoon. Discard the stringy flesh surrounding the seeds.

2 | **Rinse and Dry the Seeds:** Next, rinse the seeds thoroughly under cold water to remove any remaining pulp. Pat them dry with a paper towel and let them dry for a few days.

3 | **Mix with Honey:** After the seeds have dried, mix the papaya seeds with raw honey in a small bowl. Label and store.

NOTES:

Avoid consuming sugar, as it can feed parasites.

Consult a healthcare professional before using this remedy if pregnant, nursing, or having chronic health conditions. Some individuals may be allergic to papaya seeds. Discontinue use if you experience any allergic reactions. If taking medications, consult a healthcare provider before using this remedy, as papaya seeds may interact with certain medications.

DOSAGE:

Start with one tablespoon of the mixture per day and increase the dosage gradually as needed.

Fermented Cabbage Juice
(Best Probiotic)

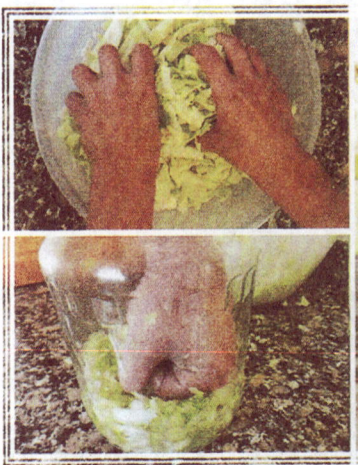

Fermented cabbage juice is a nutrient-dense beverage that can provide numerous health benefits, particularly for digestive health. Cabbage is rich in vitamins C and K, and antioxidants, and has strong anti-inflammatory properties. Drinking cabbage juice can support gut health, detoxify the body, and provide a natural boost to your immune system.

INGREDIENTS:

- 1 medium-sized cabbage (about 2-3 pounds)
- 1 tablespoon of sea salt (aim for 1.5-2% salt by weight)
- Optional: Caraway seeds or juniper berries for flavor (1-2 tablespoons)

NOTES:

Don't forget to thoroughly wash your hands and all utensils before. Cleanliness is crucial in fermentation. Some individuals may experience increased gas or bloating when first introducing cabbage juice into their diet. Start with small amounts to allow your body to adjust.

If you have a thyroid condition, consult with a healthcare provider before consuming large amounts of cabbage juice, as it contains goitrogens which can interfere with thyroid function.

Feel free to experiment with different combinations to find your favorites. These creative variations can add exciting flavors and health benefits to your meals:

Turmeric and ginger sauerkraut, beet and carrot sauerkraut, garlic and dill sauerkraut, pineapple and jalapeño sauerkraut, cranberry and rosemary sauerkraut. For added flavor, you can also try mixing the fermented cabbage juice with other vegetable juices like carrot or apple juice.

INSTRUCTIONS:

1 | **Prepare the Cabbage:** Remove the outer leaves of the cabbage and set them aside. Then, cut the cabbage into quarters and remove the core.

2 | **Shred the Cabbage:** Shred the cabbage finely using a sharp knife or a mandolin slicer.

3 | **Massage and Squeeze:** In a large bowl, combine the shredded cabbage and salt. Massage and squeeze the cabbage with your hands for about 10-15 minutes. This will help break down the cell walls and release the cabbage's natural juices.

4 | **Optional Flavoring:** If you're adding caraway seeds or juniper berries for flavor, mix them in with the cabbage.

5 | **Pack into a Jar:** Pack the cabbage mixture tightly into a clean glass or ceramic fermentation jar. Press it down firmly so that the cabbage is submerged in its own juices. Leave some space at the top of the jar to allow for expansion.

6 | **Add Cabbage Leaves on Top:** Take the cabbage leaves you set aside earlier and place them on top of the cabbage mixture. This will help keep the cabbage submerged.

7 | **Seal the Jar:** Seal the jar with a lid. If your jar has a metal lid, place a piece of parchment paper or a plastic bag between the cabbage and the lid to prevent corrosion.

8 | **Allow Fermentation:** Let the sauerkraut ferment at room temperature for about 1-2 weeks. Check it every few days to ensure the cabbage stays submerged and to taste for your desired level of fermentation. The longer you ferment, the tangier it will become. The sauerkraut can be enjoyed as a side dish, into salads, sandwiches, or as a topping for grilled meats or vegetables.

9 | **Extract the Juice:** After fermentation, strain the fermented cabbage mixture through a fine mesh sieve or cheesecloth to collect the juice. Press down on the cabbage to extract as much juice as possible.

10 | **Store the Juice:** Pour the cabbage juice into clean glass bottles or jars. Seal them tightly and store them in the refrigerator.

DOSAGE:

Start with ¼ to ½ cup of cabbage juice per day. Gradually increase the amount as your body adjusts, up to 1 cup per day. It's best consumed on an empty stomach for optimal absorption.

Forgotten Home Apothecary

De-Bloating
Yarrow Extract

Yarrow (*Achillea millefolium*) has been traditionally used for its anti-inflammatory, digestive, antibacterial, coagulant, and diuretic properties. It can help relieve bloating by promoting digestion and reducing fluid retention.

This recipe provides a simple method to make a yarrow extract that can be used to alleviate bloating and improve digestive health.

INGREDIENTS:

- 1 cup dried yarrow flowers (*Achillea millefolium*)
- 2 cups 80-proof vodka or another neutral spirit
- 1 glass jar with a tight-fitting lid

NOTES:

Do not use yarrow extract if you are pregnant, breastfeeding, or allergic to plants in the Asteraceae family.

Consult with a healthcare professional before using yarrow extract if you have any underlying health conditions or are taking other medications.

Discontinue use if any adverse reactions occur.

INSTRUCTIONS:

1 | **Prepare the Herbs:** Measure 1 cup of dried yarrow flowers and place them in the glass jar.
2 | **Add the Vodka:** Pour 2 cups of 80-proof vodka over the yarrow flowers, ensuring that the flowers are fully submerged. Feel free to scale this recipe down.
3 | **Steep:** Seal the jar tightly and place it in a cool, dark place. Allow the mixture to steep for 4-6 weeks, shaking the jar gently every few days to ensure thorough mixing.
4 | **Strain:** After 4-6 weeks, strain the mixture through a fine mesh strainer or cheesecloth into a clean glass jar. Discard the spent yarrow flowers.
5 | **Bottle and Label:** Transfer the strained extract into a dark glass bottle with a dropper for easy use. Label the bottle with the date and contents.

DOSAGE:

Take 10-20 drops of the yarrow extract in a small amount of water up to 3 times daily as needed for bloating relief.

Hemorrhoid-Alleviating
Oil

Hemorrhoids (or haemorrhoids), also known as piles, are swollen veins in your lower rectum and anus. Hemorrhoids can be caused by straining during bowel movements, chronic constipation, or pregnancy. Common symptoms include bleeding during bowel movements, itching, and discomfort. This soothing oil blend combines natural ingredients known for their anti-inflammatory and analgesic properties to help alleviate the discomfort of hemorrhoids. The blend is designed to reduce swelling, pain, and itching. Yarrow may also be added to this blend.

INGREDIENTS AND MATERIALS:

- 2 tablespoons coconut oil
- 1 tablespoon witch hazel
- 10 drops lavender essential oil
- 10 drops frankincense essential oil
- 5 drops tea tree essential oil
- A small, clean glass jar for storage

NOTES:

Test a small amount on a patch of skin before full use to ensure no allergic reactions. Discontinue use if irritation occurs.

If you have any chronic health conditions, are pregnant, or are nursing, consult with a healthcare professional before using this remedy.

INSTRUCTIONS:

1| **Melt the Coconut Oil:** In a small bowl, gently melt 2 tablespoons of coconut oil if it is solid. You can use a double boiler or microwave in short bursts.
2| **Add Witch Hazel:** Stir in 1 tablespoon of witch hazel into the melted coconut oil.
3| **Add Essential Oils:** Add 10 drops of lavender essential oil, 10 drops of frankincense essential oil, and 5 drops of tea tree essential oil. Mix well to combine all the ingredients. Use organic, high-quality ingredients for the best results.
4| **Store:** Transfer the mixture to a small, clean glass jar. Allow it to solidify at room temperature or refrigerate it for a faster setting. Keep the oil in a cool, dark place to maintain its potency.You an also refrigerate the oil if you prefer a cooling effect during application.

DOSAGE:

Apply a small amount of the oil to the affected area using a clean cotton pad or your fingertips. Use up to three times daily, especially after bowel movements and before bedtime.

Herbal Kombucha
for Gut Health

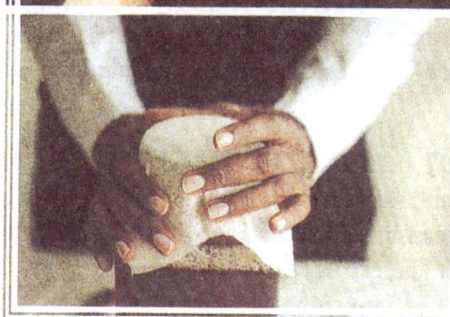

Kombucha is a probiotic-rich beverage that can enhance the balance of beneficial bacteria in your gut. This herbal kombucha is a fantastic way to combine the benefits of probiotics with digestive herbs.

INGREDIENTS AND MATERIALS:

- 1 kombucha SCOBY (Symbiotic Culture of Bacteria and Yeast)
- 4 cups of brewed black or green tea
- ½ cup of granulated sugar
- 1-gallon glass jar
- Cheesecloth or a breathable cloth for covering the jar
- Rubber band
- Filtered water
- A blend of digestive herbs (such as chamomile *Matricaria chamomilla*, fennel *Foeniculum vulgare*, and peppermint *Mentha × piperita*)

NOTES:

Be cautious with the herbal blend's proportions, as some herbs can be quite potent.

As always, ensure your equipment is clean and sanitized to prevent unwanted bacterial contamination.

INSTRUCTIONS:

1 | **Prepare the Herbal Blend:** Select your digestive herbs. For example, you can use 1 tablespoon of dried chamomile flowers, 1 tablespoon of fennel seeds, and 1 tablespoon of dried peppermint leaves. Crush the fennel seeds slightly to release their flavors.

2 | **Brew the Tea:** Brew your black or green tea using 4 cups of hot water.

3 | **Stir in the Granulated Sugar Until It Dissolves:** Add your herbal blend to the hot tea. Allow the tea to cool to room temperature. This is an important step because if you put your SCOBY in hot water, you will kill it.

4 | **Strain the Tea:** Strain the herbal tea to remove the ginger, fennel, and peppermint pieces.

5 | **Combine the Ingredients:** Place the brewed and strained herbal tea in your glass jar. Gently slide the kombucha SCOBY into the jar.

6 | **Fermentation:** Cover the jar with the cheesecloth or breathable cloth and secure it with a rubber band. Store the jar in a dark, room-temperature place for 7-10 days. Check the kombucha's taste after 7 days. If it's to your liking, it's ready. If not, continue fermenting for a few more days.

7 | **Bottling:** Once it reaches the desired taste, remove the SCOBY. Pour the herbal kombucha into individual glass bottles, leaving some space at the top. Seal the bottles tightly and let them sit at room temperature for another 2-3 days for carbonation.

8 | **Refrigeration:** After the secondary fermentation, move the bottles to the refrigerator to halt the fermentation process.

DOSAGE:

For general gut health and enjoyment, start with about 4-8 ounces (120-240 ml) of herbal kombucha per day.

Forgotten Home Apothecary

HERBAL SUPPORT
for Detox

Weight loss and detoxification are two important aspects of maintaining a healthy body, and they play a significant role in addressing the risk of obesity.

1. Weight Loss:

- **Obesity Risk:** Carrying excess weight is a major risk factor for various health problems, including heart disease, diabetes, and joint issues. Losing weight reduces these risks and improves overall well-being.
- **Improved Metabolism:** Shedding excess pounds can enhance metabolism, making it easier to maintain a healthy weight over the long term.
- **Better Cardiovascular Health:** Weight loss can lead to lower blood pressure and reduced levels of LDL cholesterol, both of which contribute to a healthier cardiovascular system.

2. Detoxification:

- **Elimination of Toxins:** Detoxification processes help the body remove accumulated toxins and waste products. This can improve overall organ function and reduce the risk of chronic diseases.
- **Enhanced Digestion:** Detoxifying the digestive system can lead to improved nutrient absorption and better digestive health.
- **Weight Management:** Some detox plans support weight loss by promoting healthy eating habits and reducing cravings for unhealthy foods.

Now, let's focus on how you can support weight loss and detoxification:

MINDFUL EATING:
- Take time to savor your meals. Chew thoroughly, and eat without distractions.
- Choose whole, unprocessed foods, and include plenty of fruits and vegetables in your diet.
- Reduce or eliminate sugar, caffeine, and alcohol.

EXERCISE REGULARLY: Engage in a mix of aerobic exercises, strength training, walking, and yoga.

HYDRATION: Drink plenty of water throughout the day.

SLEEP AND STRESS MANAGEMENT:
- Aim for 7-8 hours of quality sleep.
- Practice relaxation techniques like meditation and deep breathing.

DRY BRUSHING: Use a dry brush to gently exfoliate the skin before showering. This can stimulate the lymphatic system and improve circulation.

INTERMITTENT FASTING: Explore intermittent fasting, which can support weight loss and improve insulin sensitivity. Be aware that intermittent fasting affects men and women differently.

HERBAL SUPPORT

Green Tea (*Camellia sinensis*)
Contains catechins, particularly epigallocatechin gallate (EGCG), which may increase metabolism and aid in burning fat. It also has antioxidant properties that support detoxification.

Garcinia Cambogia (*Garcinia gummi-gutta*)
This tropical fruit extract may help suppress appetite and inhibit the formation of fat cells, potentially aiding in weight loss.

Dandelion (*Taraxacum officinale*)
Dandelion roots and leaves are known for their diuretic properties, which assist in detoxification by promoting the elimination of waste and excess water.

Milk Thistle (*Silybum marianum*)
Milk thistle supports liver health and detoxification. It can help protect the liver from toxins and promote its proper functioning.

Ginger (*Zingiber officinale*)
Ginger aids digestion and may help control appetite. It can also help reduce inflammation and support detoxification.

Turmeric (*Curcuma longa*)
Curcumin, the active compound in turmeric, has anti-inflammatory and antioxidant properties. It may support weight loss by reducing inflammation and improving metabolism.

Psyllium Husk (*Plantago ovata*)
Psyllium husk is a fiber-rich herb that can help with weight management by promoting a feeling of fullness and supporting regular bowel movements, which aids in detox.

Cinnamon (*Cinnamomum verum*)
Cinnamon helps regulate blood sugar levels, which can be beneficial for weight management. It also adds flavor to foods and can reduce sugar cravings.

Fennel (*Foeniculum vulgare*)
Fennel seeds help support digestion and reduce bloating, which can be useful during detox. They can also act as an appetite suppressant.

IMPORTANT NOTES:

Always consult with a healthcare professional before starting any herbal remedies, especially if you have underlying health conditions or are taking medications.

Herbal remedies should be used as part of a holistic approach that includes a balanced diet and regular exercise for effective weight loss and detoxification.

All-Day
Slimming Tea

This slimming tea combines gurmar, ginseng, cinnamon, black peppercorns, and oolong tea to potentially support weight management by curbing sugar cravings, boosting energy, and promoting metabolism.

INGREDIENTS:

- ½ teaspoon of gurmar powder (*Gymnema sylvestre*)
- ½ teaspoons of ginseng (*Panax ginseng*)
- ½ teaspoon of cinnamon powder (*Cinnamomum verum*)
- ½ teaspoon of black peppercorns (*Piper nigrum*)
- 1-2 teaspoons of oolong tea leaves

NOTES:

This tea is not a replacement for a healthy diet and exercise.

It should be used as a complementary measure in a weight management plan.

INSTRUCTIONS:

1. **Boil the Water:** Boil 2 cups of water.
2. **Steep Oolong Tea:** Pour 1 cup boiling water over the oolong tea leaves in a teapot. Steep for 3-5 minutes and strain. Oolong tea, like many other types of tea, has a specific optimal steeping time to bring out its flavor without making it bitter. Brewing it separately allows you to control the steeping time precisely. Steeping oolong tea for too long or at too high a temperature can result in a bitter taste.
3. **Prepare Herbal Mixture:** In a separate bowl, mix the gurmar powder, ginseng, cinnamon powder, and crushed black peppercorns. Pour 1 cup boiling water over and steep it separately for 10 minutes. Separating the tea from the herbal blend ensures that the flavors of both the tea and herbs are balanced.
4. **Combine Ingredients:** Combine the herbal mixture from Step 3 to the cup of oolong tea.
5. **Stir and Enjoy:** Stir well to ensure the herbal ingredients are properly blended with the tea. Let it cool for a few minutes and enjoy your slimming tea. You can add a touch of honey or a slice of lemon if you like.

DOSAGE:

One cup of tea in the morning. Do not drink it before going to bed as it might prevent you from falling asleep.

Bay Leaf
Water

Bay leaf water is a popular herbal remedy traditionally used to support weight management. Bay leaves contain compounds like cineole and eugenol, which can help improve digestion and relieve digestive discomfort. It is believed that bay leaf water helps reduce appetite, potentially aiding in weight management.

INGREDIENTS:

- 2-3 bay leaves (*Laurus nobilis*)
- 4 cups of water

NOTES:

Always use dried bay leaves (*Laurus nobilis*) for making bay leaf water.

Fresh bay leaves contain more moisture, which can introduce unwanted microorganisms or cause mold growth when steeped in water for an extended period, such as overnight soaking.

You can also experiment with other ingredients. Bay leaves, oregano and cinnamon tea is a popular recipe for weight loss.

INSTRUCTIONS:

1 | **Prepare Bay Leaves:** Take 2-3 bay leaves (*Laurus nobilis*) and cut or crush them into small pieces. This helps release their essential oils and flavor.
2 | **Boil the Water:** In a pot, bring ~4 cups of water to a boil.
3 | **Add Bay Leaves:** Once the water is boiling, add the small pieces of bay leaves to the pot with boiling water. The amount of water to add when making bay leaf water depends on your desired concentration and the size of your container. Generally, a standard recommendation is to use about 1 liter (approximately 4 cups) of water for 2-3 bay leaves. If you enjoy a more robust bay leaf flavor, you can use less water. For example, you can use 2 cups of water for 2-3 bay leaves. This will yield a stronger infusion.
4 | **Soak Overnight:** Cover the pot and let it soak overnight. Allowing the bay leaves to steep in the hot water for an extended period helps extract their flavors and benefits.
5 | **Strain:** The following day, strain the water to separate it from the bay leaf remnants. You can use a fine mesh strainer or a tea infuser for this.
6 | **Serve:** Your bay leaf water is now ready to be consumed.

DOSAGE:

Consume this bay leaf water once a day. Start with a small amount, such as half a cup, and adjust the quantity based on your preference and tolerance. Avoid overconsumption. Store in the refrigerator.

Flat Tummy
Capsules

There are many different combinations of herbs that can be used to make homemade flat tummy capsules, but this blend is particularly effective for supporting digestive health and weight management:

- **Fennel seeds:** Traditionally used to aid digestion and reduce bloating.
- **Ginger:** Known for supporting digestion, boosting metabolism, and reducing appetite.
- **Dandelion root:** Supports liver health, which may aid in weight management.
- **Turmeric:** Valued for its anti-inflammatory properties.
- **Cayenne pepper:** Contains capsaicin, a compound believed to increase thermogenesis (heat production in the body), which may aid in burning calories.

INGREDIENTS:

- 2-part fennel seeds (*Foeniculum vulgare*)
- 2-part ginger root (*Zingiber officinale*)
- 1 part dandelion root (*Taraxacum officinale*)
- 1 part turmeric (*Curcuma longa*)
- 1 part cayenne pepper (*Capsicum annuum*)

NOTES:

If you experience any adverse reactions, discontinue use and consult a healthcare provider.
These capsules are not a substitute for a balanced diet and exercise.
Remember to follow these steps carefully and consult with a healthcare professional before adding any herbal supplements to your routine.

INSTRUCTIONS:

1. **Prepare the Herbs:** Ensure that the herbs are completely dried to prevent moisture in the capsules and grind each of the dried herbs individually into a fine powder.
2. **Mix the Herbal Powders:** Combine the powdered herbs in the proportions mentioned in the ingredients list.
3. **Fill the Capsules:** Using either a capsule-filling machine or by hand, fill empty vegetarian or gelatin capsules with the herbal mixture.
4. **Store Your Capsules:** Store the homemade flat tummy capsules in a cool, dry place away from direct sunlight.

DOSAGE:

1 capsule before meals, up to three times a day.

Forgotten Home Apothecary

Craving-Buster
Brew

Licorice root tea is a natural remedy that may help curb sugar cravings and promote better blood sugar balance. This tea has a naturally sweet taste, making it a delightful replacement for sugary beverages.

INGREDIENTS:

- 1 tablespoon of dried licorice root (*Glycyrrhiza glabra*)
- 1 cup of boiling water
- Optional: Fresh lemon or a slice of ginger for added flavor

NOTES:

While licorice can be beneficial for curbing sugar cravings, it should be used in moderation. Excessive licorice consumption may lead to high blood pressure and potassium loss.

If you have hypertension or kidney issues, consult a healthcare professional before using licorice tea regularly.

INSTRUCTIONS:

1 | **Boil the Water:** Boil 1 cup of water using a kettle or saucepan.
2 | **Prepare Licorice Root:** If you're using a licorice root tea bag, simply place it in a heatproof cup. If you have dried licorice root, add 1 tablespoon of the dried root to the cup.
3 | **Pour Boiling Water:** Carefully pour the boiling water over the licorice root.
4 | **Steep the Tea:** Cover the cup with a saucer or small plate to trap the steam, and let the licorice root steep in the hot water for about 5-10 minutes. This allows the flavors and beneficial compounds to infuse into the water.
5 | **Optional Flavorings:** If desired, add a squeeze of fresh lemon or a slice of ginger to the tea for added flavor. Licorice root has a naturally sweet taste, but these additions can enhance the taste.
6 | **Serve and Enjoy:** Your licorice tea is ready to be enjoyed. Sip it slowly while it's still warm, especially when you experience sugar cravings.

DOSAGE:

Drink this licorice tea whenever you have sugar cravings or after a meal to curb your sweet tooth. Limit your consumption to 1-2 cups per day to avoid excessive licorice intake, as high amounts can cause side effects.

Dandelion and Burdock
Purge

This herbal elixir combines the traditional detoxifying properties of dandelion and burdock roots to support weight management and promote overall well-being. Dandelion is known for its diuretic properties, which help eliminate excess water weight and toxins from the body. Burdock root is rich in fiber, which promotes feelings of fullness and aid in weight management efforts.

INGREDIENTS:

- 2 tablespoons of dried dandelion root (*Taraxacum officinale*)
- 2 tablespoons of dried burdock root (*Arctium lappa*)
- 4 cups of filtered water
- 1 tablespoon of honey
- lemon slices for garnish (optional)

NOTES:

Please note that while this elixir may support weight loss and detoxification, it should be part of a broader healthy lifestyle that includes a balanced diet and regular physical activity.

If you prefer a more concentrated form of this herbal remedy, you can make it as a tincture. To do so, follow the directions in the first part of the book – Tincture Making.

INSTRUCTIONS:

1 | **Boil the Water:** Boil 4 cups of filtered water in a pot.
2 | **Add the Herbs:** Add 2 tablespoons of dried dandelion root and 2 tablespoons of dried burdock root to the boiling water.
3 | **Simmer the Mixture:** Reduce the heat and allow the herbal mixture to simmer for approximately 10-15 minutes. This step allows the beneficial compounds from dandelion and burdock to infuse into the water.
4 | **Cool the Elixir:** Remove the pot from heat and let the elixir cool for a few minutes before proceeding.
5 | **Strain and Remove Herbs:** Strain the elixir to separate the liquid from the dandelion and burdock roots, leaving you with your infusion.
6 | **Sweeten with Honey:** Add 1 tablespoon of raw honey to the elixir and stir until it dissolves. This step is optional but enhances the flavor.
7 | **Transfer and Cool:** Pour the elixir into a clean container and allow it to cool to room temperature. You can also refrigerate it for a cold, refreshing drink.
8 | **Garnish and Serve (Optional):** For added flavor and aesthetics, consider garnishing your elixir with lemon slices before serving.

DOSAGE:

Drink 1 cup of this elixir before meals, up to three times a day. It's recommended to follow this routine for a few weeks as part of a balanced diet and healthy lifestyle.

Metabolic
Herbal Coffee

Coffee by itself has some surprising health benefits. But when you walk into a big-name coffeehouse, order a milky latte, and start adding syrup and sugar that's when things start to change. This recipe combines herbal ingredients known for their potential to support weight management.

INGREDIENTS:

- ½ teaspoon of turmeric powder (*Curcuma longa*)
- A pinch of black pepper (*Piper nigrum*)
- ½ teaspoon of cinnamon powder (*Cinnamomum verum*)
- ¼ teaspoon of ginger powder (*Zingiber officinale*)
- 1 cup of freshly brewed coffee (*Coffea arabica* or *Coffea canephora*)
- Coconut oil MCT (optional)
- Sweetener of choice

NOTES:

Please keep in mind that while these herbs may have some beneficial effects, they should be used as part of a balanced diet and healthy lifestyle. Individual results may vary.

INSTRUCTIONS:

1 | **Brew the Coffee:** Start by brewing a cup of coffee using your preferred method. Use high-quality, organic coffee beans for the best results.

2 | **Add Turmeric and Black Pepper:** While the coffee is still hot, add ½ teaspoon of turmeric powder for its anti-inflammatory and potential fat-burning benefits. Add a pinch of black pepper to enhance the absorption of curcumin from the turmeric. Be cautious with the black pepper, as too much can make the coffee spicy.

3 | **Incorporate Cinnamon:** Mix in ½ teaspoon of cinnamon powder, which is known to help regulate blood sugar levels.

4 | **Introduce Ginger:** Add ¼ teaspoon of ginger powder for digestive benefits and flavor.

5 | **Enhance with Coconut Oil MCT (Optional):** If desired, further enhance the coffee by adding a teaspoon of coconut oil MCT for extra energy and satiation.

6 | **Sweeten to Taste (Optional):** Sweeten your coffee to taste with your preferred sweetener, but be mindful of excess sugar, as it can counteract the fat-burning effects.

DOSAGE:

Consume this fat-burning coffee in the morning or before a workout as a supplement to your regular diet. Adjust the amount of turmeric, black pepper, and sweetener to suit your taste.

Green Burn
Smoothie

This smoothie recipe incorporates herbal ingredients that offer potential benefits for boosting metabolism and aiding in weight management.

INGREDIENTS:

- 1 cup fresh spinach
- ½ cup fresh parsley
- ½ cup cucumber slices
- ½ medium-sized avocado
- ½ lemon, juiced
- 1 teaspoon grated ginger
- 1 teaspoon honey (optional, for sweetness)
- ½ medium-sized apple, chopped
- ½ teaspoon green tea leaves or green tea powder
- ½ cup cold water or milk

NOTES:

This green burn smoothie recipe contains ingredients that are high in oxalates, particularly spinach and parsley. Oxalates are naturally occurring compounds found in certain foods but can contribute to kidney stone formation in individuals who are susceptible.

- Cucumber provides hydration and adds a refreshing taste.
- Avocado offers healthy fats and fiber, contributing to a feeling of fullness.
- Spinach and parsley are rich in vitamins and minerals, supporting overall health.
- Lemon juice provides vitamin C and adds a zesty flavor.
- Ginger may help boost metabolism.
- Honey adds sweetness, but it's optional.
- Apple adds natural sweetness and fiber.
- Green tea contains compounds like catechins that have been studied for their potential to aid in weight management.

INSTRUCTIONS:

1 | **Prepare the Greens:** Wash the spinach, parsley, and cucumber thoroughly.
2 | **Prepare Other Ingredients:** Cut the avocado in half, remove the pit, and scoop out the flesh. Juice the lemon, grate the ginger, and chop the apple.
3 | **Add the Ingredients to a Blender:** In a blender, add the spinach, parsley, cucumber slices, avocado, lemon juice, grated ginger, honey (if desired), chopped apple, green tea leaves or green tea powder, and ½ cup of cold water or milk. (Dairy-free alternatives like almond milk, coconut milk, or soy milk are my favorites).
4 | **Blend Until Smooth:** Blend all the ingredients until you achieve a smooth, creamy consistency. You may need to stop and scrape down the sides of the blender to ensure everything is well mixed.
5 | **Serve and Enjoy:** Pour the green burn smoothie into a glass. You can garnish it with a parsley sprig or a slice of lemon, if desired.

DOSAGE:

You can consume this smoothie in the morning or as a snack. There's no specific dosage; adjust the ingredients and liquid quantity to suit your taste and nutritional needs.

Forgotten Home Apothecary

Forskolin Capsules
to Boost Metabolism

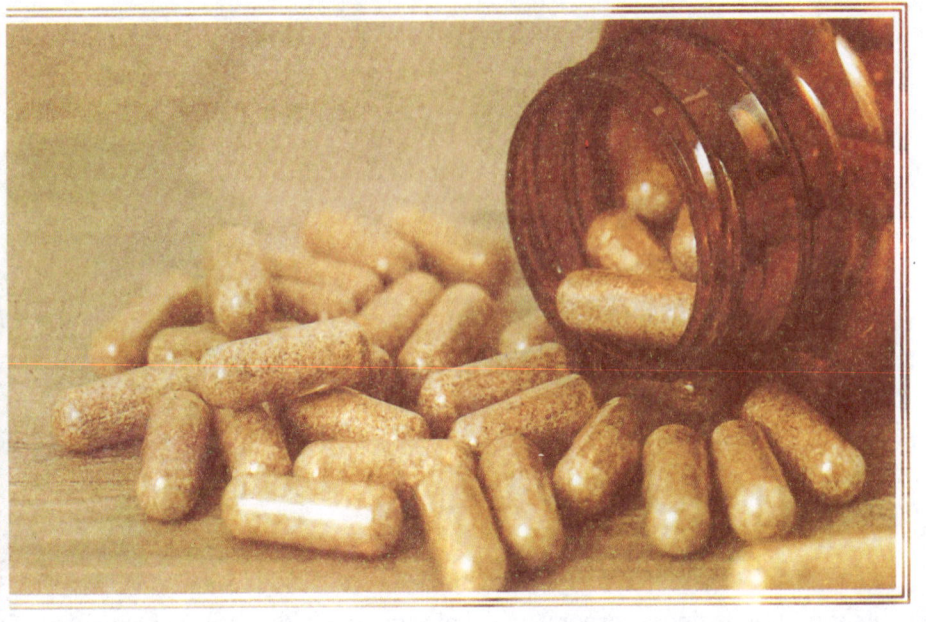

Homemade forskolin capsules offer a convenient method of consuming this herbal supplement. Forskolin, derived from the *Coleus forskohlii* plant, may help boost metabolism.

Forskolin is believed to promote the production of hormone-sensitive lipase, an enzyme involved in moving stored triglycerides and releasing fatty acids so your body can use them for energy. In simple terms, forskolin is thought to reduce the size of fat cells by promoting the breakdown of fats.

INGREDIENTS:

- 2 tbsp dried forskolin root (*Coleus forskohlii*)
- Empty vegetarian capsules

NOTES:

Forskolin may interact with certain medications and medical conditions, so consult with a healthcare provider before using it, especially if you have any underlying health concerns.

Some people may experience side effects like digestive issues or a decrease in blood pressure when taking Forskolin. Discontinue use if you experience any adverse effects.

Always use caution when preparing and handling herbal supplements, and ensure proper hygiene to avoid contamination.

INSTRUCTIONS:

1| **Prepare the Forskolin Powder:** Start by obtaining dried Coleus forskohlii root. Make sure it's completely dry. Grind the dried root into a fine powder using a coffee grinder or mortar and pestle. This will be your Forskolin powder.

2| **Fill the Capsules:** Open the empty vegetarian capsules and separate the two halves. Size "00" capsules are commonly used for herbal supplements, as they can hold a sufficient amount of powdered herbs without being too large to swallow. Using a small spoon or a capsule-filling machine, carefully fill each half of the capsules with the Forskolin powder.

3| **Assemble the Capsules:** Once both halves are filled, press them together until they snap shut. Ensure they are tightly sealed to prevent air or moisture from getting in.

4| **Store the Capsules:** Store the forskolin capsules in an airtight container in a cool, dry place, away from direct sunlight. Proper storage is essential to maintain their potency.

DOSAGE:

A common dosage is 250-500 milligrams per day.

Cleansing
Stinging Nettle Soup

Nettle soup is a nutritious and cleansing herbal dish that can be a beneficial addition to a balanced diet. Nettles are traditionally known for their diuretic properties and are rich in vitamins and minerals, making them a healthy choice for those looking to support weight management.

INGREDIENTS:

- 2 cups fresh nettle leaves (*Urtica dioica*)
- 1 medium onion, finely chopped
- 2 cloves garlic, minced
- 1 medium potato, diced
- 4 cups vegetable broth
- 1 tablespoon olive oil
- Salt and pepper to taste
- Juice of half a lemon (optional)

NOTES:

Be cautious when handling fresh nettle leaves. Wear gloves to avoid stinging.

If you have allergies or are taking medication, consult with a healthcare professional before adding nettles to your diet.

INSTRUCTIONS:

1. **Prepare the Nettles:** Wear gloves to handle fresh nettle leaves as they can cause skin irritation. Wash the nettles thoroughly, then blanch them in boiling water for about 1-2 minutes. Drain and chop them finely.
2. **Sauté the Aromatics:** In a large soup pot, heat the olive oil over medium heat. Add the chopped onion and minced garlic. Sauté until they become translucent.
3. **Add Potatoes and Nettles:** Add the diced potato and chopped nettles to the pot. Stir well.
4. **Pour in Vegetable Broth:** Pour in the vegetable broth, ensuring that the nettles and potatoes are fully submerged. Bring the mixture to a boil, then reduce the heat to a simmer. Cover and cook for about 15-20 minutes, or until the potatoes are tender.
5. **Blend the Soup:** Using an immersion blender or a regular blender (in batches), blend the soup until it's smooth and creamy.
6. **Season and Serve:** Season the soup with salt and pepper to taste. If desired, add the juice of half a lemon for extra flavor and a boost of vitamin C.
7. Alternatively, you can put the whole plant through a juicer and add an antioxidant-packed shot to your morning smoothie.

DOSAGE:

Enjoy a bowl of nettle soup as a part of your lunch or dinner. You can have this soup a few times a week as part of a balanced diet.

Forgotten Home Apothecary

Metabolic Superfood
Bars

These fat-burning bars are a delicious and nutritious snack that can support weight management. They contain ingredients like matcha and goji berries that have metabolism-boosting and appetite-suppressing properties, along with other nutrient-rich components. Oats provide fiber for a feeling of fullness. Almond butter offers healthy fats and protein. Flaxseed and chia seeds provide omega-3 fatty acids and fiber. When consuming chia seeds, it's essential to stay hydrated, as they absorb water and help with satiety. Unsweetened cocoa powder adds a chocolatey flavor with antioxidants.

INGREDIENTS:

- 1 cup rolled oats
- ½ cup almond butter
- ¼ cup honey
- ¼ cup ground flaxseed
- ¼ cup chia seeds
- ¼ cup unsweetened cocoa powder
- ¼ cup green tea powder (matcha) (*Camellia sinensis*)
- ¼ cup dried goji berries (*Lycium barbarum*)

NOTES:

Check for nut allergies when using almond butter. If allergic, consider using an alternative like sunflower seed butter.

These bars contain healthy fats and natural sugars, so be mindful of your overall calorie intake if you're watching your weight.

Green tea contains caffeine, which can vary in concentration. If you're sensitive to caffeine, consider using a decaffeinated matcha.

INSTRUCTIONS:

1. **Gather Your Ingredients:** Gather all the ingredients you'll need to make these fat-burning bars. Feel free to add other ingredients like chopped nuts, dried fruits, or a touch of vanilla extract for more flavor and texture.
2. **Mix Dry Ingredients:** Combine rolled oats, ground flaxseed, chia seeds, unsweetened cocoa powder, green tea powder (matcha), and dried goji berries in a mixing bowl.
3. **Add Wet Ingredients:** Mix in the almond butter and honey to the dry ingredient mixture.
4. **Blend and Form Mixture:** Combine the ingredients until they are well mixed and the mixture holds together.
5. **Prepare Baking Dish:** Line a square baking dish with parchment paper to make it easier to remove the bars later.
6. **Press Mixture into Dish:** Press the mixture firmly into the prepared baking dish.
7. **Refrigerate:** Place the baking dish in the refrigerator for at least 1-2 hours to allow the mixture to set.
8. **Cut into Bars:** Remove the dish from the refrigerator and cut the mixture into bars. For neat and even bars, use a sharp knife and dip it in hot water before cutting. This prevents sticking and ensures clean cuts.
9. **Store:** Store the fat-burning bars in an airtight container for later consumption.

DOSAGE:

Enjoy them as a guilt-free treat or an on-the-go energy booster.

HERBAL SUPPORT
for the Respiratory System

The respiratory system is crucial for several reasons:

- **Oxygen Exchange:** It allows the body to exchange oxygen from the air and release carbon dioxide, a waste product, ensuring proper oxygenation of the body's cells.
- **Immune Defense:** The respiratory system filters out harmful particles and pathogens, reducing the risk of infections.
- **Maintaining Acid-Base Balance:** It regulates the body's pH levels by controlling the removal of carbon dioxide, which can affect blood acidity.
- **Vocalization:** The respiratory system is essential for speech and vocalization.
- **Supporting Circulation:** It influences heart function, as efficient oxygen supply to the heart is vital.

Tips to Maintain a Healthy Digestive System:

AVOID SMOKING AND EXPOSURE TO POLLUTANTS:

Smoking and exposure to environmental pollutants can harm your respiratory system. Quitting smoking and minimizing exposure to air pollutants are essential for long-term respiratory health.

INDOOR AIR QUALITY:

Maintain good indoor air quality by ventilating your living spaces, getting an air purifier, and minimizing exposure to pollutants. Some indoor plants will help as well. The best air-purifying plants include the peace lily, aloe vera, dracaena, spider plant, Boston fern and chrysanthemums.

PRACTICE DEEP BREATHING:

Deep breathing exercises can help improve lung function and increase lung capacity. Try techniques like diaphragmatic breathing or pursed-lip breathing.

HERBAL SUPPORT

Eucalyptus (*Eucalyptus globulus*)
The leaves or oil are traditionally used to help open up the airways and provide relief from congestion. They can be used in a steam inhalation or as a topical oil.

Mullein (*Verbascum thapsus*)
Known for its anti-inflammatory properties, mullein is traditionally used to help calm coughs, open up the respiratory tract, lessen mucus, and encourage the expulsion of phlegm. It can be used as a tincture or tea.

Ginger (*Zingiber officinale*)
Ginger has anti-inflammatory properties and may help alleviate respiratory symptoms. It can be consumed as a tea or added to meals.

Turmeric (*Curcuma longa*)
Curcumin, a compound in turmeric, has anti-inflammatory and antioxidant properties that can benefit respiratory health. Consider using turmeric in cooking or taking curcumin supplements.

Peppermint (*Mentha piperita*)
Peppermint contains menthol, traditionally used to help relax the muscles of the respiratory tract and ease breathing. Peppermint can be used as a tea or oil.

Licorice Root (*Glycyrrhiza glabra*)
Licorice root has been traditionally used for respiratory issues due to its anti-inflammatory properties. It can be consumed as a tea or supplement.

Thyme (*Thymus vulgaris*)
Thyme contains compounds with antimicrobial properties that can support respiratory health. It can be used in cooking or as an herbal infusion.

Remember that while herbal remedies can be beneficial, they are not a replacement for professional medical care, especially in cases of serious or chronic respiratory conditions. When in doubt or when experiencing severe or persistent symptoms, consult with a healthcare provider for the best course of action.

Rosemary and Sage
Sore Throat Spray

This homemade sore throat spray harnesses the soothing properties of rosemary, sage, and oregano, along with essential oils, to naturally alleviate throat irritation and discomfort. Rosemary contains compounds such as rosmarinic acid, oleanolic acid, eucalyptol, caffeic acid, camphor, and alpha-pinene, which are traditionally used to support relief from sore throats and colds, and may help break down viral and bacterial biofilms. Oregano's essential oil, rich in carvacrol, is known for its traditional use in targeting throat discomfort and strep throat, and may initially cause a warming sensation. Meanwhile, sage essential oil, with alpha-thujone and camphor, is traditionally used to alleviate throat discomfort, strep throat and viruses, and to reduce pain sensitivity and inflammation.

INGREDIENTS:

- 1.5 cups of alcohol (at least 40% or 80 proof)
- 1 tablespoon of dried chopped sage (*Salvia officinalis*)
- 1 tablespoon of dried chopped rosemary (*Salvia rosmarinus*)
- 1 tablespoon of dried chopped oregano (*Origanum vulgare*)
- 10 drops of sage essential oil
- 10 drops of rosemary essential oil
- 10 drops of oregano essential oil

NOTES:
To use, shake the spray bottle well to mix the ingredients. Then, spray the herbal solution directly onto the back of your throat as needed for relief from sore throat discomfort.

INSTRUCTIONS:

1 | **Prepare the Herbs:** Measure 1 tablespoon each of dried herbs. If you have fresh herbs, double the quantity.
2 | **Warm the Alcohol:** Heat 1.5 cups of an alcohol like vodka or brandy to between 120 – 140 °F (50 – 60 °C) in a jar sitting in a pot of warm water.
3 | **Add the Herbs:** Add the 3 herbs stir and put the lid on. Maintain the heat for 2 hours and stir occasionally.
4 | **Strain the Infusion:** After steeping, Allow the liquid to cool to room temperature. Then strain the herbal infusion through a fine-mesh strainer or a piece of cheesecloth to remove the herb particles.
5 | **Add the Essential Oils:** Add 10 drops each of sage essential oil, rosemary essential oil, and oregano essential oil to the strained herbal tincture. Stir well to combine.
6 | **Transfer to a Spray Bottle:** Using a funnel if needed, carefully pour the herbal tincture with essential oils into a small spray bottle.
7 | **Label and Store:** Label the bottle with the contents and date. Store in a dark, cool location for up to 1 year. Be sure to shake before use.

DOSAGE:

The frequency of use can vary depending on the severity of your symptoms and your personal preference. Generally, you can use it every 2-4 hours, but it's essential to monitor how your throat responds and adjust accordingly.

Honey Lemon Ginger
Cough Drops

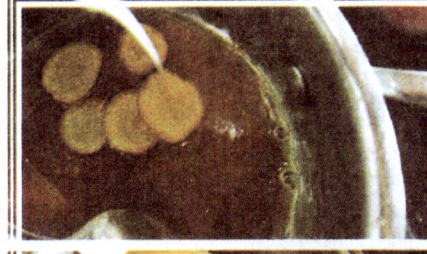

By combining these ingredients in your homemade cough drops, you create a natural remedy that not only tastes good but also provides multiple benefits for soothing coughs and sore throats. Honey's thick consistency coats the throat, providing a soothing effect and reducing irritation. It also offers natural antibacterial properties and supports the immune system. Lemon juice, rich in vitamin C and antioxidants, reduces inflammation, breaks down mucus, and adds a pleasant flavor. known for its anti-inflammatory properties, throat soothing effects, and acts as a natural cough suppressant.

INGREDIENTS:

- 4 tablespoons raw honey
- ¼ cup high-quality lemon juice (freshly squeezed is best)
- 4 to 5 slices of fresh ginger (*Zingiber officinale*)

NOTES:

Use high-quality, fresh ingredients for the best results.

While these drops are natural, avoid excessive consumption. Excessive honey intake can lead to an increase in blood sugar levels.

Raw honey should not be given to infants under one year old due to the risk of botulism. For children under one year, consult with a pediatrician for appropriate cough remedies.

INSTRUCTIONS:

1 | **Prepare the Ginger:** Wash and thinly slice the fresh ginger. You can leave the peel on for extra flavor, but make sure it's clean.
2 | **Combine Ingredients:** In a small saucepan, mix the honey, lemon juice, and sliced ginger. Heat the mixture over low heat, stirring constantly. You don't want it to boil; just warm it enough to infuse the ginger into the liquid. This should take 5-10 minutes.
3 | **Remove Ginger Slices:** Once the mixture is warm and the flavors have melded together, remove it from the heat. Take out the ginger slices, leaving you with a smooth syrup.
4 | **Form Drops:** Allow the syrup to cool slightly. While it's still warm but not hot to the touch, use a small spoon or dropper to form drops in a silicone mold or on a parchment paper-lined tray. You can make them as big or as small as you prefer.
5 | **Cool and Set:** Let the drops cool and set at room temperature for a few hours or until they are no longer sticky to the touch. This can take anywhere from 4-8 hours, depending on the size of your drops and the humidity in your environment.
6 | **Storage:** Once the drops have hardened, transfer them to an airtight container. Store them in a cool, dry place. They should stay good for several weeks.

DOSAGE:

Take these cough drops as needed. For adults, one to two cough drops every 2-4 hours is a typical dosage. For children, adjust the dosage based on their age and size, but a drop every 4-6 hours is a good starting point.

Mustard
Plaster

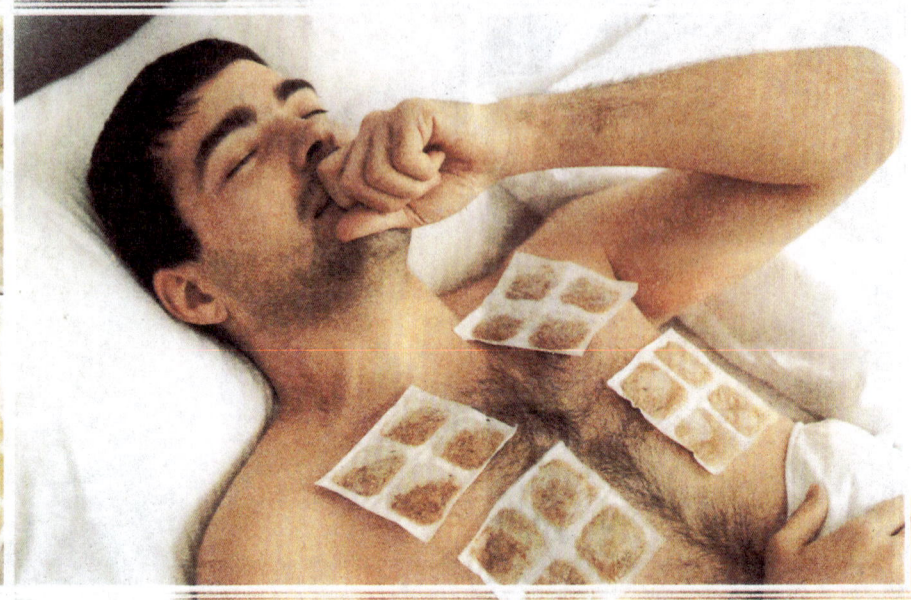

A homemade medicinal mustard plaster can be a supportive remedy for chest congestion and may provide relief from symptoms like coughing and difficulty breathing. Mustard plasters work by creating a warming sensation on the skin, which may help loosen mucus, improve circulation, and provide relief.

INGREDIENTS:

- 2 tablespoons of mustard powder. You can find mustard powder at most grocery stores or online.
- 2 tablespoons of flour
- Water (as needed to create a thick paste)

NOTES:

Mustard plasters can cause skin irritation or burns if left on for too long or if the mustard paste is too strong.

Always monitor the person closely during the treatment and remove the plaster if they experience discomfort or excessive burning. Use extra caution when applying mustard plasters to children and elderly individuals, as their skin may be more sensitive.

Do not use mustard plasters on individuals with known mustard allergies.

INSTRUCTIONS:

1 | **Gather the Materials:** You'll need a mixing bowl, a spoon for stirring, a clean cloth (such as a kitchen towel or muslin cloth), and plastic wrap or a small towel.

2 | **Prepare the Mustard Paste:** Start by measuring out approximately 2 tablespoons of mustard powder into your mixing bowl. Add an equal amount of flour (2 tablespoons) to the bowl. Gradually add water while stirring until you achieve a thick, paste-like consistency. Aim for a consistency similar to pancake batter.

3 | **Apply the Mustard Plaster:** Place the clean cloth on a flat surface. Spread the mustard paste evenly over one-half of the cloth, leaving the other half clean. Fold the cloth in half to cover the mustard paste.

4 | **Warm the Cloth:** Warm the mustard plaster by placing it in a microwave for 5-10 seconds or by heating it in a dry skillet for a few seconds. Ensure it's comfortably warm and not too hot in order to avoid burns.

5 | **Apply the Plaster:** Place the warm mustard plaster directly on the chest of the person experiencing congestion. Cover the plaster with a thin cloth or plastic wrap to protect the skin. Leave the plaster in place for about 10-15 minutes or until it starts to feel warm and the skin becomes pink but not red. Be cautious not to leave it on for too long to avoid skin irritation or burns.

6 | **Remove the Plaster:** If the person feels uncomfortable or experiences excessive burning or irritation, remove the plaster immediately. After removing the plaster, wipe the chest with a damp cloth to remove any mustard residue.

DOSAGE:

You can repeat this up to 3 times a day if needed, but it's usually not necessary to use it more than once a day.

Heating
Potato Pad

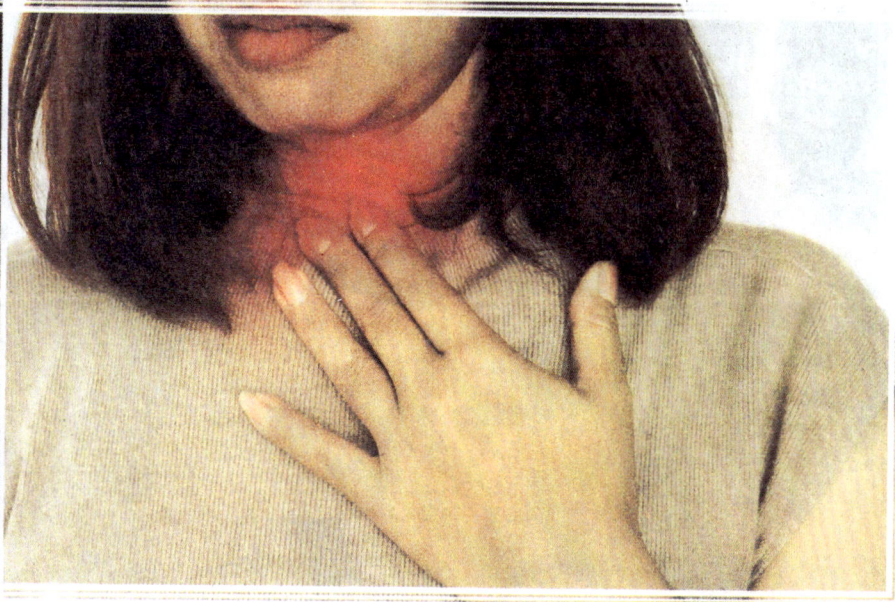

Potatoes have long been used in folk remedies for their warming properties.

This simple "Heating Potato Pad" can be made quickly to help soothe sore throats. It's a natural, pain-free, and chemical-free solution.

INGREDIENTS:

- 1-2 potatoes

NOTES:

Ensure the potatoes are not too hot before applying them to avoid burns.

Always supervise children when using this heating pad to ensure safety.

If you or your child has an allergy to potatoes, do not use this remedy.

INSTRUCTIONS:

1 | **Slice the Potatoes:** Begin by slicing the potatoes into thin rounds.
2 | **Heat the Potatoes:** Place the potato slices on the stove or in the microwave until they are hot but not too hot to handle.
3 | **Prepare the Heating Pad:** Wrap the hot potato slices in a cloth or put them in a sock.
4 | **Apply to the Neck:** Apply the wrapped potato slices to your neck. Leave it in place for a few minutes to stimulate circulation and act as a homemade heating pad.

DOSAGE:

Use this heating pad whenever you have a sore throat. Apply it for a few minutes until the potatoes start to cool down.

Amish
Cough Syrup

This Amish Cough Syrup, also known as "Snake Juice", is an old-fashioned remedy used to calm coughs, soothe sore throats, and reduce congestion. The combination of onions, lemons, honey, brandy, and peppermint schnapps provides a blend of supportive properties.

Onions are known for their antimicrobial properties, helping to reduce inflammation and fight respiratory infections. Lemons rich in vitamin C, can support the immune system. Honey acts as a natural cough suppressant with antibacterial properties that soothe the throat. Blackberry brandy contains antioxidants and provides a warming effect to ease cold symptoms, while peppermint schnapps adds a cooling sensation and helps to clear congestion.

INGREDIENTS:

- 1-2 medium onions, sliced
- 2-4 lemons, sliced
- 1 pint honey
- 1 pint peppermint schnapps
- 1 pint blackberry brandy

NOTES:

This recipe contains alcohol. Avoid giving it to children or individuals sensitive to alcohol.

For a non-alcoholic version, substitute blackberry brandy and peppermint schnapps with an equal amount of strong blackberry tea or syrup and peppermint extract.

If symptoms persist for more than a week, consult a healthcare professional.

INSTRUCTIONS:

1 | **Prepare the Ingredients:** Slice the onions and lemons thinly. In an airtight glass container, create alternating layers of onion slices and lemon slices.
2 | **Combine the Ingredients:** Pour the honey over the layers of onions and lemons. Add the peppermint schnapps and blackberry brandy, ensuring they cover the layers completely.
3 | **Infuse:** Seal the container tightly and let it sit at room temperature for three days.
4 | **Strain:** After three days, strain the mixture to remove the onion and lemon slices, keeping the liquid syrup.
5 | **Store:** Store the syrup in a cool, dark place. It can last for 6 to 12 months when stored properly.

DOSAGE:

Take 1 tablespoon every 4 hours as needed to soothe coughing and sore throat.

Mullein and Marshmallow
Cough Syrup

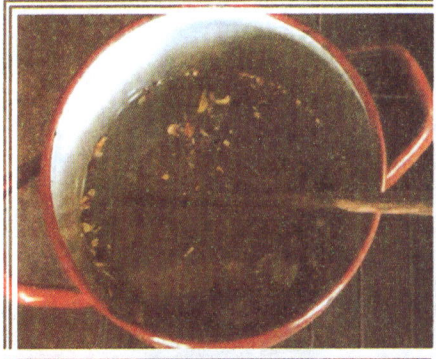

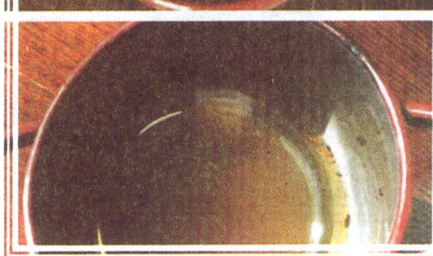

Mullein and marshmallow root are two herbal remedies often used to soothe coughs and respiratory discomfort. When combined into a homemade cough syrup, they can can provide a natural alternative to over-the-counter cough syrups.

INGREDIENTS:

- 1 tablespoon of dried mullein leaves and flowers (*Verbascum thapsus*)
- 1 tablespoon of dried marshmallow root (*Althaea officinalis*)
- 2 cups of water
- ½ to 1 cup of honey (adjust for desired sweetness)

NOTES:

If your cough persists or worsens after a few days of using the syrup, or if you experience severe symptoms, seek medical attention.

This syrup is not a substitute for professional medical advice or treatment. Be aware of any allergies to mullein or marshmallow root.

INSTRUCTIONS:

1. **Combine the Herbs:** In a small saucepan, combine 1 tablespoon of dried mullein leaves and flowers (if available) with 1 tablespoon of dried marshmallow root.
2. **Add Water:** Pour 2 cups of water into the saucepan with the herbs.
3. **Bring to a Boil:** Place the saucepan over medium-high heat and bring the mixture to a boil.
4. **Reduce Heat and Simmer:** Once it boils, reduce the heat to low, and let the herbs simmer for about 15-20 minutes. This allows the water to reduce by half.
5. **Strain the Liquid:** After simmering, strain the herbal liquid into a heat-resistant container to remove the herbs. Allow it to cool to a warm but not scalding temperature.
6. **Add Honey:** Once the liquid has cooled down, add ½ to 1 cup of honey (adjust to your desired level of sweetness). Stir well to ensure the honey is fully incorporated into the syrup.
7. **Store:** Pour the prepared syrup into a clean, airtight glass jar or bottle.
8. **Refrigerate:** Store the cough syrup in the refrigerator for freshness.

DOSAGE:

Take 1-2 tablespoons of the syrup every 4-6 hours as needed. For children (over 1 year old) you can give 1-2 teaspoons of the syrup every 4-6 hours as needed.

Sinus Relief
Eucalyptus Steam

Creating a homemade eucalyptus steam for sinus relief can be a soothing way to alleviate congestion and sinus discomfort. Eucalyptus oil is traditionally used to support respiratory health by helping to clear mucus and debris from the airways. This is why it is often found in saline nasal washes. Additionally, eucalyptus steam is believed to help promote the movement of tiny hair-like filaments in your lungs (called cilia), which sweep out mucus and debris from your airways.

INGREDIENTS AND MATERIALS:

- Enough boiling water to create a good amount of steam
- About 3-5 drops of eucalyptus (*Eucalyptus globulus*) essential oil
- A large towel to cover your head and the pot or bowl, creating a steam tent

NOTES:

Be cautious when working with boiling water to avoid burns. Keep a safe distance, and don't lean too close to the pot. Do not add too much eucalyptus oil. A few drops are usually sufficient, as eucalyptus oil is potent.

If you experience any discomfort or adverse reactions during or after steam inhalation, stop the process immediately.

INSTRUCTIONS:

1 | **Boil Water:** Start by boiling a pot of water. You'll need enough boiling water to create a good amount of steam.

2 | **Prepare a Safe Surface:** Place the pot or heatproof bowl on a stable, heat-resistant surface. Make sure you can comfortably lean over it without the risk of tipping it over.

3 | **Add Eucalyptus Oil:** Once the water has come to a boil, turn off the heat, and add a few drops (about 3-5 drops) of eucalyptus essential oil to the hot water. The steam will carry the eucalyptus scent and properties into your sinuses.

4 | **Create a Steam Tent:** Carefully drape the large towel over your head, shoulders, and the pot or bowl, creating a tent to trap the steam.

5 | **Inhale Steam:** Sit or lean over the pot/bowl, keeping your face about 12 inches (30 cm) away from the water. Close your eyes and inhale the steam deeply through your nose for about 5-10 minutes. Breathe slowly and gently to avoid discomfort.

6 | **Take Breaks:** If the steam becomes too hot or intense, take breaks as needed. Lift the towel and let some of the heat escape before resuming.

DOSAGE:

You can repeat this steam inhalation process 2-3 times a day or as often as needed to relieve sinus congestion. Alternatively, you can use eucalyptus essential oil in a nebulizer for sinus relief. Nebulizers convert liquids into a fine mist that can be inhaled directly into the respiratory system, delivering the therapeutic benefits of eucalyptus oil effectively. This method allows for controlled and consistent inhalation of eucalyptus vapor, making it a convenient option for those seeking relief from sinus congestion and discomfort.

Hot Herbal Compress
for Sinus Infections

When it comes to using aromatherapy to relieve the pain associated with a sinus headache, a combination of eucalyptus, peppermint and lavender may be beneficial. Eucalyptus contains eucalyptol, an anti-inflammatory that regulates mucus. Peppermint helps with various headaches, including sinus headaches. Lavender reduces headache frequency and severity and promotes better sleep through its calming aroma in essential oil aromatherapy.

INGREDIENTS:

- 2 tablespoons each of dried lavender flowers (*Lavandula*), chamomile flowers (*Matricaria chamomilla*), eucalyptus leaves, and peppermint leaves (*Mentha piperita*)
- 1 cup of uncooked rice or flaxseed
- A piece of natural, breathable fabric like cotton or muslin
- String or rubber bands to securely close the compress

NOTES:

Always be cautious with the temperature to prevent burns. If your sinus infection persists or worsens, consult a healthcare provider for appropriate medical treatment. Make sure the fabric and herbs are clean and free from contaminants to avoid skin irritation or infection.

INSTRUCTIONS:

1 | **Mix the Herbs:** In a bowl, combine the dried herbs: 2 tablespoons each of lavender, chamomile, eucalyptus, and peppermint.
2 | **Prepare the Compress:** Lay a 10x10-inch cotton cloth flat on a clean surface.
3 | **Fill the Compress:** Place 1 cup of uncooked rice or flaxseed onto one half of the cloth to ensure that the compress holds heat effectively. Then, evenly distribute the herbal mixture over the filling.
4 | **Fold and Secure:** Fold the other half of the cloth over the filling to create a pouch. Secure the edges with string or rubber bands, ensuring that the herbs and filling are well-contained.
5 | **Heat the Compress:** Place the compress in the microwave for 20-30 seconds. Carefully check the temperature, ensuring it's comfortably warm, not too hot.
6 | **Check the Temperature:** Always test the compress on your wrist or the back of your hand to make sure it's safe for your face. It should be comfortably warm, not scalding.
7 | **Apply the Compress:** Lie down and place the warm compress over your sinuses, typically located on either side of your nose, below your eyes. You can also apply it to your forehead and cheekbones. Keep it in place for 10-15 minutes or until it cools down.
8 | **Store** the herbal compress in a cool, dry place when not in use. You can reuse it several times, but replace the herbs if they lose their aroma or effectiveness.

DOSAGE:

You can use this compress multiple times a day to help relieve sinus congestion and discomfort. However, never reheat the same compress immediately after use to avoid overheating.

Forgotten Home Apothecary

Herbal Gargle
for Throat Infections

A homemade herbal gargle can be a supportive way to soothe a sore throat, reduce inflammation, and potentially help prevent infections. Thyme has antibacterial properties and can help relieve coughs and sore throats. Sage has antimicrobial and anti-inflammatory properties. Peppermint has a soothing effect and can help relieve throat discomfort. Salt has natural antibacterial properties and can help soothe a sore throat. Honey is known for its antibacterial properties and helps soothe the throat. Lemon juice contains vitamin C and has antimicrobial properties.

INGREDIENTS:

- 1 cup of warm water
- ½ teaspoon of salt
- 1-2 tablespoons of honey
- Juice of half a lemon
- Your choice of herbs (select one or two): thyme (*Thymus vulgaris*), sage (*Salvia officinalis*), or peppermint (*Mentha piperita*)

NOTES:

Ensure that the water is comfortably warm for gargling. Water that is too hot can scald the throat, so test the temperature before using it.

Hydration: In addition to gargling, staying well-hydrated by drinking water and herbal teas can also help soothe a sore throat.

INSTRUCTIONS:

1. **Prepare Warm Water:** Boil the water and allow it to cool slightly until it's warm but not too hot to gargle.
2. **Add Salt and Dissolve:** Add ½ teaspoon of salt to the warm water and stir until it dissolves.
3. **Incorporate Honey:** Add 1-2 tablespoons of honey to the mixture, depending on your taste preferences.
4. **Squeeze Lemon Juice:** Squeeze the juice of half a lemon into the mixture.
5. **Infuse with Herbs:** For thyme: Add a few sprigs of thyme or a teaspoon of dried thyme leaves. For sage: Add a few sage leaves or a teaspoon of dried sage. For peppermint: Add a few fresh peppermint leaves or a teaspoon of dried peppermint leaves.
6. **Stir and Steep:** Stir the mixture well to ensure the salt and honey are fully dissolved, then let it steep for a few minutes to allow the herbs to infuse.
7. **Gargle Safely:** Once the mixture is at a comfortable temperature for gargling, take a sip, tilt your head back, and gargle for about 30 seconds before spitting it out. Be careful not to swallow it.

DOSAGE:

Gargle for about 30 seconds to a minute, ensuring that the mixture reaches the back of the throat. Repeat the gargling process every few hours or as needed for relief.

Forgotten Home Apothecary

Soothing Elixir
for Cold and Flu Season

This herbal elixir features thyme, licorice root, yarrow leaves, white willow bark, and joint fir leaves, , traditionally used for the following properties. Thyme's antimicrobial and anti-inflammatory qualities, licorice root's immune-regulating effects, yarrow's fever-reducing and anti-inflammatory attributes, and white willow bark's astringent properties can help alleviate cold and flu symptoms. Joint fir leaves, while providing potential bronchodilatory benefits, should be used cautiously.

INGREDIENTS:

- 1 teaspoon of chopped thyme (*Thymus vulgaris*)
- 1 teaspoon of chopped licorice root (*Glycyrrhiza glabra*)
- 1 teaspoon of chopped yarrow leaves (*Achillea millefolium*)
- 1 teaspoon of chopped white willow bark (*Salix alba*)
- 1 teaspoon of chopped joint fir leaves (*Ephedra* spp.)
- 1 cup of water
- 3 cups of glycerin

NOTES:
Be aware of any allergies or sensitivities to these herbs. Discontinue use if you experience adverse reactions.

Use joint fir (*Ephedra*) with caution and only in small amounts due to its potential stimulant effects and possible side effects, especially in high doses.

INSTRUCTIONS:

1. **Prepare the Herbal Mixture:** Combine 1 teaspoon each of chopped thyme, licorice root, yarrow leaves, white willow bark, and joint fir leaves in a saucepan.
2. **Infuse the Herbs:** Pour 1 cup of water over the herbs in the saucepan.
3. **Simmer the Herbal Infusion:** Bring the mixture to a boil, then reduce the heat and let it simmer for about 10-15 minutes, creating an herbal infusion.
4. **Cool the Herbal Infusion:** Remove the saucepan from heat and allow it to cool until it is warm but not scalding.
5. **Strain the Herbal Infusion:** Using a fine mesh strainer or cheesecloth, strain out the herbs from the infusion, collecting the liquid in a clean glass bottle or container with a tight-fitting lid. Make sure it's large enough for the next step.
6. **Add Glycerin:** Mix 1 cup of glycerin into the warm strained herbal infusion, stirring well or shaking in the jar to combine.
7. **Store the Elixir:** Store the elixir in a cool, dark place. It should remain potent for several months.

DOSAGE:

Typically, a teaspoon or two daily is suitable for most adults.

Grandma's
"Antibiotic"

Usnea is traditionally used in herbal practices to support respiratory health and infections. It is known for its potential to aid with bronchitis, pneumonia, sinus infections, strep throat, colds, flus, and respiratory discomforts. Usnea is also commonly used to support urinary tract health, including the bladder and kidneys. Its antimicrobial properties are believed to help maintain the body's natural defenses while supporting the immune system.

INGREDIENTS:

- Dried usnea lichen
- 80 to 100 proof alcohol, 8 ounces
- Distilled water

NOTES:

While usnea is generally considered safe, it's typically recommended for short-term use. Consult a healthcare professional if you plan to use it for an extended period or have chronic respiratory conditions.

I use it as a throat spray as well, and use it for cold/flu prevention daily (due to the small amount consumed) in the cold and flu season and when traveling.

It's also useful as a spray to access spots in the throat if needed (e.g. strep).

INSTRUCTIONS:

ALCOHOL EXTRACTION

1 | **Preparation:** Begin by breaking or cutting the dried usnea lichen into smaller pieces to increase the surface area for extraction and to access the core.
2 | **Combine with Alcohol:** Place the chopped usnea lichen in a glass jar and cover it with high-proof alcohol, ensuring that the lichen is fully submerged. Use a 1:2 ratio of usnea to alcohol (e.g., 1 ounce of usnea to 2 ounces of alcohol).
3 | **Seal and Store:** Seal the jar tightly with a lid. Store it in a cool, dark place for at least 6 weeks, shaking the jar gently every few days to agitate the mixture.
4 | **Strain:** After the alcohol extraction period, strain the liquid through a cheesecloth or fine mesh strainer into a clean container, saving the usnea.

WATER EXTRACTION

1 | **Boil Water:** In a separate pot, bring distilled water to a boil.
2 | **Add Usnea:** Add your used usnea lichen from the alcohol extraction to the boiling water. Use a 1:2 ratio of usnea to water.
3 | **Simmer:** Reduce the heat to a low simmer and let it cook for about an hour.
4 | **Strain:** After simmering, strain the liquid through a cheesecloth or fine mesh strainer into another clean container.

Combine the Extracts: Mix the alcohol-based extract and the water-based extract together in a 3:1 ratio of alcoholic tincture to your water extraction. Transfer the combined tincture into dark glass bottles for storage.

DOSAGE:

Typically, 10-30 drops diluted in water or juice or taken directly in the mouth 2-3 times per day for 7-10 days.

Homemade Rub
for Easy Breathing

Making your own Vicks VapoRub ointment at home is possible using a few simple ingredients. This homemade version can provide relief from congestion, coughing, and sore muscles. Eucalyptus oil is the key ingredient in Vicks VapoRub for its menthol-like scent. Peppermint oil provides additional soothing and cooling properties. Camphor has been proven to increase blood flow and ease a cough. At first, it produces a cooling sensation on the skin, but after 10 minutes or so, it switches to a warming sensation.

INGREDIENTS:

- ½ cup coconut oil
- 2 tablespoons beeswax
- 20-drops eucalyptus essential oil (*Eucalyptus*)
- 20 drops peppermint essential oil (*Mentha piperita*)
- 20 drops camphor essential oil (*Cinnamomum camphora*)

NOTES:

This ointment is meant for external use only. Do not ingest it. If you have sensitive skin or allergies to any of the ingredients, perform a patch test on a small area of skin before applying the ointment to larger areas.

Store your homemade VapoRub in a cool, dry place with the lid tightly closed. It should last for several months, but if you notice any changes in color, consistency, or scent, it's best to make a fresh batch.

INSTRUCTIONS:

1. **Prepare Your Workspace:** Ensure your workspace is clean and well-ventilated. Wash your hands thoroughly.
2. **Melt Beeswax and Coconut Oil:** In a heat-resistant glass container or a double boiler, combine the beeswax and coconut oil. Place the container in a pot of simmering water (double boiler) or microwave in short intervals, stirring frequently until both ingredients are completely melted and well combined. Be cautious not to overheat.
3. **Add Essential Oils:** Remove the mixture from heat and let it cool slightly (but not solidify). Add the eucalyptus, peppermint, and camphor essential oils to the mixture. Adjust the number of drops according to your preference for scent and strength.
4. **Stir Well:** Use a clean utensil to stir the mixture thoroughly, ensuring the essential oils are evenly distributed.
5. **Transfer to Container:** Pour the ointment mixture into your airtight container and cover it while it's still in a liquid state.
6. **Cool and Solidify:** Let the mixture cool and solidify at room temperature. This may take a few hours.
7. **Usage:** To use your homemade VapoRub, apply a small amount to your chest, back, or throat (externally) as needed. You can also rub it onto sore muscles or the soles of your feet if you have a cough. The heat from your body will help release the soothing vapors.

DOSAGE:

Use as often as necessary, but typically 2-3 times a day is sufficient.

Forgotten Home Apothecary

Thyme and Honey
Respiratory Elixir

Homemade thyme and honey respiratory elixir is a natural remedy that combines the soothing properties of thyme and honey to help alleviate respiratory symptoms such as coughs, congestion, and sore throats. Thyme is known for its antimicrobial and anti-inflammatory properties, while honey helps soothe a sore throat and provide some relief from coughing.

INGREDIENTS:

- 1 cup fresh thyme leaves or ½ cup dried thyme (*Thymus vulgaris*)
- 1 cup raw honey

NOTES:

Be cautious if you have allergies to thyme or bee products like honey.

If you experience any allergic reactions, discontinue use and seek medical advice.

Avoid giving this elixir to infants under one year of age. Honey can pose health risks to young children due to the potential presence of botulism spores.

INSTRUCTIONS:

1 | **Harvest and Prepare Thyme:** If you're using fresh thyme, wash it thoroughly and remove the leaves from the stems. If you're using dried thyme, skip this step.

2 | **Combine Thyme and Honey:** Place the thyme leaves (or dried thyme) in a clean, dry glass jar. Pour the honey over the thyme.

3 | **Mix Well:** Stir the honey and thyme together until they are well combined.

4 | **Infuse:** Seal the jar tightly and let the mixture infuse for at least 3-4 days. You can leave it for up to a week to maximize the flavor and medicinal properties. Store the jar in a cool, dark place.

5 | **Filter the Mixture:** After the infusion period, pass the mixture through cheesecloth or a fine mesh strainer into a clean glass bottle. This will separate the thyme leaves, leaving you with the infused honey. You may find that warming the jar slightly in a warm water bath helps this process.

6 | **Store:** Seal the glass bottle with the infused honey and store it in a cool, dark place. It should remain good for several months.

DOSAGE:

Take 1-2 teaspoons as needed to soothe a sore throat or calm a cough. You can take it straight or mix it into a cup of warm water or herbal tea.

"Mighty Lungs"
Tincture

A homemade "Mighty Lungs" tincture can support respiratory health. This tincture consists of herbs and ingredients known for their lung-strengthening and soothing properties.

Mullein is known for its respiratory benefits and can help soothe irritated lungs. Lungwort is an herb that is traditionally used for lung health. Thyme is known for its antimicrobial properties and can help with respiratory congestion. Peppermint helps open up the airways and soothe the respiratory tract.

INGREDIENTS:

- ¼ cup dried mullein leaves (*Verbascum thapsus*)
- ⅛ cup dried lungwort (*Pulmonaria officinalis*)
- ⅛ cup dried thyme
- ⅛ cup dried peppermint
- 1 cup alcohol (vodka or brandy work well)

NOTES:

These measurements will yield a small batch of tincture that you can use to support respiratory health. If you want to make a larger batch, you can scale up the measurements accordingly while maintaining the equal proportions of the herbs.

Start with a small dose and monitor your body's response. Adjust the dosage as needed based on your individual preferences and needs.

INSTRUCTIONS:

1 | **Gather the Ingredients:** Collect the specified amounts of dried mullein leaves, lungwort, thyme, and peppermint. You can find these herbs in health food stores or online.

2 | **Combine the Herbs:** Mix the dried herbs together in a clean glass jar with a tight-fitting lid. Ensure that you have an equal proportion of each herb.

3 | **Add Alcohol:** Pour 1 cup of alcohol (vodka or brandy) into the jar containing the mixed herbs to cover them completely. Seal the jar tightly.

4 | **Shake and Steep:** Gently shake the jar to ensure the herbs are fully submerged in the alcohol. Then, store the sealed jar in a cool, dark place for about 4-6 weeks. Remember to shake the jar once a day to agitate the mixture.

5 | **Strain the Tincture:** After the steeping period, strain the liquid through a fine mesh strainer or cheesecloth into a clean, dark glass dropper bottle.

DOSAGE:

To use the tincture, take about 20-30 drops (approximately 1-1.5 ml) directly in the mouth or diluted in a small amount of water, tea, or juice. You can take it up to three times a day or as needed to support your respiratory health.

Cowboy Cough Syrup
(with Whiskey)

Cowboy cough syrup with whiskey is a time-tested remedy used to combat cough symptoms. It is a natural remedy that combines the soothing properties of raw honey, lemon, whiskey, and peppermint candies to ease cough symptoms. Raw honey soothes a sore throat, reduces inflammation, and provides antioxidants. Lemon breaks up mucus, relieves throat discomfort, and has anti-inflammatory properties. Whiskey numbs the throat and temporarily eases coughing. Peppermint candies provide short-term relief with menthol and analgesic effects.

INGREDIENTS:

- 4 fl oz whiskey (~120 ml)
- 2 sliced lemons (medium-sized)
- 3 tablespoons of honey
- 8 peppermint candies

NOTES:

It's important to use whiskey responsibly and avoid giving raw honey to infants.

Keep the jar in a dark place or in your fridge. This way it will keep for up to a month.

Please remember that this remedy contains alcohol, and it should be used responsibly. It's not a substitute for medical advice or prescribed medications.

If your cough persists or worsens, consult a healthcare professional.

INSTRUCTIONS:

1. **Prepare the Base:** Place 4 peppermint candies in the mason jar.
2. **Layer the Ingredients:** Add the lemon slices, covering the peppermint candies.
3. **First Honey Addition:** Add two tablespoons of honey.
4. **Add More Peppermint:** Place the remaining peppermint candies on top of the lemon slices.
5. **Layer with Lemon Slices:** Cover the candies with the second round of lemon slices.
6. **Second Honey Addition:** Add another tablespoon of honey.
7. **Pour in the Whiskey:** Pour the whiskey into the jar until you cover the rest of the ingredients.
8. **Seal and Gently Mix:** Close the lid carefully and shake it gently.
9. **Allow Mixture to Infuse:** Leave the jar in a dark place and shake it every 6 hours. After 24 hours, your cough syrup is ready to use.

This homemade cowboy cough syrup can be taken in small sips as needed for cough relief. The whiskey and peppermint help numb the throat and provide temporary relief from coughing, while the honey soothes the throat, and the lemon helps soothe and break up mucus.

DOSAGE:

Take 1 tablespoon of the mixture every 4 to 6 hours. You can also put 1-2 tablespoons of this syrup in warm water or tea.

Hot Toddy

A hot toddy is a classic warm beverage that's perfect for cold weather or soothing a sore throat.

Whiskey provides a comforting warmth, while honey sweetens the concoction and is traditionally known for its soothing properties. Fresh lemon juice adds a burst of flavor and is commonly used for its vitamin C content. Cloves contribute a hint of spice and are traditionally used for their potential anti-inflammatory effects. Cinnamon not only adds a delightful flavor but also brings potential antioxidant qualities. Including star anise in your hot toddy can introduce an additional layer of complexity and flavor, with its subtle licorice-like aroma. Star anise is traditionally valued for its potential antimicrobial and digestive properties.

INGREDIENTS:

- 2 oz whiskey (such as Scotch or bourbon)
- 1 tablespoon honey
- ½ oz fresh lemon juice
- 4 oz hot water
- 2 whole cloves
- 1 cinnamon stick
- Optional: lemon wedge for garnish and star anise

NOTES:

Exercise caution when consuming alcohol, especially if you have a low tolerance or sensitivity to its effects.

Everyone's tolerance to alcohol and its effects varies. Know your limits and listen to your body.

Consult with a healthcare professional before consuming a Hot Toddy, especially if you are taking medications that may interact with alcohol or any of the ingredients.

INSTRUCTIONS:

1. **Prepare Ingredients:** Gather your whiskey, honey, fresh lemon juice, hot water, cloves, and cinnamon stick.
2. **Warm Your Mug:** Heat a mug by rinsing it with hot water, then discard the water.
3. **Combine Ingredients:** Pour the whiskey, honey, lemon juice, cloves, and cinnamon stick into the warmed mug.
4. **Add Hot Water:** Fill the mug with hot water, leaving a bit of space at the top.
5. **Stir:** Use a spoon to stir the ingredients until the honey is fully dissolved.
6. **Steep:** Allow the cloves and cinnamon stick to steep in the mixture for a few minutes to infuse their flavors. Remove.
7. **Garnish and Serve:** If desired, garnish with a lemon wedge. Remember to stay hydrated by drinking water alongside or after enjoying a Hot Toddy, as alcohol can contribute to dehydration.

DOSAGE:

Enjoy this Hot Toddy as needed for warmth or relief. It's best enjoyed in moderation.

Forgotten Home Apothecary

Anti-Viral
Pine Neede Tincture

Pine needles contain compounds such as vitamin C, antioxidants, and certain essential oils that are known to have antiviral properties. They have up to five times the amount of Vitamin C as an orange and contain enormous amounts of Vitamin A. In addition, the natural terpenes in pine needles lend to their antibacterial, anti-microbial, and anti-inflammatory capabilities. Pine needles also contain shikimic acid, a natural compound known for its potential help with respiratory complications due to illness and it is traditionally used as an anti-viral.

INGREDIENTS:

- Fresh pine needles
- High-proof alcohol (such as 100-proof vodka or Everclear)

NOTES:

Ensure that you can positively identify the pine species.

Make sure the pine needles are from a non-toxic pine species like Eastern white pine or Scots pine.

You can use the young green pine cones and more mature pine cones to make a pine cone tincture, but the more immature cones hold more medicinal value. They should be harvested directly off the tree in late spring to early summer once nutrition levels have reached their maximum.

INSTRUCTIONS:

1. **Harvest Pine Needles:** Gather fresh, green pine needles from a healthy pine tree.
2. **Clean and Dry:** Rinse the pine needles under cool running water to remove any dirt or debris. Pat dry.
3. **Chop or Crush:** Chop the pine needles into small pieces or use a mortar and pestle to lightly crush them. This will help release the active compounds.
4. **Place in Jar:** Place the chopped or crushed pine needles in a glass jar. Fill the jar about halfway with the pine needles.
5. **Add Alcohol:** Pour the high-proof alcohol over the pine needles, making sure they are fully submerged. Seal the jar with a tight-fitting lid.
6. **Infuse:** Store the jar in a cool, dark place for at least four weeks. You can shake the jar gently every day or so to help with the extraction process.
7. **Strain:** After the infusion period, strain the tincture through a fine mesh strainer or cheesecloth to remove the pine needle solids. Transfer the liquid tincture to a clean, dark glass bottle for storage.
8. **Storage:** Store the tincture in a cool, dark place away from direct sunlight. When stored properly, it can have a shelf life of several years.

DOSAGE:

The appropriate dosage can vary, so it's crucial to consult with a healthcare professional or herbalist for guidance. I usually use this when ill, taking 1ml (~ a dropperful) 2-3x/day.

"Jello"
Flu Shots

This "Jello" flu shots recipe combines the immune-boosting properties of echinacea (*Echinacea purpurea*) with the vitamin-rich goodness of freshly squeezed apple and carrot juice.

Turning wellness remedies into jello shots offers a convenient and enjoyable way to consume immune-boosting ingredients, suitable for both adults and children. Their portability makes them ideal for on-the-go consumption, fitting into busy lifestyles, while their individual moldings allow for customizable dosage control. Additionally, these shots mask any undesirable flavors, making them palatable for those who may find herbal remedies unappealing. Furthermore, compared to fresh juices or teas, jello shots have a longer shelf life, providing a convenient option for stocking up on immune-boosting remedies.

INGREDIENTS:

- 1 cup of freshly squeezed apple and carrot juice
- 1 tablespoon of agar agar flakes
- ½ cup of echinacea tea (adjust to your preference)
- Optional: Honey or maple syrup for sweetness

NOTES:

Experiment with different variations of juice for flavor variety. Consider adding additional immune-boosting ingredients like ginger or lemon juice for added benefits.

Consult with a healthcare professional before using echinacea, especially if you have autoimmune conditions (elderberry is a good replacement) or are pregnant or nursing.

Avoid this recipe if you have allergies to any of the ingredients.

INSTRUCTIONS:

1 | **Prepare Agar Agar Mixture:** In a small saucepan, combine the agar agar flakes and the echinacea tea. Let the mixture sit for a few minutes to allow the agar agar flakes to soften.

2 | **Dissolve Agar Agar:** Heat the mixture over medium heat, stirring continuously until the agar flakes dissolve completely. This typically takes about 5–7 minutes. Be patient as the mixture thickens.

3 | **Incorporate Juice:** Once the agar agar flakes are fully dissolved, remove the mixture from the heat. Stir in the freshly squeezed apple-carrot juice until well combined.

4 | **Optional Sweetener:** If desired, add honey or maple syrup for sweetness. Note that honey is a natural throat soother and cough treatment; avoid adding it to boiling mixtures to preserve its enzymes.

5 | **Mold and Set:** Pour the mixture into silicone molds or a glass dish. Refrigerate until set, usually within 1–2 hours.

DOSAGE:

Enjoy one jello flu shot daily as a preventative measure during flu season or increase dosage as needed during illness.

Forgotten Home Apothecary

Anti-Phlegm
Holy Basil Tea

Holy basil, also known as Tulsi, is a popular herb with a long history of use in traditional medicine systems like Ayurveda. It is believed to have various health benefits, including its potential to help with respiratory issues, such as expectorating phlegm.

INGREDIENTS:

- Holy basil leaves (*Ocimum tenuiflorum*)
- 1 cup of water per serving
- Raw honey (optional): Honey can be added for flavor and to soothe a sore throat

NOTES:

While fresh holy basil leaves are preferred, dried leaves are a convenient alternative.

Fresh leaves offer a more vibrant flavor and aroma, but dried leaves are a practical option, especially when fresh ones are not readily available.

If you have allergies to basil or similar plants, be cautious when trying this remedy, and consult a healthcare professional if needed.

INSTRUCTIONS:

1. **Wash the Basil Leaves:** If using fresh leaves, wash them thoroughly to remove any dirt or contaminants.
2. **Boil the Water:** Place the water in a pot and bring it to a boil.
3. **Add Holy Basil Leaves:** Once the water is boiling, add the holy basil leaves to the pot. You can use 4-6 fresh leaves or 1-2 teaspoons of dried basil per cup of water, depending on your preference for flavor and strength.
4. **Simmer:** Reduce the heat to low and let the basil leaves simmer for about 5-10 minutes. This allows the leaves to infuse their beneficial compounds into the water. When simmering the holy basil leaves, ensure the water remains at a gentle simmer, not a rolling boil. This will help preserve the delicate flavors and beneficial compounds in the herb.
5. **Strain:** After simmering, strain the tea to remove the basil leaves. You can use a fine mesh strainer or a tea infuser.
6. **Serve:** Pour the hot holy basil tea into a cup. If desired, add honey for sweetness and to help soothe your throat.
7. **Enjoy:** Sip the tea slowly while it's still warm. In addition to holy basil tea, make sure you stay well-hydrated by drinking plenty of water, especially when dealing with respiratory issues and phlegm.

Get creative with your holy basil tea by adding other herbs like mint, ginger, or lemongrass for additional flavors and health benefits.

DOSAGE:

Drink 1 to 2 cups of holy basil tea per day, especially when you're experiencing respiratory discomfort due to excess phlegm.

Alergy Relief
Balm

Creating a homemade antihistamine balm for natural allergy relief can be a soothing and effective way to alleviate the discomfort caused by allergies. Keep in mind that while these ingredients have natural antihistamine properties, they may not be as potent as over-the-counter medications or herbs such as stinging nettle, so their effectiveness may vary from person to person. Adding garlic to your homemade antihistamine balm can enhance its anti-inflammatory and immune-boosting properties. Using stinging nettle tincture 2-3x/day in conjunction is advised.

INGREDIENTS:

- ¼ cup coconut oil
- 1-2 tablespoons beeswax
- 2-3 garlic cloves (finely minced)
- Essential oils (optional):
  - Lavender oil (*Lavandula*): 5-10 drops
  - Peppermint oil (*Mentha piperita*): 5-10 drops
  - Tea tree oil (*Melaleuca alternifolia*): 5-10 drops
  - Chamomile oil (*Matricaria chamomilla*): 5-10 drops

NOTES:
Be sure to do a patch test on a small area of your skin before applying the balm more widely to check for any adverse reactions to the garlic or essential oils.

INSTRUCTIONS:

1. **Prepare a Double Boiler:** Fill a pot with a few inches of water and place a heatproof glass or metal bowl on top, ensuring it doesn't touch the water. This creates a double boiler for melting ingredients.
2. **Melt Coconut Oil and Beeswax:** Add ¼ cup of coconut oil and 1-2 tablespoons of beeswax to the bowl. Heat the pot over low to medium heat until the oil and beeswax are completely melted, stirring occasionally.
3. **Add Minced Garlic:** Once the coconut oil and beeswax are melted, add the finely minced garlic cloves to the mixture. Stir well to incorporate the garlic into the balm.
4. **Incorporate Essential Oils:** Add the desired essential oils at this stage for added fragrance and potential antihistamine benefits. Adjust the quantity to your preference. Stir the mixture thoroughly to evenly distribute the essential oils.
5. **Pour into Containers:** Remove the mixture from heat and let it cool slightly, but not enough to solidify. Pour the liquid balm into small containers, lip balm tubes, or any suitable containers you have on hand. Allow the balm to cool and solidify at room temperature or in the refrigerator.

DOSAGE:

Whenever needed, apply the balm to affected areas of your skin or gently rub it on your chest and under your nose to inhale the soothing aroma.

Anti-Histaminic
Tea

"Anti-Histaminic Tea" is an herbal blend designed to help alleviate symptoms of allergies. This tea combines herbs known for their natural antihistamine properties, providing relief from common allergic reactions such as sneezing, itching, and congestion. Stinging nettle is traditionally used to support the body's response to allergens. Peppermint soothes respiratory discomfort and supports clearing the airways. Chamomile offers calming effects and eases allergy-related stress. Rooibos, rich in antioxidants, supports immune health. Ginger, known for its anti-inflammatory properties, aids in respiratory health.

INGREDIENTS:

- 1 teaspoon dried stinging nettle (*Urtica dioica*)
- 1 teaspoon dried peppermint (*Mentha piperita*)
- 1 teaspoon dried chamomile (*Matricaria chamomilla*)
- 1 teaspoon dried rooibos (*Aspalathus linearis*)
- 1 teaspoon dried ginger root (*Zingiber officinale*)
- 2 cups boiling water
- Honey (optional, to taste)

NOTES:

Stinging nettle, peppermint, chamomile, rooibos, and ginger may cause mild digestive issues or allergic reactions. Start with small amounts. Consult a healthcare provider if taking antihistamines, blood thinners, or blood pressure medications, and before use during pregnancy, nursing, or with chronic health conditions.

INSTRUCTIONS:

1 | **Combine the Herbs:** In a teapot or a heatproof container, combine the dried stinging nettle, peppermint, chamomile, rooibos, and ginger root. Use high-quality, organic herbs for the best results.
2 | **Boil the Water:** Bring 2 cups of water to a boil.
3 | **Steep the Tea:** Pour the boiling water over the herbs. Cover and let the tea steep for 10-15 minutes to allow the herbs to infuse their beneficial properties into the water.
4 | **Strain the Tea:** After steeping, strain the herbs from the tea using a fine mesh strainer or cheesecloth.
5 | **Serve:** Pour the strained tea into a cup. Add honey to taste if desired. Add a squeeze of fresh lemon juice to your tea for extra flavor. You can Make a larger batch of the herbal blend and store it in an airtight container for convenience.

DOSAGE:

Drink 1-2 cups of the anti-histaminic tea daily, especially during allergy season or when experiencing allergy symptoms.

Stinging Nettle Tincture
for Hay Fever

Stinging nettle is a natural remedy that some people use to alleviate the symptoms of hay fever (allergic rhinitis) and other allergies. Stinging nettle has anti-inflammatory and antihistamine properties that can help reduce the allergic response.

INGREDIENTS:

- Fresh stinging nettle leaves and stems (*Urtica dioica*)
- 80-100 proof alcohol (such as vodka or brandy)

NOTES:

When harvesting stinging nettles, wear gloves and protective clothing to avoid skin irritation from the stinging hairs on the plant.

If you have a real allergy to plants in the Urticaceae family, avoid using stinging nettle altogether, as it can trigger allergic reactions in some individuals.

INSTRUCTIONS:

1 | **Harvest the Stinging Nettle:** Wear gloves to protect your hands from stings. Harvest fresh stinging nettle leaves and stems., but younger leaves are preferred.
2 | **Chop the Nettle:** Roughly chop the nettle leaves and stems. This will increase the surface area for extraction. Letting the leaves dry first takes away the majority of the sting, making the plant easier to work with.
3 | **Fill the Jar:** Place the chopped nettle in a glass jar. Fill the jar about halfway with the nettle.
4 | **Add Alcohol:** Pour the alcohol over the nettle, making sure it covers the plant material completely.
5 | **Seal and Store:** Seal the jar tightly with its lid.
6 | **Shake and Store:** Periodically shake the jar gently to mix the alcohol and nettle. Store the jar in a cool, dark place, away from direct sunlight.
7 | **Wait and Shake:** Let the tincture sit for at least 4-6 weeks, shaking it every few days to help with the extraction process.
8 | **Strain:** After the steeping period, strain the tincture through cheesecloth or a fine mesh strainer into a clean glass container or amber dropper bottles. Squeeze out as much liquid as possible from the nettle material.
9 | **Label:** Label your tincture with the date and contents.

DOSAGE:

Take 10-20 drops of the tincture directly in the mouth for hay fever symptoms, up to three times a day. Start with a lower dose and adjust as necessary. You may take it in a small glass of water or juice, but it works better if taken orally.

Anti-Mucus
Mullein Leaf Infusion

Mullein leaf tea is a traditional remedy that has been used for centuries to alleviate respiratory issues and clear out mucus from the respiratory tract. Mullein is known for its soothing and expectorant properties. In addition to making tea, mullein can be used in herbal smoking blends for respiratory benefits. A blend can include 1 tablespoon each of dried mullein and peppermint (*Mentha piperita*), and 1/2 tablespoon of dried thyme (*Thymus vulgaris*). Combine the herbs in a bowl, mix well, and use rolling papers or a pipe for smoking. Light the blend and take slow, steady puffs, inhaling gently to avoid irritation.

INGREDIENTS:

- 1-2 tablespoons of dried mullein leaves or 1-2 fresh mullein leaves (*Verbascum thapsus*)
- 1 cup of boiling water
- Honey or lemon (optional, for taste)

NOTES:

Ensure the quality and cleanliness of the mullein leaves you use. If you're harvesting fresh leaves, pick them from a clean, pesticide-free source. When using dried leaves, make sure they are from a reputable supplier to ensure their safety and efficacy.

Use mullein tea for a maximum of 7-10 days. If your symptoms persist beyond this time frame, consult a healthcare professional. If you use the smoking blend, always ensure the herbs used are safe for smoking and sourced from reputable suppliers.

INSTRUCTIONS:

1 | **Prepare the Mullein Leaves:** If you're using fresh mullein leaves, wash them thoroughly and chop them into smaller pieces. If you're using dried mullein leaves, measure out 1-2 tablespoons.
2 | **Boil the Water:** Heat 1 cup of water to a boil. You can use a kettle or a pot for this purpose.
3 | **Steep the Mullein Leaves:** Place the mullein leaves in a teapot or a cup. Pour the boiling water over the leaves.
4 | **Cover and Steep:** Cover the teapot or cup with a lid or a saucer to trap the steam and let the tea steep for about 10-15 minutes. This steeping time allows the beneficial compounds in the mullein leaves to infuse into the water.
5 | **Strain the Tea:** After steeping, use a fine-mesh strainer or a tea infuser to remove the mullein leaves from the tea. You can discard the used leaves.
6 | **Optional Flavoring:** If desired, you can add honey or lemon to your mullein leaf tea to improve the taste and add extra soothing properties. Raw honey, in particular, can help soothe your throat.
7 | **Cool and Enjoy:** Let the tea cool down to a comfortable drinking temperature, and then sip it slowly. You can have this tea 2-3 times a day as needed to help clear mucus and alleviate respiratory discomfort.

DOSAGE:

Start with 1-2 cups of mullein tea per day. If your symptoms are severe, you can increase the dosage to 3-4 cups of mullein tea per day.

Fever-Breaking
Onion Socks

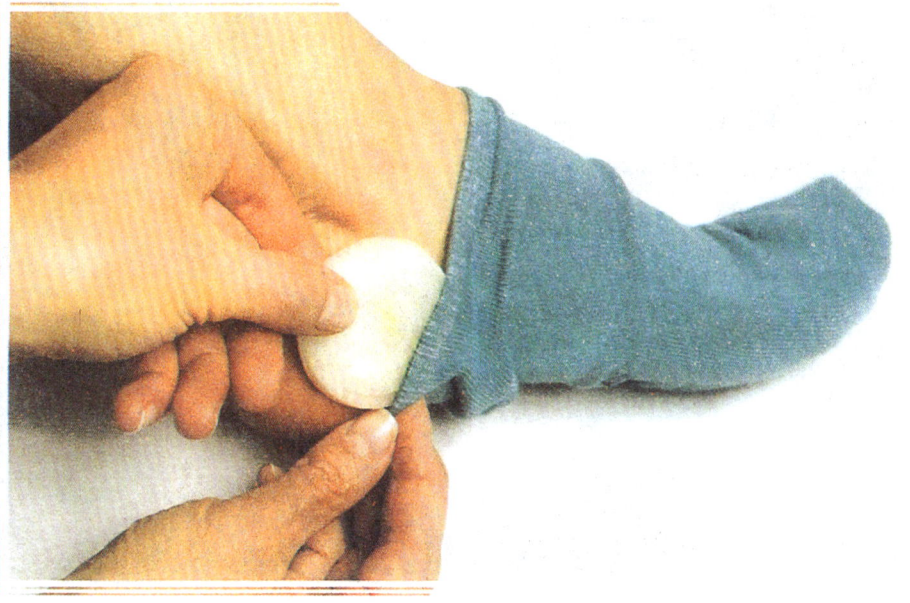

Onion socks are a traditional home remedy believed to help reduce fever and alleviate symptoms of illnesses like the common cold and flu. The idea behind onion socks is that the natural compounds in onions, such as sulfur compounds, can have anti-inflammatory and antimicrobial properties, which may assist in lowering fever and improving overall comfort.

INGREDIENTS AND MATERIALS:

- 1 onion (preferably red or white)
- 1 pair of thin cotton socks
- 1 pair of thick wool or fleece socks

NOTES:

This remedy is believed to work by drawing heat and toxins away from the body, potentially helping to reduce fever and alleviate some symptoms. However, scientific evidence supporting the effectiveness of onion socks is limited, and it may not work for everyone.

If you have high fever, another thing to do is to soak your socks in vinegar.

Keep them on your feet for about 20 minutes, and refresh them every half hour until the temperature begins to drop. You can use regular or apple cider vinegar.

INSTRUCTIONS:

1. **Prepare the Onion:** Start by peeling and either finely chopping or slicing the onion. Use an organic onion (you don't want pesticides being absorbed by your skin).
2. **Select Socks:** Choose a pair of thin cotton socks to help to minimize the smell and hold the onions in place.
3. **Onion Filling:** Place the chopped onion evenly in the socks, distributing it throughout both socks. Make sure the onion pieces are spread out as much as possible to maximize their contact with your feet. You can also use thin slices and put them directly in the socks. Make sure the onion slices are on the bottom of your feet, not the top, to maximize absorption.
4. **Prepare Your Feet:** Before putting on the onion-filled socks, make sure your feet are clean and dry.
5. **Put On Onion Socks:** Wear the onion-filled cotton socks.
6. **Insulate with Outer Socks:** Next, put on a pair of thick wool or fleece socks over the onion-filled socks. These outer socks will help hold the onion-filled socks in place and provide insulation.
7. **Wear Overnight:** Wear these onion socks overnight while you sleep. It's essential to keep your feet warm and covered throughout the night. If the smell of the onion bothers you, sprinkle a few drops of complementary scented essential oils on the outside of your socks or on a cotton pillowcase.
8. **Morning Removal:** In the morning, remove the onion socks and discard the onion pieces.

DOSAGE:

Whenever needed, wear these onion socks overnight while you sleep.

Forgotten Home Apothecary

Vinegar Socks

Vinegar socks are a traditional home remedy believed to help reduce fever and provide relief during colds and flu. This simple and natural method uses the cooling and antimicrobial properties of vinegar to help alleviate symptoms.

INGREDIENTS AND MATERIALS:

- 2 cups water
- ½ cup vinegar (apple cider vinegar preferred)
- 1 pair of cotton socks
- 1 pair of wool socks (optional for added warmth)

NOTES:

If you have sensitive skin, dilute the vinegar further or discontinue use if you experience any irritation or discomfort.

Consult with a healthcare professional before using this remedy, especially for children, the elderly, or if you have any chronic health conditions.

If the fever is very high or persistent, seek medical advice promptly.

INSTRUCTIONS:

1. **Prepare the Vinegar Solution:** In a bowl, mix 2 cups of water with ½ cup of vinegar. While apple cider vinegar is preferred due to its additional health benefits and pleasant aroma, other types of vinegar can also be used. White vinegar is a suitable substitute and works just as well for this remedy. If you have sensitive skin, consider diluting the vinegar more or using milder types like rice vinegar.
2. **Soak the Socks:** Soak the cotton socks in the vinegar solution until they are thoroughly saturated.
3. **Wring Out Excess Liquid:** Remove the socks from the solution and wring out any excess liquid so that they are damp but not dripping.
4. **Apply the Socks:** Put the damp cotton socks on your feet. For added warmth and comfort, you can layer a pair of dry wool socks over the damp socks.
5. **Rest and Relax:** Lie down and rest with your feet elevated if possible. Leave the socks on until they are dry. Ensure the room is warm enough to prevent chilling while using this remedy. You can also use this method in conjunction with other fever-reducing techniques, such as drinking plenty of fluids and resting.

DOSAGE:

Use the vinegar socks remedy as needed to help reduce fever and alleviate symptoms of cold and flu. It can be repeated several times a day if necessary.

Anti-Fever
Elixir

For a fever elixir, we can use herbs known for their antipyretic (fever-reducing) properties. One effective combination includes peppermint (*Mentha piperita*) and elderflower (*Sambucus nigra*). Peppermint is widely recognized for its cooling effect on the body and its ability to reduce fever, while elderflower has been traditionally used to support the immune system and ease symptoms of colds and fevers. If the fever is high, yarrow is an excellent addition.

INGREDIENTS:

- 2 cups water
- 1 tablespoon dried peppermint leaves (*Mentha piperita*)
- 1 tablespoon dried elderflower (*Sambucus nigra*)
- 1 tablespoon honey (optional, for taste)

NOTES:

Consult with a healthcare professional before giving herbal remedies to children, pregnant women, or individuals with pre-existing medical conditions.

Peppermint may cause heartburn or allergic reactions in some individuals. Discontinue use if any adverse reactions occur.

INSTRUCTIONS:

1 | **Prepare the Herbs:** In a small saucepan, bring the water to a boil.
2 | **Infusion:** Once boiling, remove from heat and add the dried peppermint leaves and elderflower to the water. Cover the saucepan and let the herbs steep for about 10-15 minutes to extract their beneficial properties.
3 | **Strain:** After steeping, strain the mixture to remove the herb residues. Use a fine mesh strainer or cheesecloth for this step.
4 | **Sweeten (Optional):** If desired, add honey to the strained liquid and stir until it dissolves. Honey not only adds sweetness but also possesses its own antimicrobial properties. For additional flavor and immune-boosting benefits, consider adding a slice of fresh lemon or a dash of ginger to the elixir.
5 | **Cooling:** Allow the elixir to cool to a lukewarm temperature before consumption. It can be consumed warm or chilled, according to preference.
6 | **Store:** Store any leftover elixir in a sealed container in the refrigerator for up to 24 hours. Reheat gently before consuming.

DOSAGE:

Drink ½ to 1 cup of the elixir every 4-6 hours as needed to reduce fever. Maintain proper hydration by drinking plenty of water in addition to the elixir to support the body's natural healing process.

Herbal
Fever Compress

Plantain (*Plantago major*) is a common weed traditionally known for its anti-inflammatory and cooling properties. This herbal compress may help reduce fever by providing a soothing and cooling effect when applied to the skin. I often add yarrow leaves and flowers to this mixture as well.

INGREDIENTS:

- Fresh plantain leaves (*Plantago major*)
- A clean cloth or cheesecloth
- A bandage or strip of cloth to secure the compress

NOTES:

Test a small amount of crushed plantain on your skin before full use to ensure you do not have an allergic reaction. Discontinue use if irritation occurs.

If you have any chronic health conditions, are pregnant, or are nursing, consult with a healthcare professional before using this remedy.

If the fever is very high or persistent, seek medical advice promptly.

INSTRUCTIONS:

1 | **Prepare the Plantain Leaves:** Plantain is a common weed found in many areas, making it an accessible and easy-to-find remedy. Gather a handful of fresh plantain leaves. Wash them thoroughly to remove any dirt or contaminants.

2 | **Crush the Leaves:** Using a mortar and pestle or a clean utensil, crush the plantain leaves to release their juices. You can also chop them finely and mash them to achieve a similar effect.

3 | **Make the Compress:** Place the crushed leaves onto a clean cloth or cheesecloth. Fold the cloth to create a small, secure bundle that can be easily applied to the skin.

4 | **Apply the Compress:** Place the plantain compress on the forehead, back of the neck, or the soles of the feet. Secure it in place with a bandage or strip of cloth.

5 | **Leave in Place:** Leave the compress in place for 20-30 minutes, or until the leaves begin to dry out. Replace with fresh leaves if needed. For added cooling, you can refrigerate the leaves before using them in the compress.

DOSAGE:

Use the compress as needed to help reduce fever and provide a cooling, soothing effect. I often add yarrow tincture internally to help reduce fever.

Snore Relief
Jelly

Snoring can be disruptive to both the snorer and their sleeping partner. While there are various causes of snoring, including nasal congestion, relaxed throat muscles, or sleep position, using a snore relief jelly can help alleviate the symptoms by lubricating the throat and nasal passages, reducing irritation and potential obstruction.

Here's a simple recipe for a snore relief jelly using peppermint (*Mentha piperita*) and eucalyptus (*Eucalyptus globulus*) essential oils, which are known for their decongestant and soothing properties.

INGREDIENTS:

- ½ cup water
- 1 tablespoon agar-agar powder (natural gelatin alternative)
- 5 drops peppermint (*Mentha piperita*) essential oil
- 5 drops eucalyptus (*Eucalyptus globulus*) essential oil

NOTES:

Adjust the essential oil quantities according to personal preference, but be cautious not to use too much, as it may cause skin irritation.

Avoid applying the jelly to broken or irritated skin.

Discontinue use if any adverse reactions occur.

Keep out of reach of children and pets.

INSTRUCTIONS:

1 | **Prepare the Agar Mixture:** In a small saucepan, bring the water to a gentle boil. Slowly sprinkle the agar-agar powder over the boiling water while stirring continuously to prevent clumping. Allow the mixture to simmer for 2-3 minutes until the agar-agar is fully dissolved.

2 | **Add Essential Oils:** Once the agar mixture is smooth and free of lumps, remove the saucepan from heat. Add the peppermint and eucalyptus essential oils to the mixture, stirring well to ensure they are evenly distributed.

3 | **Pour into Molds:** Carefully pour the liquid jelly mixture into a jar, small silicone molds or an ice cube tray.

4 | **Allow to Set:** Place the molds in the refrigerator and let the jelly set for at least 1 hour, or until firm.

5 | **Usage:** Before bedtime, remove a portion of the snore relief jelly from the mold. Gently massage a small amount onto the throat and chest area, and/or beneath the nostrils for nasal congestion relief. This jelly can also be used as a natural vapor rub for respiratory congestion relief during cold and flu season.

DOSAGE:

Use as needed, preferably before bedtime.

Turmeric Tonic
for Inflamation

This tonic is traditionally used to support overall wellness, and many people find it helpful during the cold and flu season. Additionally, it's a great way to start your day feeling energized and refreshed. Turmeric is a spice long valued for its anti-inflammatory, antioxidant, and immune-supporting properties. You can adjust the quantities to suit your taste and tolerance. Some people prefer a milder flavor, while others like it stronger.

INGREDIENTS:

- 1 tablespoon fresh turmeric (*Curcuma longa*)
- 1 tablespoon fresh ginger (*Zingiber officinale*)
- A pinch of black pepper (*Piper nigrum*)
- Juice of 1 lemon (about 3 tablespoons)
- 3 cups of water
- 1-2 teaspoons honey (optional, for sweetness)

NOTES:

Remember that turmeric can stain surfaces and clothing, so handle it carefully and clean up any spills promptly.

Additionally, be mindful of the potential staining of your teeth, which can occur due to the natural pigments in turmeric.

INSTRUCTIONS:

1 | **Prepare the Turmeric and Ginger:** Wash and peel the fresh turmeric and ginger. Grate or finely chop them. The finer you chop, the more flavor they'll release.

2 | **Boil the Water:** In a saucepan, bring 3 cups of water to a boil.

3 | **Add Turmeric and Ginger:** Once the water is boiling, add the grated or chopped turmeric and ginger to the water.

4 | **Add Black Pepper:** Add a pinch of black pepper to the mixture. Black pepper contains piperine, which enhances the absorption of curcumin, the active compound in turmeric.

5 | **Simmer:** Reduce the heat to low, and let the mixture simmer for about 15-20 minutes. This will allow the flavors and medicinal properties to infuse into the water.

6 | **Strain:** After simmering, strain the liquid to remove the turmeric and ginger pieces. You can use a fine mesh strainer or a piece of cheesecloth.

7 | **Add Lemon Juice:** Squeeze the juice of one lemon into the turmeric-ginger-infused water. Stir well to combine.

8 | **Sweeten (Optional):** If you'd like to sweeten your turmeric tonic, add 1-2 teaspoons of raw honey. Adjust to your taste.

9 | **Serve:** Pour the turmeric tonic into a mug or glass. You can enjoy it hot, like a tea, or let it cool and serve it over ice for a refreshing drink.

10 | **Enjoy:** Sip on your homemade turmeric tonic to relish the health benefits and flavors of this invigorating drink.

DOSAGE:

You can drink this turmeric tonic 2-3 times a day when you have cold or flu symptoms. It can be helpful to have a warm cup in the morning and evening, and possibly a milder version during the day. If you make a larger batch, store in a sealed glass jar in the fridge up to 3 days.

HERBAL SUPPORT
for the Nervous System

The nervous system serves as the body's control center, ensuring that all other systems work together harmoniously. Its ability to sense, process, and respond to internal and external stimuli is crucial for maintaining health, adapting to changes, and responding to challenges in the environment. This complex network of communication and control is essential for the overall well-being of the body.

Tips to support a healthy nervous system:

BALANCED DIET:

Eat a nutritious diet rich in whole grains, lean proteins, healthy fats, and a variety of fruits and vegetables. Nutrients like omega-3 fatty acids, B vitamins, magnesium, and antioxidants support nerve function.

REGULAR EXERCISE:

Engage in physical activity regularly to reduce stress and promote overall health. Aerobic exercises, yoga, and tai chi are excellent choices for nervous system health.

BRAIN EXERCISES:

Keep your mind active with puzzles, reading, learning new skills, and engaging in cognitive challenges.

ADEQUATE SLEEP:

Prioritize quality sleep to support cognitive function and emotional well-being.

STRESS MANAGEMENT:

Practice stress-reduction techniques such as meditation, deep breathing, and mindfulness.

SOCIAL CONNECTIONS:

Foster positive relationships with friends and family to support emotional well-being.

HOBBIES AND RELAXATION:

Engage in activities you enjoy to reduce stress and boost mood.

AVOID TOXINS:

Minimize exposure to environmental toxins and pollutants.

HERBAL SUPPORT

Ashwagandha (Withania somnifera)
An adaptogenic herb, ashwagandha is thought to help reduce stress and anxiety by supporting the adrenal glands. It can be taken as a powdered supplement or tincture.

Lion's Mane Mushroom (Hericium erinaceus)
This mushroom is believed to support nerve health by encouraging the production of Nerve Growth Factor (NGF). It may help with sleep issues, mood, cognitive function, energy levels, gut health, and stress symptoms. It is commonly used as a dual-extracted tincture.

Lemon Balm (Melissa officinalis)
Lemon balm is associated with improvements in memory, mood, and age-related cognitive performance, a reduction in stress and anxiety, and improved clarity and focus. lemon balm is an antioxidant, helping to protect nerves. Lemon balm also inhibits the brain's levels of acetylcholinesterase (AChE), an enzyme that helps break down acetylcholine (Ach), a critical neurotransmitter involved in cognition and memory. It can be consumed as a tea or tincture.

Passionflower (Passiflora incarnata)
Passionflower is known for its calming effects and can help alleviate anxiety and promote better sleep. It is typically used as a tea or tincture at night.

Ginkgo Biloba (Ginkgo biloba)
Ginko biloba may improve cognitive function and blood circulation to the brain. It is available as a supplement or tincture.

Waterhyssop (Bacopa monnieri)
Bacopa monnieri is believed to support cognitive function and memory. It can be taken as a supplement or tincture.

Memory Elixir

This memory elixir combines five herbs traditionally used for their cognitive and memory-enhancing properties. Rosemary, ashwagandha, lemon balm, ginseng and ginkgo biloba are all renowned for their ability to support mental clarity, reduce stress, and improve overall brain function.

INGREDIENTS:

- 1 tablespoon dried rosemary (*Rosmarinus officinalis*)
- 1 tablespoon dried ashwagandha root (*Withania somnifera*)
- 1 tablespoon dried lemon balm (*Melissa officinalis*)
- 1 tablespoon dried ginseng root (*Panax ginseng*)
- 1 tablespoon dried ginkgo biloba (*Ginkgo biloba*)
- 4 cups of water

NOTES:

Whether using fresh or dried herbs, ensure they are of high quality and free from pesticides or contaminants. If harvesting from your garden, do so when the herbs are at their peak potency.

INSTRUCTIONS:

1. **Prepare the Ingredients:** Measure and prepare all the dried herbs: rosemary, ashwagandha, lemon balm, ginseng, and ginkgo biloba.
2. **Boil the Water:** Add 4 cups of water to a pot and bring it to a boil. Once boiling, add one tablespoon each of the prepared herbs to the pot.
3. **Simmer:** Lower the heat to a simmer and let the mixture simmer for 15 minutes. This allows the herbs to release their beneficial compounds into the water.
4. **Steep:** After 15 minutes of simmering, turn off the heat completely.
5. Cover the pot and let the mixture steep for an additional 30 minutes. This ensures maximum extraction of the herbal properties.
6. **Strain:** After 30 minutes of steeping, strain the mixture through a fine mesh strainer or cheesecloth into a clean container to remove the herbal material.
7. **Serve:** Pour the elixir into cups and enjoy. You can store the remaining elixir in a glass jar in the refrigerator for up to 3 days. For added flavor, consider adding a teaspoon of honey or a slice of lemon to each cup.
8. **Store:** Store the elixir in a sealed container in the refrigerator to maintain its freshness and potency.

DOSAGE:

Do not drink more than two cups of this elixir per day.

Brain Boosting
Tonic

In the quest for optimal cognitive function, this brain-boosting tonic combines herbs known for their cognitive-enhancing properties. *Ginkgo biloba*, known for its distinctive fan-shaped leaves, has long been celebrated for its ability to enhance blood circulation to the brain, thereby improving memory and concentration. *Bacopa monnieri* is rooted in its support for cognitive function, anxiety reduction, and memory enhancement. Gotu kola, with its historical use in traditional medicine, contributes by improving memory, increasing mental clarity, and alleviating anxiety. Finally, sage, an herb with cognitive-enhancing properties, further enriches the concoction, promoting memory and concentration.

INGREDIENTS:

- 1 teaspoon of dried *Ginkgo biloba* leaves
- 1-2 teaspoons of dried *Bacopa monnieri*
- 1-2 teaspoons of dried gotu kola (*Centella asiatica*)
- 1-2 teaspoons of dried Sage (*Salvia officinalis*)

NOTES:

Regularly incorporate brain-boosting foods like blueberries, walnuts, and fatty fish into your diet for added benefits.

Herbs can interact with medications you may be taking. *Ginkgo biloba*, for example, can interact with blood thinners. Ensure there are no contraindications with your current medications.

INSTRUCTIONS:

1 | **Herbal Infusion Preparation:** Boil 4 cups of water in a pot.
2 | **Add the Herbs:** Once the water is boiling, add the specified amounts of dried *Ginkgo biloba* leaves, *Bacopa monnieri*, gotu kola, and sage to the pot.
3 | **Simmer and Steep:** Reduce the heat to a simmer and cover the pot. Allow the herbs to steep for 10-15 minutes.
4 | **Strain the Infusion:** After the steeping period, carefully strain the infusion into a glass or container, removing the herbs. This will leave you with the herbal tonic.
5 | **Sweeten and Serve:** Add honey or stevia to sweeten the herbal tonic to your liking. You can store any leftover infusions in the refrigerator for up to 2 days.

Before indulging in this brain-boosting elixir, it's wise to incorporate other brain-friendly foods into your diet, such as blueberries, walnuts, and fatty fish.

DOSAGE:

Consume 1 cup of this tonic daily, preferably in the morning, to enhance cognitive function.

Forgotten Home Apothecary

Natural
Brain Booster

This recipe creates a "brain booster" powder that combines ingredients traditionally valued for their cognitive support properties. Using rosemary, fennel seeds, walnuts, and pumpkin seeds, this blend is rich in antioxidants, omega-3 fatty acids, and other nutrients believed to support brain health and mental clarity.

INGREDIENTS:

- 2 tbsp of dried rosemary
- 1 tsp fennel seeds
- ¾ cup walnuts
- ½ cup pumpkin seeds
- Stevia or monkfruit (to taste)
- Grinder or blender
- Jar for storage

NOTES:

Adjust the amount of sweetener based on your preference for sweetness.

For an additional flavor boost and extra nutritional benefits, consider adding a sprinkle of cinnamon or cocoa powder to the mix.

INSTRUCTIONS:

1 | **Blend the Ingredients:** Place the dried rosemary, fennel seeds, walnuts, pumpkin seeds, and a suitable amount of stevia or monkfruit into your blender or grinder.
2 | **Grind to a Powder:** Process all the ingredients until they are fully pulverized into a fine powder. This ensures that the flavors and nutrients are well-mixed and easily consumable.
3 | **Storage:** Transfer the resulting powder into a clean and sterile jar. Seal the jar tightly to preserve freshness.
4 | **Refrigeration:** Keep the jar in the fridge to maintain its potency and freshness for up to 4 months.
5 | **Serve:** Incorporate 2 teaspoons of the brain booster powder into your daily diet by adding it to a glass of milk, coffee, or a smoothie.

DOSAGE:

You can consume it in the morning before a meal or before bedtime to suit your routine.

Forgotten Home Apothecary

Brain Power
Mushroom Elixir

Lion's mane is a remarkable mushroom traditionally used for its potential cognitive-supporting properties. It contains compounds such as hericenones and erinacines that support brain health, making it a popular choice for addressing brain fog. This recipe combines the double extraction method using alcohol and water with the spagyric method to maximize the full benefits of lion's mane.

INGREDIENTS:

- 4 oz dried and ground lion's mane mushroom (*Hericium erinaceus*)
- 2 cups high-proof alcohol
- 2 cups distilled water

NOTES:

Be aware of any potential allergic reactions, especially if you have known mushroom allergies. Discontinue use if you experience adverse effects.

If you are particularly sensitive to the taste, you can dilute the tincture with a small amount of water or juice.

These mushrooms are also delicious in soups, cut finely as an alternative to meat in light spring rolls, or simply cooked in wild garlic butter for delightful simplicity. You can also make teas, or you can find them in supplements.

INSTRUCTIONS:

1. **Alcohol Extraction:** Begin by finely grinding the dried lion's mane mushroom. Place the ground mushroom in a glass jar and cover it with the high-proof alcohol. Seal the jar tightly and store it in a cool, dark place for at least 5-6 weeks, shaking it gently every day. After 5-6 weeks, strain the liquid through a fine mesh strainer or cheesecloth into a clean glass container. This is your alcohol extract.

2. **Water Extraction:** Take the strained mushroom material from the alcohol extraction and place it in a pot. Add 2 cups of distilled water. Simmer the mixture for about 1 hour, ensuring the liquid reduces to half its original volume. Strain the liquid through a fine mesh strainer into a separate container. This is your water extract.

3. **Combine Extracts:** Mix the alcohol extract and water extract together in a glass container (my ratio is usually a 3:1 ratio of alcoholic extract to water extract; you can do 2:1 if you start with a high percentage alcohol, like Everclear).

4. **Spagyric Method:** To extract the full spectrum of minerals and compounds, you can incorporate the spagyric method as well. Burn the leftover mushroom material from the alcohol extraction to ash. Then add the ash to the combined extracts.

5. **Aging and Bottling:** Seal the container and allow it to age for an additional 2-4 weeks if you are using the spagyric method. After aging, strain the tincture one more time to remove any remaining particulates. Transfer the tincture into dark glass bottles, and label them with the date and ingredients. Store the tincture in a cool, dark place to preserve its potency.

DOSAGE:

Start with 1-2 ml (about 20-40 drops) of lion's mane tincture, 1-3 times per day.

Forgotten Home Apothecary

The Mind-Sharpening
Infusion

Yerba mate, scientifically known as *Ilex paraguariensis*, is a South American herb known for its stimulating and cognitive-enhancing properties. It contains caffeine and theobromine, which can help improve mental alertness and focus.

The instructions for preparing yerba mate described below refers to the traditional way, but you may prepare it any way you like. The simplest method is to treat yerba mate like any other loose tea, prepared in a regular cup or glass, prepared with a brewer, or by using French press.

INGREDIENTS:

- 1 tablespoon of dried yerba mate leaves
- 8 ounces (about 240 ml) of hot water around 160-180°F (70-80°C)

NOTES:

The flavor and strength of yerba mate depends on where the yerba is taken from, its drying and toasting process, the time of year, and the proportion of stems versus leaves. Each one has a different taste, so you will need some testing to find your favorite.

You can flavor your yerba mate tea with citrus, honey, or mint for added taste.

Yerba mate contains caffeine, so avoid excessive consumption, especially in the evening, as it may disrupt your sleep.

INSTRUCTIONS:

1 | **Prepare the Gourd:** Put the dried yerba mate into the mate gourd. Adjust the amount based on how strong you want the infusion.

2 | **Shake to Remove Dust:** Cover the mate gourd with your hand, turn it upside down, and shake. This helps remove some of the dust to prevent clogging the bombilla's filter. Skip this step if your yerba mate has no twigs or dust.

3 | **Create a Mound:** Return the mate gourd to its initial position and tilt it to form a "mound" of dried mate on one side while exposing the bottom of the gourd.

4 | **Insert the Bombilla:** Place the bombilla (metal straw with a filter) on the mound with the filter facing down, so it touches the bottom of the mate gourd.

5 | **Position the Gourd:** Carefully bring the mate gourd to an upright position, ensuring that the dried mate doesn't cover the bottom.

6 | **Add Cool Water:** Pour a small amount of cool water over the yerba mate, aiming for the exposed bottom of the mate gourd. Wait for the liquid to soak into the dried leaves.

7 | **Pour Hot Water:** Fill the mate gourd with hot water, around 160-180°F (70-80°C). Avoid using boiling water, as it can make the tea bitter. If the bombilla isn't already in the gourd, insert it, plugging the tip with your thumb to avoid clogging. Yerba mate will brew for about 5 minutes, longer steeping results in a stronger, more bitter infusion. You can pour water over the dried mate multiple times until it loses its flavor.

DOSAGE:

Consume 1-2 cups of yerba mate tea a day for improved mental alertness.

Forgotten Home Apothecary

Ginko Biloba
Focus Fuel

Ginkgo biloba has a long-standing history of use in improving cognitive function. It has been used in Traditional Chinese Medicine since at least the 11th Century to treat dementia and other ailments. The main active ingredients in *Ginkgo biloba* leaf and fruit are terpene lactones, phenolic acids, and flavonoid glycosides.

It's particularly renowned for its ability to increase blood flow to the brain. This increased circulation aids in better oxygen and nutrient delivery, which is vital for maintaining cognitive health. Ginkgo also possesses antioxidant properties, which help protect the brain from oxidative damage, a key factor in age-related cognitive decline.

INGREDIENTS:

- 2 teaspoons of dried ginkgo (*Ginkgo biloba*) leaves
- 1 cup of boiling water

NOTES:

Just because a remedy is natural or plant-based does not necessarily mean it is safe for everybody. There are records of adverse reactions to Ginkgo and even reactions to the pollen.

In addition, certain individuals or groups should avoid this plant.

- Those who are taking blood-thinning medications
- Pregnant and breastfeeding women
- Individuals who are allergic to mangoes, cashews, and poison ivy
- Patients taking SSRIs/MAOIs/antidepressants (*e.g.*, Prozac and Zoloft)
- NSAIDS - analgesics such as Ibuprofen and Tylenol.

INSTRUCTIONS:

1. **Boil the Water:** Boil one cup of water.
2. **Prepare *Ginkgo Biloba* Leaves:** While the water is boiling, place 2 teaspoons of dried ginkgo biloba leaves in a teapot or heatproof container.
3. **Pour Boiling Water:** Once the water has boiled, pour it over the *Ginkgo biloba* leaves.
4. **Steep *Ginkgo Biloba* Tea:** Cover the container and let the tea steep for about 10-15 minutes. This allows the beneficial compounds to infuse into the water.
5. **Strain the Tea:** After steeping, strain the tea to remove the leaves. You can add a touch of honey or lemon for added flavor, if desired.

To enhance the effectiveness of *Ginkgo biloba* for cognitive health, you can also make a tincture by combining ¼ cup of finely chopped dried *Ginkgo biloba* leaves with 1 cup of 80-proof alcohol. This method yields a concentrated form of the herb. Let steep for 4-6 weeks before straining.

DOSAGE:

Consume this tea 1-2 times a day for cognitive support. It's best to drink in the morning for a mental boost.

Anti-Migraine
Syrup

Migraines are debilitating headaches often accompanied by nausea, sensitivity to light, and other symptoms. Herbal remedies can offer relief by targeting inflammation, reducing pain, and calming the nervous system. One effective remedy is a homemade anti-migraine syrup containing feverfew (*Tanacetum parthenium*) and ginger (*Zingiber officinale*), both known for their anti-inflammatory and analgesic properties.

INGREDIENTS:

- 1 cup water
- ¼ cup dried feverfew (*Tanacetum parthenium*) leaves
- 2 tablespoons fresh ginger (*Zingiber officinale*) root, grated
- ½ cup honey

NOTES:

Avoid this syrup if you are allergic to any of its ingredients.

Consult with a healthcare professional before using this syrup, especially if you are pregnant, breastfeeding, or taking any medications.

Discontinue use if any adverse reactions occur and seek medical attention.

INSTRUCTIONS:

1. **Boil the Water:** Boil 1 cup of water in a saucepan.
2. **Infuse Feverfew:** Add ¼ cup of dried feverfew leaves to the boiling water.
3. **Simmer:** Reduce heat and let simmer for 10 minutes to infuse the water with feverfew's medicinal properties.
4. **Strain:** Strain the mixture to remove the feverfew leaves, leaving only the infused liquid.
5. **Add Ginger:** Return the infused liquid to the saucepan and add 2 tablespoons of grated fresh ginger.
6. **Simmer Again:** Simmer for an additional 5 minutes to incorporate the ginger's benefits.
7. **Cool:** Remove from heat and let the mixture cool slightly.
8. **Add Honey:** Once cooled, stir in ½ cup of honey until fully dissolved. Use raw honey for its additional antimicrobial properties. Consider adding a squeeze of lemon juice for flavor.
9. **Store:** Transfer the syrup to a clean, airtight container for storage. Store the syrup in the refrigerator for extended shelf life.

DOSAGE:

Take 1 tablespoon of the syrup at the onset of migraine symptoms. Repeat every 4-6 hours as needed, not exceeding 4 doses in a 24-hour period. Some people use this syrup as a preventative measure for migraines, especially when paired with butterbur.

Herbal Blend
for Headache Relief

INGREDIENTS:

- 1 teaspoon of feverfew (*Tanacetum parthenium*) leaves
- 1 teaspoon of chamomile (*Matricaria chamomilla*) flowers
- 1 teaspoon of peppermint (*Mentha piperita*) leaves
- ½ teaspoon of white willow (*Salix alba*) bark
- 1 cup of water

NOTES:

Allergies to any of the herbs used can occur, so if you experience any adverse reactions, discontinue use.

Pregnant or nursing individuals should consult with a healthcare provider before using this herbal blend.

Since white willow contains salicin, avoid this blend if you are allergic to aspirin or taking blood-thinning medications, as it may potentiate the effects.

This tea blend combines herbs traditionally used for their potential to provide relief from headaches.

- Feverfew is believed to help reduce the frequency and severity of migraines.
- Chamomile is known for its calming and anti-inflammatory properties, which may help alleviate stress-related tension headaches by relaxing muscles.
- Peppermint is valued for its analgesic properties, which can help relax constricted muscles, promote blood flow, and relieve headache discomfort.
- White Willow, containing salicin, is traditionally used as a pain reliever and anti-inflammatory agent, addressing various types of headaches. To prepare white willow, gather freshly grown buds from a willow tree and store them in a jar. Chewing some of these buds is a traditional method to potentially help alleviate headache discomfort. The bark is also commonly used.

INSTRUCTIONS:

1. **Boil the Water:** Bring one cup of water to a rolling boil in a pot.
2. **Add the Herbs:** Once the water is boiling, remove it from heat and add the feverfew leaves, chamomile flowers, peppermint leaves, and white willow bark to the hot water.
3. **Steep:** Cover the pot with a lid and let the herbs steep for about 10-15 minutes.
4. **Strain:** After steeping, strain the tea into a cup, removing the herb materials.
5. **Let it Cool:** Allow the tea to cool slightly but ensure it's still warm enough to drink comfortably.
6. **Sweeten (Optional):** You can sweeten the tea with honey or lemon if desired.
7. **Enjoy:** Relax in a quiet, dimly lit room while sipping this tea to maximize its headache-relief effects.

Keep hydrated and maintain a healthy diet to prevent future headaches.

DOSAGE:

Drink this tea when you experience a headache, up to two times a day.

Forgotten Home Apothecary

Moon Milk
for Better Sleep

Moon milk is a traditional Ayurvedic remedy that includes herbs known for their relaxing properties. Ashwagandha, a key ingredient in moon milk, is an adaptogenic herb known for its ability to reduce stress and anxiety. It helps your body adapt to stressors, making it easier to unwind and prepare for a restful night's sleep. The process of making moon milk is also a calming and meditative ritual. You can customize it with other adaptogens like astragalus (not recommended for those with autoimmune issues). The addition of virgin coconut oil or ghee enhances the absorption of turmeric, as it is fat-soluble.

INGREDIENTS:

- 1 cup of whole milk or unsweetened nut milk
- ½ teaspoon of ground cinnamon (*Cinnamomum verum*)
- ½ teaspoon of ground turmeric (*Curcuma longa*)
- ¼ teaspoon of ground ashwagandha (*Withania somnifera*)
- 2 pinches of ground cardamom (*Elettaria cardamomum*)
- 1 pinch of ground ginger (*Zingiber officinale*)
- 1 pinch of ground nutmeg (*Myristica* spp.)
- A pinch of freshly ground black pepper
- 1 teaspoon of virgin coconut oil or ghee
- 1 teaspoon of raw honey

NOTES:
While ashwagandha is generally safe, consult with a healthcare professional if you are pregnant, nursing, or have specific health concerns.

INSTRUCTIONS:

1 | **Simmer the Milk:** Simmer your choice of milk in a small saucepan over medium-low heat.
2 | **Add the Spices:** Whisk in the turmeric, cinnamon, ashwagandha, ginger, cardamom, nutmeg, and freshly ground black pepper. Whisk vigorously to prevent lumps and clumps.
3 | **Incorporate Healthy Fats:** Add the virgin coconut oil or ghee, reduce the heat to low, and continue to cook for about 5-10 minutes. The longer you simmer, the stronger the infusion will be.
4 | **Cool and Sweeten:** Remove the mixture from the heat and allow it to cool slightly. Then, stir in the raw honey. Do not heat the honey, as it retains its healing properties when used raw.
5 | **Serve and Enjoy:** Pour your Moon Milk into a mug, ensuring it's warm but not too hot, and enjoy it before heading to bed, allowing it to gently guide you into a restful night's sleep.

One of the wonderful aspects of Moon Milk is its adaptability. Moon Milk boasts versatile variations, each with distinct benefits for relaxation and sleep: *Rose Moon Milk*, with rose petals, calms the mind; *Lavender Moon Milk* uses lavender for stress reduction. *Saffron Moon Milk* adds an earthy, mood-enhancing twist. *Blue Moon Milk*'s vivid blue hue comes from butterfly pea flowers, believed to reduce stress. Finally, *Chocolate Moon Milk* combines cocoa with traditional ingredients, providing a comforting and relaxing flavor.

DOSAGE:

Enjoy your Moon Milk about 30 minutes before bedtime.

Forgotten Home Apothecary

Nature's "Aspirin"

Making a homemade willow bark tincture can be a rewarding way to to explore the traditional uses of willow bark, which contains natural salicylates (similar to aspirin) and has been used for centuries to relieve back pain, muscle pain and headaches. Given aspirin's recognized role in heart health, willow bark is also traditionally used in ways that may support similar benefits.

INGREDIENTS:

- Willow bark (*Salix alba*)
- You can gather willow bark from willow trees in your area or purchase dried willow bark from herbal stores or online.
- High-proof alcohol like vodka, brandy, or rum. Aim for at least 80-100 proof (40-50% alcohol content)

NOTES:

Individuals with conditions such as asthma, stomach ulcers, diabetes, gout, hemophilia, hypoprothrombinemia, or kidney or liver disease may be sensitive to aspirin and similarly to willow bark, due to its effects on blood clotting. It's important to be cautious with willow bark as it could increase bleeding during and after surgery. Therefore, it is advisable to stop using willow bark at least two weeks before any scheduled surgery.

INSTRUCTIONS:

1 | **Prepare the Willow Bark:** If you're using fresh willow bark, chop it into small pieces. There is an outer layer of bark, and an inner which has a greenish color to it, this is what holds the most medicine, while the darker wood beneath it all should be discarded. If using dried willow bark, you can use it as is.

2 | **Measure Ingredients:** For every 1 part of dried willow bark, use 5 parts of alcohol. For example, if you have 1 ounce of dried willow bark, use 5 ounces of alcohol.

3 | **Combine Ingredients:** Place the willow bark in the glass jar and pour the alcohol over it. Ensure that the willow bark is completely submerged in the alcohol. Seal the jar with a lid and label.

4 | **Shake and Store:** Give the jar a good shake to mix the ingredients thoroughly. Store it in a cool, dark place like a cupboard or pantry.

5 | **Steeping Time:** Allow the mixture to steep for at least 4-6 weeks, shaking the jar gently every few days. The longer it steeps, the stronger the tincture will be.

6 | **Strain and Bottle:** After the steeping period, strain the liquid through a fine mesh strainer or cheesecloth into a clean glass bottle. Squeeze out as much liquid from the willow bark as possible. It will last several years if stored properly.

DOSAGE:

Start with 1-2 ml (approximately 20-40 drops) of the tincture diluted in a small amount of water or juice, taken orally. You can take this dose up to three times a day.

Deep Sleep
Banana Tea

Bananas may seem like an unusual choice, but they can be a valuable herbal remedy for promoting deep and restful sleep.

Banana is a rich source of potassium, magnesium, and tryptophan. Potassium and magnesium are minerals that are associated with better sleep. These minerals improve the length of your sleep as well as the quality. Moreover, it helps relax the muscles so that your sleep will be calmer. Tryptophan is an amino acid. This amino acid plays an important role in the production of serotonin and melatonin, two hormones that help induce sleep.

INGREDIENTS:

- 1 whole ripe banana or banana peel
- 2 cups of water
- A dash of cinnamon (optional)
- Honey (optional)

NOTES:

Bananas don't seem to have any known negative health effects, but they may cause allergic reactions in some individuals with a latex allergy.

Use washed organic bananas, when possible, as they are free from pesticides and chemicals.

Eating a moderate amount of bananas should not raise blood sugar levels significantly. However, diabetics should be careful with fully ripe bananas.

INSTRUCTIONS:

1 | **Prepare the Banana:** Start by washing the banana thoroughly to remove any surface dirt. Cut off both ends of the banana and discard them, then can cut the whole banana in half or in 1-2-inch slices. If you are controlling your sugar levels and you find the above preparation too sweet, then you can forego using the fruit (use only the peel). If you use only the peels, carefully remove the peel, ensuring that you're left with the inner, white part.

2 | **Boil the Banana:** Place the banana/banana peel in a pot of water. Bring the water to a boil and then reduce the heat to a simmer. Let it simmer for about 10-15 minutes.

3 | **Add Optional Ingredients:** If desired, add a dash of cinnamon to the mixture for extra flavor. You can sweeten the tea with honey if you prefer a sweeter taste.

4 | **Strain and Serve:** Remove the banana/banana peel from the pot. Strain the liquid into a cup or a teapot. Your deep sleep banana tea is ready to drink.

DOSAGE:

Drink this tea approximately 30 minutes before bedtime for the best results.

Soothing
Herbal Soak

Nothing soothes the soul like a good warm bath - especially when the bath contains herbs, nourishing essential oils, and salts. Any herb that you can use in herbal tea to drink can be used for a tub tea.

This blend offers a harmonious fusion of lavender's calming influence, chamomile's stress-relieving properties, and calendula's soothing benefits for your skin, making it an ideal choice for unwinding and self-care. If you want to elevate the experience, you can add dry or fresh rose petals, which will help to tone the skin. Epsom salts help relax muscles and relieve pain in the shoulders, neck, and back. Adding powdered milk softens and soothes the skin while loosening any dead skin cells and baking soda is traditionally used to soothe certain itchy skin conditions.

INGREDIENTS:

- ⅛ cup lavender (*Lavandula* spp.) flowers
- ⅛ cup chamomile (*Matricaria chamomilla*) flowers
- ⅛ cup calendula (*Calendula officinalis*) flowers
- 2 cups Epsom salt
- 1 cup baking soda
- ½ cup powdered milk
- 15-20 drops of your choice of essential oils (*e.g.*, jasmine, sandalwood)
- Reusable muslin tea bags or cheesecloth

NOTES:

Perform a patch test before using the tub tea if you suspect allergies to any ingredients. Discontinue use if skin irritation or allergies occur.

Avoid contact with eyes when using the tub tea. If contact occurs, flush the eyes with clean water. If irritation persists, seek medical attention.

INSTRUCTIONS:

1 | **Prepare the Herbal Blend:** Grind the lavender, chamomile and calendula buds into a fine mixture using a coffee grinder or mortar and pestle.
2 | **Combine the Dry Ingredients:** In a mixing bowl, combine the ground herbal blend, Epsom salt, baking soda, and powdered milk. Mix well.
3 | **Add Essential Oils:** Add 15-20 drops of your chosen essential oils to the mixture. Mix thoroughly to distribute the fragrance evenly.
4 | **Store Your Tub Tea:** Transfer the mixture to an airtight container or small sachets for storage. Store in a cool, dry place away from direct sunlight. They make a great gift as sachets.
5 | **Usage:** Tie the mixture in a tea bag, muslin bag, or cheesecloth to prevent debris in the bath if not already in a sachet. Place it in the tub or drape it over the faucet. Let the water run through it while the tub fills. Allow the herbs to infuse in the bathwater for around 15 to 20 minutes. Be cautious when using the tub tea, as the essential oils and powdered ingredients may make the bathtub surface slippery. To prevent accidents, clean the tub thoroughly after use.

DOSAGE:

Use ½ to 1 cup of the herbal tub tea per bath. Adjust the amount to your preference.

Forgotten Home Apothecary

St. John's Wort and Linden
Calming Infusion

By blending these herbs into a vinegar-based tincture, we create a concentrated, accessible remedy to combat anxiety naturally. St. John's wort is traditionally used to support mood stability and alleviate feelings of restlessness. Its active compounds may influence neurotransmitters related to mood regulation, potentially offering support for feelings of anxiety and nervousness. Linden, or lime blossom, is known for its calming effects. Rich in flavonoids, it is believed to help reduce tension and promote relaxation, making it a valuable ally during times of stress.

INGREDIENTS:

- ½ cup of dried St. John's wort flowers (*Hypericum perforatum*)
- ½ cup of dried linden flowers (*Tilia platyphyllos* or *Tilia cordata*)
- 2 cups of apple cider vinegar

NOTES:

Do not drive or operate heavy machinery after consuming the tincture, as it may cause drowsiness. St. John's wort may interact with certain medications, such as indinavir (used to treat HIV), cyclosporine (used to prevent organ transplant rejection), birth control pills, SSRIs, and more, so it's essential to consult with a healthcare provider beforehand.

If you experience any adverse effects, discontinue use, and seek medical advice.

INSTRUCTIONS:

1 | **Prepare the Herbs:** Start by finely chopping the dried St. John's wort and linden flowers.
2 | **Combine the Ingredients:** Place the chopped herbs in a glass jar.
3 | **Add Vinegar:** Pour the apple cider vinegar over the herbs until they are fully submerged. Ensure that there's about an inch of extra vinegar above the herbs.
4 | **Seal the Jar:** Close the jar tightly with the lid.
5 | **Infusion Period:** Let the mixture sit in a cool, dark place for about 4-6 weeks. Shake the jar gently every day.
6 | **Strain:** After the infusion period, strain the liquid through a fine mesh strainer or cheesecloth into a clean, dark glass bottle. This is your St. John's Wort and Linden vinegar tincture.
7 | **Store:** Store the tincture in a cool, dark place to maintain its potency. Keep a record of how the tincture affects your anxiety symptoms to adjust the dosage if needed.

DOSAGE:

Take 1-2 teaspoons of the tincture directly in the mouth or in a small glass of water up to three times a day.

Nature's Sedative

This herbal liquid sedative is a blend of traditionally used herbs known for their calming properties.

Ashwagandha root, lavender, chamomile, and lemon balm have been used in various cultures for their soothing effects. This recipe provides a simple way to combine these herbs into a potent liquid form that may support relaxation and help ease occasional restlessness.

INGREDIENTS:

- 2 tablespoons of dried Ashwagandha root (*Withania somnifera*)
- 1 tablespoon of dried lavender (*Lavandula angustifolia*)
- 1 tablespoon of chamomile (*Matricaria chamomilla*)
- 1 tablespoon of lemon balm (*Melissa officinalis*)
- 2 cups of water

NOTES:

Consult with a healthcare provider before using this tea if you are pregnant, nursing, taking medications (especially for thyroid issues, blood pressure, or anxiety), or have chronic health conditions. Be aware of potential allergies, particularly to chamomile and lavender. This tea may cause drowsiness, so avoid driving or operating heavy machinery after consumption.

INSTRUCTIONS:

1. **Combine Herbs:** In a medium-sized pan, add the herbs.
2. **Simmer:** Pour 2 cups of water over the herbs. Place the pan on the stove and bring to a gentle simmer. Let the mixture simmer for 20 minutes, ensuring it doesn't boil.
3. **Rest:** Remove the pan from heat and let the mixture rest for 1 hour. Stir occasionally to ensure the herbs are well-infused.
4. **Strain:** After the mixture has rested, strain the liquid using a mesh strainer or cheesecloth into a clean container.
5. **Store:** Transfer the strained liquid into a bottle. Store the Liquid Sedative in the refrigerator. It can be kept for up to 4 weeks.

DOSAGE:

Start with a small dose of 1 teaspoon to assess your body's response. If needed, you may gradually increase the dosage to up to 1 tablespoon.

Stress-Free
Elixir

Lavender and lemon balm are two well-regarded herbs for their calming and soothing properties.

Lavender, known for its calming and soothing properties, is a versatile herb that goes beyond its pleasant fragrance. The gentle sedative effect of lavender makes it an excellent choice for promoting relaxation. Documented benefits include calming the nervous system, alleviating insomnia, and reducing anxiety. Lemon balm is celebrated for its ability to soothe the mind, reduce stress, and lift the spirits. It has been used for generations to combat anxiety, restlessness, and sleep disorders. When combined with lavender, its lemony aroma complements the floral notes of lavender, creating a harmonious and comforting blend. Lemon balm may also be used as a tincture.

INGREDIENTS:

- 1 teaspoon dried lavender (*Lavandula angustifolia*) flowers
- 1 teaspoon dried lemon balm (*Melissa officinalis*) leaves
- 1 cup of hot water
- Honey (optional, for sweetening)

NOTES:

If you have allergies to plants in the Lamiaceae family, be cautious.

If you are taking any medications, especially sedatives, consult with a healthcare provider before regularly consuming lavender and lemon balm, as they can potentially interact with certain medications.

INSTRUCTIONS:

1 | **Boil the Water:** Boil a cup of water and allow it to cool slightly, to around 180°F (82°C).
2 | **Measure the Herbs:** Place one teaspoon of both dried lavender flowers and lemon balm leaves in a teapot or infuser.
3 | **Add Hot Water:** Pour the hot water over the herbs in the teapot.
4 | **Steep:** Cover the teapot and steep for about 5-7 minutes to release the flavors and therapeutic properties. Steeping longer may make the tea too bitter, but feel free to experiment with the steeping time to find your preferred balance of flavors.
5 | **Strain:** Strain the tea into a cup.
6 | **Optional Additions:** If desired, add honey for sweetening. Stir until it dissolves. To enhance the flavor, add a slice of lemon or a few fresh lavender flowers. Adjust honey and additional ingredients to suit your taste.

DOSAGE:

Consume this herbal calming tea as needed for relaxation. One cup in the evening may help promote better sleep.

Stress Relief
Herbal Candle

Indulging in the gentle flicker of a herbal candle can be a profound ritual for relaxation and unwinding. Lavender is an herb known for its calming properties. When used in aromatherapy, it may help reduce stress and support a peaceful state of mind. Its soothing scent is often used to calm racing thoughts and promote restful sleep. Sage has been appreciated for centuries for its ability to clear the mind, enhance focus, and release mental tension. The aroma of sage carries a sense of tranquility, making it an excellent companion for moments of relaxation and contemplation.

INGREDIENTS AND MATERIALS:

- 1 cup of soy wax flakes
- Lavender essential oil
- Sage essential oil
- Dried lavender (*Lavandula* spp.) flowers
- Dried sage (*Salvia officinalis*) leaves
- Wick
- Glass container

NOTES:

Experiment with the lavender and sage essential oil ratios to achieve your preferred scent intensity.

Never leave a burning candle unattended. Place the candle on a heat-resistant surface.

Keep out of reach of children and pets.

Use the candle in a well-ventilated room and enjoy the herbal aroma.

INSTRUCTIONS:

1 | **Prepare Your Work Area:** Set up a clean and safe workspace for making the candle. Ensure all materials are within reach.
2 | **Prepare the Container:** Place the wick in the center of the glass container and secure it using a bit of melted wax.
3 | **Melt the Wax:** Melt the soy wax flakes using a double boiler or microwave. The ideal temperature for melting soy wax is around 170°F (77°C). This process usually takes about 10-15 minutes. Be careful while handling hot wax.
4 | **Add Essential Oils:** For a standard-sized candle, add 10-15 drops of Lavender essential oil and 5-10 drops of Sage essential oil to the melted wax. Stir the oils into the wax thoroughly to ensure an even distribution.
5 | **Add Dried Herbs:** Sprinkle some dried Lavender flowers and Sage leaves into the wax for a delightful visual and aromatic effect.
6 | **Pour Wax into Container:** Carefully pour the scented wax into the prepared glass container, ensuring the wick remains centered.
7 | **Let It Cool:** Allow the candle to cool and solidify. This may take a few hours.
8 | **Trim the Wick:** Trim the wick to about ¼ inch above the wax surface.

DOSAGE:

Light the candle and let it burn for a few hours. You can use the candle during meditation or before bedtime to enhance relaxation.

At-Home Sedative
to Alleviate Panic Attacks

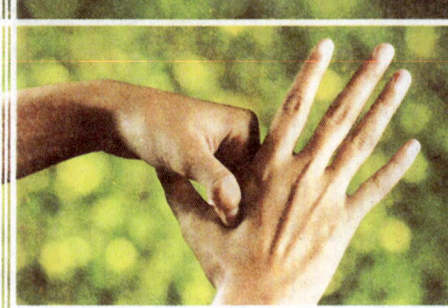

This anxiety-relieving massage oil combines a blend of essential oils known for their calming properties. Utilizing oil massage can effectively reduce anxiety and alleviate stress and tension, particularly when combined with the stimulation of specific acupressure points.

These points include the LI4 point, located between your thumb and pointer finger, and the P6 point, just above your inner wrist. Additional acupressure points that may help alleviate stress are situated between your eyebrows, at your temples, ears, the tops of your feet, and in the area between your neck and shoulder.

INGREDIENTS:

- 10 drops lavender (*Lavandula angustifolia*) essential oil
- 8 drops clary sage (*Salvia sclarea*) essential oil
- 6 drops ylang ylang (*Cananga odorata*) essential oil
- 1 oz (30ml) carrier oil (*e.g.*, sweet almond oil, jojoba oil)

NOTES:

Essential oils are potent; ensure you're not allergic to any of them. Do not use undiluted essential oils directly on your skin.

If you're new to acupressure, it's a good idea to seek guidance from a qualified acupressure practitioner or a healthcare professional. They can help you identify the right points and techniques for your specific needs.

INSTRUCTIONS:

1 | **Preparation:** Ensure a clean and sterile workspace. Use a dark glass bottle to store your massage oil, protecting the oils from UV light and preserving their potency. For easy application, you can also use a roll-on bottle. The rollerball design of the roll-on bottle can be used to apply controlled pressure to acupressure points.

2 | **Blend the Essential Oils:** In the dark glass bottle or roll-on, add the lavender, clary sage, and ylang ylang essential oils. coriander, sweet basil, and bergamot are also excellent anxiety-relieving essential oils.

3 | **Add Carrier Oil:** Pour the carrier oil (*e.g.*, organic sweet almond or jojoba oil) into the bottle with the essential oils.

4 | **Mix Thoroughly:** Seal the bottle and gently roll it between your palms to mix the oils.

5 | **Allow the Blend to Mature:** Store the bottle in a cool, dark place for 24-48 hours. This allows the oils to blend and intensify their aroma.

6 | **Test and Adjust:** Before using the massage oil, do a patch test on a small area of skin to ensure you don't have any allergic reactions. If the scent is too strong, add more carrier oil to dilute it.

DOSAGE:

Apply a small amount of massage oil to your skin and gently massage it in. If you use the roll-on bottle, gently roll the ball over the pressure points in a circular or up-and-down motion. Use as needed for relaxation and anxiety relief.

Restorative Tablets
to Ease Mental Pressure

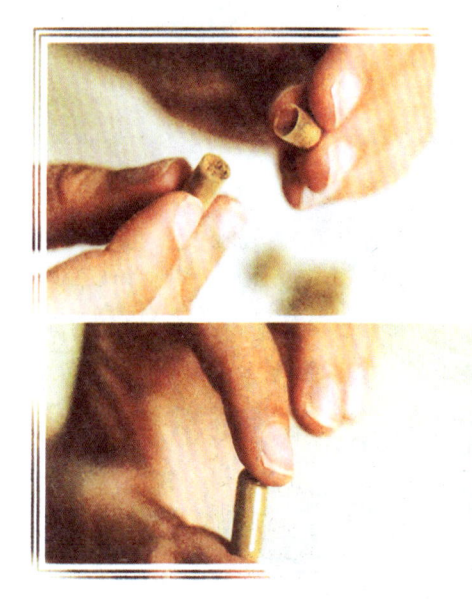

Ashwagandha, often referred to as Indian ginseng, boasts a history steeped in Ayurvedic medicine and is aptly named "somnifera" due to its capacity to promote restful sleep and alleviate stress-related insomnia. This adaptogen is valued for its potential to provide relief from stress and anxiety, making it an useful tool for individuals seeking to regain balance in challenging situations. Additionally, ashwagandha is renowned for its immune-enhancing effects. Rhodiola, also known as golden root, is celebrated for its ability to enhance stress resilience and increase energy levels. Its stimulating properties are traditionally used to help alleviate fatigue and improve mood, making it beneficial for those seeking to combat tiredness and stress-related discomfort. Furthermore, it has shown promise in improving physical performance and cognitive function, making it a versatile addition to the stress management toolkit. When combined, ashwagandha and rhodiola offer a comprehensive approach to stress reduction, striking a balance between relaxation and increased energy, ultimately promoting overall well-being.

INGREDIENTS AND MATERIALS:

- Ashwagandha root powder (*Withania somnifera*)
- Rhodiola root powder (*Rhodiola rosea*)
- Vegetarian capsules (size 00)
- Capsule filling machine (optional, but recommended)

NOTES:

As with any supplement, it's essential to consult a healthcare professional before starting a new regimen, especially if you have any medical conditions.

Note that rhodiola may be too stimulating for individuals with autoimmune disorders.

Rhodiola should be avoided by people with bipolar disorder.

INSTRUCTIONS:

1 | **Prepare the Herbs:** Measure the desired amount of ashwagandha and rhodiola root powders. A common ratio is 2:1, so you can use 2-part ashwagandha to 1-part rhodiola or adjust according to your preference.

2 | **Fill the Capsules:** If you have a capsule-filling machine, follow the manufacturer's instructions to fill the capsules with the herbal powders. This will ensure precise and consistent dosages. If you don't have a filling machine, you can fill the capsules manually. To do this, open a capsule and hold one half in each hand. Use a small spoon to scoop the herbal powders into one half of the capsule. Gently press the other half over it, so the capsules close securely.

3 | **Store:** Store the capsules in a cool, dry place, away from direct sunlight.

DOSAGE:

The specific dosage will depend on the size of the capsules and the ratio of ashwagandha to rhodiola used. A common dosage is 500-1000 mg per day. Since rhodiola is a stimulating herb, it's best when taken in the morning or early afternoon.

Forgotten Home Apothecary

"Sweet Dreams"
Herbal Pillow

This herbal pillow is designed to promote sweet dreams and a restful night's sleep. Mugwort has been used for centuries to enhance dream clarity and encourage peaceful sleep while lavender offers a soothing and relaxing aroma. Essential oils will further enhance the calming effect.

INGREDIENTS AND MATERIALS:

- 1 cup dried mugwort leaves (*Artemisia vulgaris*)
- 1 cup dried lavender flowers (*Lavandula angustifolia*)
- Essential oils of your choice
- Fabric for the pillowcase
- Sewing machine or a needle and thread
- Scissors and pins
- Measuring tape or ruler
- Closure method (buttons, zipper, or Velcro)

NOTES:

To enhance the effectiveness of your herbal pillow, try using it in conjunction with other relaxation techniques such as deep breathing or meditation.

Refresh the pillow by adding a few drops of essential oil to it every few weeks.

INSTRUCTIONS:

1 | **Prepare the Herbs:** Begin by drying the mugwort leaves and lavender flowers if they are not already dried. You can do this by spreading them on a clean, dry surface for a few days.

2 | **Mix the Herbs:** In a mixing bowl, combine the dried mugwort leaves and dried lavender flowers. Gently mix them together.

3 | **Add Essential Oils:** In a separate small bowl, select your preferred essential oils. You can choose from options like ylang ylang, chamomile, cedarwood, vetiver, and clary sage. Add a total of 10-15 drops of your chosen essential oils to the dried herb mixture. Mix well to ensure even distribution.

4 | **Make the Pillowcase:** Measure and cut two identical pieces of fabric. Generally, a 6" x 6" square works well for a small herbal pillow.

5 | **Sew the Pillowcase:** Place the two pieces of fabric right sides together. Pin around three sides, leaving one side open. Using your sewing machine or a needle and thread, sew along the three pinned sides, using a ½-inch seam allowance. Turn the pillowcase right-side out through the open side and gently push out the corners to make them sharp.

6 | **Close the Pillowcase:** Decide on your closure method (buttons, zipper, or Velcro). Sew or attach the chosen closure method to the open side of the pillowcase.

7 | **Fill the Pillowcase:** Using a funnel or a spoon, carefully fill a cloth pouch or pillowcase with the herb and essential oil mixture. Pack it firmly but not too tightly to allow for some movement of the herbs.

DOSAGE:

Place the herbal pillow under your regular pillow or near your head as you sleep. Enjoy the soothing aroma as you drift off to sleep.

Forgotten Home Apothecary

Herbal
Sleeping Pills

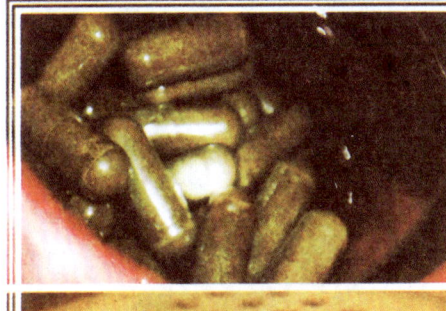

For those nights when sleep seems just out of reach and restlessness takes over, gentle, natural remedies can provide comfort. Inspired by traditional herbal practices, the following recipe combines well-regarded herbs known for their calming properties. This blend of hop flowers (*Humulus lupulus*), valerian root (*Valeriana officinalis*), lemon balm (*Melissa officinalis*), and passionflower (*Passiflora incarnatahas*) has been used historically to support relaxation and help ease the mind into a more peaceful state.

INGREDIENTS AND MATERIALS:

- 1 oz (25 g) of dried hop flowers
- 2 oz (50 g) of dried valerian root
- 1 oz (25 g) of dried lemon balm leaves
- 1 oz (25 g) of dried passionflower
- Empty capsules (size suitable for herbal use)
- Mortar and pestle or coffee grinder

NOTES:

It is advisable not to operate vehicles or heavy machinery after taking these herbal capsules due to the relaxing effects of the herbs used, especially valerian root.

Remember, it's important to consult with a healthcare provider before starting any new herbal regimen, especially if you are pregnant, nursing, or on medication.

INSTRUCTIONS:

1 | **Prepare of Ingredients:** Measure out the herbs as specified: 1 oz each of dried hop flowers, lemon balm, and passionflower, and 2 oz of dried valerian root.
2 | **Grind:** Using a clean mortar and pestle or a coffee grinder, grind each of the herbs separately into a fine powder. This allows for a more uniform texture and helps in evenly mixing the herbs.
3 | **Mix:** Combine the ground hop flowers, valerian root, lemon balm, and passionflower in a bowl. Mix thoroughly to ensure an even distribution of each herb.
4 | **Filling Capsules:** Carefully fill the empty capsules with the mixed herbal powder. Depending on the size of the capsules, the amount of powder needed per capsule will vary.
5 | **Storage:** Place the filled capsules in a sterilized jar. Store the jar in a cool, dark place to help preserve the potency and effectiveness of the herbs. Properly stored, these capsules can remain effective for up to one to two years.

DOSAGE:

Take 1-2 capsules approximately 30 minutes to an hour before bedtime.

Bath Salt Mix
for Relaxation

Enjoy the therapeutic benefits of these bath salts—a blend crafted for relaxation and skin nourishment.

Chamomile, known for its calming properties, combines with the exotic fragrance of neroli essential oil to offer a soothing bath experience. Neroli essential oil, extracted from bitter orange blossoms, contributes a fragrant element recognized for its calming effects. Enhanced by the mineral-rich composition of Epsom and Himalayan salts, this bath salt mix aims to provide practical benefits for both your muscles and overall well-being.

INGREDIENTS:

- ½ cup of Epsom salt
- ½ cup of Himalayan salt
- ¼ cup of dried chamomile flowers (*Matricaria chamomilla* or *Chamaemelum nobile*)
- 10-15 drops of neroli essential oil (*Citrus aurantium*)

NOTES:

Individuals with sensitive skin should exercise caution. If irritation occurs, discontinue use. Be aware of potential allergies to essential oils, especially Neroli. If you have a history of allergic reactions to citrus oils, a patch test is advisable.

Consult a healthcare professional if you are pregnant or have any medical conditions before using this product.

INSTRUCTIONS:

1. **Combine the Salts and Chamomile:** In a mixing bowl, combine the Epsom salt, Himalayan salt, and dried chamomile flowers. Epsom salt, rich in magnesium, helps relax muscles, while Himalayan salt adds minerals to your bath. The soothing chamomile flowers will infuse the bathwater with their calming essence.
2. **Add the Neroli Fragrance:** Carefully add the neroli essential oil to the mixture. Neroli oil, derived from bitter orange blossoms, has a sweet and comforting aroma. Stir the blend thoroughly to evenly distribute this delightful fragrance throughout the salts.
3. **Store for Later Use:** Transfer the blend to an airtight container. It's essential to ensure the container is tightly sealed to preserve the aroma and properties of the salts and herbs. Store the container in a cool, dry place, away from direct sunlight.

Create a spa-like atmosphere by dimming the lights and playing calming music during your bath.

DOSAGE:

Add ¼ to ½ cup of these bath salts to your warm bathwater. Soak for at least 20 minutes to experience their full benefits.

Kava Extract
to Unwind and Get Relief

Kava is a traditional Polynesian beverage with numerous health benefits. The active compounds found in kava, known as kavalactones, play a pivotal role in delivering the array of beneficial effects associated with this traditional beverage. These kavalactones are the essence of what makes kava a cherished and valued drink in many cultures. Kava is said to elevate mood, well-being, and contentment, and produce a feeling of relaxation. It is often used to support the management of anxiety, insomnia, and related nervous discomfort.

INGREDIENTS AND MATERIALS:

- Kava root powder (*Piper methysticum*)
- Warm water
- A fine mesh strainer or cloth bag

NOTES:

Pregnant or nursing women should avoid kava.

Do not mix kava with alcohol or other sedatives.

If you have liver issues, consult a healthcare professional before using kava.

When purchasing kava, it is important to check the number of kavalactones in the product. It may be listed either in milligrams or as a percentage.

It is considered safe to consume less than 250 mg daily for several months, but long-term use is not recommended.

INSTRUCTIONS:

1 | **Measure Ingredients:** For a single serving, measure out 2-4 tablespoons of kava root powder. Adjust the quantity to suit your taste.
2 | **Prepare the Kava:** Add the kava root powder to a strainer cloth and place it into a bowl.
3 | **Add Hot Water:** Pour warm water, approximately 1 cup for each tablespoon of kava, into the cloth. Using warm water in this traditional preparation improves the emulsification of kavalactones from the root particles into the liquid. Let the kava steep in the bag in the bowl for 5-10 minutes.
4 | **Knead the Kava:** Twist the top of your kava strainer closed and press out all of the air. Alternate between kneading the kava and squeezing the bag to strain the liquid into the bowl. The water in the bowl will turn a nice milky brown color and begin to look like chocolate milk.
5 | **Strain the Mixture:** After 5-10 minutes of kneading, wring the bag tight, straining all the liquid into your cup.
6 | **Enjoy:** Wait until it cools down and enjoy. You may notice a mild numbing sensation on your tongue.

DOSAGE:

Drink one ½ cup of kava on an empty stomach. Take at least 15-minute-long breaks between servings as it may take a while for the kavalactones to start acting and for you to feel the effects.

Forgotten Home Apothecary

The Legal Narcotic
You Can Make at Home

Mugwort is sometimes colloquially referred to as a "legal narcotic" due to its psychoactive properties. Mugwort contains compounds such as thujone, cineole, and camphor, which contribute to its medicinal properties. It is known for its calming and relaxing effects, making it a popular choice for herbal preparations aimed at promoting sleep and relaxation. Additionally, mugwort is believed to enhance dream vividness and recall, leading to its use in traditional practices like lucid dreaming and divination.

INGREDIENTS:

- 1 tablespoon dried mugwort leaves (*Artemisia vulgaris*)
- 1 cup water
- Honey or another sweetener (optional, to taste)

NOTES:

Mugwort should be avoided by pregnant women as it may stimulate the uterus and potentially lead to miscarriage.

Individuals with allergies to plants in the Asteraceae family (such as ragweed, marigolds, and daisies) may also be allergic to mugwort and should avoid its use.

Excessive consumption of mugwort may cause adverse effects due to its thujone content. It's essential to adhere to recommended dosages.

INSTRUCTIONS:

1 | **Preparation:** Boil 1 cup of water in a small saucepan.
2 | **Add Mugwort:** Once the water reaches a boil, reduce the heat to low and add 1 tablespoon of dried mugwort leaves to the water.
3 | **Simmer:** Allow the mugwort to simmer in the water for about 5-10 minutes. This will help extract the beneficial compounds from the herb. For a stronger infusion, steep the mugwort leaves for a longer duration or increase the amount of mugwort used.
4 | **Strain:** After simmering, remove the saucepan from the heat and strain the mugwort infusion using a fine mesh strainer or cheesecloth to remove the leaves.
5 | **Sweeten (Optional):** If desired, add honey or another sweetener to taste while the infusion is still warm.
6 | **Serve:** Pour the mugwort infusion into a mug and enjoy it warm.

Mugwort may also be prepared as a tincture by soaking the dried herb in alcohol (such as vodka or grain alcohol) for 4-6 weeks to extract its medicinal properties. In Traditional Chinese medicine (TCM), mugwort is often used in moxibustion therapy, where dried mugwort leaves are burned near acupuncture points to stimulate circulation and promote healing. Moxibustion is believed to have various therapeutic effects, including pain relief and immune system support.

DOSAGE:

1 cup per day, preferably in the evening before bedtime. It's advisable to start with a small amount and gradually increase the dosage as needed. Avoid excessive consumption.

Happiness Hormone
Booster

Catnip (*Nepeta cataria*), also known as catmint, is a herbaceous plant belonging to the mint family. While commonly associated with its effects on cats, catnip also possesses medicinal properties for humans. It contains compounds that can induce relaxation, reduce anxiety, and promote feelings of well-being. When combined with other herbs, catnip can act as a natural booster for oxytocin, often referred to as the "love hormone." Oxytocin is associated with bonding, trust, and social interactions.

INGREDIENTS:

- 2 teaspoons dried catnip (*Nepeta cataria*)
- 1 teaspoon dried passionflower (*Passiflora incarnata*)
- 1 teaspoon dried chamomile (*Matricaria chamomilla*)
- 2 cups water

NOTES:

While catnip and passionflower are generally safe for consumption, they may cause drowsiness. Exercise caution, especially if operating heavy machinery or driving after consuming this tea. Pregnant or breastfeeding women should consult with a healthcare professional before using this herbal remedy. If you have any known allergies to plants in the mint family, avoid using catnip.

INSTRUCTIONS:

1 | **Preparation:** Gather all the dried herbs: catnip, passionflower, and chamomile. Ensure they are of good quality for optimal results.
2 | **Boil the Water:** Bring 2 cups of water to a gentle boil in a saucepan.
3 | **Add the Herbs:** Once the water reaches a boil, add 2 teaspoons of dried catnip, 1 teaspoon of dried passionflower, and 1 teaspoon of dried chamomile to the saucepan.
4 | **Steep:** Reduce the heat to low and let the herbs simmer for about 10 minutes, allowing their medicinal compounds to infuse into the water.
5 | **Strain:** After simmering, remove the saucepan from the heat and strain the herbal mixture to separate the liquid from the solids. You can use a fine mesh strainer or cheesecloth for this step.
6 | **Cool:** Allow the herbal infusion to cool to a comfortable drinking temperature. Enjoy the tea in a calm and relaxing environment to enhance its soothing effects. For added flavor, you can sweeten the tea with honey or a natural sweetener of your choice.
7 | **Store:** Any leftover herbal infusion in a sealed container in the refrigerator for up to 2 days for freshness.

DOSAGE:

Consume 1 cup of this herbal tea per day, preferably in the evening.

Worry-Relieving
Tincture

This herbal tincture blends skullcap, holy basil, and blue vervain. These herbs are traditionally used for their calming effects. Skullcap is often employed to support the nervous system and may assist in easing feelings of anxiety, contributing to relaxation. Holy basil is recognized as an adaptogen that is traditionally used to help the body adapt to stress and to promote a sense of calm and balance. Blue vervain is commonly used to help alleviate stress and to support restful sleep through its mild calming effects. This blend is intended to offer support for managing anxiety and fostering improved sleep quality, utilizing historical herbal practices.

INGREDIENTS AND MATERIALS:

- 1 part dried skullcap (*Scutellaria lateriflora*)
- 1 part dried holy basil (*Ocimum sanctum*)
- 1 part dried blue vervain (*Verbena hastata*)
- 80-proof alcohol
- Glass jar with a tight-fitting lid
- Cheesecloth or fine mesh strainer

NOTES:

Skullcap can cause drowsiness, so avoid driving or operating heavy machinery after taking this tincture. Holy Basil may lower blood sugar levels; consult with a healthcare professional before use if you have diabetes or are on medication for blood sugar control. Pregnant and breastfeeding women should avoid this tincture unless approved by a healthcare provider.

INSTRUCTIONS:

1 | **Prepare the Herbs:** Measure equal parts of dried skullcap, dried holy basil, and dried blue vervain. Crush the herbs slightly to increase their surface area for extraction. Combine these herbs in the glass jar, filling it about halfway.

2 | **Combine the Herbs and Alcohol:** Place the crushed Pour vodka, brandy, or vegetable glycerin over the herbs in the jar until the herbs are completely submerged and there is some extra liquid on top (typically about 1-2 inches above the herbs).

3 | **Seal and Infuse:** Seal the jar with a tight-fitting lid. Store the jar in a cool, dark place for at least 4 to 6 weeks. Shake the jar gently every day to agitate the contents.

4 | **Strain:** After the infusion period, strain the tincture through a cheesecloth or fine mesh strainer into a clean glass container. Squeeze out as much liquid as possible from the herbs. If you find the taste too strong, you can dilute the tincture in water or juice when taking it.

5 | **Label and Store:** Label the bottle with the herb's name, date, and other relevant information. Store your tinctures in a cool, dark place.

DOSAGE:

For anxiety relief, take 1-2 droppers (about 30-60 drops) of the tincture diluted in a small amount of water or juice, 2-3 times a day as needed. For sleep support, take 1-2 droppers of the tincture diluted in a small amount of water or juice, about 30 minutes before bedtime.

Lemon Balm and Skullcap
Relaxing Tisane

Lemon balm and American/blue skullcap are two wonderful herbs known for their calming and relaxing properties.

Lemon balm exerts its calming effects through GABA modulation, antioxidants, and improved sleep, making it effective for anxiety and stress. American skullcap, on the other hand, acts as a nervine tonic, regulates GABA receptors, relaxes muscle tension, and has mild sedative qualities, collectively reducing anxiety and promoting relaxation. Together, they create a delightful tisane, providing a natural and soothing way to unwind and relieve stress.

INGREDIENTS:

- 2 teaspoons of dried lemon balm leaves (*Melissa officinalis*)
- 1 teaspoon of dried American/blue skullcap leaves (*Scutellaria lateriflora*)
- 1 cup of hot water
- Honey (optional, for sweetness)

NOTES:

If you are taking medications for anxiety, depression, or sleep disorders, consult a healthcare professional before using this tisane to avoid any adverse interactions.

Due to the relaxing properties of lemon balm and American skullcap, exercise caution if you are sensitive to sedatives or other substances that induce drowsiness.

INSTRUCTIONS:

1 | **Gather Your Herbs:** Begin by gathering dried lemon balm leaves and American skullcap leaves.
2 | **Boil Water:** Boil 1 cup of water to a near boil, then let it cool for a minute or two. It's important not to use boiling water as it can damage the delicate compounds in these herbs.
3 | **Combine Herbs:** Place the lemon balm and American skullcap leaves in a teapot or a heatproof container.
4 | **Pour Hot Water:** Pour the hot (but not boiling) water over the herbs.
5 | **Steep:** Cover the container and let the herbs steep for about 5-7 minutes. This will allow the herbs to release their soothing properties.
6 | **Strain:** After steeping, strain the tisane to remove the herb leaves.
7 | **Sweeten (Optional):** If you prefer your tisane a bit sweeter, you can add honey to taste.

DOSAGE:

Sip this tisane in the evening to promote relaxation. 1 cup is a standard serving, but you can adjust according to your preference. It's advisable not to use American skullcap continuously for more than a few weeks without a break.

Peaceful Mind
Drops

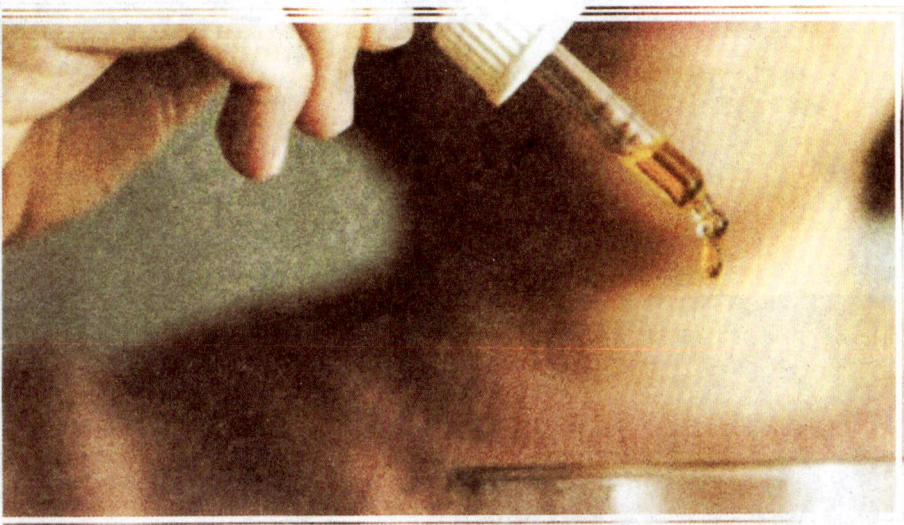

"Peaceful Mind Drops" is a calming herbal glycerite designed to help reduce stress and promote relaxation, using a glycerin base instead of alcohol. This makes it suitable for those who are sensitive to alcohol. This blend uses herbs and flowers known for their soothing properties, providing a natural way to support mental wellness.

INGREDIENTS AND MATERIALS:

- ½ cup dried skullcap (*Scutellaria lateriflora*)
- ½ cup dried lemon balm (*Melissa officinalis*)
- ¼ cup dried chamomile flowers (*Matricaria chamomilla*)
- ¼ cup dried rose petals (*Rosa* spp.)
- 2 cups vegetable glycerin
- ½ cup distilled water
- A glass jar with a tight-fitting lid
- A piece of cheesecloth or a fine mesh strainer
- A dark glass dropper bottle

NOTES:

Consult a healthcare professional before using this glycerite, especially if pregnant, nursing, or having chronic conditions. Test a small amount first and discontinue if allergic reactions occur. If taking sedatives, antidepressants, or anti-anxiety drugs, consult your provider. Skullcap has rare associations with liver damage; consult your provider if you have liver conditions or take liver-affecting medications.

INSTRUCTIONS:

1 | **Combine the Herbs:** In a clean, dry glass jar, combine the dried skullcap, lemon balm, chamomile flowers, and rose petals. Ensure the jar is large enough to accommodate the herbs and liquid with about an inch of space at the top.

2 | **Prepare the Glycerin Solution:** Mix 2 cups of vegetable glycerin with ½ cup of distilled water to create a glycerin solution.

3 | **Add Glycerin Solution to Herbs:** Pour the glycerin solution over the herbs, making sure they are completely submerged. Use a clean utensil to press the herbs down if necessary.

4 | **Seal and Store:** Seal the jar tightly with its lid. Store the jar in a cool, dark place for 4-6 weeks. Shake the jar gently every few days to mix the contents and enhance the infusion process.

5 | **Strain the Mixture:** After 4-6 weeks, strain the mixture through cheesecloth or a fine mesh strainer into a clean bowl, squeezing the herbs to extract as much liquid as possible. Discard the used herbs.

6 | **Transfer to Dropper Bottle:** Using a small funnel, carefully transfer the strained liquid into a dark glass dropper bottle for storage. Label the bottle with the name "Peaceful Mind Drops" and the date of preparation. Make sure the dropper bottle is properly sealed to prevent evaporation and contamination.

7 | **Storage and Shelf Life:** Store the glycerite in a dark, cool place to maintain its potency and extend its shelf life. Properly sealed and stored glycerite should last up to two years. Ensure the dropper bottle is tightly sealed to prevent contamination and evaporation

DOSAGE:

Take 1-2 droppers full (approximately 20-40 drops) up to three times a day, as needed. You can take it directly under the tongue for quick absorption or mix it with a small amount of water or your favorite tea.

Forgotten Home Apothecary

HERBAL SUPPORT
for the Auditory and Visual System

Your auditory and visual systems are essential for overall well-being and the way we experience the world. As we age, it's a natural process for our eyes and hearing to begin to degrade. Therefore, it becomes even more critical to take extra care of these sensory systems.

Tips to Maintain Healthy Auditory and Visual Systems:

PROTECT YOUR EARS:

Avoid exposure to loud noises or wear ear protection, such as earplugs or noise-canceling headphones, when in noisy environments to prevent hearing damage.

PROTECTIVE EYEWEAR:

Use protective eyewear, such as sunglasses with UV protection, to shield your eyes from harmful UV rays and reduce the risk of cataracts and other eye conditions.

AVOID COTTON SWAB USAGE:

Refrain from inserting cotton swabs or other objects into your ears, as this can damage the delicate structures of the ear canal.

LIMIT EARBUD/HEADPHONE USAGE:

Avoid prolonged use of headphones or earbuds at high volumes, as this can contribute to hearing loss over time.

REGULAR EYE EXAMS:

Schedule regular eye exams to monitor your visual health and address any issues promptly.

PROPER LIGHTING:

Ensure adequate lighting when reading or working to reduce eye strain.

BALANCED DIET:

Consume a diet rich in nutrients like omega-3 fatty acids, vitamin D, magnesium, and antioxidants to support the overall health of the auditory system. Consume foods rich in vitamins A, C, E, zinc, and omega-3 fatty acids to support eye health and reduce the risk of age-related macular degeneration (AMD) and other eye conditions.

HERBAL SUPPORT

Ginko *(Gingko biloba)*
This herb may support blood circulation to the eyes and ears, potentially benefiting vision and hearing health. Use as a supplement or tincture.

Bilberry *(Vaccinium myrtillus)*
Bilberry contains antioxidants that may support visual health, especially night vision. Use as a supplement or tincture.

Eyebright *(Euphrasia)*
Traditionally used to support eye health, eyebright can be used as an herbal eyewash or in supplement form.

Ginger *(Zingiber officinale)*
Ginger's anti-inflammatory properties might benefit both auditory and visual health. It can be consumed as part of your diet or as a supplement.

Turmeric *(Curcuma longa)*
Curcumin, found in turmeric, has antioxidant and anti-inflammatory properties that may be beneficial for both the eyes and ears. Consider incorporating turmeric into your diet or using curcumin supplements or tinctures.

Ear Oil
to Soothe Irritation, Inflammation, and Infection

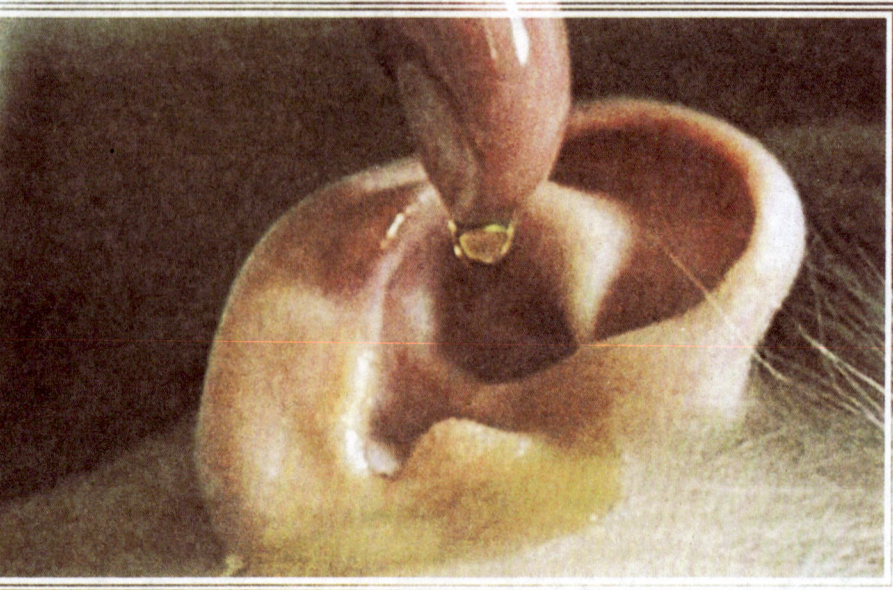

Mullein and garlic are two powerful herbal allies known for their medicinal properties.

When combined, mullein and garlic oil may help reduce swelling and congestion within the lymph system, allowing fluid to flow and releasing any build-up in the ears. The olive oil can help soften earwax, making it easier to remove, while garlic is known for its natural cleansing properties. This combination can be used to support ear health. I used this for my children whenever they had an ear infection; adding yarrow flowers and/or leaves for additional support.

INGREDIENTS:

- ¼ cup dried mullein flowers (*Verbascum thapsus*)
- 2 cloves of fresh garlic (*Allium sativum*)
- ½ cup olive oil (preferably extra virgin)

NOTES:

Ensure the dropper you use is clean and sterile.

Do not use this oil if you have a perforated eardrum or if there's any discharge from the ear.

Consult a healthcare professional if symptoms persist or worsen.

Always perform a patch test to check for allergies.

INSTRUCTIONS:

1. **Prepare the Ingredients:** Begin by gathering all ingredients, then finely chop the two fresh garlic cloves.
2. **Infuse the Oil:** In a small saucepan, combine the chopped garlic, dried Mullein flowers, and the ½ cup of olive oil.
3. **Gentle Heating:** Heat the mixture over low heat, allowing it to infuse for approximately 1-2 hours. Remember to stir occasionally to prevent burning.
4. **Cooling:** After the oil has absorbed the beneficial properties of mullein and garlic, remove it from heat and let it cool.
5. **Strain the Oil:** Strain the oil through a fine mesh strainer or cheesecloth into a clean, sterile glass container. Squeeze the herbs to extract all the infused oil.
6. **Storage:** Store the mullein and garlic ear oil in a dark, cool place. Ensure it's labeled with the date of preparation for reference.

DOSAGE:

To use the oil, warm a few drops to room temperature. Using a clean dropper, place 2-3 drops in the affected ear 2-3 times per day. Gently massage the earlobe to help distribute the oil.

Custom Spray
to Relieve Ear Aches and Infections

Calendula officinalis, commonly known as pot marigold or calendula, is a herb traditionally valued for its many beneficial properties. Its anti-inflammatory, antimicrobial, and soothing effects make it an excellent choice for maintaining ear health. This calendula ear spray can help nourish your ears and provide relief from discomfort.

INGREDIENTS:

- 1 tablespoon dried Calendula flowers (*Calendula officinalis*)
- ¼ cup olive oil
- 1 cup distilled water
- 1 tablespoon witch hazel (optional, for added astringent properties)

NOTES:

While this recipe uses dried Calendula petals, you may also use fresh flowers. However, dried flowers are preferred for infusions as they have lower moisture content and are less likely to introduce water into the oil, which can lead to spoilage.

If ear pain or discomfort persists, consult a healthcare professional.

Before using the spray, perform a sensitivity test by applying a small amount to the inside of your wrist.

INSTRUCTIONS:

1 | **Herbal Infusion:** Place the dried calendula flower petals in a clean, dry glass jar. Pour the olive oil over the calendula flowers, ensuring they are fully submerged. Seal the jar tightly and shake it gently to distribute the flowers evenly.

2 | **Solar Infusion:** Place the jar in a sunny windowsill for 3 to 4 weeks, allowing the sun's warmth to infuse the oil with the medicinal properties of calendula. The longer you let the calendula infuse in the oil, the more potent the ear drops will be. If you prefer a milder infusion, aim for 2 weeks, but for a stronger product, go for a full 4 weeks. Shake the jar gently daily.

3 | **Straining:** After the infusion period, strain the oil through a fine-mesh strainer or cheesecloth into a clean glass container. Squeeze the petals to extract all the infused oil.

4 | **Mixing:** In a spray bottle, combine 1 tablespoon of the infused calendula oil with 1 cup of distilled water. Add 1 tablespoon of witch hazel if using. Shake well to combine all ingredients.

5 | **Storage:** Store the calendula spray in a cool, dark place to preserve its potency.

6 | **Usage:** Shake the bottle well before each use. Spray the calendula ear spray into the ear canal as needed. Warm the spray slightly by placing the bottle in a bowl of warm water before use for added comfort. Avoid using the spray if it is too cold, as cold drops can cause dizziness.

DOSAGE:

Spray into the affected ear as needed, up to three times a day.

Forgotten Home Apothecary

Glycerite
to Calm Ear Ringing and Tinnitus

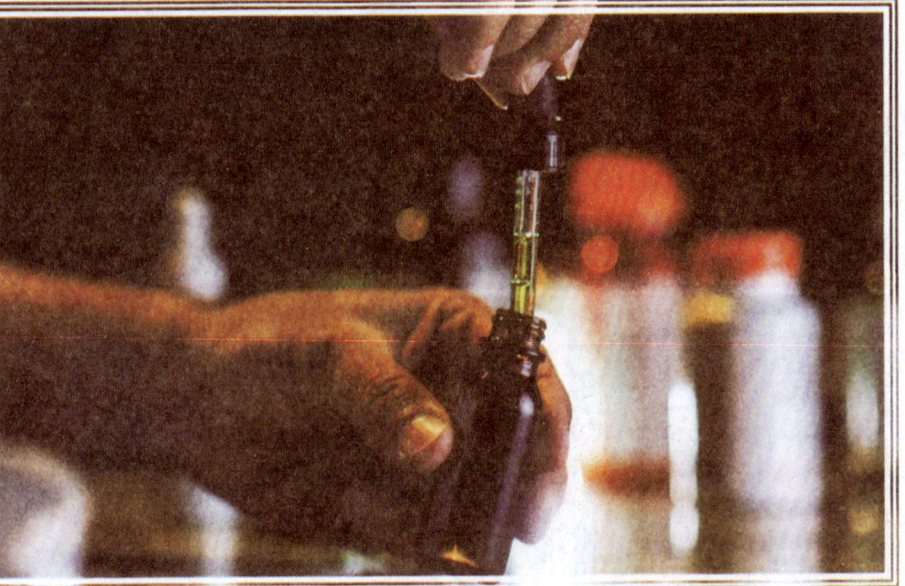

Tinnitus, the persistent perception of ringing or buzzing in the ears, poses a significant challenge for those who experience it. While chronic or long-term tinnitus may signal an underlying medical issue, herbal remedies like the ginger and mullein glycerite offer potential relief. Ginger (*Zingiber officinale*) is known for its anti-inflammatory properties, which can help reduce ear inflammation. It also improves circulation, potentially addressing problems related to poor blood flow in the ear. Mullein (*Verbascum thapsus*) is traditionally recognized for its soothing effects, making it useful for addressing ear discomfort. In addition to its primary use for respiratory support, Mullein's gentle nature contributes to overall ear health. Note that vasodiliators such as cordyceps, reishi, and lion's mane mushroom tinctures are also helpful for tinnitus.

INGREDIENTS:

- 2 tablespoons of dried mullein leaves (*Verbascum thapsus*)
- 1-inch piece of fresh ginger root (*Zingiber officinale*), grated
- Vegetable glycerin
- 1-ounce dark glass bottle with a dropper

NOTES:

Tinnitus, especially when chronic or persistent, warrants thorough medical evaluation, as it could be indicative of an underlying health issue.

It is crucial not to rely solely on herbal remedies.

A comprehensive assessment by a healthcare professional is essential for appropriate diagnosis and management.

INSTRUCTIONS:

1 | **Prepare the Mullein Infusion:** Place 2 tablespoons of dried mullein leaves in a clean glass jar. Pour enough vegetable glycerin over the mullein to completely cover it. Seal the jar and shake it gently to ensure the glycerin covers the mullein.
2 | **Prepare the Ginger Extract:** Grate a 1-inch piece of fresh ginger root.
3 | **Squeeze the Grated Ginger to Extract Its Juice:** You should have about 1 teaspoon of ginger juice.
4 | **Combine the Ingredients:** After 4-6 weeks of steeping, strain the Mullein-infused glycerin into a clean bowl. Add 1 teaspoon of fresh ginger juice to the mullein glycerite. Mix well.
5 | **Bottle the Glycerite:** Using a funnel, pour the glycerite into a 1-ounce dark glass bottle with a dropper.
6 | **Store:** Store the glycerite in a cool, dark place to maintain its potency. Shake the bottle before each use to ensure the ingredients are well mixed.

DOSAGE:

Take 1-2 droppers (approximately 20-40 drops) of the glycerite up to three times a day as needed. If you prefer to enhance the flavor of the glycerite, you can mix it with lemon juice.

Forgotten Home Apothecary

Herbal Oil
for Vertigo

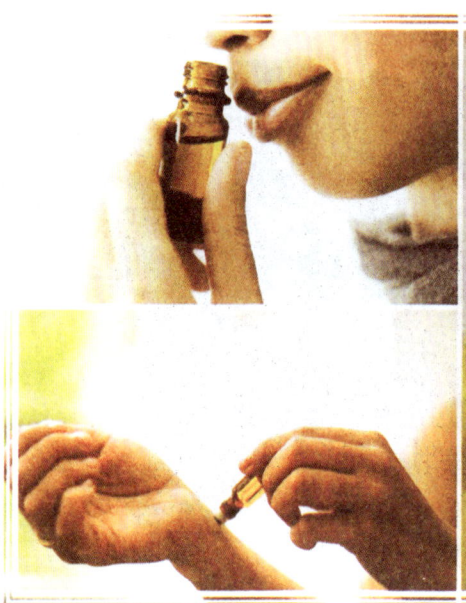

While vertigo can be life-altering, this remedy may help you regain control of your life. Ginger (*Zingiber officinale*), lemon balm (*Melissa officinalis*), and peppermint (*Mentha piperita*) oils are renowned for their therapeutic benefits. In this blend, you can harness their unique properties to ease vertigo symptoms. Ginger oil aids in reducing dizziness, while lemon balm and peppermint oils provide a calming effect on the nervous system. Note that gotu kola is an excellent internal herb to try for vertigo.

INGREDIENTS:

- 5 drops of ginger (*Zingiber officinale*) essential oil
- 5 drops of lemon balm (*Melissa officinalis*) essential oil
- 5 drops of peppermint (*Mentha piperita*) essential oil
- 1 tablespoon of carrier oil (*e.g.*, sweet almond oil)

NOTES:

Always perform a patch test before using essential oils on your skin to ensure you don't have any allergies or sensitivities.

Do not ingest the essential oils.

If irritation occurs, discontinue use immediately.

Practice deep breathing exercises alongside the application of the oil blend for better results.

INSTRUCTIONS:

1. **Choose a Container:** Begin by selecting a clean, empty glass bottle or rollerball container for your oil blend.
2. **Add Ginger Essential Oil:** Add 5 drops of ginger (*Zingiber officinale*) essential oil to the bottle. Ginger oil is effective in reducing feelings of dizziness and nausea associated with vertigo.
3. **Add Lemon Balm Essential Oil:** Follow by adding 5 drops of lemon balm (*Melissa officinalis*) essential oil. Lemon balm oil has calming properties that can help alleviate stress and anxiety linked to vertigo.
4. **Add Peppermint Essential Oil:** Lastly, add 5 drops of peppermint (*Mentha piperita*) essential oil to the blend. Peppermint oil is known for its ability to relieve nausea and dizziness, making it a valuable addition.
5. **Mix in Carrier Oil:** Pour 1 tablespoon of a carrier oil (such as sweet almond oil) into the bottle. The carrier oil serves to dilute the essential oils, ensuring safe topical application.
6. **Shake to Combine:** Seal the bottle and shake it gently to thoroughly mix the oils.
7. **Apply the Oil Blend:** Apply a small amount of the blend to your wrists, temples, and behind your ears. You can also massage it on your neck and shoulders.
8. **Inhale and Relax:** Inhale the soothing aroma and take deep breaths. This can help alleviate dizziness and promote relaxation.

DOSAGE:

Apply the oil blend as needed but avoid excessive use. A couple of times a day is usually sufficient.

Parsley Patches
for Tinnitus

Parsley is a common herb known for its culinary uses, but it also has traditional applications in herbal remedies. This recipe utilizes parsley's potential anti-inflammatory and circulatory benefits to help alleviate the symptoms of tinnitus, a condition characterized by ringing or buzzing in the ears.

INGREDIENTS:

- Fresh parsley leaves
- Cheesecloth or a clean, thin cloth
- Medical tape or adhesive bandages

NOTES:

Before using the parsley patch, test a small amount of crushed parsley on your skin to ensure you do not have an allergic reaction. If you experience redness, itching, or irritation, discontinue use

Consult with a healthcare professional before using this remedy, especially if you are pregnant, nursing, or have any chronic health conditions. If your tinnitus persists or worsens, seek advice from a healthcare provider, as it may indicate an underlying condition that requires medical attention.

INSTRUCTIONS:

1 | **Prepare the Parsley:** Wash a handful of fresh parsley leaves thoroughly to remove any dirt or contaminants. Pat them dry with a clean towel. Use fresh parsley leaves for the best results, as they contain the highest levels of beneficial compounds.

2 | **Crush the Parsley:** Using a mortar and pestle or a clean utensil, gently crush the parsley leaves to release their juices.

3 | **Make the Parsley Patch:** Place the crushed parsley leaves onto a piece of cheesecloth or a clean, thin cloth. Fold the cloth to create a small, secure patch that can be easily placed over the ear. You can prepare multiple patches in advance and store them in an airtight container in the refrigerator for up to 24 hours.

4 | **Apply the Patch:** Place the parsley patch over the ear, ensuring it covers the area where you experience tinnitus. Secure the patch in place with medical tape or an adhesive bandage.

5 | **Leave in Place:** Leave the parsley patch in place for at least 30 minutes to an hour. Combine this remedy with other relaxation techniques, such as deep breathing or meditation, to enhance its calming effects.

DOSAGE:

Apply the parsley patch once or twice a day as needed. You can use it whenever you experience discomfort related to tinnitus.

Anti-Inflammatory
Ear Compress

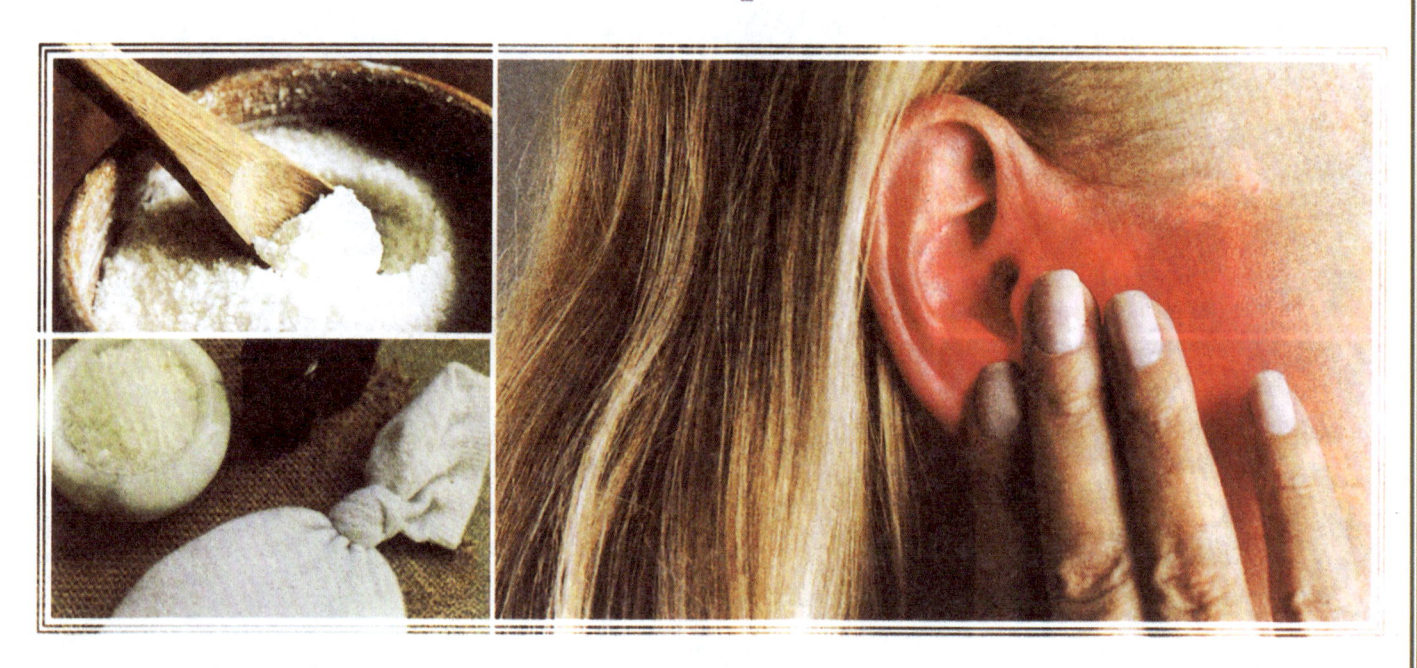

Beyond its role as a kitchen staple for flavoring food, salt has been utilized for centuries for its beneficial properties. In the context of earaches, a warm salt compress serves as a simple and traditional remedy. This technique uses the principles of osmosis to draw excess fluid out of the ear canal, potentially offering relief from ear discomfort. When the warm salt pouch is applied to the ear, it helps balance the solute concentration on both sides of the eardrum.

INGREDIENTS:

- 1 cup of coarse salt
- A clean, dry cloth or sock

NOTES:

Make sure the compress is not too hot to avoid burning your skin.

This remedy can provide relief from pressure and discomfort associated with earaches, serving as a temporary measure until you can see a doctor for professional care. If your earache persists or worsens, consult a healthcare professional immediately.

Adjust the essential oil concentration for children, and always consult with a pediatrician before using herbal remedies for children.

INSTRUCTIONS:

1 | **Preparation:** Begin by heating the coarse salt in a microwave-safe container for approximately 1-2 minutes. Periodically check and shake the salt to ensure even heating. Ensure that the salt is warm enough for comfort but not too hot to touch.

2 | **Fill the Cloth/Sock:** Take the warm salt and place it in the cloth or sock. Tie the open end of the cloth or sock securely, creating a salt-filled pouch. For added comfort, consider using a moist heat option by slightly dampening the cloth before filling it with salt. You can also enhance the experience by adding a few drops of lavender or chamomile essential oil to the salt for a soothing aromatherapy effect.

3 | **Test Temperature:** Before using, test the temperature of the salt pouch on the inside of your wrist to ensure it's not too hot.

4 | **Application:** Lie down on the side where you have the earache. Place the salt-filled pouch over the affected ear. Leave it on for 15-20 minutes, or until it cools down. You can repeat this process as needed for relief.

DOSAGE:

Use the salt hot compress as needed, typically no more than 3-4 times a day.

Antibiotic
Eye Drops

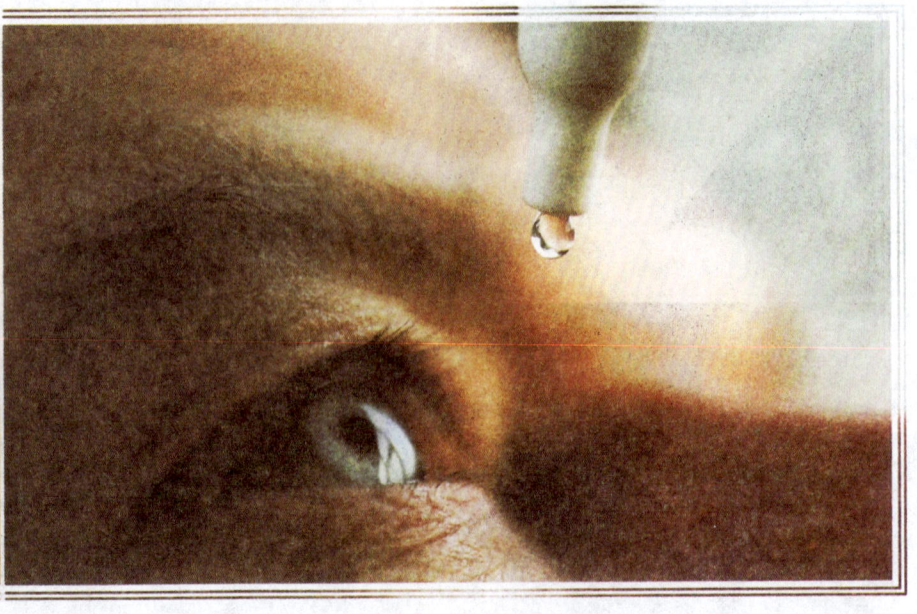

Eyebright and chamomile are two wonderful herbs traditionally known for their eye-soothing properties. As the name suggests, eyebright is often used to treat eye conditions like inflammation, blepharitis, conjunctivitis, red eye, styes, itchy eyes, stinging eyes, and weak vision, while chamomile offers anti-inflammatory and calming effects.

The combination of these herbs in the form of eyebright and chamomile drops provides a gentle yet effective remedy for soothing and supporting overall eye well-being.

INGREDIENTS:

- 1 teaspoon dried eyebright herb (*Euphrasia officinalis*)
- 1 teaspoon dried chamomile flowers (*Matricaria chamomilla*)
- ½ cup distilled water
- A clean, airtight glass dropper bottle

NOTES:

Ensure the dropper tip doesn't touch your eye to prevent contamination.

Do not use if you are allergic to either eyebright or chamomile.

If you experience any adverse reactions, discontinue use and consult with a healthcare professional.

INSTRUCTIONS:

1 | **Herbal Infusion:** Place the dried eyebright and chamomile in a heatproof glass or ceramic bowl. Boil the distilled water and pour it over the herbs. Cover the bowl and let it steep for 15-20 minutes.
2 | **Strain:** After steeping, strain the infusion through a fine mesh or cheesecloth into a clean container. Allow the liquid to cool to room temperature.
3 | **Fill the Dropper Bottle:** Using a funnel, pour the herbal infusion into the glass dropper bottle.
4 | **Store:** Store the bottle in a cool, dark place to maintain the freshness of the infusion.

You can also make a compress from a decoction of eyebright, used to give relief from redness, swelling, and visual disturbances due to eye infections. A tea is sometimes given internally along with the topical treatment. It is also used for the treatment of eye fatigue and other disturbances of vision.

DOSAGE:

Use as needed for eye irritations or discomfort. For general eye health and soothing, apply 2-3 drops into each eye up to three times a day. Always exercise caution and seek professional advice if you encounter any unexpected reactions.

Calendula and Rose Water
Eye Wash

Calendula officinalis, commonly known as pot marigold, and *Rosa damascena*, the Damask rose, are two botanical gems known for their skin-soothing and anti-inflammatory properties.

These botanicals combine perfectly to create a gentle formula tailored to bring relief to irritated eyes and refresh them when your eyes feel fatigued. This eye wash offers a practical addition to your eye care routine, providing a soothing and refreshing stuch for your eyes.

INGREDIENTS AND MATERIALS:

- 1 teaspoon dried calendula (*Calendula officinalis*) flowers
- 1 cup distilled or filtered water
- 1 teaspoon Damask rose (*Rosa damascena*) water (hydrosol)
- Cotton balls or cotton pads

NOTES:

Ensure that the water you use is pure and sterile to avoid contamination.

If eye irritation persists or worsens, consult a healthcare professional.

Store any leftover calendula and rose water solution in a clean, airtight container in the refrigerator for future use.

Always use clean cotton balls or pads to prevent contamination.

INSTRUCTIONS:

1. **Prepare the Calendula Infusion:** Boil the water and let it cool to a lukewarm temperature. Place the dried *Calendula officinalis* flowers in a clean, heatproof container. Pour the lukewarm water over the Calendula flowers, covering them completely. Allow the infusion to steep for 15-20 minutes.
2. **Strain the Calendula Infusion:** Strain the infusion through a fine mesh strainer or cheesecloth into a clean container to remove the flower petals.
3. **Mix with Rose Water:** Add 1 teaspoon of Damask rose hydrosol to the calendula infusion.
4. **Soak Cotton Ball or Pad:** Immerse a clean cotton ball or cotton pad in the calendula and rose water solution. Squeeze out excess liquid to avoid dripping.
5. **Apply to Eyes:** Gently close your eyes and place the soaked cotton ball or pad over your closed eyelids. Allow it to sit for a few minutes as it provides soothing relief to your eyes. Repeat as needed for both eyes.

DOSAGE:

Use this eye wash pads as needed for eye irritation. It's gentle and safe for regular use.

Forgotten Home Apothecary

Aloe Vera and Cucumber Mix
for Tired Eyes

Life's demands can often take a toll on your eyes, leaving them tired and puffy.

Aloe vera, cucumber, and green tea are all-natural ingredients renowned for their soothing and rejuvenating properties. This DIY eye mask is designed to provide a pampering experience, offering relief to tired and puffy eyes.

INGREDIENTS AND MATERIALS:

- 2 tablespoons aloe vera gel (*Aloe barbadensis miller*)
- 4 fresh cucumber slices
- 1 green tea bag (*Camellia sinensis*)
- Cotton pads or soft clot

NOTES:

Avoid getting the mixture into your eyes, as it may cause irritation.

If you have a known allergy to aloe vera, cucumbers, or green tea, do not use this eye mask.

Perform a patch test on a small area of skin before applying the eye mask

For added comfort and a spa-like experience, chill the mixture in the refrigerator before applying.

INSTRUCTIONS:

1 | **Extract Aloe Vera Gel:** Begin by carefully extracting the gel from an aloe vera leaf. To do this, cut a mature aloe leaf and squeeze out the gel. Make sure you use pure aloe vera gel without any added chemicals. Measure 2 tablespoons of aloe vera gel and place it in a clean bowl.

2 | **Brew Green Tea:** Boil a cup of water and steep a green tea bag in it for about 5 minutes. Allow the tea to cool to room temperature. Remove the tea bag and measure 2 tablespoons of green tea.

3 | **Blend Ingredients:** Combine the 2 tablespoons of aloe vera gel, 2 tablespoons of green tea, and the four cucumber slices in a blender. Blend the mixture until it forms a smooth, consistent paste.

4 | **Application:** Soak a cotton pad or a soft cloth in the blended mixture. Gently apply the soaked cotton pad or cloth to the area under your eyes. Lie down, relax, and leave the eye mask on for 15-20 minutes.

5 | **Store:** If you have leftover mixture, store it in the refrigerator for future use. Ensure the container is airtight to preserve its freshness.

DOSAGE:

Use this homemade eye mask whenever your eyes feel tired or puffy. Apply once a day or as needed.

Billberry Glycerite
to Enhance Night Vision and Circulation to the Eyes

Bilberry, a renowned herb with a rich history of traditional use, is valued for its capacity to promote eye health and enhance night vision. These beneficial effects can be attributed to various actions of bilberries, including stabilizing tear production, strengthening collagen fibers within capillaries, and supporting the development of robust blood vessels. This, in turn, contributes to improved circulation to the eyes. Additionally, the high anthocyanin content in bilberries has been demonstrated to stimulate the production of rhodopsin, a light-sensitive pigment crucial for aiding the eyes in adapting to changes in light and potentially enhancing night vision.

INGREDIENTS:

- 1 cup of dried bilberry (*Vaccinium myrtillus*) berries
- 1.5 cups of food-grade vegetable glycerin
- ½ cup distilled water

NOTES:

Consult a healthcare professional before using if you have any specific medical conditions or are taking medications.

Bilberry is generally safe for most people, but it's essential to consult with a healthcare provider before starting any herbal remedy, especially if you are pregnant, nursing, or have underlying health concerns.

Allergic reactions to bilberry are rare but possible. If you experience any adverse effects, discontinue use and seek medical attention.

INSTRUCTIONS:

1 | **Preparation:** Measure 1 cup of dried bilberry berries. Ensure that the berries are clean and free from debris. If they are not already crushed, lightly crush the berries using a mortar and pestle or a clean cloth to break them open, allowing the glycerin to extract the beneficial compounds more effectively.

2 | **Mix:** Place the crushed bilberry in a glass jar. Pour ½ cup of warmed distilled water and then 1.5 cups of food-grade vegetable glycerin over the berries, ensuring they are completely submerged. Stir the mixture well to combine the water, glycerin, and berries.

3 | **Maceration:** Seal the jar tightly and store it in a cool, dark place. Shake the jar gently every day for ~4 weeks to promote the extraction of the herb's beneficial compounds.

4 | **Strain:** After the maceration period, strain the mixture through a fine mesh strainer or cheesecloth into a clean, dry glass bottle. Squeeze out as much liquid from the herbs as possible to maximize your extract.

5 | **Store:** Store the bilberry glycerite in a cool, dark place to maintain its potency.

6 | **Label:** Label the bottle with the contents, date of preparation, and dosage instructions for easy reference.

DOSAGE:

The recommended dosage is typically 20-30 drops, taken 2-3 times a day.

Ginkgo Biloba Tincture
to Support Retinal Health and Blood Flow

Ginkgo biloba is a popular herbal remedy known for its potential benefits in supporting retinal health and improving blood flow. By promoting consistent blood flow and helping to keep intraocular eye pressure low, *Ginkgo biloba* may support overall eye health. It is believed to help with maintaining visual acuity and supporting the prevention of issues related to macular health and diabetic eye concerns.

INGREDIENTS:

- ¼ cup dried *Ginkgo biloba* leaves
- 1 cup of 80-proof vodka (40% alcohol by volume)

NOTES:

Ginkgo biloba may interact with certain medications or medical conditions.

Consult with a healthcare provider before using this tincture, especially if you're pregnant, nursing, or taking other medications.

Discontinue use and consult a healthcare professional if you experience any adverse reactions.

INSTRUCTIONS:

1 | **Prepare the Glass Jar:** Start by thoroughly cleaning a glass jar with a tight-fitting lid to ensure it's sterilized.
2 | **Measure *Ginkgo biloba* Leaves:** Measure and place ¼ cup of dried *Ginkgo biloba* leaves into the glass jar.
3 | **Add Vodka:** Pour 1 cup of 80-proof vodka (40% alcohol by volume) over the dried *Ginkgo biloba* leaves in the jar, ensuring they are completely submerged.
4 | **Seal the Jar:** Seal the jar with the lid tightly.
5 | **Maceration Period:** Allow the mixture to macerate in a cool, dark place for about 4-6 weeks. Shake the jar gently every few days to agitate the ingredients.
6 | **Straining:** After the maceration period, strain the tincture through a fine-mesh strainer or cheesecloth into a clean, dark glass bottle. Squeeze the plant material to extract all the liquid.
7 | **Store:** Store the tincture in a cool, dark place to maintain its potency.

DOSAGE:

15-30 drops (0.5-1 ml) in a glass of water or directly in the mouth, up to three times a day.

Antioxidant
Vision Protection

The active component in turmeric, known as curcumin, is a polyphenolic compound that has gained widespread recognition for its potent antioxidant and anti-inflammatory properties. These qualities are particularly significant when it comes to eye health, as the eyes are highly susceptible to oxidative stress and inflammation, which can contribute to various vision problems.

INGREDIENTS:

- 1 teaspoon of dried turmeric (*Curcuma longa*) root powder
- 1 cup of water
- A pinch of black pepper
- Honey or stevia to taste (optional)

NOTES:

If you are taking other medicinal herbs or dietary supplements, be aware of potential interactions. Some combinations can be beneficial, while others may have adverse effects. Consult with a healthcare provider or herbalist to ensure safe combinations.

Turmeric, especially in high doses, may cause gastrointestinal discomfort. If you have a sensitive stomach or a history of gastrointestinal issues, start with a small amount and monitor your body's response.

INSTRUCTIONS:

1. **Prepare the Turmeric Mixture:** In a small saucepan, add one cup of water. Mix in one teaspoon of dried turmeric root powder. Using fresh Turmeric root is a viable alternative. Simply grate or finely chop the fresh root and use it in the recipe. Add a pinch of black pepper to enhance the absorption of curcumin. Adding a bit of healthy fat, like coconut oil or ghee, can further enhance curcumin absorption.
2. **Stir:** Stir the mixture well.
3. **Simmer:** Place the saucepan over low heat and let the mixture simmer for 15-20 minutes. As the mixture simmers over low heat, it allows the turmeric to release its beneficial compounds into the liquid. This gentle simmering process not only enhances the flavor but also ensures that the curcumin is effectively extracted. The longer simmering time allows the infusion of more curcumin, making this tea even more potent to support eye health. Stir occasionally.
4. **Strain and Sweeten:** Remove the saucepan from heat and strain the liquid into a cup. Sweeten your turmeric tea with honey or stevia if desired.
5. **Enjoy:** Sip and enjoy while it's warm. The warm and soothing nature of this tea makes it an ideal addition to your daily routine, whether enjoyed in the morning, as a mid-day pick-me-up, or as a relaxing evening beverage.

DOSAGE:

You can consume this turmeric tea daily to support vision health. One cup per day is a typical recommendation.

HERBAL SUPPORT
for Musculoskeletal Health

The musculoskeletal system is vital for movement and our body's structure. Comprised of bones, muscles, tendons, ligaments, and joints, it enables mobility, supports the body's framework, and safeguards crucial organs. Additionally, the bone marrow within produces essential blood components. Maintaining the health of this system is key to a vibrant and active life.

Tips to Maintain a Healthy Musculoskeletal System:

REGULAR EXERCISE:
Engage in weight-bearing exercises such as walking, running, and weightlifting to strengthen bones and muscles. Incorporate flexibility and balance exercises like yoga and Pilates to maintain joint health.

BALANCED DIET:
Consume a diet rich in calcium, vitamin D, and other essential nutrients to support bone health. Include sources of lean protein to promote muscle maintenance and growth.

ADEQUATE HYDRATION:
Proper hydration is essential for joint lubrication and overall body function. Drink enough water to keep joints and muscles functioning smoothly. Make sure to get enough minerals, like magnesium, potassium, calcium, and zinc.

POSTURE AWARENESS:
Maintain good posture to reduce stress on your spine and joints.

REGULAR CHECK-UPS:
Visit a healthcare professional for routine check-ups, especially if you have musculoskeletal concerns. Early diagnosis and treatment can prevent issues from worsening.

AVOID OVERUSE AND INJURY:
Pay attention to your body's signals. If you experience pain, rest and seek medical advice. Prevent injuries by using proper techniques in sports and daily activities.

WEIGHT MANAGEMENT:
Maintain a healthy weight to reduce the strain on your joints, particularly those in the lower body.

PROPER FOOTWEAR:
Choose supportive and comfortable footwear that fits well to prevent issues with your feet, knees, and lower back.

ERGONOMICS:
If you have a desk job, set up an ergonomic workspace with proper chair height, keyboard placement, and monitor height to prevent strain on your muscles and joints.

STRETCHING:
After exercise or strenuous activities, perform stretching exercises to reduce the risk of strains and injuries. Daily stretching is recommended, regardless of exercise.

QUALITY SLEEP:
Ensure you get adequate and restful sleep. Sleep is essential for muscle recovery and overall health.

HERBAL SUPPORT

Turmeric (*Curcuma longa*)
Turmeric contains curcumin, which has anti-inflammatory properties that may help alleviate joint pain and reduce inflammation. Consider using turmeric in cooking or taking curcumin supplements or tinctures.

Ginger (*Zingiber officinale*)
Ginger also has anti-inflammatory effects and may provide relief from muscle soreness and joint pain. Include ginger in your diet or take it as a supplement.

Boswellia/Indian Frankincense (*Boswellia serrata*)
Boswellia extract may help reduce inflammation and alleviate joint pain. Use as a supplement or tincture.

Devil's Claw (*Harpagophytum procumbens*)
Devil's claw has been used traditionally to support joint health and reduce pain. Use as a supplement or tincture.

Arnica (*Arnica montana*)
Arnica is used topically as a cream or gel to relieve muscle aches, stiffness, and bruising. External use only.

White Willow (*Salix alba*)
White willow bark contains salicin, a compound similar to aspirin, providing pain relief. Use as a supplement or tincture.

Cayenne Pepper (*Capsicum annuum*)
Cayenne contains capsaicin, which can help reduce pain by blocking pain signals. It's used topically in creams or ointments.

Comfrey (*Symphytum*)
Comfrey has been used for centuries to support bone and joint health. It can be applied topically as a cream or used in compresses. External use only.

Painkiller
in a Jar

Wild lettuce (*Lactuca virosa*) has been valued for its traditional use in herbal practices. Often overlooked as a weed, this common plant is believed to have properties that can help with pain.

This recipe, "Painkiller in a Jar," is a simple way to incorporate wild lettuce into your natural wellness routine.

INGREDIENTS:

- 20 fresh leaves of wild lettuce
- 80-proof vodka
- A clean glass jar with a lid
- Sieve or cheesecloth
- Dark dropper bottle

NOTES:

Wild lettuce can cause drowsiness. Do not drive or operate heavy machinery after taking this remedy. Consult with a healthcare professional before using wild lettuce if you are pregnant, nursing, or have any chronic health conditions.

If you are taking any medications, consult with a healthcare provider before using this remedy, as wild lettuce may interact with certain medications.

INSTRUCTIONS:

1 | **Harvest Wild Lettuce:** Harvest approximately 20 fresh leaves of wild lettuce.
2 | **Prepare the Leaves:** Chop the leaves into thin slices and fill half of your glass jar with these chopped leaves.
3 | **Fill the Jar:** Pour 80-proof vodka over the leaves, filling the jar to the top. Label and date.
4 | **Seal and Store:** Seal the jar tightly with its lid and store it in a cool, dark place for 4-6 weeks, shaking the jar daily to help the extraction process.
5 | **Strain the Liquid:** After 4-6 weeks, strain the liquid through a sieve or cheesecloth into a dark dropper bottle. Label your dropper bottle with the name and the date it was made. Store the dropper bottle in a cool, dark place to maintain its potency.

DOSAGE:

Do not take more than 10 drops per day, as wild lettuce can have sedative effects in larger quantities. Start with a smaller dose to see how your body reacts before taking the full dosage.

Forgotten Home Apothecary

Amish Ibuprofen

The Amish community is renowned for their use of natural remedies and a holistic approach to health. This "Amish Ibuprofen" recipe utilizes the medicinal properties of dandelion and rosemary to create a natural pain-relieving tonic. By infusing these herbs in raw apple cider vinegar, you can harness their potential benefits in a simple, homemade remedy. This traditional approach offers a natural alternative to conventional pain relief methods and is rooted in centuries of herbal wisdom.

INGREDIENTS AND MATERIALS:

- ½ cup dried dandelion flowers, leaves, and roots (1 cup fresh)
- ¼ cup dried rosemary leaves (½ cup fresh)
- 2 cups raw apple cider vinegar (with "the mother")
- A glass jar with a tight-fitting lid
- A piece of cheesecloth or a fine mesh strainer
- A dark glass bottle for storage

NOTES:

Consult a healthcare professional before using this remedy, especially if pregnant, nursing, or having chronic health conditions.

Discontinue use if you experience any allergic reactions.

If taking medications, consult a healthcare provider as herbs may interact with them.

INSTRUCTIONS:

1 | **Combine the Herbs and Vinegar:** Place half a cup of dried dandelions and a quarter cup of rosemary into a glass jar. Fill the jar with raw apple cider vinegar, ensuring that the herbs are fully submerged.
2 | **Seal the Jar:** Seal the jar with a tight-fitting lid. If you are using a jar with a metal lid, cover the top of the jar with plastic wrap, cheesecloth, or baking paper before screwing on the metal lid to prevent corrosion and rusting.
3 | **Store and Shake:** Store the jar in a cool, dark place or in the refrigerator for 2 weeks. Shake daily. During this time, the dandelions and rosemary will infuse their healing properties into the apple cider vinegar.
4 | **Strain the Mixture:** After 2 weeks, strain the mixture through a piece of cheesecloth or a fine mesh strainer, making sure to squeeze out as much liquid as possible.
5 | **Transfer to Storage Bottle:** Transfer the strained liquid to a dark glass bottle with a plastic lid for storage. You can store it in the fridge or in a dark, cool location. If you are using fresh herbs, this remedy will last about 6 months. If you are using dried herbs, it should last closer to 9 months.

DOSAGE:

When needed, mix 2 teaspoons of the "Amish Ibuprofen" with a glass of water or your favorite herbal tea. Consume up to three times a day.

Cartilage Support
Cream

Arnica is a well-known herbal remedy valued for its potential anti-inflammatory and pain-relieving properties, making it a popular choice for addressing muscle discomfort and inflammation. Its active compounds, such as helenalin, are believed to help reduce swelling and inhibit pain signals, providing relief from muscle and cartilage discomfort caused by strains, sprains, or overexertion. Arnica is also thought to support improved blood circulation to the affected area, aiding in nutrient delivery and waste removal, which may support the healing process. When applied early after an injury, it can minimize the discoloration (bruising) and swelling that often accompany muscle and cartilage trauma.

INGREDIENTS:

- ½ cup of *Arnica montana*-infused oil
- ⅛ cup of beeswax
- 5-10 drops of peppermint essential oil
- ⅛ teaspoon of vitamin E oil (optional)

NOTES:

Arnica should never be ingested. Consuming Arnica can lead to severe health risks, including gastrointestinal distress, dizziness, and even poisoning. Keep it out of reach of children and pets.

Do not apply to broken skin or open wounds. Avoid contact with eyes and mucous membranes.

Before using arnica products, perform a patch test on a small area of the skin to check for any allergic reactions. Discontinue use if you experience itching, redness, or swelling.

INSTRUCTIONS:

1 | **Prepare Arnica-Infused Oil:** Begin by making arnica-infused oil. Do this by loosely filling a clean, dry jar with freshly-dried Arnica montana flowers and covering them with a carrier oil, such as organic olive, jojoba, hemp, or almond oil. Seal the jar and place it in a warm, dark place for 4-6 weeks, shaking it daily. Once your oil is ready, strain out the arnica flowers, leaving you with arnica-infused oil.
2 | **Melt Beeswax:** In a double boiler, melt the beeswax.
3 | **Add Arnica-Infused Oil:** Once the beeswax is completely melted, add the arnica-infused oil and stir well.
4 | **Add Peppermint Essential Oil (Optional):** Add the peppermint essential oil for fragrance and a cooling effect.
5 | **Add Vitamin E Oil (Optional):** If desired, add vitamin E oil as an optional preservative to extend the shelf life of your salve.
6 | **Pour into Containers:** Pour the mixture into clean, dry labeled containers or jars.
7 | **Let it Cool and Solidify:** Allow the salve to cool and solidify in the containers.
8 | **Store:** Store Arnica salve in a cool, dark place and keep it tightly sealed to maintain its effectiveness. Keep away from direct sunlight and heat sources.

DOSAGE:

Apply the arnica salve to the affected area, as needed, up to 3 times a day.

Comfrey and Lavender
Herbal Oil for Joint Support

Comfrey and lavender are two powerful herbs known for their beneficial properties. Comfrey is traditionally used for its ability to support joint health, reduce inflammation, and ease discomfort. Lavender is cherished for its soothing aroma and anti-inflammatory properties. Combining these herbs in an herbal oil can provide relief for joint-related issues.

INGREDIENTS:

- 3/4 cup of dried comfrey leaves (*Symphytum officinale*)
- ¼ cup of dried lavender flowers (*Lavandula angustifolia*)
- 2 cups of carrier oil (such as organic olive or almond oil)

NOTES:

This oil can be especially handy for on-the-go use and for targeting specific areas with joint discomfort.

Do not use comfrey on open wounds or broken skin.

Lavender is generally considered safe, but it can make your skin more sensitive to sunlight. Avoid prolonged sun exposure after applying the oil, especially if you have fair or sensitive skin.

INSTRUCTIONS:

1 | **Preparation:** Start by ensuring that your comfrey and lavender herbs are completely dry. Moisture can lead to mold growth in your herbal oil.

2 | **Combining the Herbs:** In a clean glass jar, combine the dried comfrey leaves and lavender flowers.

3 | **Adding the Carrier Oil:** Pour the carrier oil over the herbs, making sure they are fully submerged.

4 | **Infusion:** Seal the jar tightly and place it in a warm, sunny spot for about 4-6 weeks. This allows the herbs to infuse into the oil. Shake gently daily (or at least a few times a week).

5 | **Straining:** After the infusion period, strain the oil through a fine mesh strainer or cheesecloth to remove the plant material. Squeeze out as much oil as possible. You can enhance the aromatic properties of the oil by adding a few drops of lavender essential oil after straining.

6 | **Storage:** Transfer the infused oil to a dark glass bottle, which helps protect it from light. Store it in a cool, dark place.

You can easily transform your comfrey and lavender herbal oil into a salve for convenient application. This salve will have a thicker consistency, making it easier to apply to your joints. Simply melt some beeswax (I use a 4:1 ratio of oil to beeswax) and combine it with your herbal oil over low heat. Once combined, pour into tins for easy application.

DOSAGE:

Apply the herbal oil to the affected joints as needed, massaging gently for best results. Use a small amount and increase as necessary.

"Better Than Collagen"

Collagen, the protein responsible for skin's elasticity and youthful appearance, naturally decreases with age, leading to wrinkles and sagging skin. To counteract this, these homemade collagen-boosting gummies incorporate key ingredients known for their collagen-enhancing properties. Rosehips are rich in vitamin C, essential for collagen synthesis; agar-agar provides calcium and iron for skin health; raw honey moisturizes and contains antioxidants; and amla, acerola cherry, orange, and pineapple are vitamin C powerhouses, vital for collagen production. These gummies offer a delicious way to support collagen production, maintain skin elasticity, reduce signs of aging, and provide a tropical twist to your daily skincare routine.

INGREDIENTS AND MATERIALS:

- ½ cup rosehips (*Rosa canina*) decoction
- 2 tablespoons agar-agar powder
- ¼ cup raw honey
- ¼ cup fresh orange juice
- ¼ cup fresh pineapple juice
- 1 tablespoon amla/Indian gooseberry (*Phyllanthus emblica*) powder
- 1 teaspoon acerola cherry (*Malpighia emarginata*) powder
- Gummy molds

NOTES:

If you have allergies to any of the ingredients, avoid consuming these gummies.

Consult a healthcare professional before adding new supplements to your diet, especially if you're pregnant, nursing, or have underlying health conditions.

INSTRUCTIONS:

1 | **Prepare Rosehip Decoction:** Start by making a rosehip decoction. Boil ½ cup of water in a covered pot, turn to low, and add ½ cup of crushed dried rosehips; cover so to not lose the water and simmer for 15-20 minutes. Strain and put back into the pot.
2 | **Mix Agar-Agar:** In the pot, mix 2 tablespoons of agar-agar powder with the rosehip decoction. Stir well.
3 | **Heat and Dissolve:** Heat the mixture over low heat, stirring constantly until the agar-agar is completely dissolved.
4 | **Add Honey:** Remove from heat and add ¼ cup of raw honey. Stir until fully incorporated.
5 | **Add Juices and Powders:** Mix in ¼ cup of fresh orange juice, ¼ cup of fresh pineapple juice, 1 tablespoon of amla powder, and 1 teaspoon of acerola cherry powder. Stir until the mixture is smooth.
6 | **Pour into Molds:** Pour the mixture into gummy molds. Try using silicone molds for fun shapes.
7 | **Cool and Set:** Allow the gummies to cool and set at room temperature for about an hour.
8 | **Remove from Molds:** Once they are set, gently remove the gummies from the molds and store them in an airtight container in the refrigerator to maintain freshness.

DOSAGE:

Take 2-3 gummies daily for collagen-boosting benefits.

Forgotten Home Apothecary

Herbal Liniment
for Sports Injuries and Strains

This herbal liniment combines the benefits of dried arnica, calendula, and myrrh to create a soothing and effective solution for sports injuries and strains.

Arnica montana is well-known for its anti-inflammatory properties, *Calendula officinalis* helps in the healing process of damaged skin, and myrrh offers additional anti-inflammatory and beneficial properties.

INGREDIENTS AND MATERIALS:

- 1 tablespoon dried arnica (*Arnica montana*) flowers
- 1 tablespoon dried calendula (*Calendula officinalis*) flowers
- 1 tablespoon dried myrrh resin (*Commiphora myrrha*)
- 1 cup (240 ml) witch hazel extract
- 1 glass jar and 1 glass bottle with tight-sealing lids

NOTES:

For external use only.

Be cautious when applying herbal liniments to sensitive or broken skin and avoid contact with the eyes and mucous membranes. Always do a patch test on a small area of skin to ensure you don't have an adverse reaction to the liniment.

INSTRUCTIONS:

1 | **Prepare the Glass Bottle:** Start by sterilizing the glass jar and ensure it's completely dry before proceeding.

2 | **Combine Dried Herbs:** In the glass bottle, place the freshly-dried *Arnica montana* flowers, dried *Calendula officinalis* flowers, and dried myrrh resin.

3 | **Add Witch Hazel:** Pour the witch hazel extract over the dried herbs in the jar. Witch hazel will act as a carrier for the liniment and help extract the herbal properties. You may use rubbing alcohol instead.

4 | **Seal and Infuse:** Seal the bottle tightly and give it a good shake to mix the ingredients. Let the mixture infuse for at least two weeks, shaking the bottle gently once a day to encourage the extraction of herbal properties.

5 | **Strain and Store:** After the infusion period, strain the mixture to remove the dried herbs. Transfer the herbal liniment into a clean glass bottle for storage. Store the liniment in a cool, dark place to prolong its shelf life.

6 | **Application:** Apply a small amount of the liniment to the affected are and gently massage it into the skin.

DOSAGE:

Use as needed, but not more than 3-4 times a day

Grandma's Hot Salve
for Back Pain

Muscle, joint, and back pain can disrupt our daily lives, making simple tasks a challenge. This cream is specifically formulated to provide soothing relief from discomfort and inflammation.

Cayenne pepper, known for its capsaicin content, desensitizes pain receptors, reducing discomfort. When applied topically, it enhances blood circulation for muscle recovery. Ginger, with gingerol, an anti-inflammatory compound, reduces swelling and eases muscle and joint pain. Its warming effect synergizes with cayenne pepper, enhancing the cream's pain-relief properties. Rosemary essential oil is traditionally known for its analgesic and anti-inflammatory properties, which may help alleviate pain.

INGREDIENTS:

- ¼ cup of cayenne pepper (*Capsicum annuum*) powder
- ¼ cup of ginger (*Zingiber officinale*) powder
- ¼ cup of beeswax
- ¼ cup of coconut oil
- 10 drops of rosemary (*Rosmarinus officinalis*) essential oil
- ¼ cup of aloe vera gel

NOTES:

Avoid contact with eyes, mucous membranes, or open wounds. Wash hands thoroughly after application. Discontinue use if irritation or a burning sensation occurs. Do not use on children or pets.

Consult a healthcare professional before use if you have sensitive skin, allergies, or any medical conditions.

INSTRUCTIONS:

1. **Gather the Ingredients:** First, assemble all the ingredients you'll need to prepare your cream.
2. **Prepare the Base:** Begin by melting ¼ cup of beeswax and ¼ cup of coconut oil in a double boiler. Heat the mixture until both ingredients are fully combined.
3. **Add the Herbs:** Once the beeswax and coconut oil are fully melted, add ¼ cup of cayenne pepper powder and ¼ cup of ginger powder to the mixture. Stir thoroughly to ensure even distribution of the herbal powders.
4. **Incorporate Essential Oils and Aloe Vera:** After mixing in the herbal powders, remove the mixture from heat and let it cool for a few minutes. Now add the 10 drops of rosemary essential oil (note: frankinscence also works well). Next add your ¼ cup of aloe vera gel, which contributes to the cream's soothing and hydrating properties.
5. **Transfer and Cool:** Transfer the herbal cream into a clean, airtight container. Allow it to cool completely before sealing the container.

DOSAGE:

To use, apply a small amount of the pepper cream to the affected area. Gently massage it into the skin until fully absorbed. Use as needed, but do not exceed three applications per day. Wash hands after application so as not to get it into your eyes.

Mobility Maintenance Tincture
for Arthritis

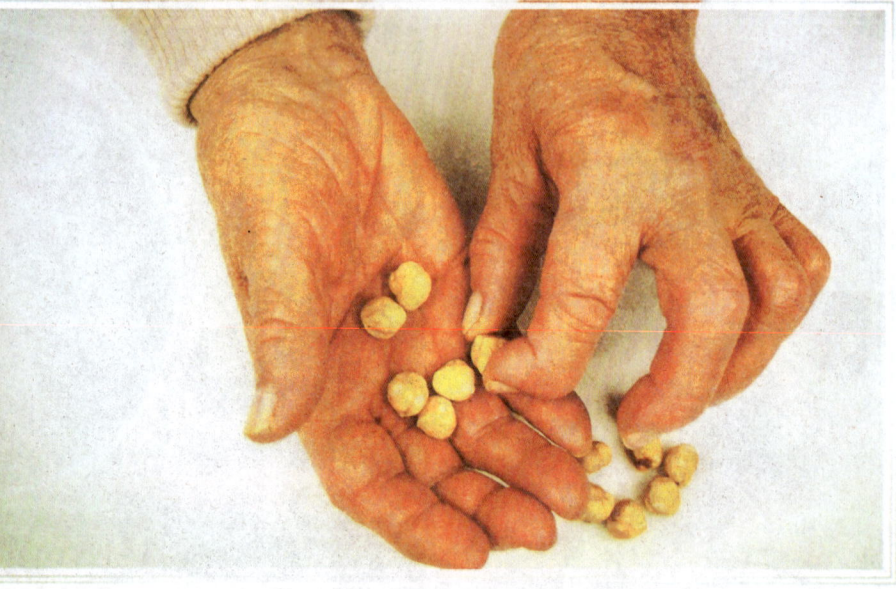

This herbal tincture combines several herbs traditionally known for their supportive anti-inflammatory and analgesic properties, which may help reduce the discomfort associated with arthritis. Devil's claw is known for its anti-inflammatory and pain-relieving abilities, traditionally used in African medicine to alleviate joint pain. Turmeric boasts potent anti-inflammatory effects with curcumin, which can reduce joint inflammation and pain. Ginger possesses anti-inflammatory properties, easing arthritis-related discomfort and swelling. Willow bark contains salicin, akin to aspirin, offering natural pain relief. Boswellia is renowned for its anti-inflammatory benefits, especially in managing osteoarthritis and rheumatoid arthritis. The pinch of black pepper helps with the bioavailablity of the curcumin. Taking a daily stinging nettle tincture in conjunction with this tincture is recommended, especially for those seeking additional support.

INGREDIENTS:

- 2-parts devil's claw (*Harpagophytum procumbens*)
- 1-part turmeric (*Curcuma longa*)
- 1-part ginger (*Zingiber officinale*)
- 1-part willow bark (*Salix* spp.)
- 1-part boswellia (*Boswellia serrata*)
- A pinch of black pepper
- 40% (80-proof) alcohol, such as vodka or brandy

NOTES:

Avoid this tincture if you are allergic to any of the ingredients.

Discontinue use if you experience any adverse reactions.

Combine this tincture with a balanced diet and regular exercise for better results in managing arthritis.

INSTRUCTIONS:

1 | **Herb Preparation:** Finely chop or grind the selected herbs to enhance their surface area, allowing for better extraction of their beneficial compounds during the tincture-making process.
2 | **Infusion:** In a glass jar, combine the chopped herbs, ensuring an accurate ratio of the ingredients and filling the jar ⅓-½ full of total herbal ingredients. Fill the jar with 40% alcohol, such as vodka or brandy, making sure all the herbs are completely submerged. Label.
3 | **Steeping Period:** Seal the glass jar tightly, and place it in a cool, dark location. Allow the herbs to steep in the alcohol for approximately 4-6 weeks. During this period, gently shake the jar every few days to ensure thorough extraction.
4 | **Straining and Storing:** After the steeping period, strain the tincture through a fine mesh or cheesecloth, collecting the liquid extract in a clean glass container. Store the tincture in a dark glass bottle in a cool, dark place (like a cupboard) for future use.

DOSAGE:

Take 1-2 ml (approximately 30-60 drops) of the tincture, directly in the mouth or diluted in a small amount of water, three times a day. Adjust the dosage as needed, but do not exceed the recommended daily dose.

Joint Pain Reliever

The pain-relieving power in mint lies with its menthol compounds. Many mint plants contain some amount of menthol; peppermint has the highest concentrations. Spearmint also has menthol, and like peppermint, has carvacrol and limonene. These pain-killing plants have been traditionally used for pain relief for centuries. More recently, their analgesic qualities have been recognized for providing safe support for osteoarthritis and other chronic musculoskeletal discomforts.

INGREDIENTS:

- 3 tablespoons grated beeswax
- 3 tablespoons flaked coconut
- ½ cup peppermint leaf infused oil
- 30 drops mint essential oil (*Mentha piperita*)
- 15 drops spearmint essential oil (*Mentha spicata*)

NOTES:

For external use only.

Do not apply to broken skin. If you experience any irritation or discomfort, discontinue use.

The salve is also excellent for reducing headaches. Place a small amount at the base of your skull and around your ears and temples to help with headaches.

INSTRUCTIONS:

1 | **Prepare Your Work Area:** Ensure your workspace is clean and sanitized. Gather all the ingredients and equipment.
2 | **Melt the Beeswax and Oils:** In a double boiler, melt the 3 tablespoons of grated beeswax over low heat until it's completely liquid. Add the 3 tablespoons of cold, flaked coconut and ½ cup of mint-infused oil to the melted beeswax. ** To prepare mint-infused oil, fill a glass jar with freshly-dried mint leaves (peppermint or spearmint) and cover them with your chosen carrier oil (like olive or coconut oil). Seal the jar, place it in a sunny spot for 2-4 weeks, shaking daily. After infusing, strain out the leaves, leaving you with mint-infused oil, perfect for culinary and herbal uses.
3 | **Stir:** Stir well to combine. Heat this mixture until everything is well incorporated. Remove from heat.
4 | **Adding Mint Essential Oils:** Allow the mixture to cool slightly, but not solidify. Add 30 drops of peppermint essential oil and 15 drops of spearmint essential oil. Stir thoroughly.
5 | **Pour into Containers:** Pour the mixture into 3 one-ounce containers. Ensure they are clean and dry. Let the salve cool and solidify for a few hours. Label your containers/tins.

DOSAGE:

Apply a small amount of the mint salve to the affected area and gently massage it in until absorbed. Use as needed, up to 3-4 times a day.

Three-Herb Poultice
for Arthritis Pain

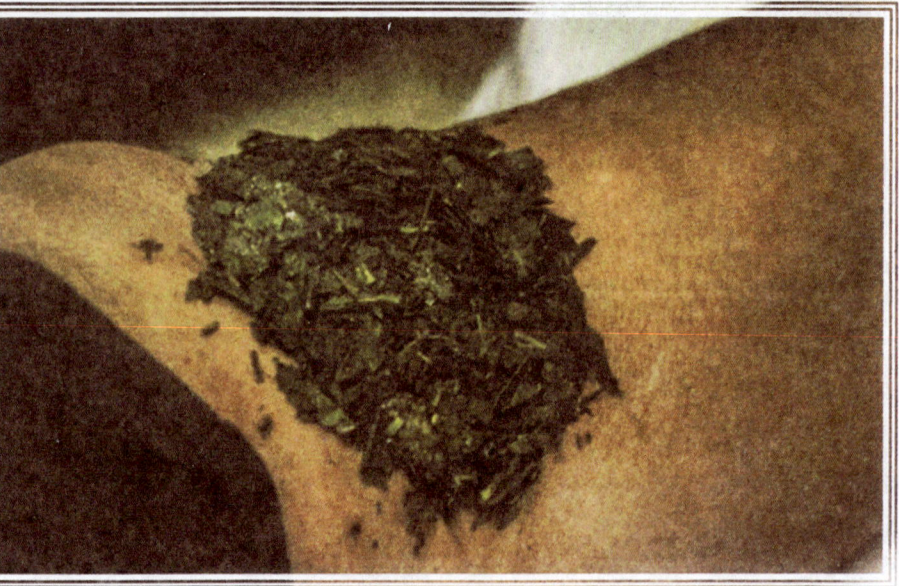

Creating an arthritis poultice involves combining natural ingredients traditionally recognized for their therapeutic properties. Green clay is used for its ability to draw out impurities and reduce inflammation. Comfrey leaves offer soothing effects and may help decrease swelling, while arnica flowers are valued for their anti-inflammatory and pain-relieving properties. Turmeric is included for its potent anti-inflammatory effects, thanks to curcumin, which may alleviate joint pain and swelling. Together, these ingredients form a poultice aimed at providing relief from the discomfort associated with arthritis.

INGREDIENTS:

- ½ cup of green clay
- ¼ cup of fresh or dried comfrey leaves (*Symphytum officinale*)
- ¼ cup of fresh or dried arnica flowers (*Arnica montana*)
- 2 tablespoons of turmeric powder (*Curcuma longa*)
- Warm water, enough to form a paste
- Gauze or clean cloth

NOTES:

Always test a small amount on your skin first to check for any allergic reactions.

Arnica should only be used topically and not on broken skin, as it can be irritating and is toxic if ingested.

Consult with a healthcare provider before using any new treatments, especially if you have sensitive skin or are on medication.

INSTRUCTIONS:

1 | **Prepare the Herbs:** If using fresh herbs, wash and finely chop them. If using dried herbs, crumble them into smaller pieces.
2 | **Mix the Ingredients:** In a bowl, combine the green clay, comfrey leaves, arnica flowers, and turmeric powder. Gradually add warm water and stir until you create a paste of spreadable consistency.
3 | **Heat the Poultice (Optional):** If desired, you can gently heat the mixture in a double boiler just until warm but not hot to enhance the poultice's soothing effects.
4 | **Apply the Poultice:** Spread the mixture onto a piece of gauze or clean cloth. Fold the cloth to encase the mixture fully.
5 | **Position the Poultice:** Place the poultice directly onto the affected area. If the skin is sensitive, you may place a thin cloth between the poultice and the skin.
6 | **Secure the Poultice:** Use additional cloth or an elastic bandage to hold the poultice in place.
7 | **Leave in Place:** Keep the poultice on for up to an hour, checking occasionally to ensure comfort and safety.
8 | **Remove and Cleanse:** After removing the poultice, gently wash the area with warm water and pat dry.

DOSAGE:

Apply the poultice up to two times daily, as needed, to relieve arthritis discomfort.

Forgotten Home Apothecary

Anti-Inflammatory Tincture for Joints

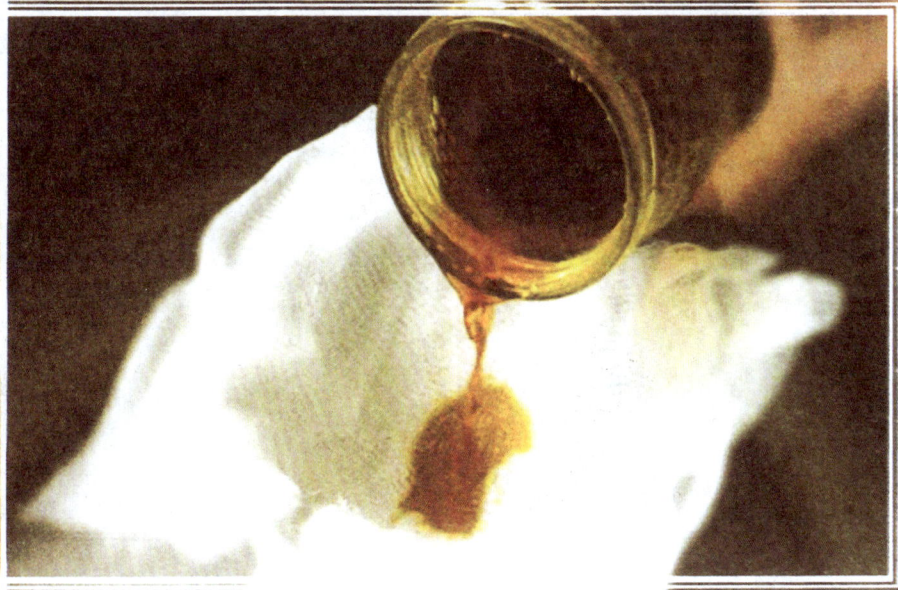

This recipe for an anti-inflammatory tincture uses natural ingredients traditionally recognized for their potential to support joint health and reduce inflammation. By infusing these ingredients in vodka, you create an extract that may help manage joint discomfort.

INGREDIENTS:

- 1 fresh ginger root (*Zingiber officinale*)
- 1 fresh turmeric root (*Curcuma longa*)
- 3 fresh cayenne peppers (*Capsicum annuum*)
- A handful of fresh peppermint leaves (*Mentha piperita*)
- Vodka (enough to cover the ingredients)

NOTES:

Always consult with a healthcare provider before starting any new treatment, especially if you have existing health conditions or are taking other medications.

Tinctures containing high concentrations of active ingredients like cayenne can interact with medications and affect individuals differently.

INSTRUCTIONS:

1 | **Prepare the Ingredients:** Peel and chop one ginger root and one turmeric root into small pieces to maximize their surface area. Slice three cayenne peppers carefully, wearing gloves to avoid irritation. Roughly chop a handful of peppermint leaves to release their oils.

2 | **Combine in a Jar:** Place the chopped ginger, turmeric, cayenne peppers, and peppermint leaves into a clean glass jar.

3 | **Cover with Alcohol:** Pour enough vodka over the ingredients to completely submerge them. Vodka is preferred due to its neutral flavor and high alcohol content, which is excellent for extracting the active compounds from the ingredients.

4 | **Seal and Store:** Tightly seal the jar and place it in the refrigerator. Let the mixture infuse for four to six weeks. Shake the jar occasionally to mix the contents and promote extraction.

5 | **Strain and Preserve:** After the infusion period, remove the jar from the refrigerator. Strain out the solid ingredients using a fine mesh strainer or cheesecloth, saving the liquid. Transfer the liquid tincture to a clean, sealed bottle or jar for storage. Store your tincture in a cool, dark place. Because it's alcohol-based, it will remain potent and preserve its therapeutic properties for years without refrigeration.

DOSAGE:

Tinctures are highly concentrated, so typically, just a few drops to a dropperful are needed per dose. Begin with a small amount to see how your body responds. You can gradually increase the dosage until you find what works best for you.

Forgotten Home Apothecary

DYI Relieving
Balm

DYI Relieving Balm is a popular topical ointment known for its soothing properties, combining several key ingredients traditionally used for pain relief:

- **White Camphor** essential oil produces a cooling sensation when applied to the skin, followed by a warming effect. This dual action can help distract the mind from pain or discomfort.
- **Menthol,** found in peppermint and spearmint essential oil, provides a cooling effect, which can alleviate pain by numbing the skin's surface.
- **Cinnamon or Cassia essential oil** is known for its warming properties. It helps increase blood flow to the applied area, providing relief for sore muscles and joints.
- **Clove essential oil** is another strong warming oil with analgesic properties. It can help reduce pain and inflammation in muscles and joints.
- **Cajeput essential oil** has warming properties and is traditionally used for pain relief, particularly for muscle aches and joint discomfort.

INGREDIENTS:

- White camphor essential oil (*Cinnamomum camphora*) (15%)
- Menthol (*Mentha* spp.) in the form of peppermint and/or spearmint essential oil (15%)
- Cinnamon or cassia essential oil (*Cinnamomum* spp.) (10%)
- Clove essential oil (*Eugenia caryophyllata*) (10%)
- Cajeput essential oil (*Melaleuca cajuputi*) (7%)
- A base, such as coconut oil or beeswax

NOTES:

For external use only.

Avoid contact with eyes, mucous membranes, and open wounds. Do a patch test on a small area of skin to check for any adverse reactions before widespread use. Discontinue use if irritation occurs.

INSTRUCTIONS:

1 | **Preparing the Base:** Measure out your base (beeswax) according to your desired batch size. It will make up the remaining percentage of your balm. Typically, a 57% base to 43% essential oils ratio is recommended for this balm. You can eyeball ~60% base to ~40% essential oils if easier. Or use a small measuring cup for each, then mix.

2 | **Mixing the Essential Oils:** In a clean, dry container, mix the essential oils in recommended percentages.

3 | **Combine the Base and Essential Oils:** In a double boiler or microwave, melt your base (coconut oil or beeswax) until it's completely liquid. Once melted, add the mixture of essential oils and stir thoroughly to ensure even distribution.

4 | **Cooling and Storing:** Allow the mixture to cool slightly. Pour the balm into clean, airtight containers.

DOSAGE:

Apply a small amount of this homemade balm to the affected area. Massage it into the skin in a circular motion until fully absorbed. Wash hands post-application.

Forgotten Home Apothecary

Pineapple
Painkilling Extract

Bromelain, an enzyme derived from pineapple, is known for its pain-relieving properties. It has anti-inflammatory and analgesic effects, making it a natural choice for managing pain.

INGREDIENTS AND MATERIALS:

- Fresh pineapple, including the stem
- Juicer
- Cheesecloth

NOTES:

If you prefer a topical application, you can also use the extract as a poultice on the affected area.

If you're allergic to pineapple or bromelain, do not use this extract.

Avoid consuming large quantities as it may cause digestive discomfort in some individuals.

Consult a healthcare professional before using bromelain if you are pregnant, nursing, or taking medications, as it can interact with certain drugs.

INSTRUCTIONS:

1 | **Preparation:** Begin by selecting a fresh pineapple, including the stem. Cut the pineapple into small chunks. remove and discard any damaged, soft, or discolored pieces of the pineapple. These signs indicate rotting and can affect the quality of the bromelain.
2 | **Juicing:** Run all the pineapple chunks, including the stem, through a juicer to extract the juice. This method ensures you get the most concentrated form of bromelain.
3 | **Straining:** After juicing, pour the pineapple juice through a cheesecloth or a fine mesh strainer to remove any remaining pulp. This step will give you a clear and pure extract.
4 | **Store:** You can freeze the extract in ice cube trays for longer storage. Storing your fresh pineapple bromelain extract properly is crucial to retain its enzymatic activity. Maintain a temperature that is below -4 degrees Celsius (24.8 degrees Fahrenheit). This temperature is essential to preserve the enzymatic activity of the bromelain.

You can also create a pineapple bromelain tincture with vodka by simply mixing the fresh pineapple pieces with high-proof vodka (100-proof) in a 1:2 ratio (1 part pineapple to 2 parts vodka). Allow this mixture to infuse in a sealed container for 4-6 weeks, shaking it periodically. Strain and store the tincture in an amber glass bottle for easy dosing. Take 1-2 droppers (approximately 1-2 ml) under the tongue or in water up to three times a day for pain relief.

DOSAGE:

For pain relief, consume 1-2 tablespoons of the pineapple bromelain extract on an empty stomach up to three times a day.

Forgotten Home Apothecary

Backyard Calming Pills

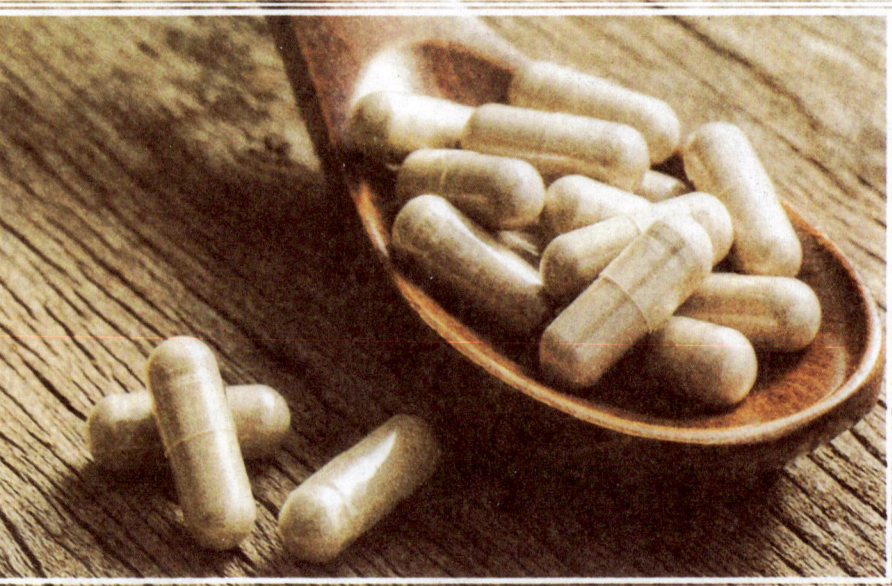

These "Backyard Calming Pills" are crafted using mugwort (*Artemisia vulgaris*), an herb traditionally used for its calming properties and to help alleviate occasional discomfort. This simple recipe provides a natural way to support relaxation and soothe mild pain.

INGREDIENTS:

- 1/2 cup of dried mugwort (*Artemisia vulgaris*)
- Honey or glycerin (for binding)
- Empty capsules (size 00 recommended)

NOTES:

Always consult with a healthcare provider before starting any new herbal regimen, especially if you are pregnant, nursing, or taking other medications.

Be aware of potential allergies to mugwort. Do not exceed the recommended dosage to avoid potential side effects. Keep out of reach of children.

INSTRUCTIONS:

1 | **Prepare Mugwort:** Using a mortar and pestle or a coffee grinder, finely grind the dried mugwort into a fine powder. Using 1/2 cup of dried mugwort, you should be able to make approximately 50-60 capsules, depending on how firmly they are packed.
2 | **Mix and Bind:** In a bowl, add a small amount of honey or glycerin to the mugwort powder. Mix thoroughly to create a slightly sticky consistency. This will help the powder adhere together when forming the pills.
3 | **Form Pills:** Using a small spoon, fill each empty capsule with the mugwort mixture, packing it firmly but not overfilling. Alternatively, you can form small pea-sized balls with the mixture if you prefer not to use capsules. Using 1/2 cup of dried mugwort, you should be able to make approximately 50-60 capsules, depending on how firmly they are packed.
4 | **Store:** Store the filled capsules or formed pills in an airtight container in a cool, dark place. They can be kept for up to 6 months.

DOSAGE:

Take 1-2 capsules or pills as needed for calming mild pain. Start with a lower dose to assess your body's response.

Magnesium Rub
for Leg Cramps

Magnesium is an essential electrolyte in the body, responsible for muscle relaxation and preventing cramps. It's lost through sweat and urination, along with other vital minerals like sodium, potassium, and iron.

Many people don't get enough magnesium in their diets, and factors like medication use and certain medical conditions can exacerbate deficiencies. One of the best ways to relieve these symptoms is to supplement with magnesium. But if some of the symptoms you're experiencing are muscle-related, such as soreness, cramping, restless legs, and pain, making a magnesium muscle rub can help.

INGREDIENTS:

- ¼ cup magnesium flakes
- ¼ cup warm distilled water
- 10 drops of lavender essential oil
- 1 tablespoon of coconut oil

NOTES:

Avoid applying the spray to broken or irritated skin.

If you have allergies or skin sensitivities, perform a patch test before using the spray more extensively.

If you're pregnant or nursing, consult a healthcare professional before using this remedy.

INSTRUCTIONS:

1 | **Prepare Magnesium Spray:** Begin by mixing ¼ cup of magnesium flakes and ¼ cup of warm distilled water in a clean bowl. Stir well until the magnesium flakes are fully dissolved.

2 | **Add Essential Oils:** Add 10 drops of Lavender essential oil to the magnesium spray. Lavender's calming properties will enhance the spray's effectiveness. Feel free to experiment with different essential oils to customize the scent to your liking.

3 | **Include Coconut Oil:** To make the rub more spreadable, include 1 tablespoon of coconut oil. Mix everything thoroughly to ensure the oils are well combined.

4 | **Transfer to Spray Bottle:** Carefully pour the magnesium rub mixture into a spray bottle or dropper bottle. Make sure the bottle is clean and dry before transferring the mixture. Label.

DOSAGE:

Spray a small amount or apply a few drops of the magnesium rub directly onto the area of your leg affected by cramps. Gently massage it into the skin. Use as needed when you have leg or foot cramps.

Fermented Red Clover
(Can Help You Rebuild Bone Mass)

Red clover (*Trifolium pratense*), an herbal gem, is believed to be beneficial for bone health due to its rich content of isoflavones and phytoestrogens. These natural compounds may support the rebuilding of bone mass by assisting with bone density and hormonal balance.

INGREDIENTS:

- ¼ cup dried red clover blossoms (*Trifolium pratense*)
- A little less than 1 quart (32 fl oz) purified water (need 24 oz)
- ¼ cup sugar
- ¼ cup organic red clover honey (optional, for flavor)

NOTES:

If you have a history of hormone-related conditions, such as estrogen-sensitive cancers (*e.g.*, breast, ovarian, uterine), endometriosis, or uterine fibroids, please consult with a healthcare provider before using red clover. Please consult with your doctor if you are pregnant or breastfeeding.

INSTRUCTIONS:

1 | **Prepare the Glass Jar:** Begin by sterilizing a quart-sized glass jar and its lid to ensure cleanliness.

2 | **Add Red Clover Blossoms:** Add ¼ cup of dried red clover blossoms (*Trifolium pratense*) to the sterilized jar.

3 | **Water Infusion:** Pour 24 fl. oz of room temperature purified water over the red clover blossoms in the jar. Make sure the water is not too cold or hot, as extreme temperatures can affect the fermentation process.

4 | **Sweeten with Sugar:** Add ¼ cup of sugar to the jar and stir gently to dissolve. Use a glass jar and bottle for fermentation to avoid any chemical reactions with plastic containers.

5 | **Optional Honey:** For enhanced flavor and sweetness, you can also add ¼ cup of organic red clover honey (optional but recommended) at this stage.

6 | **Partially Cover and Begin Fermentation:** Cover the jar with its sterilized lid, leaving a small gap for gas to escape (or use a fermentation jar).

7 | **Extended Fermentation:** Place the jar in a cool, dark place, away from direct sunlight, and at room temperature for an extended fermentation period of 5-7 days. This longer fermentation time allows for a more potent infusion.

8 | **Strain and Store:** After the extended fermentation period, strain the liquid into a clean glass bottle, discarding the Red Clover blossoms. Seal the bottle and store it in the refrigerator. It's ready to use after about one week of fermentation.

DOSAGE:

Consume 1-2 tablespoons of fermented red clover daily. You can dilute it with water or add it to your favorite beverage or salad dressing.

Dandelion Salve
for Sore Muscles and Joints

This healing dandelion salve is specifically formulated to soothe sore joints and provide relief. Dandelion's potent anti-inflammatory properties, courtesy of flavonoids and polyphenols, can help alleviate joint pain and stiffness by reducing inflammation. Additionally, this herb is a nutritional powerhouse rich in vitamins (A, C, and K) and minerals like calcium and potassium, supporting joint health and tissue repair. Dandelion's diuretic effects assist in eliminating excess fluids and toxins, providing relief for swollen joints. Furthermore, its antioxidants, including beta-carotene and polyphenols, combat harmful free radicals, safeguarding joint tissues from damage and pain.

INGREDIENTS:

- ½ cup dried dandelion flowers
- 1 cup coconut oil
- ½ cup sweet almond oil
- 1.5 oz beeswax
- 1 oz shea butter
- 10-15 drops of essential oil of your choice (*e.g.*, jasmine)

NOTES:

To enhance joint health, consider drinking dandelion tea as well. This dual approach can provide comprehensive support for your joints.

Before applying the salve, you'll want to warm up the salve to make it easier to apply. Place a small amount of salve in your hands rub it gently until it melts.

Perform a patch test before applying the salve to a larger area to ensure there are no adverse reactions.

INSTRUCTIONS:

1 | **Harvest Dandelion Flowers:** Pick 1 cup of dandelion flowers. Ensure they are free from pesticides and thoroughly wash them. Dry them prior to infusing them in oil.

2 | **Prepare Herbal Infusion:** Place the dandelion flowers in a clean, dry glass jar. Melt the coconut oil and sweet almond oil together until they are warm but not boiling. Pour the warm oils over the dandelion flowers in the jar. Seal the jar and let it sit in a sunny spot for ~2 weeks to infuse. Shake the jar gently daily.

3 | **Strain the Herbal Oil:** After the infusion period, strain the oil through a fine-mesh strainer or cheesecloth to remove the dandelion flowers.

4 | **Create the Salve:** In a double boiler, melt the beeswax and shea butter together.

5 | **Combine the Ingredients:** Once melted, add the dandelion-infused oil to the beeswax and shea butter mixture. Stir well to combine.

6 | **Add Essential Oil:** Add 10-15 drops of your chosen essential oil (*e.g.*, jasmine) for a pleasant fragrance and added benefits.

7 | **Pour into Containers:** Pour the mixture into clean, airtight containers (such as small tins or glass jars). Let the salve cool and solidify. Label.

DOSAGE:

Apply the dandelion salve to sore joints as needed. Gently massage it into the affected areas

Forgotten Home Apothecary

Watercress Broth
to Strenghten Your Joints and Bones

Watercress, a small leaf with a big taste, is traditionally known to support bone health and reduce inflammation in the joints. One cup of watercress contains 85 micrograms of vitamin K, which represents 106% of the recommended daily dose. Vitamin K aids the absorption of calcium in the body and stops it from being eliminated through urine.

INGREDIENTS:

- 2 cups loosely packed watercress (*Nasturtium officinale*)
- ½ cup sliced carrots
- 3 garlic cloves, thinly sliced
- 1 white potato peeled and cut into ½-inch dice
- 1-quart (1 liter) of water
- Salt and pepper to taste
- A few slices of ginger (*Zingiber officinale*) for extra flavor and vitamins

NOTES:

If you have any allergies or sensitivities to the ingredients used in this recipe, replace those items.

If you have a history of kidney stones or kidney issues, be cautious with watercress as it contains oxalates, which can contribute to kidney stone formation. Limit your intake or consult a healthcare provider.

INSTRUCTIONS:

1 | **Prepare the Watercress:** Begin by washing and thoroughly cleaning the watercress to remove any dirt or impurities. If you're preparing watercress for a salad, you may want to trim off the stems. For this soup, however, include the stems. Drain and set it aside.

2 | **Assemble the Ingredients:** Gather and prepare the ingredients. In a large pot, combine the water, sliced carrots, thinly sliced garlic, and diced white potato.

3 | **Add Ginger:** Optionally, add a few slices of ginger to enhance the flavor and provide additional vitamins.

4 | **Boil:** Bring the mixture to a boil over medium-high heat. Once it starts boiling, reduce the heat to a simmer, cover, and let it cook for about 20-25 minutes until the vegetables are tender.

5 | **Add the Watercress:** Once the other vegetables are tender, add the 2 cups of watercress to the pot. Continue to simmer until the watercress wilts, which should take an additional 5-7 minutes.

6 | **Season:** Season the broth with salt and pepper to taste.

7 | **Blend:** Remove the pot from heat and let it cool slightly. You can either eat it as it is or blend it together for a smoother texture (my preference). Using a blender or an immersion blender, carefully puree the mixture until it becomes a smooth and creamy soup.

8 | **Serve:** For an extra nutritional boost, add a squeeze of fresh lemon juice or a drizzle of olive oil before serving.

9 | **Store:** This broth can be stored in the refrigerator for a few days, so you can prepare a batch and enjoy it throughout the week.

DOSAGE:

Consume a cup of this watercress soup daily to help strengthen your joints and bones.

Bone-Strenghtening
Juice

Creating a bone-strengthening juice with plant-based ingredients rich in calcium can naturally support bone health. Kale provides calcium and vitamin K, which are crucial for bone health, while spinach offers additional calcium and vital minerals. Oranges boost vitamin C, aiding calcium absorption and adding a mild flavor to the juice. Celery contributes calcium and anti-inflammatory properties, and apples add natural sweetness and fiber. Chia seeds and sesame seeds are rich sources of calcium, omega-3 fatty acids, and other essential minerals.

INGREDIENTS:

- 1 cup kale
- 1 cup spinach
- 1 orange, peeled
- 1 small cucumber
- 2 celery stalks
- 1 apple
- 1 tablespoon chia seeds
- 1 teaspoon ground sesame seeds

NOTES:

While plant-sourced calcium may offer benefits, it should not be seen as a treatment or cure for medical conditions but rather as a complement to a balanced diet and healthy lifestyle. This juice provides various nutrients traditionally known to support bone health. Regular consumption of a balanced diet with adequate physical activity is essential for maintaining healthy bones. Always discuss dietary changes with a healthcare provider, especially if you have pre-existing health conditions or dietary concerns.

INSTRUCTIONS:

1 | **Prepare Ingredients:** Wash all the vegetables and fruits thoroughly. Roughly chop the kale, spinach, cucumber, celery, and apple into chunks that will easily blend.
2 | **Juicing:** Add the kale, spinach, orange, cucumber, celery, and apple to your juicer. Process these ingredients until smooth. If the juice is too thick, adjust the consistency by adding a little water or ice to blend further or thin it out.
3 | **Add Seeds:** After juicing, stir in the chia seeds and ground sesame seeds into the juice. Let it sit for a few minutes to allow the chia seeds to swell and thicken the juice slightly.
4 | **Serve:** Pour the juice into a glass and enjoy immediately. For an extra nutritional boost, add a squeeze of fresh lemon juice or a drizzle of olive oil before serving.
5 | **Store:** This broth can be stored in the refrigerator for a few days, so you can prepare a batch and enjoy it throughout the week.

Variations: You can add fresh herbs like parsley or mint for additional flavor and nutrients. Nettle leaf is a great addition if you have access. Using bok choy and mustard greens instead of kale and spinach can help minimize the dietary intake of oxalates, which may enhance the bioavailability of calcium in the juice. This adjustment is particularly beneficial for individuals concerned with oxalate intake due to specific health issues like kidney stones.

DOSAGE:

Consume one glass of this bone-strengthening juice daily to support bone health.

Forgotten Home Apothecary

Cabbage "Socks"
for Inflammation and Joint Pain

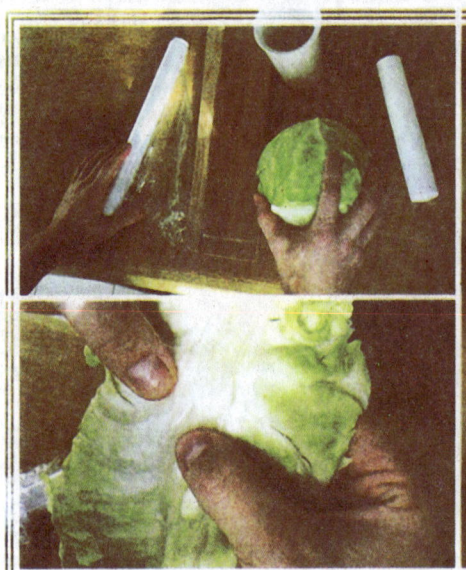

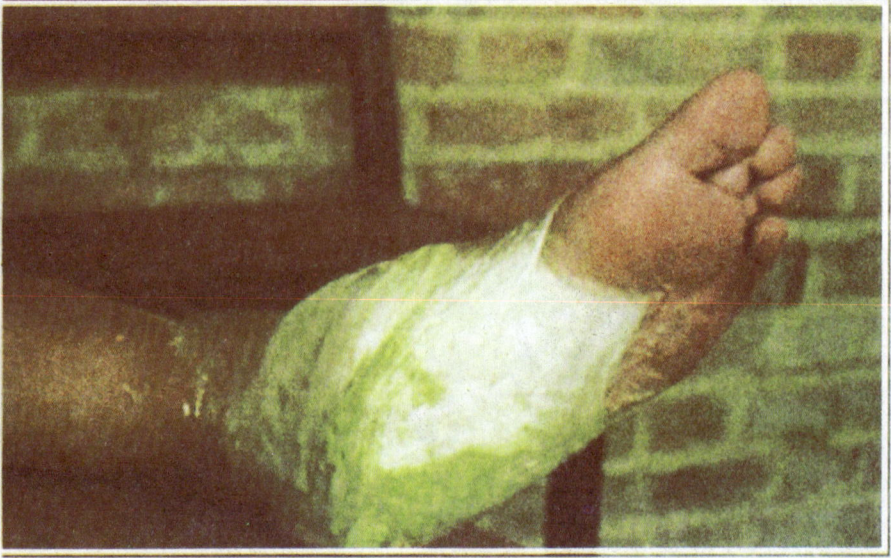

Cabbage has been used for centuries in traditional herbal medicine for its anti-inflammatory properties. It contains various beneficial compounds, including antioxidants and sulfur-containing compounds like glucosinolates. When used externally, cabbage leaves are thought to help reduce inflammation and alleviate joint pain.

INGREDIENTS AND MATERIALS:

- Fresh cabbage leaves
- Plastic wrap or bandage
- Clean cloth or gauze

NOTES:

If you have a known allergy to cabbage or any related vegetables in the Brassica family, refrain from using cabbage bandages. Always perform a patch test by applying a small piece of cabbage leaf to your skin.

In addition to joint pain, cabbage leaves are also used to alleviate breast engorgement in lactating mothers. If you're experiencing breast engorgement, follow a similar process to apply cabbage leaves to your breasts. Ensure they cover the affected areas but avoid the nipple area.

INSTRUCTIONS:

1 | **Select and Prepare the Cabbage Leaves:** Choose fresh cabbage leaves, preferably organic, as they are free from pesticides and unwanted chemicals. Look for leaves that are pliable and not wilted. Wash the leaves under running water to remove any dirt or impurities.

2 | **Soften the Cabbage Leaves:** You can put the leaves directly on the skin, but boiling water or microwaving is often used to soften the cabbage leaves and make them more flexible for application. Fill a pot with enough water to submerge the cabbage leaves and bring it to a boil. Submerge the cabbage leaves in the boiling water for about 2-3 minutes. This blanching process makes the leaves easier to mold to the joint and may enhance their effectiveness. After blanching, remove the leaves carefully using tongs and let them cool until they reach a comfortable temperature for application. To release more of the cabbage juices, gently bruise the leaves with a rolling pin or a meat hammer.

3 | **Apply the Cabbage Bandage:** Lay the cabbage leaves on the affected joint area, such as the knee, ankle, or elbow. Ensure the leaves cover the joint and the surrounding area where you're experiencing pain. Place the leaves in such a way that they overlap slightly for better coverage. To secure the cabbage leaves in place, cover them with plastic wrap or a bandage. This will help keep them in contact with the skin. Avoid wrapping it too tightly to allow for proper circulation and comfort.

DOSAGE:

Apply the cabbage bandage for at least an hour, depending on your preference and the level of pain you're experiencing. You can repeat this treatment once a day or as needed for pain relief. The cabbage poultice can be left on overnight for extended relief.

Forgotten Home Apothecary

Pine Needle Infused Oil
for Rheumatism and Arthritis Pain

Pine needles (*Pinus* spp.) are well-known for their traditional uses. They contain compounds like turpentines and pinenes, which have anti-inflammatory and analgesic effects, making them beneficial for rheumatism and arthritis. When considering the use of pine for medicinal purposes, it's important to choose the right species. Not all pine species are suitable for herbal use, and some may be toxic. Here are a few common pine species that are typically considered safe for herbal and medicinal applications: Eastern white pine (*Pinus strobus*), Scots pine (*Pinus sylvestris*), and Ponderosa pine (*Pinus ponderosa*).

INGREDIENTS:

- 1 cup fresh pine needles (*Pinus* spp.)
- 1 cup carrier oil (such as olive oil or coconut oil)

NOTES:

Perform a patch test before using to check for any allergic reactions. If irritation occurs, discontinue use.

While pine needles do have medicinal properties and can be used topically, ingesting them can be risky.

Pine needles contain compounds like turpentines and pinenes, which, when consumed in large quantities, may irritate the digestive system and mucous membranes, leading to stomach discomfort, nausea, and potential poisoning.

INSTRUCTIONS:

1. **Harvest the Pine Needles:** Gather fresh pine needles. Ensure they are clean and free of debris.
2. **Prepare the Pine Needles:** Wash the pine needles thoroughly and pat them dry with a clean cloth.
3. **Crush the Pine Needles:** Use a mortar and pestle to gently crush the pine needles. This helps release the essential oils and compounds.
4. **Infusion Process:** In a glass jar, add the crushed pine needles. Pour the carrier oil over the pine needles, ensuring they are fully submerged. Seal the jar tightly.
5. **Sunlight Infusion Method:** Place the jar in a sunny windowsill or outdoors in a place where it will receive direct sunlight for about 2-4 weeks. This will allow the oil to infuse with the pine needles.
6. **Shake Daily:** Shake the jar gently every day to ensure thorough infusion.
7. **Strain the Oil:** After the infusion period, strain the oil through a fine mesh strainer or cheesecloth into a clean glass container. Label.
8. **Storage:** Store the pine needle infused oil in a cool, dark place in an airtight container.

DOSAGE:

For external use, apply a small amount of the oil to the affected area and massage gently. Use as needed.

Willow Bark Bath Salts
for Inflammation

Named after the *Salix* genus, willow bark contains salicin, a natural precursor to aspirin, which is traditionally known for its analgesic and anti-inflammatory properties. When used in bath salts, salicin eases muscle tension and joint discomfort as it permeates the skin during a relaxing soak. Additionally, Epsom salts, rich in magnesium and sulfate, complement these benefits. Magnesium relaxes muscles, and sulfate supports detoxification processes, further enhancing relief during a warm bath.

INGREDIENTS:

- 1 cup Epsom salt (Magnesium sulfate)
- ½ cup sea salt (Sodium chloride)
- ¼ cup dried and ground willow bark (*Salix alba*)
- 10-15 drops of your favorite essential oil (optional, for fragrance)

NOTES:

If you are allergic to aspirin or have a known sensitivity to salicylates, it's advisable to avoid using willow bark bath salts. Salicin is a natural form of salicylate and may cause adverse reactions such as skin rashes. Consult with a healthcare professional if you are pregnant, nursing, or have any medical conditions before using this product.

INSTRUCTIONS:

1 | **Prepare the Willow Bark:** Begin by finely grinding the dried willow bark into a powder. You can use a coffee grinder or mortar and pestle for this. If you can't find dried willow bark, you may purchase willow bark extract and add a few drops to the bath salts mixture.

2 | **Mix the Salts:** In a mixing bowl, combine the Epsom salt, sea salt, and the ground willow bark. Make sure to blend them thoroughly to distribute the willow bark evenly throughout the mixture.

3 | **Add Essential Oils:** If you want to add a pleasant fragrance to your bath salts, add 10-15 drops of your favorite essential oil. Lavender or chamomile essential oil complements the natural scent of willow bark. Mix the essential oil into the salts until well distributed. You can customize the fragrance of your bath salts by using different essential oils. Just ensure they are safe for use on the skin.

4 | **Store Your Bath Salts:** Transfer the mixture into a sealed glass jar to preserve its freshness and scent. When ready to indulge in a soothing bath, pour the salt mixture into a muslin bag and hang it below the faucet or let it float in your bath.

DOSAGE:

For a standard bath, add approximately ¼ to ½ cup of these bath salts to your warm bathwater. Soak for at least 20-30 minutes to enjoy the soothing effects.

Patches
with Nature's "Ibuprofen"

Cayenne pepper (*Capsicum annuum*) and turmeric (*Curcuma longa*) are both renowned for their anti-inflammatory properties. When combined with olive oil and beeswax, they create a soothing patch that can help alleviate various types of pain, including muscle soreness and joint pain.

INGREDIENTS AND MATERIALS:

- 3 tablespoons of cayenne powder
- 3 tablespoons of turmeric
- ½ cup of olive oil
- ½ cup of beeswax pellets
- Gauze pads
- Waterproof paper tape
- Glass Mason jars

NOTES:

Avoid contact with eyes and mucous membranes. Avoid using on broken or irritated skin. Discontinue use if any adverse reactions occur. Wash hands thoroughly after handling the patches.

Keep out of reach of children and pets.

Consult with a healthcare professional before use, especially if pregnant, nursing, or taking medication.

INSTRUCTIONS:

1 | **Mix the Ingredients:** Mix the cayenne powder and turmeric with ½ cup of olive oil in a medium-sized bowl until evenly distributed.

2 | **Heat the Mixture:** Pour the mixed contents into a small- or medium-sized pot. Warm over medium heat for a few minutes, but do not let it come to a boil. Pour ½ cup of beeswax pellets into the mixture on the stove and stir until melted evenly. Avoid fumes coming into contact with eyes. You may use a lid on the pot, but keep an eye on it to prevent burning.

3 | **Dip the Gauze Pads:** Take your gauze pads and dip them fully into the warm mixture, then place them into your glass Mason jar. They won't stick together once cooled. You may cool them first on wax paper if needed.

4 | **Cool:** Place the Mason jar (or wax paper) with the gauze pads in the refrigerator to cool for at least 30 minutes before use. The patches should be cool to the touch when ready to use.

5 | **Store:** Always store the patches in the refrigerator. You may also save the remaining mixture by pouring it into another glass Mason jar and storing it in the refrigerator. This can be used as a salve/cream by spooning the mixture onto a bandage or rubbing it into your skin.

6 | **Apply and Use:** Once cooled, place a patch on the affected areas. Cover the patch with either sports tape, or with a large bandage or similar. Leave the patch on for 1-2 hours, or overnight for prolonged relief.

DOSAGE:

Apply the patch to the affected area as needed for pain relief.

Forgotten Home Apothecary

Soothing Herbal Blend
for Fibromyalgia Pain

Fibromyalgia is a chronic condition characterized by widespread pain, tenderness, and a range of other symptoms. This herbal remedy incorporates herbs traditionally known for their supportive properties in managing discomfort, inflammation, and promoting relaxation.

Turmeric has anti-inflammatory properties to help reduce the pain and discomfort associated with fibromyalgia. Ginger has anti-inflammatory and analgesic properties, which can provide relief from pain. White willow bark contains salicin, a compound similar to aspirin, which can help with pain management. Chamomile has calming properties, which can help ease the psychological aspects of fibromyalgia.

INGREDIENTS:

- 1 tablespoon of dried turmeric (*Curcuma longa*)
- 1 tablespoon of dried ginger (*Zingiber officinale*)
- 1 tablespoon of dried white willow bark (*Salix alba*) or 2 teaspoons if using powdered form
- 1 tablespoon of dried chamomile (*Matricaria chamomilla*) flowers
- 4 cups of water

NOTES:

Incorporating regular exercise, stress management techniques, and maintaining a balanced diet complements herbal treatments and contributes to an improved quality of life for individuals with fibromyalgia. Consult with a healthcare professional for a comprehensive fibromyalgia management plan tailored to your needs.

INSTRUCTIONS:

1. **Mix the Herbs:** Combine the selected herbs, creating the base for your herbal blend. Add all of the gathered herbs into a pot or saucepan.
2. **Add Water:** Pour 4 cups of water into the pot with the herbs to create the herbal decoction. Place the pot on the stove, and turn the heat to medium-high.
3. **Bring to a Boil:** As the mixture heats, wait until it comes to a gentle boil.
4. **Simmer and Extract:** Once the mixture reaches a boil, reduce the heat to low, and let it simmer for 15-20 minutes. This simmering process will help extract the medicinal compounds from the herbs.
5. **Strain the Herbal Blend:** Remove the pot from the heat. Using a fine-mesh strainer or cheesecloth, strain the liquid into a cup or glass jar. This is your herbal decoction.
6. **Enjoy Your Herbal Blend:** Your soothing herbal decoction blend for fibromyalgia pain is ready to be consumed.

DOSAGE:

Drink 1 cup of this herbal blend two times a day, preferably in the morning and before bedtime. If you prefer a tincture, simply infuse these herbs into an 80-proof alcohol, such as vodka (see Mobility Maintenance Tincture for Arthritis in the Herbal Support for Musculoskeletal Health chapter).

HERBAL SUPPORT
for a Healthy Immune System

A strong immune system is crucial for maintaining overall health. It acts as your body's defense mechanism against infections, diseases, and foreign invaders. The immune system is composed of various components, including white blood cells, antibodies, and lymphoid tissues, all working in harmony to identify and neutralize threats.

Tips and Herbal Remedies to Boost Your Immune System:

HEALTHY DIET:

A well-balanced diet rich in fruits, vegetables, lean proteins, and whole grains provides essential vitamins and minerals necessary for immune function. Key nutrients include vitamin C (found in citrus fruits), vitamin D (from sunlight and fortified foods), and zinc (in nuts and seeds).

ADEQUATE HYDRATION:

Staying well-hydrated supports the body's natural detoxification processes and helps the immune system function optimally. Aim for at least 8 cups (64 oz) of water daily.

REGULAR EXERCISE:

Physical activity promotes good circulation, which helps immune cells move through the body more effectively. Aim for 150 minutes of moderate-intensity exercise per week.

QUALITY SLEEP:

Quality sleep is essential for immune health. Aim for 7-9 hours of restful sleep per night to allow your body to repair and regenerate.

AVOID SMOKING AND EXCESSIVE ALCOHOL:

Both smoking and excessive alcohol consumption can weaken the immune system.

HAND HYGIENE:

Good hygiene practices, such as regular handwashing and avoiding close contact with sick individuals, help prevent the spread of infections.

AVOID ANTIBIOTIC OVERUSE:

Use antibiotics only when prescribed by a healthcare professional, as overuse can weaken the immune system's ability to fight infections.

HERBAL SUPPORT

Echinacea *(Echinacea purpurea)*
Echinacea is believed to stimulate the immune system and may help reduce the severity and duration of cold symptoms. Use as a supplement, tea, or tincture. Do not use or use with care if you have an autoimmune condition.

Astragalus *(Astragalus membranaceus)*
Astragalus is an adaptogen that helps enhance immune function and protect against stress. It's often used in traditional Chinese medicine and can be taken as a supplement, tea, or tincture. Do not use or use with care if you have an autoimmune condition.

Garlic *(Allium sativum)*
Garlic contains compounds that have immune-boosting properties. Include fresh garlic in your diet and/or take garlic supplements.

Ginseng *(Panax ginseng)*
Ginseng is an adaptogen that may enhance immune responses and help the body cope with stress. Use as a supplement or tincture.

Turmeric *(Curcuma longa)*
Curcumin in turmeric has anti-inflammatory and antioxidant effects that can support immune health. Incorporate turmeric into your cooking or take curcumin supplements or tinctures.

Oregano Oil *(Origanum vulgare)*
Oregano oil has antimicrobial properties and may help support immune function. It can be taken as a supplement, but use caution as it's potent.

Mushrooms
Certain mushrooms like reishi, turkey tail, cordyceps, lion's mane, shiitake, and maitake contain compounds that support immune function. They can be consumed as part of your diet or as a dual-extracted tincture.

Elderberry *(Sambucus nigra)*
Elderberry has been used traditionally to alleviate cold and flu symptoms. It's available as a syrup, extract, tincture, or supplement.

Licorice Root *(Glycyrrhiza glabra)*
Licorice root has immune-modulating and antiviral properties. Use as a supplement or herbal tea.

Immune-Boosting
Elderberry Syrup

Elderberries are rich in antioxidants and and are traditionally known for their supportive anti-viral properties during cold and flu seasons. For those seeking variation, there's ample room for creativity with this recipe. To enhance shelf stability, you can increase the sugar content or introduce a small amount of alcohol, like vodka or brandy. Additionally, you can explore a world of flavors by incorporating various herbs, extracts, or flavorings. For instance, brighten your syrup with lemon or citrus, or infuse it with the comforting smoothness of vanilla bean. By tailoring this recipe to your preferences, you can create a unique and delightful elixir that not only supports your immune health but also pleases your taste buds.

INGREDIENTS:

- 1 cup dried black elderberry (*Sambucus nigra*)
- 2 cups fresh spring water
- 2 cinnamon sticks
- 1 tablespoon whole cloves
- 3 slices ginger root
- ½ cup raw local honey

NOTES:

Never consume raw or unprocessed elderberries, as they can cause cyanide poisoning symptoms, including nausea, vomiting, diarrhea, and, in severe cases, respiratory distress.

Children and those with compromised health are especially susceptible to these effects.

Ensure that you accurately identify the black elderberry (*Sambucus nigra*) and avoid using potentially toxic species.

INSTRUCTIONS:

1 | **Prepare the Elderberries:** Rinse the dried black elderberries thoroughly under cold water and put them in a medium-sized pot.

2 | **Boil the Berries:** Add the 2 cups of fresh spring water to the pot with the elderberries. Bring the mixture to a boil, then reduce the heat to a simmer. Allow it to simmer for about 30 minutes, until the liquid is reduced by half.

3 | **Add Spices:** Once the liquid has reduced, add the 2 cinnamon sticks, 1 tablespoon of whole cloves, and 3 slices of ginger root to the pot. Continue to simmer for an additional 20-30 minutes.

4 | **Strain the Mixture:** Remove the pot from the heat and allow it to cool for a few minutes. Then, strain the liquid through a fine-mesh strainer or cheesecloth into a clean glass container. Discard the solids.

5 | **Add Raw Honey:** After the liquid has cooled to a lukewarm temperature, add ½ cup of raw local honey. Stir until the honey is completely dissolved. You can also add a splash of lemon juice for an extra vitamin C boost.

6 | **Store:** Transfer the elderberry syrup to a glass jar with a lid. Store it in the refrigerator. Label and date your elderberry syrup for reference.

DOSAGE:

For immune support, adults can take 1 tablespoon daily, while children can take 1 teaspoon daily. If you feel like you're coming down with something or are ill, you can take the same dose every 2-3 hours.

Forgotten Home Apothecary

Turmeric Golden Milk
(Anti-Inflammatory)

Golden milk, also known as "Haldi Doodh" in India, is a traditional herbal remedy used for its anti-inflammatory properties. The key ingredient in this recipe is turmeric, scientifically known as *Curcuma longa*. Turmeric contains an active compound called curcumin, which has been widely-studied for its anti-inflammatory effects.

INGREDIENTS:

- 1 cup whole milk
- ½ teaspoon ground turmeric (*Curcuma longa*)
- ¼ teaspoon ground black pepper
- ½ teaspoon honey (optional)
- A pinch of cinnamon (*Cinnamomum verum*) for flavor (optional)

NOTES:

People with gallbladder issues should avoid the use of turmeric. Turmeric may worsen gallstones or obstruct the bile duct.

Do not use turmeric if you have liver issues/disease as it may worsen the problem. Also, the herb may inhibit iron absorption. Thus, it should be avoided by people with iron deficiency anemia or other iron-related problems.

INSTRUCTIONS:

1 | **Warm the Milk:** Start by heating 1 cup of whole milk in a small saucepan over low heat. Do not bring it to a boil. You can substitute whole milk with almond milk, coconut milk, or any other plant-based milk if you are lactose intolerant or prefer a dairy-free option.

2 | **Add Turmeric and Black Pepper:** Add ½ teaspoon of ground turmeric and ¼ teaspoon of ground black pepper to the milk. Stir well. You may use fresh turmeric root if available. Grate a 1-inch piece and add it to the milk for a more intense flavor.

3 | **Simmer and Infuse:** Simmer the mixture for about 5 minutes, allowing the flavors to meld and the turmeric to infuse into the milk. If you prefer a thicker consistency, consider adding a touch of coconut oil or cream for a creamy texture.

4 | **Sweeten:** If you prefer a slightly sweet taste, add ½ teaspoon of honey. You can use maple syrup, agave nectar, or a sweetener of your choice. Adjust the sweetness level to suit your taste. Some people prefer it without any sweetener.

5 | **Optional Spices:** If desired, sprinkle a pinch of cinnamon for added flavor and aroma. Nutmeg, vanilla, or cardamom can be used as alternatives to cinnamon for a different flavor profile. Experiment with various spices to find your favorite combination.

6 | **Strain:** Strain the golden milk into a cup to remove any sediment. Be cautious with staining, as turmeric can leave yellow marks on surfaces and clothing.

DOSAGE:

Drink this soothing golden milk once a day, preferably before bedtime, to help with inflammation.

Forgotten Home Apothecary

"Penicillin" Soup

"Penicillin" soup derives its name from the comparison of its therapeutic properties to those of penicillin, a widely used antibiotic. However, instead of relying on pharmaceuticals, this soup harnesses the natural antibacterial properties of garlic. Garlic contains allicin, a compound known for its antimicrobial effects. This herb has been valued for centuries for its ability to support immune function. In this soup, garlic's beneficial qualities are combined with a variety of vegetables to create a nourishing dish that is not only flavorful but also supportive of overall health.

INGREDIENTS:

- 50 cloves of garlic (*Allium sativum*), peeled and minced
- 4 tablespoons olive oil
- 6 cups vegetable/chicken broth
- 1 cup carrots, diced
- 1 cup celery, diced
- 1 cup onion, diced
- 1 teaspoon dried thyme (*Thymus vulgaris*)
- Salt and pepper to taste
- Fresh parsley for garnish

NOTES:

Garlic may interact with certain medications, particularly blood-thinning drugs.

Consult with your healthcare provider if you have any concerns or medical conditions.

INSTRUCTIONS:

1. **Prepare Ingredients:** Peel and mince the 50 cloves of garlic. Dice the carrots, celery, and onion.
2. **Sauté Garlic:** Heat olive oil in a large pot over medium heat. Add minced garlic and sauté for 1-2 minutes until fragrant, being careful not to burn it.
3. **Add Vegetables:** Add diced carrots, celery, and onion to the pot. Cook for another 5 minutes until vegetables are slightly softened.
4. **Add Broth and Seasonings:** Pour in the vegetable broth. Stir in dried thyme, salt, and pepper to taste.
5. **Simmer Soup:** Bring the soup to a boil, then reduce heat to low and let it simmer for 15-20 minutes until the vegetables are tender and the flavors meld together.
6. **Serve:** Ladle the garlic soup into bowls. Garnish with fresh parsley for added flavor and presentation. This soup freezes well, so you can make a large batch and store it for later use.

DOSAGE:

Enjoy a bowl of garlic soup whenever you feel like supporting your immune system or seeking comfort during the cold or flu season.

Echinacea and Astragalus Tincture
for a Strong Immune System

Echinacea and astragalus are two well-regarded herbs traditionally known for their immune-supporting properties. Echinacea is commonly used to support the body's defenses against infections and may help reduce the severity and duration of colds and respiratory ailments. Astragalus is valued for its ability to enhance the immune system, support adaptability to stressors, and promote long-term wellness. Together, echinacea's immediate immune support and astragalus' long-term benefits create a synergistic combination that can help fortify the immune system.

INGREDIENTS:

- 1-part dried echinacea root (*Echinacea purpurea*)
- 1-part dried astragalus root (*Astragalus membranaceus*)
- 80 proof (40% alcohol by volume) vodka or grain alcohol

NOTES:

Echinacea and astragalus are immune-stimulating herbs, which may not be suitable for individuals with autoimmune conditions such as rheumatoid arthritis, lupus, or multiple sclerosis.

If you have an autoimmune condition, consult a healthcare practitioner before using these herbs. Alternative herbs that are generally considered more immune-balancing and less stimulating include: elderberry and turkey tail mushroom.

INSTRUCTIONS:

1 | **Preparation:** Start by measuring your herbs in parts. For example, if you have 1 ounce of echinacea root, you should also have 1 ounce of astragalus root.
2 | **Combining Herbs:** Place the dried echinacea and astragalus roots in a glass jar. Ensure the herbs are finely chopped or crushed for maximum extraction. Fill the jar ⅓rd full with your herbs.
3 | **Alcohol and Herbs:** Pour enough alcohol into the jar to completely cover the herbs. Seal the jar with a tight-fitting lid.
4 | **Shake and Store:** Shake the jar gently to make sure the herbs are well-soaked. Store it in a cool, dark place for about 6-8 weeks. Shake the jar daily to agitate the mixture.
5 | **Strain:** After the maceration period, strain the tincture through a cheesecloth into a clean container.
6 | **Bottling:** Use a dark, glass container to store the tincture, as this protects it from light, which can degrade its potency.
7 | **Store:** Store your tincture in a cool, dark place to maintain its effectiveness. Label with the name of the tincture and the date it was made.

DOSAGE:

Take 1-2 ml (approximately 20-40 drops) of the tincture in a glass of water 2-3 times a day when needed for immune support.

Antiviral
Herbal Honey

Garlic, lemon, and honey have been used for centuries for their potential immune-boosting properties. Garlic contains allicin, which is believed to have antimicrobial and immune-enhancing effects. Lemons are a rich source of vitamin C and antioxidants, and honey has natural antioxidants and soothing properties. Ginger contains compounds with anti-inflammatory properties, which can help reduce inflammation throughout the body. This is particularly beneficial when looking to support overall health and the immune system. It also adds a pleasant, warm, and slightly spicy flavor to the elixir.

INGREDIENTS:

- 5-6 cloves of fresh garlic (*Allium sativum*)
- 1 lemon
- 1 cup of raw honey
- 1 small piece of fresh ginger (*Zingiber officinale*)

NOTES:

Do not give honey or honey-based elixirs to infants under 1 year of age due to the risk of botulism.

If you have allergies to garlic, lemon, ginger, or honey, consult a healthcare professional before using this elixir.

You can add a teaspoon of this elixir to warm water or herbal tea for a soothing drink.

INSTRUCTIONS:

1 | **Prepare the Garlic:** Peel and finely chop the garlic cloves.
2 | **Prepare the Lemon:** Wash the lemon thoroughly and cut it into slices.
3 | **Prepare the Ginger:** Peel and finely chop the small piece of ginger.
4 | **Mix the Ingredients:** In a clean glass jar, combine the chopped garlic, lemon slices, and ginger.
5 | **Add Honey:** Pour the raw honey over the garlic, lemon, and ginger mixture.
6 | **Infusion time:** Stir the mixture thoroughly until all ingredients are well coated with honey. Seal the glass jar with a lid and let the mixture infuse for at least 3-4 days. Allowing the elixir to infuse for a longer time will intensify the flavors and potential health benefits. It can be left at room temperature during this time.
7 | **Strain:** After the infusion period, strain the elixir to separate the liquid from the garlic, lemon, and ginger pieces. Store the liquid in a clean, airtight container.

DOSAGE:

Take 1-2 teaspoons of the elixir daily, especially during the cold and flu season, to support your immune system.

Immunity
Mushroom Blend

This Immunity mushroom blend incorporates three key mushrooms, each renowned for their immune-boosting properties. Reishi mushrooms are antiviral and contain compounds that stimulate white blood cell production and reduce oxidative stress. Shiitake mushrooms are rich in lentinan and beta-glucans, enhancing immune response and providing essential nutrients. Maitake mushrooms offer immune-modulating beta-glucans and antioxidants that combat inflammation and support immune function. This blend combines these powerful mushroom varieties to create a potent synergy of immune-enhancing compounds, making it a valuable addition to your daily wellness routine.

INGREDIENTS:

- 2 tablespoons of dried reishi mushrooms (*Ganoderma lucidum*)
- 2 tablespoons of dried shiitake mushrooms (*Lentinula edodes*)
- 2 tablespoons of dried maitake mushrooms (*Grifola frondosa*)

NOTES:

If you are pregnant, nursing, or have any medical conditions, consult with a healthcare provider before using this blend.

Discontinue use and seek medical advice if you experience any adverse reactions.

To add a zesty twist and extra warmth to your immune-boosting blend, include chili flakes.

INSTRUCTIONS:

1 | **Prepare the Mushrooms:** Start by gathering your dried reishi, shiitake, and maitake mushrooms. Ensure they are clean and free from any debris. If you purchase the mushrooms, it's essential to purchase high-quality, organic dried mushrooms for the best result.

2 | **Grinding the Mushrooms:** Grind each type of mushroom individually into a fine powder using a clean coffee grinder. Make sure each type is very finely ground.

3 | **Combine the Mushroom Powders:** In a bowl, combine the powdered reishi, shiitake, and maitake mushrooms. Mix them thoroughly to create your immunity mushroom blend.

4 | **Store the Blend:** Transfer the blend to an airtight container, preferably a glass jar, and store it in a cool, dark place.

5 | **Serve:** You can incorporate this mushroom blend into smoothies, soups, coffee, or sprinkle it on your meals for an added immune boost.

DOSAGE:

Take ½ to 1 teaspoon of the immunity mushroom blend daily, mixed into your favorite beverage or food.

Immuni-Tea

This recipe explores the synergy of aloe vera, pine needles, mint, and rosemary, all of which have unique properties that contribute to a healthy immune system.

Aloe vera, though optional, offers soothing and anti-inflammatory qualities, promoting overall well-being. Fresh or dried pine needles provide a rich source of vitamin C, a vital nutrient known for its immune-boosting potential. Mint adds a refreshing element to the blend while contributing antimicrobial and digestive benefits. Rosemary, with its robust flavor, brings antioxidants and anti-inflammatory properties to the mix, enhancing the tea's immune-supporting properties. By combining these herbs in this Immuni-Tea, we create a flavorful elixir that empowers your immune system to face daily challenges with vitality and strength.

INGREDIENTS:

- 1 tablespoon of aloe vera gel (optional)
- 1 tablespoon of fresh pine needles (*Pinus* spp.) or 1 teaspoon of dried pine needles
- 1 tablespoon of fresh Mint (*Mentha* spp.) or 1 teaspoon of dried mint
- 1 tablespoon of fresh rosemary (*Rosmarinus officinalis*) or 1 teaspoon of dried rosemary leaves

NOTES:

The choice of pine species can vary, and it's important to ensure that you select a pine species that is safe and suitable for consumption.

While many pine species are edible and have vitamin C content, the most used pine species for culinary and herbal purposes are Eastern white pine (*Pinus strobus*) and Scots pine (*Pinus sylvestris*).

INSTRUCTIONS:

1 | **Prepare Your Herbs:** If using fresh pine needles, mint, and rosemary, finely chop or crush them to release their aromatic compounds. If using dried herbs, use a mortar and pestle to slightly crush them to enhance their flavor.* If you're foraging for pine needles, make sure they come from a tree that hasn't been treated with pesticides or other chemicals.

2 | **Boil the Water:** Bring 2 cups (16 ounces) of water to a boil in a pot.

3 | **Steep the Herbs:** Add the fresh or dried pine needles, mint, and rosemary to the boiling water. Reduce the heat to a simmer and let the herbs steep for about 5-7 minutes. Adjust the strength of your tea by varying the amount of dried herbs or steeping time according to your taste.

4 | **Strain the Tea:** After steeping, strain the tea to remove the herb particles, leaving you with a clear liquid.

5 | **Aloe Vera Addition (Optional):** If desired, add 1 tablespoon of aloe vera gel to the strained tea. Stir well to combine.

DOSAGE:

Consume 1-2 cups of this Immuni-Tea daily to support your immune system. It's best enjoyed warm.

Forgotten Home Apothecary

Anti-Inflammatory
Root Infusion

This herbal tea blend is a delightful combination designed to support your immune system. Turmeric, celebrated for its anti-inflammatory and antioxidant benefits, works synergistically with ginger, known for its anti-inflammatory and immune-boosting properties. Calendula contributes to the blend with its soothing and anti-inflammatory effects, enhancing overall immune support. Cinnamon not only adds delightful flavor but also brings antioxidant properties that promote a healthy immune system. Rooibos, rich in antioxidants, forms a soothing base for this harmonious herbal infusion, providing a gentle and caffeine-free option for immune well-being.

INGREDIENTS:

- 1 teaspoon ground turmeric (*Curcuma longa*)
- 1 teaspoon fresh ginger, sliced (*Zingiber officinale*)
- 1 teaspoon dried calendula petals (*Calendula officinalis*)
- 1 teaspoon dried rooibos (*Aspalathus linearis*)
- 1 cinnamon stick (or ½ teaspoon ground cinnamon
- 1 cup water

NOTES:

When using this herbal tea, be mindful of potential allergic reactions and consult a healthcare professional if pregnant, breastfeeding, or having liver or gallbladder issues.

Turmeric may cause stomach upset or worsen gallbladder issues; ginger can increase bleeding risk; and calendula should be avoided by those allergic to plants in the Asteraceae family.

INSTRUCTIONS:

1| **Boil the Water:** Begin by bringing 1 cup of water to a boil in a kettle or pot.
2| **Add the Herbs:** As the water reaches a boil, incorporate 1 teaspoon of ground turmeric, 1 teaspoon of sliced fresh ginger, 1 teaspoon of dried calendula petals, a cinnamon stick (or ½ teaspoon of ground cinnamon), and 1 teaspoon of dried rooibos into the boiling water. If you prefer a caffeinated version, consider replacing rooibos with green tea in the herbal tea recipe. This adds a gentle caffeine boost along with the antioxidant benefits of green tea. Adjust the steeping time according to your green tea preferences and enjoy the energizing twist to this immune-supportive blend.
3| **Steep:** Allow the herbal blend to steep in the boiling water for 7-10 minutes. This step extracts the beneficial compounds from the herbs.
4| **Strain:** After the steeping period, strain the tea into a cup using a fine mesh strainer or tea infuser. This helps remove the solid herb particles, leaving you with a smooth, flavorful liquid. Sweeten it with raw honey or a splash of almond milk for added flavor.

DOSAGE:

Savor 1 cup of this herbal tea daily. Adjust the frequency based on your preferences and consult with your healthcare provider if you have specific health concerns.

Forgotten Home Apothecary

Anti-Inflammatory
Golden Salve

Turmeric is a potent herb known for its anti-inflammatory properties. This golden salve combines the benefits of turmeric with the soothing properties of carrier oils and the skin-nourishing effects of beeswax. Applying the salve topically allows the skin to absorb the beneficial compounds directly. The skin, being the body's largest organ, plays a crucial role in immune defense. By promoting skin health and reducing inflammation locally, the salve indirectly supports the overall immune system.

INGREDIENTS:

- 6 teaspoons of dried turmeric powder (*Curcuma longa*)
- 8 tablespoons of organic carrier oil (olive oil or a mixture of different plant-based oils)
- 1 oz (28 g) of beeswax

NOTES:

Perform a patch test before widespread use to check for any allergic reactions.

Avoid contact with eyes, mucous membranes, and broken skin.

Consult with a healthcare professional if pregnant, nursing, or under medical supervision.

Discontinue use if irritation occurs.

INSTRUCTIONS:

1 | **Turmeric Infusion:** Combine 6 teaspoons of dried turmeric powder with 8 tablespoons of your chosen organic carrier oil in a heat-resistant bowl. Gently heat to infuse the oil with turmeric.

2 | **Strain:** Once heated, strain the turmeric-infused oil using a fine mesh sieve or cheesecloth to remove any solid particles (this step is needed for fresh grated turmeric but is usually not needed for powdered turmeric).

3 | **Melt Beeswax:** In a separate heat-resistant container, melt 1 oz of beeswax using a double boiler (preferred) or microwave.

4 | **Combine Ingredients:** Slowly add the turmeric-infused oil to the melted beeswax, stirring continuously for even incorporation.

5 | **Cooling Phase:** Remove the mixture from heat and let it cool slightly before pouring it into clean, sterilized jars or tins.

6 | **Solidification:** Allow the salve to solidify completely before sealing the containers. Label.

7 | **Proper Storage:** Store the salve in a cool, dark place to prolong its shelf life.

DOSAGE:

Apply a small amount of the golden salve topically to the affected area, massaging gently until absorbed. Repeat 2-3 times daily, or as needed for relief.

Homemade
Quinine

This recipe combines a variety of flavorful and beneficial ingredients, making it both healthful and enjoyable. Quinine, derived from the bark of the cinchona tree, has been traditionally used for its potential immune-supporting properties. The bark of the cinchona tree contains quinine alkaloids, such as quinine and cinchonidine, which are believed to have immune-boosting effects. Quinine (in larger doses) is still used for malaria treatment, often in conjunction with other medications.

INGREDIENTS:

- 4 cups filtered water
- 2 teaspoons powdered cinchona bark
- Zest of 1 orange
- Zest of 2 lemons
- 2 star anise pods
- 1 lemongrass stalk
- 2 tablespoons citric acid
- 1 teaspoon coriander powder (or 1 ¼ teaspoon coriander seeds)
- 10 drops liquid stevia
- Water/sparkling water (to mix with once the quinine mixture is ready)

NOTES:

Keep in mind that while homemade preparations may not be as standardized as pharmaceutical products, you can still make a simple quinine tonic at home. Consult with a healthcare professional before using quinine, as it has many possible (and serious) side effects. Do not use if you have myasthenia gravis.

INSTRUCTIONS:

1| **Infuse the Cinchona:** In a saucepan, combine 4 cups of filtered water with 2 teaspoons of powdered cinchona bark.
2| **Add Aromatic Zest and Spices:** Introduce the zest of 1 orange, zest of 2 lemons, 2 star anise pods, and 1 lemongrass stalk to the mixture. Sprinkle in 2 tablespoons of citric acid to elevate the tonic's tanginess.
3| **Simmer to Infuse Flavors:** Bring the mixture to a gentle boil, then reduce heat and simmer for 15-20 minutes, allowing the flavors to meld. Take it off the heat and let it cool to room temp.
4| **Aging Process:** Pour the quinine mixture into a container, preferably a glass jar with the lid securely fastened. Place it in the refrigerator for 72 hours, giving it a gentle shake a few times each day. This step allows the infusion to intensify, enhancing the overall flavor and potency of the tonic.
5| **Strain:** After the infusion period, pour the infused mixture through a cheesecloth-covered sieve, allowing the liquid to pass through while catching any remaining solids.
6| **Sweeten with Stevia:** Add 10 drops of liquid stevia to sweeten the tonic naturally.
7| **Thoroughly Mix:** Stir the concoction well to ensure all ingredients are thoroughly mixed.
8| **Serve:** For a refreshing twist, mix the quinine tonic with water or sparkling water to create a revitalizing beverage (1 part quinine to 2 parts water/sparkling water). You can keep the tonic in a sealed container in the refrigerator for up to one month.

DOSAGE:

Take 1-2 tablespoons of the homemade quinine tonic for immune support after consulting with a healthcare professional. It is widely considered safe in this dosage but best to get a consult first.

Forgotten Home Apothecary

White Cell
Boosting Juice

Carrots and beets are rich in antioxidants, vitamins, and minerals, including vitamin C, vitamin A, and potassium, which support overall immune function. These vegetables also contain phytonutrients like beta-carotene and betalains, which have been shown to have immune-boosting properties and may help increase the production of white blood cells, thus enhancing the body's ability to fight off infections and illnesses. Additionally, parsley is a good source of vitamin C and vitamin K, as well as flavonoids and antioxidants, which further support immune health.

Adding astragalus (*Astragalus membranaceus*) or echinacea (*Echinacea purpurea*) extract enhances the immune-boosting benefits, while ginger adds a touch of warmth and depth to the flavor profile. Together, they create a delicious and nutritious juice. Elderberry and Japanese honeysuckle extracts/tinctures may be also be used (see side note).

INGREDIENTS:

- 1 liter of natural orange juice (approximately 8-12 freshly squeezed oranges)
- 1 medium carrot, chopped
- 1 medium beet, chopped
- 1-inch piece of ginger (*Zingiber officinale*), peeled
- A handful of parsley leaves
- 1 teaspoon of honey or sweetener (optional)
- Astragalus or echinacea extract/tincture

NOTES:

If you are pregnant, nursing, or have any underlying health conditions, consult with a healthcare professional before consuming this juice.

If you have an autoimmune condition best to replace astragalus and echinacea with elderberry and Japanese honeysuckle, as the former herbs may be too immunostimulatory.

INSTRUCTIONS:

1 | **Gather and Prepare Ingredients:** Prepare the ingredients as directed. In a blender, combine the natural orange juice, chopped carrot, chopped beet, peeled ginger, and parsley leaves. Use freshly squeezed orange juice for the best flavor and nutritional content.

2 | **Sweeten:** Add the honey or sweetener if desired for additional sweetness. Exercise caution if using honey or sweetener, especially if managing blood sugar levels.

3 | **Include the Extract:** Add 10-15 drops of astragalus and/or echinacea extract to the blender.

4 | **Blend:** Blend on high speed until the ingredients are well combined and the mixture is smooth.

5 | **Strain:** If necessary, strain the juice using a fine mesh strainer or cheesecloth to remove any pulp.

6 | **Serve:** Pour the juice into a glass and serve chilled or over ice.

DOSAGE:

Enjoy a glass of this immune-boosting juice daily for optimal health benefits.

Herbal Antibiotic
Capsules

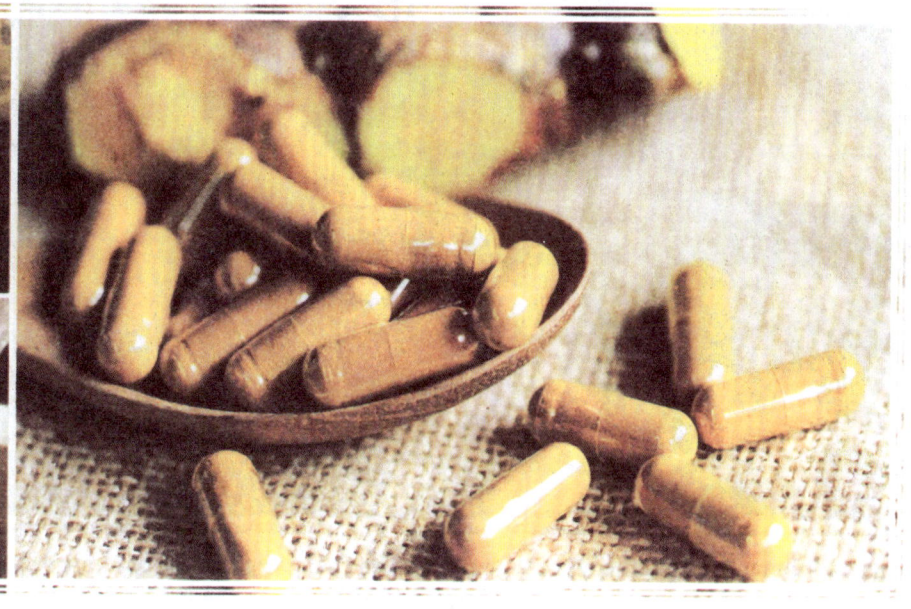

This recipe offers a natural alternative to conventional antibiotics, utilizing the unique properties of various herbs. From the pungent kick of jalapeño peppers to the robust earthiness of grated horseradish, each ingredient contributes to a holistic approach to wellness. The concoction includes antioxidant-rich turmeric, immune-boosting echinacea, and nutrient-packed moringa leaves.

INGREDIENTS:

- ¼ cup chopped onion
- 2 hot jalapeño peppers
- 2 tbsp grated horseradish
- ¼ cup grated ginger (*Zingiber officinale*)
- 2 tbsp turmeric powder (*Curcuma longa*)
- ¼ cup chopped garlic
- ¼ cup moringa leaves (*Moringa oleifera*)
- ¼ cup echinacea (*Echinacea purpurea*)
- 3 cups apple cider vinegar
- Empty gelatin capsules (size 0 or 00)

NOTES:

Regularly check the drying process to prevent burning. The mixture is sufficiently dried when it turns brown and exhibits a crumbly texture.

If making capsules regularly, consider investing in a capsule filling tray for efficiency.

INSTRUCTIONS:

1 | **Blend the Ingredients:** Chop all ingredients and place them in a blender. Pour apple cider vinegar into the blender last. Blend on high until a smooth, consistent liquid is achieved, similar to the texture of a smoothie.

2 | **Infusion Period:** Pour the blended liquid into jars and store them in a cool, dark place for two weeks.

3 | **Thickening Process:** After 2 weeks have passed, pour the liquid into a metal baking dish and place it in the oven at low heat. Allow the moisture to evaporate and the liquid to thicken to a consistency thicker than a cake batter, ensuring it won't run.

4 | **Spread and Dry:** Cover a cookie sheet with parchment and spread the thickened mixture in an even layer. Return the mixture to the oven on low heat to thoroughly dry, avoiding burning. It will turn brown when dry.

5 | **Powdering the Mixture:** Break up the dry mixture and place it in a jar blender (or regular blender). Chop it at high speed into a fine powder.

6 | **Capsule Filling:** Using a spoon or scoop, fill the inner part of the gelatin capsules until the powder is flush with the edge. Cap it with the outer part of the capsule.

7 | **Storage and Dosage:** Keep the finished antibiotic capsules in a sealed, moisture-proof jar. If available, include a silica desiccant package in the jar to protect the capsules from moisture. Capsules can last up to a year or more if stored correctly.

DOSAGE:

Start with one capsule a day and adjust the dosage based on individual response. Omit or replace echinacea if you have an autoimmune disorder. Elderberry, oregano, and yarrow are good alternatives.

Amish
Fire Cider

This traditional Amish remedy is a type of fire cider that combines the unique properties of onions, garlic, horseradish, honey, black pepper, and apple cider vinegar to create a natural tonic. Onions, rich in quercetin and sulfur compounds, are known for their supportive analgesic and anti-inflammatory effects. Garlic, abundant in allicin, is traditionally used for its supportive anti-inflammatory properties. Horseradish contributes its antibacterial qualities, while honey's natural properties aid in microbial control. Black pepper's piperine enhances nutrient absorption, potentially amplifying the benefits of the entire blend. Feel free to customize the recipe to suit your preferences and specific needs. You can adjust the quantities of ingredients to achieve your desired potency or flavor profile. Additionally, you may explore adding other herbs or spices known for their supportive properties, such as ginger, turmeric, lemon, and/or cayenne pepper.

INGREDIENTS:

- 1 medium onion, finely chopped
- 3 cloves garlic, minced
- 2 tablespoons horseradish, grated
- ¼ cup raw honey
- Dash of ground black pepper
- Apple cider vinegar, enough to cover the ingredients

NOTES:

Consult with a healthcare professional before using this remedy, especially if you have any underlying health conditions or are pregnant or nursing.

Discontinue use if any adverse reactions occur.

Adjust the amount of honey and pepper to suit your taste preferences.

For a smoother tonic, blend the strained liquid before transferring it to a storage container.

INSTRUCTIONS:

1 | **Prepare Ingredients:** Finely chop the onion, mince the garlic cloves, grate the horseradish.
2 | **Combine Ingredients:** In a clean glass jar, layer the chopped onion, minced garlic, and grated horseradish. Pour honey over the layered ingredients. Add a dash of ground black pepper.
3 | **Cover with Apple Cider Vinegar:** Pour apple cider vinegar over the mixture until all ingredients are completely covered.
4 | **Mix Well:** Use a spoon to gently stir the ingredients, ensuring they are evenly distributed.
5 | **Seal and Store:** Seal the jar tightly with a lid. Label and date. Store the jar in a cool, dark place for up to 1 month to allow the flavors to meld and the medicinal properties to infuse into the vinegar.
6 | **Strain and Transfer:** After 1 month, strain the mixture through a fine mesh sieve or cheesecloth to remove solids. Transfer the liquid to a clean glass jar or bottle for storage.

DOSAGE:

Take 1 tablespoon of this cider up to three times per day as needed for pain relief and inflammation.

Blue Tea
to Ease Inflammation

Butterfly pea flower, scientifically referred to as *Clitoria ternatea*, earns recognition not just for its striking blue appearance but for its anti-inflammatory properties. The flowers make a great anti-inflammatory tea thanks to the plant's anthocyanins - antioxidant compounds that give the flowers their vibrant blue color. The ternatin anthocyanins found in the flowers help to fight chronic inflammation, which is a precursor to many diseases. This also helps reduce pain and swelling for conditions such as rheumatoid arthritis. This recipe takes it a step further by incorporating lemon, not only for a color-changing effect but also to enhance the overall health benefits of the concoction.

INGREDIENTS:

- 2 teaspoons dried butterfly pea flowers (*Clitoria ternatea*)
- 1 cup hot water
- 1 tablespoon fresh lemon juice

NOTES:

Individuals with known allergies to pea flowers or citrus should exercise caution or avoid this tea.

For a refreshing twist on hot summer days, try serving the butterfly pea flower and lemon tea over ice. This simple addition transforms the herbal infusion into a cool and invigorating beverage, perfect for staying hydrated while enjoying the anti-inflammatory and antioxidant benefits of butterfly pea flowers.

INSTRUCTIONS:

1 | **Infusion Process:** Boil 1 cup of water. Place the dried butterfly pea flowers in a teapot. Pour the hot water over the flowers, initiating the extraction of beneficial compounds and imparting a vivid blue color. Allow the infusion to steep for 5-7 minutes. Experiment with steeping times to achieve the desired intensity of color and flavor.

2 | **Strain and Serve:** Strain the tea to remove flower remnants, leaving behind the visually stunning blue liquid. Pour the tea into a cup.

3 | **Add lemon:** Squeeze half a lemon into each mug and watch the color change from bright blue to a purple hue. Since the tea has lemon juice in it, remember to rinse your mouth out with water after each mug you drink to remove the acid and protect your tooth enamel.

4 | **Optional Additions:** Sweeten with honey if a touch of sweetness is preferred. You can also play around by adding extra ingredients and flavor combinations (e.g. mint, lemongrass, or ginger). As this tea has such a subtle flavor it lends itself to many additions so choose ones that you like and are beneficial to your health.

DOSAGE:

For those seeking its anti-inflammatory benefits, consider consuming 1-2 cups daily.

Herbal
Vitamin Bars

Crafted to support and enhance your immune system, this vitamin bar incorporates a blend of nutrient-rich herbs. Bilberry, known for its antioxidant properties and richness in anthocyanins, contributes to immune health. Elderberries, renowned for its anti-viral and antioxidant properties, is a staple in herbal remedies for overall well-being. Licorice root, with its anti-inflammatory and antiviral properties, is included to bolster the immune system. Packed with essential nutrients, pumpkin seeds provide a dose of zinc vital for immune function, while sunflower seeds, high in vitamin E, contribute to maintaining a robust immune system. Cocoa powder not only adds a rich flavor but also contains flavonoids that may have immune-supporting effects.

INGREDIENTS:

- 4 oz dried pitted dates
- 5 oz mixed nuts
- 1 heaped tsp bilberry powder
- 1 tsp elderberry extract
- 1 tsp licorice root extract
- 1 tbsp pumpkin seeds
- 1 tbsp sunflower seeds
- 2 tbsp pure cocoa powder
- 2 tbsp raw honey

NOTES:

Customize the nut mix based on your preferences and dietary restrictions.

Store the vitamin bars in an airtight container in the refrigerator for prolonged freshness.

Individuals with known allergies to any of the listed ingredients should avoid consumption.

INSTRUCTIONS:

1| **Prepare the Base:** In a food processor, combine dried pitted dates and mixed nuts. Blend until you achieve a sticky and cohesive mixture. Press the mixture into a lined pan to create an even base for your vitamin bar.

2| **Herbal Infusion Layer:** In a small bowl, mix bilberry powder, elderberry extract, and licorice root extract. Spread this herbal blend evenly over the prepared base.

3| **Nutrient-Rich Toppings:** Sprinkle pumpkin seeds, sunflower seeds, and pure cocoa powder over the herbal layer.

4| **Sweeten and Set:** Drizzle honey evenly across the top, providing natural sweetness. Keep the mixture in the freezer for 30 minutes.

5| **Cut and Serve:** Once the herbal vitamin bar has set in the freezer, use a sharp knife to carefully cut it into individual squares or bars. For a clean cut, run the knife under hot water before slicing each portion. Store in portioned containers for convenient daily consumption.

DOSAGE:

Consume one square of the herbal vitamin bar daily for optimal immune support. The calories per serving will vary based on the specific ingredients you use, their nutritional content, and the size of the bars.

Forgotten Home Apothecary

Lymphatic Cleanser

The lymphatic system plays a crucial role in immune function, helping to remove waste and toxins from the body. Herbs such as cleavers and red clover are traditionally used to support lymphatic health by promoting lymphatic drainage and circulation.

- For added flavor and benefits, incorporate other lymphatic-supporting herbs such as burdock root or dandelion leaf.
- Consider adding a splash of lemon juice or a drizzle of honey to enhance the taste of the infusion.
- Pairing this herbal remedy with gentle exercise, such as yoga or walking, can further support lymphatic circulation.

INGREDIENTS:

- 2 tbsp dried cleavers (*Galium aparine*)
- 2 tbsps dried red clover blossoms (*Trifolium pratense*)
- 4 cups water

NOTES:

Cleavers may interact with certain medications, particularly blood thinners. Use caution if you are on medication or have a bleeding disorder.

Red clover may have estrogenic effects and should be avoided by individuals with hormone-sensitive conditions such as breast cancer, uterine fibroids, or endometriosis.

INSTRUCTIONS:

1 | **Prepare the Herbs:** Combine the dried cleavers and red clover blossoms in a teapot or heatproof container.
2 | **Infusion:** Bring 4 cups of water to a boil. Pour the boiling water over the herbs. Cover and let steep for 15-20 minutes to extract the beneficial compounds.
3 | **Strain:** After steeping, strain the herbal infusion using a fine mesh strainer or cheesecloth into a clean container.

DOSAGE:

Drink 1-2 cups of the herbal infusion daily. For a more intense cleanse, you may drink up to 3 cups per day for a limited period, typically 1-2 weeks.

Mushroom Extract
to Help with Viral Infections

The selected mushrooms, including reishi (*Ganoderma lucidum*), shiitake (*Lentinula edodes*), maitake (*Grifola frondosa*), and turkey tail (*Trametes versicolor*), are traditionally used for their immunomodulatory and anti-viral properties, thus potentially helping address HPV (Human Papillomavirus) infections.

Reishi, rich in beta-glucans, may enhance immune cell activity; Shiitake, containing lentinan, has immunomodulatory effects; Maitake, with beta-glucans, supports immune function; Turkey tail, housing polysaccharopeptides (PSP) and polysaccharide-K (PSK), contributes to immunomodulation. Together, these mushrooms may create a synergistic effect, aiding the immune system's ability to recognize and combat viral infections, potentially inhibiting HPV. Additionally, their anti-inflammatory properties may help modulate immune responses and reduce inflammation associated with HPV persistence.

INGREDIENTS:

- 1 ounce dried reishi mushroom (*Ganoderma lucidum*)
- 1 ounce dried shiitake mushroom (*Lentinula edodes*)
- 1 ounce dried maitake mushroom (*Grifola frondosa*)
- 1 ounce (dried) turkey tail mushroom (*Trametes versicolor*)
- 2 cups vodka (at least 40% alcohol)
- 2 cups distilled water

NOTES:

While promising, more research specific to HPV is needed, and individual responses vary.

Consult with a healthcare professional before use, especially if you have existing medical conditions. Monitor for any adverse reactions and discontinue use if any occur.

INSTRUCTIONS:

1. **Preparing the Mushrooms:** Ensure all mushrooms are clean and chopped or ground into small pieces. Place the dried reishi, shiitake, maitake, and turkey tail mushrooms in a glass jar.
2. **Alcohol Extraction:** Pour 2 cups of vodka over the mushrooms, ensuring they are fully submerged. Seal the jar tightly and store it in a cool, dark place for 6-8 weeks, shaking periodically.
3. **Water Extraction:** After the alcohol extraction period, strain the alcohol extract into a separate container. Take the strained mushrooms and place them in a saucepan. Add 2 cups of distilled water to the saucepan and simmer for 1-2 hours, simmering off half the water.
4. **Combining Extractions:** Strain the water extract, squeezing out any remaining liquid from the mushrooms. Combine the alcohol and water extracts in a glass container using a ratio of 3 parts alcoholic tincture to 1 part water extraction.
5. **Label and Store:** Label the tincture with the date of preparation. Store the tincture in a dark glass bottle in a cool, dark place.

DOSAGE:

Consume 1 teaspoon of the double extraction tincture daily. Dilute it in water or juice or take directly in the mouth.

Nature's "Amoxicillin"

"Nature's Amoxicillin" is an herbal concoction designed to support immunity and promote overall health. Packed with natural ingredients renowned for their antimicrobial and anti-inflammatory properties, this recipe harnesses the power of herbs like ginger (*Zingiber officinale*), turmeric (*Curcuma longa*), garlic (*Allium sativum*), and more, combined with the acidic punch of apple cider vinegar. The addition of fresh pineapple and honey not only enhances the flavor but provides additional health benefits. Experiment with different herbs and spices to customize the recipe to your liking.

INGREDIENTS:

- 2/3 cup apple cider vinegar (ACV)
- ½ cup fresh pineapple, washed and cut into half-inch cubes
- 2-inch piece of ginger, peeled
- 1-inch piece of turmeric root, peeled (or ½ to ¾ tsp turmeric powder)
- 2 to 3 cloves of garlic
- 1 medium-sized onion
- ¼ organic lime or lemon with peel, chopped
- 1 ½ tbsp honey
- ⅛ tsp cayenne pepper
- A pinch of black pepper

NOTES:

While this herbal concoction is generally safe for consumption, individuals with allergies to any of the ingredients or those with underlying health conditions, pregnant, or breastfeeding should consult with a healthcare professional before use.

INSTRUCTIONS:

1. **Prepare Ingredients:** Wash and chop the pineapple, ginger, turmeric, garlic, onion, and lime (or lemon) as specified. Ensure all ingredients are fresh and organic for maximum potency and health.
2. **Blend:** Place all the prepared ingredients in a blender, including the apple cider vinegar and honey. You can also use fresh cayenne pepper instead of powder for a spicier cider. Blend until smooth and well combined.
3. **Strain (Optional):** If desired, strain the mixture through a fine mesh strainer to remove any pulp and extract just the liquid. However, consuming the pulp provides additional health benefits.
4. **Store:** Transfer the strained or unstrained juice to a clean glass mason jar for storage. Seal the jar tightly and refrigerate. The fire cider shot can be kept in the fridge for up to 2 weeks.

- Take a shot glass of Nature's "Amoxicillin" tonic before meals to support digestion and boost immunity.
- Incorporate the tonic into salad dressings or marinades for an added flavor kick and health benefits.
- Mix with sparkling water for a refreshing and health-supportive cocktail.

DOSAGE:

1 shot glass (approximately 1-2 ounces) per day.

Nail-Fungus
Herbal Cream

Nail fungus, or onychomycosis, is a prevalent and persistent condition that can be challenging to address. This homemade cream combines natural ingredients known for their antifungal properties and skin-nourishing effects. Other strong antifungal options include usnea lichen (an oil-infusion or a tincture in a spray bottle works well) and black walnut hull as an oil-infusion. Simply replace the 2T of each oil with one or both of these antifungal oils, making the recipe even stronger.

INGREDIENTS:

- 2 tablespoons of olive oil
- 2 tablespoons of soybean oil
- ⅓ ounce (10 g) of beeswax
- 1 teaspoon of arrowroot powder
- 30 drops of essential oil

NOTES:

In addition to using the cream, maintain good nail hygiene practices.

Regularly trim infected nails to promote faster healing. Keep feet dry and well-ventilated to create an inhospitable environment for fungal growth.

Conduct a patch test before widespread use to check for any adverse reactions.

Avoid contact with eyes and mucous membranes.

INSTRUCTIONS:

1 | **Double Boiler Method:** Utilize a double boiler to melt the beeswax. Once melted, add the olive oil and soybean oil. Stir the mixture thoroughly until all ingredients are well combined. To ensure a successful homemade nail fungus treatment, it's important to consider how to maximize the skin's absorption so that the cream is delivered deeper into the skin. Olive oil improves the absorption of the outer skin layers (the epidermis), while soybean oil penetrates both the epidermis as well as the dermis underneath.

2 | **Arrowroot Addition:** Gradually add the arrowroot powder to the mixture, stirring continuously to prevent the formation of lumps. This step is crucial for thickening the cream.

3 | **Antifungal Essential Oils:** Allow the mixture to cool slightly before adding 10 drops of each: cinnamon bark, oregano oil, and lavender oil. Stir the oils into the mixture for a uniform blend. **Cinnamon Bark Oil:** contains cinnamaldehyde, known for its antifungal and antibacterial properties. **Oregano Oil:** Rich in carvacrol, which has potent antifungal and antimicrobial effects. **Lavender Oil:** Exhibits antifungal and soothing properties, promoting overall skin health.

4 | **Pouring and Cooling:** Transfer the cream into a clean, airtight container, and allow it to cool and solidify. This process may take a few hours, depending on the ambient temperature.

DOSAGE:

Apply a small amount of the cream to the affected nails twice daily. Before each application, ensure the affected area is clean and dry. For stubborn infections, consider adding in usnea and/or black walnut hull.

Anti-Fungal Powder
for Toenail Fungus

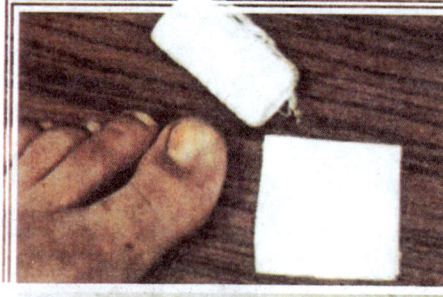

This DIY anti-fungal powder uses natural ingredients known for their anti-fungal and anti-inflammatory properties. Bentonite clay is used traditionally to help drawing out toxins and impurities, while cayenne pepper stimulates circulation and has anti-fungal properties. Cinnamon, clove, and frankincense essential oils are renowned for their anti-fungal and antimicrobial effects. Together, these ingredients create a blend that may help support the management of toenail fungus.

INGREDIENTS AND MATERIALS:

- ½ cup Bentonite clay
- 2 teaspoons cayenne pepper powder
- 6 drops cinnamon essential oil
- 6 drops clove essential oil
- 6 drops frankincense essential oil
- A container with holes for dispensing (*e.g.*, a salt shaker)

NOTES:

Test a small amount on a patch of skin before full use to ensure you do not have an adverse reaction. Discontinue use if irritation occurs. Do not touch your face or eyes after handling the powder, especially due to the cayenne pepper. Wash hands thoroughly after use. If you have any chronic health conditions or are pregnant or nursing, consult a healthcare professional before using this remedy.

INSTRUCTIONS:

1 | **Combine Ingredients:** Measure ½ cup of Bentonite clay into a bowl or food processor. Add 2 teaspoons of cayenne pepper powder. Wear gloves when handling the powder to avoid irritation from the cayenne pepper.
2 | **Add Essential Oils:** Add 6 drops each of cinnamon, clove, and frankincense essential oils to the mixture.
3 | **Mix Thoroughly:** Process on low for about 30 seconds in a food processor or mix well by hand with a fork or whisk to ensure the oils are evenly distributed.
4 | **Store:** Transfer the finished powder to a container that is easy to scoop or shake out, such as a salt shaker. Store the powder in a dry place. If it becomes moist, add dry rice to the container.

DOSAGE:

Sprinkle the powder on your feet or in your socks twice a day for 1-2 weeks. You can also apply it before bedtime, ensuring to wear socks.

Forgotten Home Apothecary

Anti-Fungal
Salve

This antifungal salve harnesses the potent properties of garlic, oregano, thyme, and marjoram to create a natural remedy for combating fungal infections on the skin. Each of these herbs are traditionally used for their antifungal properties, making them making them valuable in addressing various fungal pathogens. Garlic is renowned for its antimicrobial and antifungal effects, while oregano contains compounds such as carvacrol and thymol, known for their powerful antifungal properties. Thyme and marjoram also contribute to the salve with their antimicrobial and soothing qualities, providing additional support for skin health. By combining these herbs with beeswax and coconut oil, we create a soothing and effective salve that can be applied topically to support the management of fungal issues and promote skin wellness.

INGREDIENTS:

- 3 tablespoons beeswax
- ½ cup coconut oil
- 1 tablespoon dried oregano (*Origanum vulgare*)
- 1 tablespoon dried thyme (*Thymus vulgaris*)
- 1 tablespoon dried marjoram (*Origanum majorana*)
- 3 cloves garlic, finely minced (*Allium sativum*)
- 10 drops tea tree oil
- 10 drops lavender essential oil

NOTES:

For external use only.

Avoid contact with eyes.

Consider doing a patch test on a small area of skin before using the salve more extensively.

Keep out of reach of children.

If pregnant, nursing, or under medical supervision, consult a healthcare professional before use.

INSTRUCTIONS:

1 | **Prepare Your Work Area:** Clean and sterilize all utensils, containers, and work surfaces before you begin.

2 | **Infuse the Coconut Oil:** In a double boiler or a heatproof bowl set over a pot of simmering water, melt the coconut oil. Add the dried oregano, thyme, marjoram, and minced garlic to the melted coconut oil. Let the mixture simmer gently for 30 minutes, stirring occasionally to ensure thorough infusion.

3 | **Strain the Infused Oil:** After 30 minutes, remove the infused oil from the heat and strain it through a fine-mesh sieve or cheesecloth to remove the solid herbs and garlic. Return the infused oil to the double boiler.

4 | **Add the Beeswax and Essential Oils:** Add the beeswax to the infused oil in the double boiler and continue to heat until the beeswax is fully melted, stirring occasionally. Once melted, remove the mixture from the heat and add the tea tree oil and lavender essential oil. Stir well.

5 | **Pour Into Containers:** Carefully pour the melted mixture into clean, sterilized containers. Allow the salve to cool and solidify completely before sealing the containers. Label and date.

DOSAGE:

Apply a small amount of the salve directly to the affected area 2-3 times daily.

Wart "Freezing" *Spray*

One herb known for its potential wart-removing properties is *Thuja occidentalis*, commonly known as Arborvitae or white cedar. It contains compounds, such as thujone and flavonoids, that possess antimicrobial and antiviral properties, making it a popular choice for addressing viral infections like warts. The essential oil from this herb is believed to inhibit the growth of the human papillomavirus (HPV), which causes warts. This recipe creates a convenient spray form for easy application.

INGREDIENTS:

- 3-4 drops *Thuja occidentalis* essential oil
- 1 tablespoon witch hazel
- 2 tablespoons of distilled water
- Small spray bottle

NOTES:

Other home remedies for wart removal include: applying apple cider vinegar (ACV), using crushed garlic secured with a bandage, placing banana peel on the wart, applying aloe vera gel multiple times a day, diluting tea tree oil with a carrier oil for daily use, employing duct tape occlusion for about six days followed by gentle exfoliation, creating a baking soda paste for regular application, using castor oil covered with a bandage, and using diluted oregano oil regularly.

INSTRUCTIONS:

1 | **Clean the Area:** Start by cleaning the affected area around the wart with mild soap and water. Pat it dry gently with a clean towel.
2 | **Prepare the Solution:** In a small mixing bowl, combine 3-4 drops of Thuja occidentalis essential oil with 1 tablespoon of witch hazel. Mix well. Add 2 tablespoons of distilled water to the mixture and stir until fully blended.
3 | **Fill the Spray Bottle:** Pour the mixture into a small spray bottle. Ensure the lid is tightly secured and shake the bottle vigorously to ensure that all ingredients are well combined.
4 | **Apply the Spray:** Spray a modest amount directly onto the wart, making sure to cover it thoroughly. It's important to perform a patch test on a small area of skin first to ensure there are no adverse reactions. Avoid contact with eyes and mucous membranes.
5 | **Cover the Area:** After application, cover the wart with a sterile bandage or gauze pad. This prevents the solution from rubbing off on clothes or bedding and helps in keeping the treated area clean.
6 | **Be Patient:** Allow time for the remedy to take effect. Natural treatments can take longer to show results. If the wart persists or if there is any sign of irritation, consult a healthcare professional for advice.

DOSAGE:

Perform this application once or twice daily, preferably in the morning and evening. Consistency is key.

Forgotten Home Apothecary

Cleaning Ointment
(for Candida)

Candida overgrowth can cause a variety of health issues, including yeast infections, digestive problems, and fatigue. It can also manifest externally, leading to skin issues such as yeast infections and fungal rashes. To support the body in managing Candida, you may create a soothing ointment using herbs traditionally known for their antifungal properties. One effective combination includes tea tree oil (*Melaleuca alternifolia*) and garlic (*Allium sativum*), both known for their potent antifungal properties. Additionally, addressing internal digestive balance may involve focusing on dietary adjustments, probiotics, and herbs taken internally. For internal support, consider incorporating Japanese honeysuckle (*Lonicera japonica*), turmeric, and/or caprylic acid.

INGREDIENTS:

- 1 tablespoon of coconut oil
- 3 drops of tea tree oil (*Melaleuca alternifolia*)
- 1 clove of garlic (*Allium sativum*), minced

NOTES:

Avoid applying the ointment to broken skin or sensitive areas, as it may cause irritation.

Perform a patch test before using the ointment extensively to ensure you do not have an allergic reaction to any of the ingredients.

If irritation occurs, discontinue use and consult a healthcare professional.

INSTRUCTIONS:

1. **Melt the Coconut Oil:** Place the coconut oil in a small saucepan and heat it gently until it becomes liquid.
2. **Add the Tea Tree Oil:** Once the coconut oil is melted, remove it from the heat and add the drops of tea tree oil. Stir well to combine.
3. **Mix in the Minced Garlic:** Add the minced garlic to the oil mixture and stir thoroughly to distribute it evenly.
4. **Cool and Solidify:** Allow the mixture to cool down until it solidifies into a firm ointment consistency. Transfer to a container: Once the ointment has reached the desired consistency, transfer it into a clean, airtight container suitable for storage.
5. **Store:** Store the ointment in a cool, dark place to prolong its shelf life. Consider adding other antifungal herbs such as oregano (*Origanum vulgare*) or thyme (*Thymus vulgaris*) for added effectiveness.

DOSAGE:

Apply a small amount of the ointment to affected areas up to three times daily.

Soothing Anti-Viral Oil
for Herpes Sores and Shingles Rashes

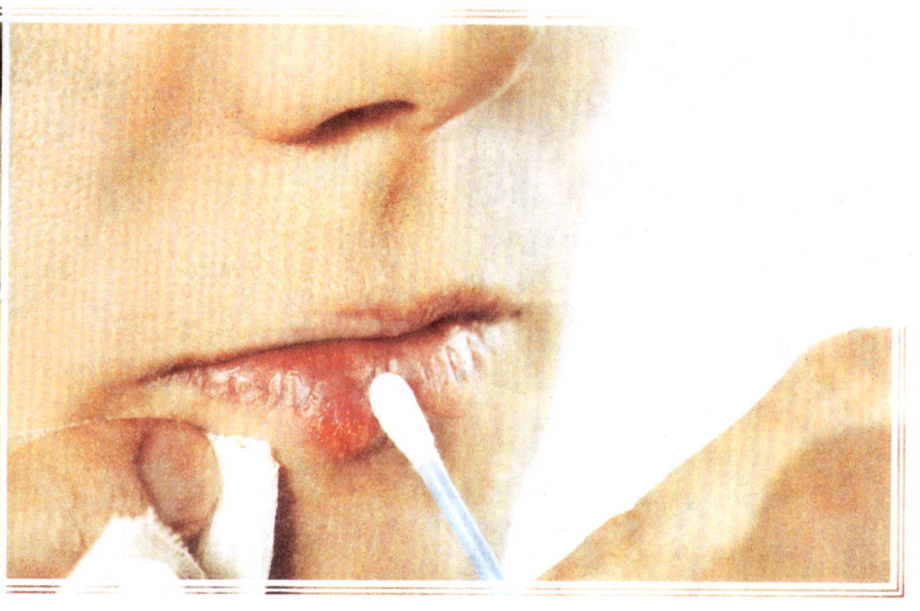

This soothing oil, traditionally used for its potential antiviral properties, may support the management of herpes outbreaks. Lemon balm demonstrates significant antiviral activity against both HSV-1 and HSV-2, while also calming the nervous system and reducing stress, common triggers for outbreaks. Heal-all contains antiviral compounds and anti-inflammatory properties to alleviate discomfort. Sage aids in drying out and healing herpes sores and shingles lesions. Rosemary exhibits antiviral properties against herpes viruses. Calendula soothes and helps heal herpes sores and shingles lesions, promoting skin regeneration. Geranium essential oil offers rapid pain relief, particularly for shingles-related discomfort. These herbs work together to provide relief and support for those managing skin outbreaks.

INGREDIENTS:

- Equal parts lemon balm, heal-all (self-heal/*Prunella vulgaris*), sage, rosemary, calendula
- Organic almond or olive oil
- Geranium essential oil (*Pelargonium graveolens*)

NOTES:

Perform a patch test before applying the oil to a larger area of the skin to check for any allergic reactions.

Avoid contact with eyes and mucous membranes.

Consult a healthcare professional before using if pregnant, nursing, or have any underlying medical conditions.

Best paired with internal tinctures of lemon balm and the following medicinal mushrooms: turkey tail, reishi, and cordyceps.

INSTRUCTIONS:

1 | **Prepare the Herbs:** Tear or crush the lemon balm, heal-all, sage, rosemary, and calendula. Lightly pack the herbs into a sterilized glass jar.
2 | **Infusion:** Fill the jar ⅓ full with the dried herbs. Pour organic almond or olive oil over the herbs, filling the jar to within a ½ inch (1.25 cm) of the top.
3 | **Storage:** Cap the jar tightly and label it with the contents and date. Store the jar in a cool, dark location for 6 to 8 weeks (no longer) to allow the herbs to infuse into the oil.
4 | **Straining:** After the infusion period, strain the oil using cheesecloth into a clean, sterilized glass jar. Label and date.
5 | **Add Essential Oil:** Add ~10 drops of geranium oil to the mixture. Mix well to remove any air bubbles.
6 | **Storage and Usage:** Store the strained oil in a cool, dark location. When stored properly, the oil will last for 1 to 2 years.

DOSAGE:

Apply a small amount of the oil topically to the affected area as needed.

Herbal Balm
for Herpes Sores

Creating herbal balm designed to soothe skin irritations can be beneficial, especially when it includes ingredients traditionally used for their calming properties. The primary herbs used are lemon balm, which is known for its antiviral properties, and St. John's wort, which is also a known anti-viral and helps in reducing inflammation. Additionally, lavender and tea tree essential oils are included for their soothing and antiseptic properties.

INGREDIENTS:

- ¼ cup dried lemon balm (*Melissa officinalis*)
- ¼ cup dried St. John's Wort (*Hypericum perforatum*)
- ½ cup coconut oil
- ¼ cup beeswax pellets
- 10 drops lavender essential oil (*Lavandula angustifolia*)
- 10 drops tea tree essential oil (*Melaleuca alternifolia*)

NOTES:

Perform a patch test before first use to ensure no allergic reactions occur. Avoid use on broken skin or open wounds. If irritation or adverse reactions occur, discontinue use immediately and consult a healthcare professional.

Not recommended for use during pregnancy or breastfeeding without consulting a healthcare provider.

INSTRUCTIONS:

1 | **Prepare the Infusion:** Combine the dried lemon balm and St. John's wort in a heatproof jar. Add the coconut oil to the jar, ensuring the herbs are fully submerged. Place the jar in a double boiler or a saucepan with water and heat gently for 2-3 hours, keeping the water at a simmer. This allows the herbs to infuse into the oil.

2 | **Strain the Infused Oil:** After 2-3 hours, strain the oil through a fine mesh strainer or cheesecloth into a clean heatproof bowl, squeezing out as much oil as possible from the herbs.

3 | **Melt the Beeswax:** Add the beeswax pellets to the infused oil and place the bowl back into the double boiler. Heat gently until the beeswax is completely melted, stirring occasionally. For a firmer balm, increase the amount of beeswax slightly; for a softer balm, reduce the beeswax.

4 | **Add Essential Oils:** Once the beeswax is melted, remove the bowl from the heat. Add the lavender and tea tree essential oils to the mixture, stirring thoroughly to combine.

5 | **Pour and Settle the Balm:** Pour the mixture into small, clean containers, tins, or empty lipstick tubes for easy application. Allow the balm to cool and solidify completely before capping the containers. Store the balm in a cool, dark place to extend its shelf life.

DOSAGE:

Apply a small amount of balm directly to the affected area 2-3 times daily during an outbreak. For preventative use, apply once daily to areas prone to outbreaks.

Forgotten Home Apothecary

Heavy Metal
Detoxifier

This heavy metal detoxifier is designed to help remove accumulated heavy metals from the body using natural ingredients known for their detoxifying properties. This smoothie combines powerful ingredients like moringa, ginger, cilantro, parsley, and more to support your body's detox processes.

INGREDIENTS:

- ¾ cup papaya
- 1 tablespoon moringa powder
- ½ inch piece of ginger root
- Small handful of cilantro
- A small handful of parsley
- 1 orange, segmented
- 1 teaspoon cinnamon
- 1 teaspoon vanilla powder
- 2 tablespoons chia seeds
- 1 cup prepared bone broth (or vegetable broth for a vegan option)
- 1 cup ice
- 2 tablespoons honey
- 4 tablespoons date sugar or 4 raw dates

NOTES:
Consult a healthcare professional before starting any detox regimen, especially if pregnant, nursing, or having chronic conditions. Ensure no allergies to ingredients and stop if reactions occur. Consult your provider if on medications.

INSTRUCTIONS:

1 | **Soak Chia Seeds:** Combine the chia seeds with the bone broth and let them soak while preparing the other ingredients. Use vegetable broth if you are vegan or cannot find bone broth.
2 | **Prepare Ingredients:** Gather all your ingredients. Measure and cut everything into small pieces. Use fresh, organic ingredients whenever possible.
3 | **Add Ice to Blender:** Add the ice to the blender.
4 | **Add Remaining Ingredients:** Add the soaked chia seeds and broth, papaya, moringa powder, ginger root, cilantro, parsley, orange segments, cinnamon, vanilla powder, honey, and date sugar (or dates) to the blender.
5 | **Blend:** Blend until smooth.
6 | **Serve:** Pour into a glass and Drink immediately for best results. If you need to store it, keep it in an airtight container in the refrigerator and consume it within 24 hours.

DOSAGE:

Drink this smoothie as often as desired. For best results, consume on an empty stomach and wait at least one hour before eating or taking medication.

Mushroom Drops
for an Overactive Immune System

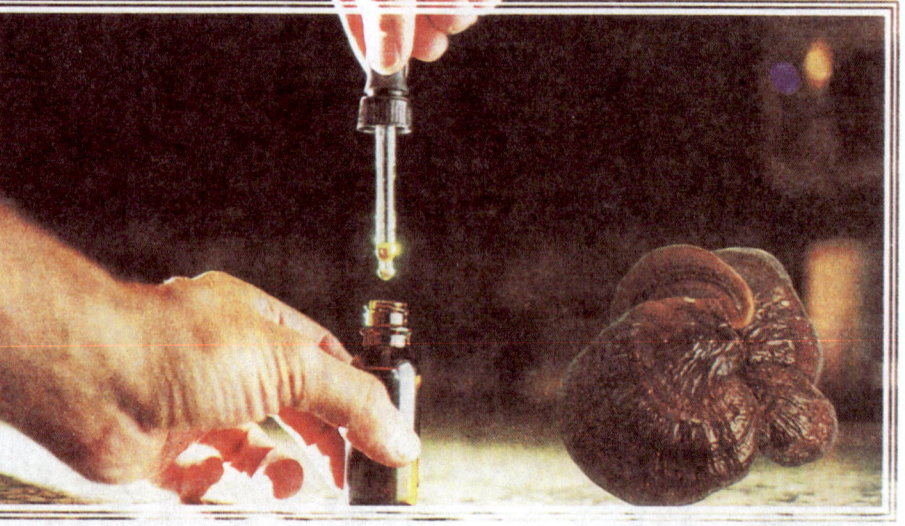

Mushroom drops are a natural remedy aimed at supporting the immune system and managing autoimmune disorders. The primary mushrooms used in this tincture are reishi, known for its immunomodulatory properties, and turkey tail, recognized for its immune-regulating and anti-inflammatory benefits. These mushrooms work synergistically to help balance the immune response and reduce inflammation associated with autoimmune conditions. A double extraction method ensures that both the water-soluble and alcohol-soluble compounds are effectively extracted.

INGREDIENTS:

- ¼ cup dried Reishi mushrooms (*Ganoderma lucidum*)
- ¼ cup dried Turkey Tail mushrooms (*Trametes versicolor*)
- 2 cups vodka (80-proof)
- 2 cups distilled water
- 1 pint mason jar
- Dropper bottles for storage

NOTES:

It's important to note that this is not intended to treat, cure, or prevent any autoimmune disorders, but rather to support general health as part of a holistic wellness strategy. Always consult with a healthcare provider before starting any new health regimen, especially if you have an autoimmune disorder.

Do not use if you are allergic to mushrooms. Pregnant or breastfeeding women should avoid using mushroom tinctures without medical advice.

If any adverse reactions occur, discontinue use immediately and seek medical attention.

INSTRUCTIONS:

1 | **Preparation of Mushrooms:** Chop or grind the dried mushrooms into small pieces to increase their surface area for extraction.

2 | **Alcohol Extraction:** Place the chopped mushrooms in a clean pint mason jar. Pour the vodka over the mushrooms, ensuring they are fully submerged. Seal the jar tightly and shake well. Label and date. Store the jar in a cool, dark place for 6-8 weeks, shaking gently every few days.

3 | **Strain the Alcohol Tincture:** After 6-8 weeks, strain the alcohol tincture through a fine mesh strainer or cheesecloth into a clean bowl, squeezing out as much liquid as possible from the mushroom pieces. Set the strained alcohol tincture aside.

4 | **Water Extraction:** Place the strained mushroom pieces in a saucepan. Add 2 cups of distilled water and bring to a simmer. Simmer gently for 1-2 hours, ensuring the water does not evaporate completely. Add more water if necessary to keep the mushrooms submerged.

5 | **Straining the Water Tincture:** After simmering, strain the water extract through a fine mesh strainer or cheesecloth into a clean bowl, again squeezing out as much liquid as possible from the mushroom pieces. Allow the water extract to cool completely.

6 | **Combining the Extracts:** Combine the alcohol and water extracts in a clean glass container. The ratio should be roughly 3:1 of your alcoholic tincture to your water extraction. Mix well to ensure thorough combination.

7 | **Bottling the Tincture:** Transfer the combined tincture into dropper bottles for easy use. Store the dropper bottles in a cool, dark place to preserve the tincture's potency.

DOSAGE:

1-2 dropperfuls (approximately 30-60 drops) 2-3 times daily. Start with a lower dose and gradually increase it to assess tolerance and effectiveness. For maximum efficacy, take these drops directly in the mouth. If the taste is too strong, you may add drops to water, juice, or tea.

HERBAL SUPPORT
for Skin Problems and Wounds

The skin is the largest organ of the body and plays a crucial role in protecting the body from external elements, regulating temperature, and serving as a barrier against infections.

Tips for promoting Skin Health:

CLEANSE GENTLY:
Use a gentle cleanser to remove dirt, oil, and makeup without stripping your skin's natural oils. Over-cleansing can lead to dryness and irritation.

EXFOLIATION:
Exfoliate 1-2 times a week to remove dead skin cells and promote skin renewal. Avoid over-exfoliating, which can lead to sensitivity.

SUN PROTECTION:
Use broad-spectrum sunscreen with at least SPF 30 daily, even on cloudy days. Sun protection helps prevent premature aging and reduces the risk of skin cancer.

HYDRATION:
Drink plenty of water to keep your skin hydrated from within. Moisturize your skin to maintain its moisture barrier.

HEALTHY DIET:
- **Antioxidant-Rich Foods:** Consume foods high in antioxidants, such as fruits, vegetables, nuts, and green tea. Antioxidants help protect your skin from damage caused by free radicals.
- **Vitamin C:** Foods rich in vitamin C, like citrus fruits, berries, and bell peppers, help promote collagen production and protect against UV damage. Proper hydration and nutrition are also important for efficient wound healing.

HERBAL SUPPORT

Aloe Vera *(Aloe barbadensis miller)*
Aloe vera gel may soothe irritated and burnt skin, support skin recovery, and provide hydration.

Arnica *(Arnica spp.)*
Arnica is commonly used for bruises, aches, sprains, swelling, and pain relief, and is often utilized for conditions like arthritis and carpal tunnel.

Calendula *(Calendula officinalis)*
Calendula is used topically to soothe irritated or inflamed skin. It supports skin health with its anti-inflammatory, antimicrobial, astringent, antifungal, and antiviral properties. Calendula is traditionally used for minor wounds, conjunctivitis, cuts, scrapes, chapped or chafed skin, bruises, burns, athlete's foot, acne, yeast imbalances, bee stings, diaper rash, and other minor skin irritations.

Chamomile *(Matricaria chamomilla)*
Chamomile has anti-inflammatory and calming properties. It can be used as a topical treatment or consumed as a tea to help with skin irritation.

Comfrey *(Symphytum)*
Comfrey is traditionally used to support wound recovery due to its cell-regenerating properties. It is used externally and is beneficial for set broken bones. It is not recommended for deep puncture wounds.

Cottonwood Bud Oil (Balm of Gilead)
Cottonwood buds are anti-fungal, anti-microbial, & anti-inflammatory. It is used externally for pain relief from arthritis, strains, and muscle pains, and is beneficial for sunburns.

Green Tea *(Camellia sinensis)*
Green tea is rich in antioxidants that help protect the skin from damage. Apply cooled green tea bags to your skin or drink green tea.

Lavender *(Lavandula officinalis)*
Lavender essential oil has calming effects and may help reduce skin irritation. Dilute it before applying to the skin.

Plantain *(Plantago major)*
Plantain is traditionally used externally for swollen joints, sore muscles, sprains, insect bites and stings, snake bites, and sore feet. Its tannins may help stop bleeding, and it is known as a drawing herb. Warning: For snake bites, it is crucial to seek immediate medical attention, as plantain is not a substitute for professional medical treatment.

Raw Honey
Manuka honey has natural antibacterial properties and can be applied to wounds to prevent infection and and support skin recovery. It is also beneficial for burns.

Rosehip Oil *(Rosa canina)*
Rosehip oil is rich in vitamins and fatty acids that support skin regeneration and hydration. It is often used as a facial oil.

Turmeric *(Curcuma longa)*
Turmeric contains curcumin, which has anti-inflammatory and antioxidant properties. It can be used topically or consumed to support skin health.

Witch Hazel *(Hamamelis virginiana)*
Witch hazel has astringent properties and can help tone the skin and reduce inflammation.

Antiseptic Balm

This chaparral salve blends the beneficial qualities of chaparral leaves with nourishing plant-based oil and beeswax, offering a natural option for supporting skin health. Historically, it has been used to address skin infections and to soothe sunburns and skin-related issues.

INGREDIENTS:

- 1 ½ cup of high-quality organic plant-based oil
- 1 cup of dried chaparral leaves (*Larrea tridentata*)
- ¼ cup of beeswax pellets
- Essential oil (optional, for added fragrance)

NOTES:

Do not use this preparation on a very recent burn as oil may seal in the heat which will allow damage to continue or lead to a more severe burn.

Perform a patch test before widespread use to ensure no allergic reactions.

Avoid using on deep wounds or open sores without consulting a healthcare professional.

INSTRUCTIONS:

1 | **Infusing the Oil:** In a clean, dry glass jar, combine the chosen plant-based oil (*e.g.* olive, hemp, almond, jojoba) and dried chaparral leaves. Choosing the right plant-based oil tailored to your specific skin condition is crucial for optimizing the benefits of the chaparral salve. (More about carrier oils and their benefits under the **Oil Infusions** section of this book). Ensure that the leaves are fully submerged in the oil. Seal the jar tightly and place it in a warm, sunny spot for about 4-6 weeks to allow the infusion to occur. Shake the jar occasionally. After the infusion period, strain the oil to remove the chaparral leaves, ensuring only the infused oil remains.

2 | **Or Quick Oil Infusion:** In a saucepan, combine the plant-based oil and dried chaparral leaves. Heat the mixture over low heat, maintaining a gentle simmer for 1-2 hours. Stir occasionally. Allow the oil to cool slightly before straining to remove the chaparral leaves.

3 | **Create the Salve:** In a double boiler, melt the beeswax pellets over low heat. Once melted, add the chaparral-infused oil to the beeswax and stir well. If desired, add a few drops of essential oil for fragrance.

4 | **Pouring and Cooling:** Pour the melted mixture into clean, sterile jars or containers. Allow the salve to cool and solidify.

DOSAGE:

Apply a small amount of chaparral salve topically to the affected area 2-3 times daily.

Nature's "Betadine"

Nature offers herbal antiseptic solutions that can serve as alternatives to commercial antiseptics.

This recipe uses ingredients traditionally known for their antimicrobial and soothing properties. This homemade solution may be used for minor cuts, scrapes, and abrasions to clean the area and support the body's natural healing processes. Below is a recipe using natural ingredients like tea tree oil and witch hazel, which are popular in folk medicine for their antiseptic qualities.

INGREDIENTS:

- 2 tablespoons dried thyme (*Thymus vulgaris*)
- 2 tablespoons dried goldenseal root (*Hydrastis canadensis*)
- 1 tablespoon dried lavender flowers (*Lavandula angustifolia*)
- 1 cup distilled water
- ¼ cup witch hazel extract (optional for added astringent effect)
- - 10 drops tea tree essential oil (*Melaleuca alternifolia*)

NOTES:

Do not use on deep or severe wounds; seek medical attention for serious injuries.

Patch test before use to ensure no allergic reaction occurs.

Discontinue use if irritation or adverse reactions occur. Pregnant or breastfeeding women should consult ahealthcare provider before use.

INSTRUCTIONS:

1 | **Preparare the Herbal Infusion:** Boil 1 cup of distilled water. Add 2 tablespoons of dried thyme, 2 tablespoons of dried goldenseal root, and 1 tablespoon of dried lavender flowers to the boiling water. Remove from heat and let the mixture steep for 30 minutes.

2 | **Strain:** Strain the mixture through a fine mesh strainer or cheesecloth into a clean container, ensuring no plant material remains in the liquid.

3 | **Mix:** Allow the infusion to cool to room temperature. Add ¼ cup of witch hazel extract if using. Add 10 drops of tea tree essential oil to the cooled mixture and stir well.

4 | **Storage:** Transfer the antiseptic solution to a sterilized glass jar or bottle with a tight-fitting lid. Store in a cool, dark place for up to two weeks. For longer storage, refrigerate and use within a month.

5 | **Apply:** Clean the wound with mild soap and water. Apply the natural antiseptic solution to the affected area using a clean cotton ball or gauze.

DOSAGE:

Apply as needed, ensuring to keep the wound clean and covered with a sterile bandage if necessary.

Black Drawing Salve
for Boils, Splinters, and Tick Bites

Black drawing salve is a traditional remedy known for its ability to draw out impurities from the skin, making it effective for treating boils, tick bites, and removing splinters. The combination of activated charcoal and bentonite clay works as a dynamic duo to pull out impurities and toxins from the skin. Herbal-infused oils, such as plantain, calendula, and comfrey, contribute their anti-inflammatory and skin-nourishing properties to aid in the healing process.

Essential oils such as tea tree and lavender not only provide a pleasant aroma but also deliver antimicrobial benefits, defending against potential infections. The beeswax in the salve creates a protective layer on the skin, assisting in maintaining the skin's integrity and preventing further damage.

INGREDIENTS:

- 3 tbsp infused oil
- 3 tbsp coconut oil
- 2 tbsp castor oil
- 2 tbsp beeswax
- 1 tbsp activated charcoal
- 1 tbsp bentonite clay
- 25 drops of lavender essential oil
- 15 drops of tea tree essential oil

NOTES:

This salve is a great natural remedy, but it is not a replacement for medical care when needed. Consult a doctor before using if you have any health conditions or concerns.

Prolonged or excessive use of this salve may result in dryness, especially in individuals with sensitive or naturally dry skin. If you experience dryness, reduce the frequency of application to allow the skin to regain its natural moisture balance.

INSTRUCTIONS:

1 | **Combine and Melt Ingredients:** In a double boiler, melt the chosen herbal infused oil (*e.g.* calendula, comfrey, and/or plantain), coconut oil, castor oil, and beeswax together. My favorite is plantain (*Plantago* spp.) for its drawing abilities.

2 | **Add Absorbers:** Once melted, add activated charcoal and bentonite clay, stirring continuously to avoid clumps. Activated charcoal tends to stain fabric, so you don't want it touching your clothing or furniture.

3 | **Essential Oil Blend:** Remove from heat and add lavender and tea tree essential oils, ensuring even distribution.

4 | **Jar the Salve:** Pour the mixture into sterilized jars and let it cool before sealing.

5 | **Application:** Apply a small amount of the salve to the affected area, covering it with a bandage if needed. You can leave the salve on the spot overnight. In the case of splinters and other foreign bodies, check if it's moved enough to grab it with tweezers. For tick and insect bites, you can remove the salve after a couple hours, clean the spot, and then either let it be open to the air or cover it with another bandage.

6 | **Moisturize:** Apply a gentle, hydrating moisturizer to the treated area after using the salve if needed.

DOSAGE:

Use 1-2 times daily until the issue resolves.

Soothing Chickweed and Vinegar Bath
for Rashes

Chickweed is a common herb traditionally used for its soothing properties, especially for skin-related issues. When combined with vinegar, this bath recipe may support relief for rashes and irritated skin. Chickweed contains compounds like flavonoids and saponins, which are known to help with skin discomfort, providing hydration through its mucilage content and soothing itchiness. Additionally, chickweed is traditionally known for its wound-healing properties and mild antimicrobial benefits. Apple cider vinegar is commonly used in skincare for balancing the skin's pH levels, acting as a gentle exfoliant with acetic acid, and offering antimicrobial properties. It is also known to help with sunburned skin.

INGREDIENTS:

- 1 cup of fresh chickweed leaves (*Stellaria media*) or ½ cup of dried chickweed
- 2 cups of apple cider vinegar

NOTES:

If you are allergic to chickweed or vinegar, refrain from using this bath.

Avoid getting the herbal infusion in your eyes.

Apple cider vinegar can cause irritation and may not be suitable for all types of eczema. Speak with a doctor or naturopath before using it, dilute the vinegar, and do a patch test first.

INSTRUCTIONS:

1 | **Prepare Chickweed Infusion:** Harvest fresh chickweed leaves, ensuring they are free from pesticides and thoroughly washed. Alternatively, use ½ cup of dried chickweed. In a large pot, bring 4 cups of water to a boil. Add the washed chickweed leaves or dried chickweed to the boiling water. Let it simmer for 10-15 minutes. Strain the chickweed-infused water into a bathtub filled with warm water.

2 | **Add Vinegar:** Add 2 cups of apple cider vinegar to the bath. Vinegar helps balance the skin's pH and provides additional soothing properties. Consider using organic apple cider vinegar.

3 | **Mix and Soak:** Stir the bathwater gently to ensure an even distribution of chickweed and vinegar. Soak in the bath for 15-20 minutes, allowing the herbal infusion to soothe the skin. Pat your skin dry after the bath; do not rub vigorously.

DOSAGE:

Take this bath once a day until the rash or irritation subsides.

Forgotten Home Apothecary

Antibiotic
Restorative Cream

There are several OTC antiseptic ointments to choose from at the local market, which are normally applied directly to the wound. They are meant to prevent infection from developing. While these options often work and the products have some helpful ingredients, they also have some unnecessary ingredients, so they can be mass-produced.

This herbal salve combines the soothing properties of beeswax, almond oil, and a blend of herbs and essential oils known for their antibacterial and skin-nourishing qualities. The ingredients are chosen for their potential to promote skin health and provide a natural alternative to commercial products like Neosporin.

INGREDIENTS:

- 2 oz. beeswax
- 1 cup yarrow-infused organic almond oil
- 0.5 tsp tea tree oil
- 25 drops of vitamin E oil
- 20 drops of lavender essential oil
- 10 drops of lemon essential oil

NOTES:

For external use only.

Perform a patch test to check for allergies before widespread use. Discontinue use if irritation occurs.

For those who do not like the smell of lemon or lavender, you can substitute either one, or both. Lavender can be replaced with chamomile essential oil, and lemon can be replaced with fir essential oil.

INSTRUCTIONS:

1 | **Melt Beeswax:** In a double boiler, melt the beeswax until fully liquid (beeswax pellets melt quicker than solid beeswax).

2 | **Add Yarrow-Infused Almond Oil:** Once the beeswax is melted, slowly pour in the yarrow-infused organic almond oil (or chosen substitute like organic olive oil) while stirring continuously. Use our oil-infusion recipe to infuse the yarrow.

3 | **Incorporate Essential Oils:** Remove the mixture from heat and add tea tree oil, lavender essential oil, and lemon essential oil. Stir thoroughly to ensure even distribution.

4 | **Add Vitamin E Oil:** Add vitamin E oil and stir again. Vitamin E contributes to stabilizing the herbs, helping to maintain their potency and therapeutic benefits. The inclusion of vitamin E significantly extends the shelf life of the herbal healing salve by preventing the oils from becoming rancid.

5 | **Cooling and Storage:** Allow the mixture to cool but not solidify completely. Pour it into salve containers or jars. Let it solidify at room temperature. Store in a cool, dark place to prolong shelf life.

DOSAGE:

Apply a small amount to the affected area. Repeat 2-3 times a day or as needed.

Calendula and Comfrey
Skin Salve

Calendula (*Calendula officinalis*) and comfrey (*Symphytum officinale*) are two powerful herbs known for their skin-soothing properties. Calendula is recognized for its anti-inflammatory and antimicrobial effects, making it excellent for promoting wound healing and reducing skin irritation. Comfrey, with its high content of allantoin, is valued for its ability to support cell regeneration and support the recovery process.

INGREDIENTS:

- 1 cup of calendula-infused oil (organic olive oil base)
- ¼ cup of comfrey-infused oil (organic olive oil base)
- 2.5 oz of beeswax
- 10 drops of lavender essential oil (optional for added fragrance and antibacterial properties)

NOTES:

Do not use on lacerations or on deep open wounds.

Consider conducting a patch test before widespread use to ensure no allergic reaction. Discontinue use if irritation occurs.

Consult with a healthcare professional before use, especially for pregnant or breastfeeding individuals.

INSTRUCTIONS:

CALENDULA-INFUSED OIL:
To prepare, fill a jar with dried calendula flowers and cover them with olive oil. Let the mixture sit for ~4 weeks, shaking daily. Strain out the flowers, and you have your infused oil.

COMFREY-INFUSED OIL:
Follow the same process as with calendula, using dried comfrey leaves and/or root.

1. **Double Boiler Setup:** Set up a double boiler by placing a heatproof bowl over a pot of simmering water.
2. **Combine Oils:** In the bowl, combine the calendula-infused oil, Comfrey-infused oil, and beeswax. Heat gently until the beeswax melts, stirring occasionally.
3. **Add Essential Oil (Optional):** If desired, add 10 drops of lavender essential oil to enhance the salve's fragrance and provide additional antibacterial properties.
4. **Pour into Containers:** Once the mixture is well-combined, pour it into small, clean jars or tins. Label.
5. **Cooling and Solidifying:** Allow the salve to cool and solidify at room temperature. This may take a few hours.

DOSAGE:

Apply a small amount of the salve to clean, dry skin as needed.

Forgotten Home Apothecary

Yarrow
Stop-Bleeding Powder

Yarrow, known scientifically as *Achillea millefolium*, is a versatile herb with a rich history in traditional medicine.

Renowned for its styptic properties, yarrow has been used for centuries to promote wound healing and control bleeding. The active compounds in yarrow, such as tannins and flavonoids, contribute to its hemostatic effects, making it an excellent choice for creating a styptic powder to staunch bleeding from minor cuts and wounds.

Kaolin clay, a natural mineral known for its absorbent and soothing properties, enhances the effectiveness of styptic powder. You may also use yarrow powder on its own. I often store yarrow powder in a sealed straw for portability when in the woods.

INGREDIENTS:

- 2 tablespoons of dried yarrow (*Achillea millefolium*) powder
- 1 tablespoon of Kaolin clay

NOTES:

For external use only.

Consult a healthcare professional for deep or serious wounds.

Cayenne pepper is another potent natural remedy for controlling bleeding. Rich in capsaicin, it promotes blood clotting and acts as a powerful hemostatic agent. To use, apply a small amount of cayenne pepper directly to the bleeding wound. The capsaicin stimulates blood flow, helping to seal the wound and prevent excessive bleeding.

INSTRUCTIONS:

1 | **Prepare the Herbs:** Grind the dried yarrow into a fine powder using a mortar and pestle or a coffee grinder. Harvest yarrow from pesticide-free areas for the highest quality.
2 | **Combine Ingredients:** In a bowl, thoroughly mix the yarrow powder and kaolin clay.
3 | **Store the Powder:** Transfer the mixture into a clean, airtight container for storage.
4 | **Application:** Clean the wound thoroughly before application.
Apply a small amount of the yarrow and kaolin clay styptic powder directly to the bleeding area. Gently press the powder onto the wound until the bleeding stops. Repeat as needed.

Alternatively, you can create a yarrow poultice using freshly harvested leaves—crush or chew and apply directly to the wound.

DOSAGE:

Apply as needed.

Lavender Infused Oil
for Skin Regeneration

Lavender (*Lavandula angustifolia*) is a versatile herb known for its calming aroma and numerous health benefits. Infusing lavender into oil can create a potent concoction for promoting skin regeneration. The essential oil derived from lavender contains compounds like linalool and linalyl acetate, which have antimicrobial and antioxidant properties, making it beneficial for skin health.

INGREDIENTS:

- 1 cup of carrier oil (such as sweet almond oil or jojoba oil)
- ¼ cup dried lavender flowers (*Lavandula angustifolia*)

NOTES:

Perform a patch test before widespread use to check for any allergic reactions.

If irritation occurs, discontinue use immediately.

Avoid contact with eyes.

If the oil comes into contact with the eyes, rinse thoroughly with water.

INSTRUCTIONS:

1 | **Prepare the Ingredients:** Gather 1 cup of your chosen carrier oil and ¼ cup of dried lavender flowers.
2 | **Infusion Process:** In a clean and dry glass jar, combine the carrier oil and dried lavender flowers. Ensure that the lavender flowers are fully submerged in the oil. Seal the jar tightly and place it in a cool, dark place for at least 4-6 weeks to allow for proper infusion.
3 | **Strain the Oil:** After the infusion period, strain the oil using cheesecloth or a fine mesh sieve to remove the lavender flowers, ensuring only the infused oil remains.
4 | **Store the Infused Oil:** Transfer the lavender-infused oil to a dark glass bottle to protect it from light. Store it in a cool, dark place for extended shelf life.

To transform this into a salve, melt beeswax (around 2 ounces per cup of oil) in a double boiler, then combine it with the lavender-infused oil until well mixed. Adjust the ratio for desired consistency. Test on a plate for texture, pour into dark glass jars or tins, and let it cool. Label and store the salve in a cool, dark place. Adjust the beeswax quantity to achieve the preferred texture of the salve.

DOSAGE:

Apply a small amount of lavender-infused oil to the affected skin area. Gently massage the oil into the skin in circular motions.

Chamomile Lotion
for Scars

Chamomile (*Matricaria chamomilla*, also known as *Chamomilla recutita*) is renowned for its anti-inflammatory and skin-soothing properties, making it an excellent choice for scar healing. The carrier oil used in this recipe is rosehip seed oil, valued for its high content of essential fatty acids and antioxidants, which promote skin regeneration and reduce the appearance of scars. Known for its anti-inflammatory and regenerative properties, helichrysum oil supports skin healing and can aid in reducing the appearance of scars. It is also praised for its antioxidant content, which helps protect the skin from free radical damage. Frankincense essential oil has been traditionally used for its skin-rejuvenating properties. It may promote cell regeneration and improve the appearance of scars. Frankincense essential oil also has anti-inflammatory effects, contributing to overall skin health.

INGREDIENTS:

- 1 cup chamomile-infused rosehip seed oil (made with - 1 cup rosehip seed oil and - 2 tablespoons dried chamomile flowers)
- ¼ cup beeswax
- ¼ cup shea butter
- 5 drops helichrysum essential oil
- 5 drops frankincense essential oil

NOTES:

Perform a patch test before widespread use to ensure no allergic reactions.

Avoid contact with eyes.

Discontinue use if irritation occurs.

Consult with a healthcare professional for persistent or worsening skin conditions.

INSTRUCTIONS:

1 | **Prepare Chamomile-Infused Rosehip Seed Oil:** In a heatproof jar, combine 2 tablespoons dried chamomile flowers with 1 cup of rosehip seed oil. Place the jar in a sunny windowsill for 4-6 weeks, shaking it daily. Strain the oil to remove the chamomile flowers. You can also use the quick infusion method.

2 | **Create the Lotion:** In a double boiler, melt ¼ cup beeswax and ¼ cup shea butter with 1 cup of chamomile-infused rosehip seed oil. Stir the mixture well and remove from heat.

3 | **Add Essential Oils:** Incorporate 5 drops of helichrysum essential oil and 5 drops of frankincense essential oil. Mix thoroughly to ensure even distribution.

4 | **Cool and Blend:** Allow the mixture to cool for a few minutes. Use a hand blender to whip the lotion until it reaches a creamy consistency.

5 | **Store in Containers:** Transfer the lotion into sterilized jars or bottles. Label.

DOSAGE:

Apply a small amount of the chamomile salve to the scarred area twice daily. Massage gently until absorbed.

Honey Oat Soap
for Eczema and Skin Rashes

Honey and oats are well-known for their soothing and moisturizing properties, making them excellent ingredients for a homemade soap to alleviate symptoms of eczema and soothe irritated skin. Honey is renowned for its antimicrobial and healing properties, while oats provide gentle exfoliation and help retain skin moisture.

INGREDIENTS:

- ½ cup oats
- 2 tablespoons raw and unprocessed honey
- 1 cup olive oil
- ½ cup coconut oil
- 2.2 ounces lye (Sodium hydroxide)
- ½ cup water
- 1 tablespoon almond oil

NOTES:

Use a soap calculator to ensure accurate measurements. You can use an online soap calculator like SoapCalc or any other calculator you prefer.

If you prefer a simpler version, you might find using a glycerin soap base advantageous. Glycerin bases are readily available, require less handling of lye, and can be melted and customized with herbs and essential oils to create a straightforward herbal soap.

INSTRUCTIONS:

1. **Prepare the Oats:** Grind the oats into a fine powder using a blender or food processor.
2. **Prepare the Lye Solution:** In a heat-resistant container, add the lye to the water. Stir carefully and allow the solution to cool while ensuring the area is well-ventilated. Wear protective gear, including gloves and safety glasses, when working with lye. Lye solution gets hot fast and puts off strong fumes for a few moments that you should avoid breathing in.
3. **Prepare Oils:** In a separate container, combine olive oil, coconut oil, and almond oil.
4. **Mix Lye Solution and Oils:** Once the lye solution and oils are at a similar temperature (around 100-110°F), slowly pour the lye solution into the oils, stirring continuously.
5. **Blend Ingredients:** Use a stick blender to mix the ingredients until it reaches trace - a thickened consistency resembling runny pudding.
6. **Add Honey and Oats:** Add the ground oats and honey to the mixture. Stir thoroughly to evenly distribute these ingredients.
7. **Pour into Mold:** Pour the soap mixture into molds. Tap the molds gently to remove air bubbles.
8. **Curing:** Cover the mold with a lid or plastic wrap and insulate it to keep the heat in. Allow the soap to cure for 24-48 hours.
9. **Cut into Bars:** Once the soap has hardened, cut it into bars of your desired size.
10. **Additional Curing:** Allow the bars to cure for 4-6 weeks. This ensures the lye fully reacts with the oils, creating a milder and harder soap.

DOSAGE:

Use the soap as needed during your regular bath or shower routine. Rinse thoroughly.

Psoriasis Irritation Relief
Herbal Ointment

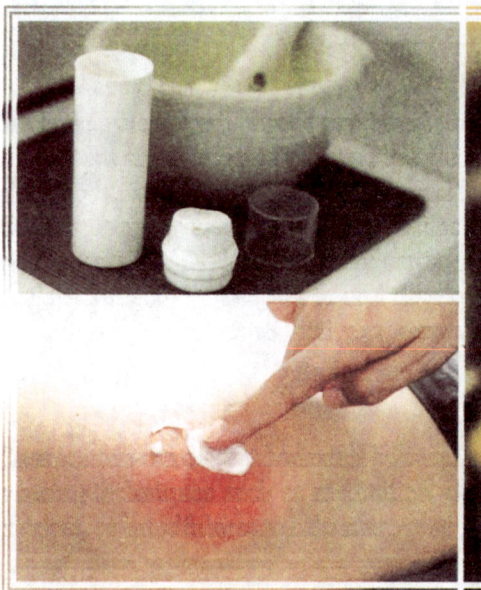

Mahonia aquifolium, commonly known as Oregon grape, is a versatile herb with anti-inflammatory and antimicrobial properties. It has been traditionally used to address various skin conditions, including psoriasis. Its active compounds, such as berberine, confer its therapeutic effects. The peppermint oil brings additional benefits, such as cooling relief and potential anti-itch properties.

INGREDIENTS:

- ½ cup Oregon grape (*Mahonia aquifolium*) root decoction
- ¼ cup coconut oil
- 2 tablespoons beeswax
- 1 tablespoon shea butter
- 10 drops peppermint essential oil

NOTES:

Perform a patch test before widespread use to check for potential allergic reactions. Apply a small amount of the ointment on a small area of skin and wait for 24 hours to observe any adverse reactions.

Exercise caution to prevent contact with eyes and mucous membranes. If accidental contact occurs, rinse thoroughly with water. Do not ingest the ointment.

INSTRUCTIONS:

1| **Prepare the Extract:** Combine ½ cup of *Mahonia aquifolium* root with 1 cup of water in a saucepan. Bring the mixture to a gentle boil and then reduce heat to simmer for 15 minutes. Strain the mixture to obtain the liquid extract of *Mahonia aquifolium*.

2| **Create the Ointment Base:** In a double boiler, melt ¼ cup coconut oil, 2 tablespoons beeswax, and 1 tablespoon shea butter. Stir the mixture continuously until all ingredients are fully melted and well combined.

3| **Combine Ingredients:** Add ½ cup of the prepared Oregon grape root extract to the melted base. Stir thoroughly to ensure the even distribution of the herbal extract within the ointment.

4| **Add Peppermint Essential Oil:** Add 10 drops of peppermint essential oil into the mixture. Stir continuously to evenly distribute the peppermint oil throughout the ointment.

5| **Cool and Store:** Allow the ointment mixture to cool at room temperature until it solidifies. Once solid, transfer the ointment into a clean, airtight container for storage. Use a clean spatula or applicator to avoid contamination when scooping out the ointment.

DOSAGE:

Apply a thin layer of the ointment to affected areas twice daily, or as needed.

Arnica and Calendula
First Aid Spray

Arnica (*Arnica montana*) and calendula (*Calendula officinalis*) are two herbs traditionally recognized for their beneficial properties. Arnica is renowned for its anti-inflammatory and pain-relieving effects, while Calendula is celebrated for its antimicrobial and skin-soothing qualities. Combining these herbs in a first aid spray helps create a supportive solution for addressing minor injuries, bruises, and skin irritations. This natural blend can be a valuable addition to your wellness routine for promoting skin health and comfort.

INGREDIENTS:

- 1 cup distilled water
- 2 tablespoons dried arnica flowers
- 2 tablespoons dried calendula petals
- 1 tablespoon witch hazel extract
- 1 teaspoon aloe vera gel
- 10 drops lavender essential oil
- 5 drops tea tree essential oil

NOTES:

Avoid applying the spray to open wounds or broken skin.

Discontinue use if any irritation occurs.

Prior to use on children or pregnant individuals, consult with a healthcare professional.

INSTRUCTIONS:

1 | **Prepare the Herbal Infusion:** Bring the distilled water to a boil. Pour the hot water over the dried arnica flowers and calendula petals in a heatproof bowl. Cover the bowl and allow the herbs to steep for 20 minutes to extract their medicinal properties. Strain the infusion, separating the herbal water from the plant material, resulting in a concentrated herbal water base.

2 | **Create the First Aid Solution:** Combine 1 cup of the herbal water with witch hazel extract and aloe vera gel. Add 10 drops of lavender essential oil and 5 drops of tea tree essential oil to enhance the spray's healing properties. Stir the mixture thoroughly to ensure even distribution of the ingredients.

3 | **Pour into a Spray Bottle:** Use a funnel to carefully pour the herbal solution into a clean and sterilized spray bottle. Ensure the bottle is tightly sealed to prevent contamination. Label.

DOSAGE:

To apply, hold the spray bottle approximately 6 inches away from the affected area. Spritz the affected area 2-3 times per application. Repeat the application 2-3 times a day or as needed for relief.

Forgotten Home Apothecary

Cooling Herbal Gel
for Burn Relief

Sunburns can be alleviated with the soothing properties of herbal remedies. St. John's wort (*Hypericum perforatum*) and chaparral (*Larrea tridentata*) are renowned for their healing effects. St. John's wort possesses anti-inflammatory properties, while Chaparral offers antioxidants and analgesics. Aloe vera is included in this formula for its cooling and moisturizing properties. Combining these herbs into a cooling gel provides a convenient and effective way to relieve sunburn discomfort.

INGREDIENTS:

- ½ cup St. John's wort infused oil
- ½ cup chaparral infused oil
- ¼ cup aloe vera gel
- 2 tablespoons beeswax pellets
- 10 drops lavender essential oil (*Lavandula angustifolia*)
- 5 drops peppermint essential oil (*Mentha piperita*)

NOTES:

For an extra cooling sensation, store the gel in the refrigerator.

Perform a patch test before widespread use to check for allergies Discontinue use if irritation or allergic reaction occurs.

Avoid contact with eyes.

INSTRUCTIONS:

1 | **Prepare Infused Oils:** Combine ½ cup of dried St. John's wort flowers with 1 cup of organic olive oil. Combine ½ cup of dried chaparral leaves with 1 cup of organic grapeseed oil. Allow both mixtures to infuse in a dark, cool place for 4-6 weeks, shaking daily. Strain the oils using cheesecloth or a fine mesh sieve.

2 | **Create the Cooling Gel:** In a heat-resistant bowl, combine ½ cup of St. John's wort infused oil and ½ cup of chaparral infused oil. Add ¼ cup of aloe vera gel and mix well. In a separate heat-resistant container, melt 2 tablespoons of beeswax pellets over low heat. Once melted, slowly add the beeswax to the oil mixture, stirring continuously.

3 | **Incorporate Essential Oils:** Allow the mixture to cool slightly before adding 10 drops of lavender essential oil and 5 drops of peppermint essential oil. Stir thoroughly to ensure even distribution.

4 | **Transfer to a Jar:** Pour the gel into a clean, airtight glass jar. Let it cool and solidify before sealing the jar. Label.

5 | **Application:** Apply the cooling herbal gel to sunburned areas as needed, gently massaging into the skin.

DOSAGE:

Use the gel up to three times a day or as needed for sunburn relief.

Bug-Off
Spray

In this "Bug-Off" spray recipe, we're incorporating three essential oils known for their insect-repelling properties. The combination of citronella (*Cymbopogon nardus*), peppermint (*Mentha piperita*), and lemongrass (*Cymbopogon citratus*) oils creates an effective and natural solution to keep bugs away. These oils work together to provide a practical and chemical-free option for outdoor protection.

INGREDIENTS:

- 15 drops of citronella essential oil
- 8 drops of peppermint essential oil
- 10 drops of lemongrass essential oil
- 1 cup distilled water
- ¼ cup witch hazel

NOTES:

Perform a patch test before widespread use to ensure no allergic reactions.

Avoid contact with eyes; if contact occurs, rinse thoroughly with water.

Do not ingest the spray.

Consider wearing long sleeves and pants in addition to using the spray for enhanced protection.

INSTRUCTIONS:

1. **Gather Ingredients:** Ensure you have all the ingredients ready: citronella, peppermint, and lemongrass essential oils, distilled water, and witch hazel.
2. **Mix Essential Oils:** In a small bowl, combine 15 drops of citronella essential oil, 8 drops of peppermint essential oil, and 10 drops of lemongrass essential oil. Stir well for even distribution.
3. **Prepare Base:** In a separate container, mix 1 cup of distilled water with ¼ cup of witch hazel. This forms the base of the spray.
4. **Combine and Shake:** Add the mixed essential oils to the water and witch hazel base (you may also add the oils directly to this mixture and skip Step 2). Secure the lid and shake the mixture thoroughly to blend all the ingredients.
5. **Transfer to Spray Bottle:** Using a funnel, pour the mixture into a spray bottle. Label. A spray bottle makes application easy and convenient. Store the "Bug-Off" Spray in a cool, dark place to maintain its potency.

DOSAGE:

Apply the "Bug-Off" spray generously on exposed skin before heading outdoors. Reapply every 2 hours or as needed for continuous protection.

Anti-Mosquito
Salve

This salve harnesses the power of various essential oils known for their insect-repelling properties, combined with nourishing base ingredients. Known for its refreshing aroma, peppermint oil (*Mentha piperita*) contains compounds like menthol that naturally repel mosquitoes and other insects. Lemongrass (*Cymbopogon citratus*) oil has a citrusy scent and contains citronella, a well-known insect repellent. The uplifting scent of sweet orange oil (*Citrus sinensis*) masks body odors that attract mosquitoes, making it an effective natural repellent. Lavender (*Lavandula angustifolia*) oil has calming and soothing properties, while its floral scent repels mosquitoes and promotes relaxation. Basil (*Ocimum basilicum*) oil contains eugenol, which has insect-repelling properties and adds a pleasant herbal aroma to the salve.

INGREDIENTS:

- ¼ cup coconut oil
- ⅛ - ¼ cup beeswax pellets
- ¼ cup shea butter
- 2 tbsp castor oil
- 30 drops peppermint essential oil
- 15 drops lemongrass essential oil
- 10 drops sweet orange essential oil
- 10 drops lavender essential oil
- 5 drops basil essential oil

NOTES:

For added moisturizing benefits, you can increase the amount of shea butter in the recipe.

Avoid contact with eyes and mucous membranes.

Perform a patch test before using the salve, especially if you have sensitive skin or allergies. Discontinue use if any irritation occurs.

Keep out of reach of children and pets.

INSTRUCTIONS:

1 | **Melt the Base Ingredients:** In a double boiler or a heatproof bowl placed over a pot of simmering water, melt the coconut oil, beeswax pellets/pastilles, shea butter, and castor oil together. Stir occasionally until completely melted and well combined. Start with ⅛ cup of beeswax, adding more if needed (test a small drop in your tin to see if you like the consistency once solidified; more beeswax will make the consistency harder).

2 | **Add Essential Oils:** Once the base ingredients are melted, remove the mixture from heat. Allow it to cool slightly, but not solidify. Add the drops of peppermint, lemongrass, sweet orange, lavender, and basil essential oils to the mixture. Stir well to ensure the essential oils are evenly distributed throughout the mixture.

3 | **Pour into Containers:** Carefully pour the mixture into clean, sterilized containers or tins. Leave some space at the top to avoid spills when closing the containers.

4 | **Allow to Cool and Solidify:** Let the salve cool and solidify at room temperature. This process may take a few hours, depending on the temperature of your surroundings.

5 | **Label and Store:** Once the salve has cooled and solidified, label each container with the name and date of preparation. Store the salve in a cool, dry place away from direct sunlight.

DOSAGE:

Apply a small amount the salve to exposed areas of skin before heading outdoors. Reapply every few hours for continuous protection.

Anti-Itch
Plantain Band-Aid

This simple yet effective herbal remedy utilizes the therapeutic potential of plantain leaves to address inflammation and promote the healing process.

Plantain is often called the "band-aid" plant as it has soothing and anti-inflammatory properties, all thanks to a natural compound found in this plant: iridoids. Plantain also contains aglycone and aucubigenin, which have documented antimicrobial properties. Overall, plantain is packed with beneficial agents for the skin and, in addition, has allantoin, which promotes skin healing. Plantain is also my #1 go-to for bites and stings.

INGREDIENTS:

- 2 tablespoons of fresh plantain leaves (*Plantago major* or *P. lanceolata*)
- ¼ cup of olive oil
- 1 teaspoon of beeswax

NOTES:

For a quick and natural alternative, consider placing a fresh plantain leaf directly over the wound. Simply clean the leaf, bruise it slightly to release its juices, and apply it directly to the affected area.

Careful while harvesting; avoid plantain that has been treated with pesticides.

Avoid using this balm on deep wounds or open sores.

Discontinue use if any irritation or allergic reaction occurs.

INSTRUCTIONS:

1 | **Prepare the Plantain Leaves:** Combine the finely chopped plantain leaves. Ensure the leaves are free of dampness - let air dry for a day or two for best results so that most of the moisture is released.

2 | **Infuse Plantain Leaves with Olive Oil:** Combine the chopped leaves with organic olive oil in a small saucepan. Heat the mixture on low heat for about 30-40 minutes, ensuring it doesn't boil. This will infuse the oil with the plantain's properties

3 | **Strain the Infused Oil:** Strain the mixture through a fine sieve or cheesecloth into a heatproof container.

4 | **Melt the Beeswax:** In another small saucepan, melt the beeswax on low heat.

5 | **Combine Beeswax with Infused Plantain Oil:** Once the beeswax is melted, add the infused plantain oil and stir well.

6 | **Pour the Mixture into a Container:** Pour the mixture into a small container or tin. Label.

7 | **Allow the Balm to Cool and Solidify:** Let it cool and solidify. You now have your plantain anti-inflammatory and anti-itch band-aid. This plantain band-aid balm recipe provides a more portable and infused solution for extended use.

DOSAGE:

Apply a small amount of the balm to the affected area as needed. Ensure the wound is clean before applying.

NATURAL ALTERNATIVES
for Personal Care Products

Using homemade personal care products with herbal ingredients can offer several benefits compared to commercial products:

CUSTOMIZATION:

You have the flexibility to customize recipes based on your skin type, preferences, and specific needs.

QUALITY CONTROL:

You can choose high-quality, organic ingredients and ensure the purity of your products.

AVOIDANCE OF HARMFUL CHEMICALS:

By using natural, herbal ingredients, you can avoid the potential negative effects of synthetic chemicals.

PRESERVATION OF HERBAL PROPERTIES:

Fresh or dried herbs in homemade products retain more of their beneficial properties.

COST-EFFECTIVENESS:

Buying bulk herbs and making your products can be more cost-effective in the long run.

Considerations for Homemade Products:

SAFETY PRECAUTIONS:

Perform patch tests to check for allergies before applying homemade products to larger areas.

STORAGE AND SHELF LIFE:

Without preservatives, homemade products might have a shorter shelf life, so it's essential to make smaller batches and store them properly.

CONSISTENCY AND TEXTURE:

Achieving the desired consistency may take some experimentation, and textures may vary between batches.

TIME AND EFFORT:

Requires time and effort, but the process can be rewarding and allows you to connect with the preparation of your personal care items.

Understanding the potential harm present in store-bought skincare products, particularly the inclusion of toxic ingredients, underscores the importance of informed decision-making. Research indicates that the average adult uses products containing up to 126 chemical ingredients daily, with topical application potentially leading to both short-term and long-term health issues.

If you can't make your own products, here is a list enumerating the toxic ingredients commonly found in store-bought skin care products that you should avoid:

CONCERNS	Contains hidden harmful chemicals; linked to irritation, allergies, and hormone disruption.
FOUND IN	Shampoo, body wash, shaving cream, deodorant, and skincare products.

CONCERNS	Carcinogenic; linked to skin rashes, shortness of breath, and breathing difficulties.
FOUND IN	Hair straightening products, nail polish, deodorants, toothpaste, and various cosmetics.

CONCERNS	Endocrine disruptors; harmful to the environment.
FOUND IN	Fragrances and plastics

CONCERNS	Facilitates the entry of toxic ingredients into the body.
FOUND IN	Hand soaps, hair products, sunscreen, and various personal care products.

CONCERNS	Harmful to the environment and endocrine system.
FOUND IN	Hair products, soaps, shaving creams, and deodorants.

TRICLOSAN

CONCERNS	Antibacterial agent; impacts reproductive hormones.
FOUND IN	Soaps, hand sanitizers, deodorants, mouthwash, shaving cream, and toothpaste.

ETHANOLAMINES

CONCERNS	Used as emulsifiers; may cause irritation.
FOUND IN	Skincare and cleaning products.

OXYBENZONE

CONCERNS	Potential endocrine disruptor.
FOUND IN	Sunscreen and products containing sunscreen.

OCTINOXATE

CONCERNS	Can be irritating to the skin.
FOUND IN	Sunscreen products.

HOMOSALATE

CONCERNS	Commonly used in sunscreens; potential endocrine disruptor; can irritate the skin.
FOUND IN	Sunscreen products.

TOLUENE, BUTYLATED HYDROXYTOLUENE (BHT)

CONCERNS	Linked to brain toxicity; especially risky for pregnant women.
FOUND IN	Nail products and hair dye.

TALC

CONCERNS	Can be contaminated with asbestos fibers; leads to respiratory irritation and cancer.
FOUND IN	Mineral-based makeup.

PARABENS

CONCERNS	Preservatives linked to endocrine disruption and reproductive harm.
FOUND IN	Moisturizers, hair care products, and shaving creams.

BHA (BUTYLATED HYDROXYANISOLE) AND BHT (BUTYLATED HYDROXYTOLUENE)

CONCERNS	Synthetic antioxidants causing skin allergies and endocrine disruptions.
FOUND IN	Moisturizing products.

DEA (DIETHANOLAMINE)

CONCERNS	Used to make products creamy or sudsy; may cause skin and eye irritation.
FOUND IN	Moisturizers, sunscreens, soaps, shampoos, and similar products.

PETROLATUM (PETROLEUM JELLY)

CONCERNS	Used to lock in moisture; may be contaminated with carcinogenic compounds.
FOUND IN	Skincare and hair products.

SODIUM LAUREL SULFATE (SLES)

CONCERNS	Commonly used in body wash, shampoo, and cleansers; may be irritating and contaminated with 1,4-dioxane.
FOUND IN	Sudsy or foaming products.

PROPYLENE GLYCOL

CONCERNS	Used as a hydrating agent; may cause irritation and dry skin.
FOUND IN	Shampoos, soaps, and skincare products.

COAL TAR DYE

CONCERNS	Used as a coloring agent; known human carcinogen linked to various health issues.
FOUND IN	Toothpaste, hair dyes, and some shampoos.

ALUMINUM

CONCERNS	Found in some cosmetics and antiperspirants; linked to central nervous system issues and Alzheimer's disease.
FOUND IN	Some cosmetics and antiperspirants.

Rosemary
Hair Growth Spray

Rosemary (*Rosmarinus officinalis*) is a fragrant herb known for its culinary uses and medicinal properties. It has been traditionally used to stimulate hair growth and improve the overall health of the scalp. Rosemary contains ursolic acid, which helps to increase circulation, promote hair thickness, and reduce hair loss.

INGREDIENTS:

- 2-3 rosemary springs (*Rosmarinus officinalis*)
- ½ cup water
- 2 tablespoons castor oil
- 5 drops of organic clove bud essential oil (*Syzygium aromaticum*)

NOTES:

Perform a patch test before applying the spray to the entire scalp to avoid potential allergic reactions.

Discontinue use if irritation occurs.

Avoid contact with the eyes.

Incorporate a nutritious diet and proper hair care practices for comprehensive results.

INSTRUCTIONS:

1 | **Prepare the Rosemary Infusion:** Rinse the fresh rosemary sprigs under cool water. In a saucepan, combine the rosemary with 1/2 cup of water. Bring the mixture to a gentle boil and let it simmer for 15-20 minutes, allowing the rosemary's properties to infuse into the water. You should notice a yellowy-green hue in the water as it simmers. Allow the infusion to cool to room temperature.

2 | **Strain the Infusion:** Strain the rosemary sprigs from the infusion, ensuring a clear liquid.

3 | **Create the Serum Base:** In a small mixing bowl, combine the cooled rosemary infusion with 2 tablespoons of castor oil. Castor oil is known for its ability to promote hair growth and add thickness. Add 5 drops of organic clove bud essential oil for its stimulating and antimicrobial properties.

4 | **Mix and Transfer:** Mix the ingredients thoroughly until a uniform serum is achieved. Transfer the serum into a small glass bottle with a dropper for easy application.

5 | **Application:** Shake the bottle gently before each use to ensure an even distribution of the ingredients. Using the dropper, apply a few drops of the serum directly onto the scalp, concentrating on areas where hair growth is desired. Gently massage the scalp to enhance absorption and stimulate circulation.

DOSAGE:

Apply the rosemary hair growth serum 2-3 times per week for optimal results. Using a dermastamp (*e.g.* at-home microneedling) before application will increase your results.

Arnica Salve
for Age Spots

Arnica (*Arnica montana*) is a perennial herb known for its anti-inflammatory properties. Its active compounds, such as helenalin, are used to reduce inflammation and promote healing. While arnica is more commonly associated with treating bruises and muscle soreness, its potential benefits for age spots may be attributed to its anti-inflammatory effects. Cocoa butter adds moisture and promotes overall skin health.

INGREDIENTS:

- ½ cup dried *Arnica montana* flowers (dried)
- 1 cup carrier oil (such as organic olive or apricot kernel oil)
- 2 tablespoons beeswax pellets
- 2 tablespoons cocoa butter

NOTES:

External use only; do not ingest.

Perform a patch test before widespread application.

Avoid application on broken or irritated skin.

Discontinue use if any adverse reactions occur.

Combine with sun protection on the skin.

INSTRUCTIONS:

1. **Prepare Arnica Infused Oil:** Crush freshly-dried arnica flowers and loosely fill a glass jar with them. Then cover them with your organic carrier oil. Seal the jar and place it in a cool, dark place for about 4-6 weeks, shaking occasionally. After infusion, strain the oil to remove the plant material.
2. **Create the Arnica and Cocoa Butter Salve:** In a double boiler, melt the beeswax pellets and cocoa butter together. Add the arnica-infused oil to the melted beeswax and cocoa butter mixture, stirring well until combined. Remove from heat and let it cool slightly.
3. **Transfer to Container:** Pour the mixture into a clean, airtight container. Allow it to cool and solidify before sealing the container.
4. **Store:** Store the salve in a cool, dark place for prolonged efficacy.

Several other plants are known for their potential to address dark spots and promote skin health: Licorice root, turmeric, ginseng, mulberry, bearberry, papaya, rosehip, chamomile, pomegranate, lemon oil, and apricot kernel oil. You can incorporate these into your serums or creams.

DOSAGE:

Apply a small amount of the arnica and cocoa butter salve to age spots. Gently massage into the skin until absorbed. Use twice daily for optimal results.

Natural
Herbal Toothpaste

Fluorides, glycerols, artificial sweeteners, triglycerides, and sulfates—ingredients found in conventional toothpaste—have sparked an ongoing debate regarding their true benefits or potential harm. Crafting your own toothpaste allows you to harness the traditionally recognized properties of various natural ingredients. Baking soda is known for its potential to remove plaque, while cocoa powder offers antioxidants. Ginger provides anti-inflammatory effects, and cinnamon is valued for its antimicrobial properties. Calendula is known for its anti-inflammatory benefits, and coconut oil adds a creamy texture along with its antimicrobial properties. Yarrow essential oil contributes antibacterial and anti-inflammatory effects, promoting overall oral well-being.

INGREDIENTS:

- 1 tablespoon of baking soda
- 1 tablespoon of cocoa powder
- 1 tablespoon of ginger powder
- ½ teaspoon of ground cinnamon
- ½ teaspoon of calendula powder
- 2 tablespoons (27 grams) of coconut oil
- a few drops of yarrow essential oil
- 2 tablespoons of water

NOTES:

There are a few other ingredients that you can include in your homemade toothpaste: Xylitol, bentonite clay, and neem.

Avoid swallowing toothpaste.

If irritation occurs, discontinue use.

INSTRUCTIONS:

1 | **Combine Dry Ingredients:** In a bowl, mix baking soda, cocoa powder, ginger powder, ground cinnamon, and calendula powder.
2 | **Add Wet Ingredients:** Melt coconut oil and add it to the dry mixture. Mix well.
3 | **Incorporate Yarrow Oil:** Add a few drops of yarrow essential oil to the mixture and stir thoroughly.
4 | **Adjust Consistency:** If the mixture is too thick, add water gradually until you achieve a toothpaste-like consistency. You can also use a blender or mixer to create the desired consistency faster.
5 | **Storage:** Transfer the toothpaste into a small, airtight container for storage. Store the toothpaste in a cool, dry place. Use within a month for freshness.

This homemade toothpaste has a distinct salty taste and doesn't produce the same foaming effect as conventional toothpaste. It may require a few brushes to adjust to the unique flavor and texture. Despite these differences, you will find that it effectively leaves the mouth feeling clean and refreshed after use.

DOSAGE:

Use a pea-sized amount of the herbal toothpaste on your toothbrush for each brushing session.

Gum-Strenghtening
Mouthwash

Maintaining strong, healthy gums is essential for overall oral health. This herbal mouthwash recipe not only cleans your teeth but also includes minerals and essential herbal oils traditionally used to support a healthy mouth microbiome. An imbalance in the mouth's microbiome can lead to various issues, including receding gums. By incorporating this herbal mouthwash into your daily routine, you can effectively support the health of your gums and maintain a balanced oral microbiome.

INGREDIENTS:

- 2 cups filtered water
- 1 teaspoon mineral sea salt
- 10 drops of organic peppermint essential oil
- 6 drops of organic tea tree essential oil
- 3 drops organic clove bud essential oil
- 6 drops liquid stevia
- A pint-and-a-half to a quart-size mason jar or another container for storage

NOTES:

This mouthwash is for external use only; do not swallow. Discontinue use if any irritation occurs and consult a healthcare professional. While this herbal mouthwash is generally safe for adults, caution should be exercised when considering its use for children.

INSTRUCTIONS:

1 | **Prepare the Herbal Solution:** Heat 2 cups of filtered water until warm. Add mineral sea salt to the warm water, stirring until fully dissolved.

2 | **Incorporate Essential Oils:** Add organic peppermint, tea tree, and clove essential oils to the saltwater mixture. Mix thoroughly to ensure even distribution of the essential oils. Adjust the essential oil quantities based on personal preferences. For additional gum strengthening, you can add a pinch of myrrh powder (*Commiphora myrrha*) to the solution, known for its astringent properties.

3 | **Sweeten with Stevia:** Integrate liquid stevia into the mixture, providing a touch of sweetness without compromising the herbal benefits. Stir well to combine.

4 | **Transfer to Storage Container:** Carefully pour the mouthwash solution into a pint-and-a-half to a quart-size mason jar or another suitable container with a tight-fitting lid. Store the mouthwash in a cool, dark place to preserve its efficacy.

DOSAGE:

Use the herbal mouthwash twice a day. Shake well before each use. Regularly massage your gums with a soft toothbrush or your fingers to enhance blood flow and support gum health.

"Better Than Botox"

Bakuchiol seed oil, derived from the babchi plant (*Psoralea corylifolia*), is gaining popularity in the skincare industry for its potential anti-aging properties. Often referred to as a natural alternative to Botox, bakuchiol oil is renowned for its ability to reduce the appearance of fine lines and wrinkles without the use of synthetic chemicals.

INGREDIENTS:

- 1 tablespoon bakuchiol (*Psoralea/Cullen corylifolia*) seed oil
- 1 teaspoon jojoba oil
- 1 teaspoon rosehip oil
- 3 drops lavender essential oil

NOTES:

Making cold-pressed bakuchiol oil at home requires specific equipment and may not be practical for everyone.

Alternatively, you can purchase it from reputable herbal product suppliers, health food stores, or online retailers. Ensure the product is containing pure bakuchiol without synthetic additives.

INSTRUCTIONS:

1. **Combine Oils:** In a small bowl, mix 1 tablespoon of bakuchiol oil with 1 teaspoon each of jojoba oil and rosehip oil.
2. **Add Essential Oil:** Incorporate 3 drops of lavender essential oil into the mixture. Stir well to ensure even distribution.
3. **Application:** After cleansing your face, apply a small amount of the oil blend to your fingertips.
4. **Gentle Massage:** Gently massage the oil onto your face using upward and outward motions. Pay special attention to areas with fine lines, avoiding contact with eyes.
5. **Allow Absorption:** Leave the oil on your skin for at least 15 minutes to allow absorption.

For a convenient and easy-to-apply skincare solution, consider transforming this recipe into a salve. To do this, melt 2 tablespoons of beeswax pellets in a double boiler, then combine it with ½ cup of the bakuchiol oil. Remove from heat and add 10-15 drops of lavender essential oil. Stir well, pour the mixture into clean containers, and allow it to cool and solidify.

DOSAGE:

Use this bakuchiol oil blend 2-3 times a week for optimal results. Combine with a sunscreen during the day to protect your skin from harmful UV rays.

Herbal Facial Oil

This herbal facial oil harnesses the unique benefits of three powerful botanicals to promote youthful, radiant skin. Calendula flowers boast anti-inflammatory and antioxidant properties, soothing irritated skin and protecting against environmental stressors. Cottonwood buds, rich in salicin and antioxidants, help to rejuvenate and firm the skin, reducing the appearance of fine lines and wrinkles. Rosehips deliver a potent dose of vitamin C, promoting collagen production and improving skin elasticity. Together, these herbal infusions, blended with organic sweet almond oil and vitamin E, create a nourishing elixir to revitalize your complexion and combat signs of aging.

INGREDIENTS:

- 1 cup calendula flowers (*Calendula officinalis*)
- 1 cup cottonwood buds (*Populus deltoides*)
- 1 cup rosehips (*Rosa* spp.)
- 3 cups organic sweet almond oil
- 1 tsp vitamin E

NOTES:

Perform a patch test before widespread use, especially if you have sensitive skin or known allergies. Discontinue use if irritation or adverse reactions occur and seek medical advice.

Avoid contact with eyes. If contact occurs, rinse thoroughly with water.

For optimal results, apply the facial oil to slightly damp skin after cleansing. Incorporate gentle massage techniques while applying the oil to enhance absorption and relaxation

INSTRUCTIONS:

1 | **Prepare Herbal Infusions:** In three separate clean, dry glass jars, divide the calendula flowers, cottonwood buds, and crushed rosehips. Pour one cup of organic sweet almond oil into each jar, ensuring the herbs are fully submerged. For the cottonwood bud infusion, initiate the process by gently heating the oil in a water bath. Use low heat to help release the resins. Monitor closely to avoid overheating. Seal the jars tightly and place them in a cool, dark area for 6-8 weeks, allowing the herbs to infuse into the oil completely. Shake the jars gently every few days to facilitate infusion. After the infusion period, strain each oil separately using a fine mesh sieve or cheesecloth to remove the spent herbs. Apply firm pressure to extract all infused oil. Note you may infuse the CW buds for much longer if desired.

2 | **Combine Infusions:** In a clean glass bottle, mix equal amounts of the calendula, cottonwood bud, and rosehip-infused oils. Add 1 teaspoon of Vitamin E to the blended oils. Seal the bottle tightly and shake vigorously to ensure thorough incorporation of ingredients.

3 | **Storage and Usage:** Transfer the mixed oil blend into amber-colored glass pump bottles for ease of use. Label the bottles clearly with the product name and preparation date. Store the facial oil in a cool, dry place, away from direct sunlight, to preserve its potency. Use within 6-12 months for maximum freshness and efficacy.

DOSAGE:

Apply a small amount of the herbal facial oil to your face, neck, décolletage, and hands, both morning and night.

Natural Deodorant
Stick

Creating your own natural deodorant stick allows you to harness the power of herbs while avoiding potentially harmful chemicals found in commercial products. In this recipe, we'll be using coconut oil, shea butter, arrowroot powder, and a blend of herbs known for their antibacterial and odor-fighting properties. The combination of coconut oil, shea butter, and beeswax creates a base, while arrowroot powder and baking soda contribute to a smooth texture. Essential oils, such as tea tree oil and lavender oil, not only add a pleasant fragrance but also bring antibacterial benefits.

INGREDIENTS:

- ¼ cup shea butter
- ¼ cup coconut oil
- ¼ cup arrowroot powder
- 2 tablespoons beeswax
- 2 tablespoons baking soda
- 10 drops tea tree oil (*Melaleuca alternifolia*)
- 5 drops lavender oil (*Lavandula angustifolia*)

NOTES:

Discontinue use if irritation occurs. Always perform a patch test before widespread application to ensure compatibility with your skin.

Avoid contact with eyes and mucous membranes.

Avoid applying the deodorant to broken or irritated skin. Allow any cuts or abrasions to heal before use.

INSTRUCTIONS:

1 | **Melt the Ingredients:** In a double boiler, gently melt together coconut oil, shea butter, and beeswax. Allow the mixture to cool, retaining its liquid state.
2 | **Add Dry Ingredients:** Stir in ¼ cup arrowroot powder and 2 tablespoons baking soda until well combined. Stir until a smooth consistency is achieved. Due to the use of natural ingredients, the color and texture of the deodorant may vary slightly from batch to batch. This is normal and does not impact the product's effectiveness.
3 | **Incorporate Essential Oils:** Add 10 drops of tea tree oil and 5 drops of lavender oil. Mix thoroughly. Adjust the essential oil amounts based on personal preference.
4 | **Pour into Containers:** Pour the mixture into deodorant containers or silicone molds.
5 | **Cool and Solidify:** Let it cool and solidify at room temperature or in the refrigerator.
6 | **Store:** Store the deodorant in a cool place to prevent melting. Extreme temperatures can affect the consistency and efficacy of the product.

DOSAGE:

Apply a small amount to clean, dry underarms as needed.

Forgotten Home Apothecary

Natural Herbal
Sunscreen

Sun exposure has dual effects on the skin, offering a natural source of vitamin D while posing risks such as sunburn, premature aging, and an increased likelihood of skin cancer due to excessive ultraviolet (UV) rays.

This herbal sunscreen provides a holistic solution by safeguarding the skin from harmful UV rays and enriching it with the benefits of selected herbs. Red raspberry seed oil contributes a high SPF through its ellagic acid content, ensuring natural sun protection. Carrot seed oil not only provides natural UV protection but also boasts antioxidant properties to prevent sun damage. Zinc Oxide serves as a mineral sunscreen ingredient, offering broad-spectrum protection by reflecting and scattering UV rays. Coconut oil adds moisturizing benefits and a mild SPF, enhancing the overall effectiveness of the sunscreen. Beeswax is incorporated for its waterproof effect.

INGREDIENTS:

- 2 tbsp red raspberry seed oil
- 1 tbsp carrot seed oil
- 2 tbsp zinc oxide
- 2 tbsp coconut oil
- 1 tbsp beeswax

NOTES:

Perform a patch test before widespread use to check for allergic reactions. Avoid contact with eyes.

When working with zinc oxide, it's advisable to wear protective gear such as gloves and a mask to prevent inhalation.

Be aware that this sunscreen may not provide as high an SPF as commercial products.

INSTRUCTIONS:

1 | **Prepare a Double Boiler:** In a double boiler, melt the beeswax and coconut oil together until well combined.
2 | **Add Red Raspberry Seed and Carrot Seed Oils:** Once melted, add the red raspberry seed oil and carrot seed oil to the mixture. Stir well.
3 | **Incorporate Zinc Oxide:** Gradually add the zinc oxide while stirring continuously to avoid clumps. Ensure it is evenly distributed.
4 | **Pour into Container:** Once everything is well mixed, pour the mixture into a container of your choice. Label.
5 | **Allow to Cool:** Let the sunscreen cool and solidify.

DOSAGE:

Apply the sunscreen liberally to all exposed skin 15 minutes before sun exposure. Reapply every two hours or more often if swimming or sweating. Combine with protective clothing and seek shade for comprehensive sun protection.

HERBAL SUPPORT
for the Endocrine System

The endocrine system plays a crucial role in maintaining homeostasis and regulating various physiological processes in the body. It consists of glands that produce hormones, which act as messengers, influencing the functions of organs and tissues. Key functions of the endocrine system include regulating metabolism, growth and development, stress response, mood, and reproductive processes.

Tips to Maintain a Healthy Endocrine System:

MANAGE STRESS EFFECTIVELY
Chronic stress can disrupt hormonal balance. Practice stress-reducing techniques such as meditation, deep breathing exercises, or mindfulness to help manage stress levels.

BALANCED BLOOD SUGAR LEVELS
Maintain stable blood sugar levels by incorporating complex carbohydrates, fiber-rich foods, and lean proteins into your diet. Avoid excessive consumption of refined sugars and processed foods.

ADEQUATE IODINE INTAKE
Ensure sufficient iodine intake, as it is crucial for the production of thyroid hormones. Good dietary sources include seaweed, fish, dairy products, and iodized salt.

HEALTHY FATS
Include sources of healthy fats, such as avocados, nuts, seeds, and olive oil, in your diet. These fats are essential for hormone production.

REGULAR EXERCISE
Engage in both aerobic and strength-training exercises. Regular physical activity helps regulate insulin levels, improve metabolism, and support overall endocrine health.

ADEQUATE SLEEP HYGIENE
Prioritize quality sleep by maintaining a consistent sleep schedule and creating a conducive sleep environment. Sleep is essential for the regulation of various hormones.

LIMIT EXPOSURE TO ENDOCRINE DISRUPTORS
Reduce exposure to environmental toxins and endocrine disruptors found in certain plastics, pesticides, and household products. Choose natural and organic alternatives when possible.

HYDRATION
Stay well-hydrated to support the transport of hormones throughout the body. Water is essential for overall endocrine function.

REGULAR MEDICAL CHECK-UPS
Schedule regular check-ups with healthcare professionals to monitor hormone levels and address any concerns promptly.

MAINTAIN A HEALTHY WEIGHT:
Achieve and maintain a healthy weight through a balanced diet and regular exercise. Excess body fat, especially around the abdomen, can contribute to hormonal imbalances.

LIMIT CAFFEINE AND ALCOHOL INTAKE:
Excessive caffeine and alcohol consumption can impact sleep patterns and hormone production. Consume these substances in moderation.

HERBAL SUPPORT

Rhodiola (*Rhodiola rosea*)
Adaptogenic herb known for enhancing stress resistance, supporting adrenal function, and promoting hormonal balance.

Siberian Ginseng (*Eleutherococcus senticosus*)
Adaptogen with anti-fatigue properties, aiding in stress management and supporting overall endocrine health.

Chaste Tree (*Vitex agnus-castus*)
Known to regulate the menstrual cycle, alleviate PMS symptoms, and support hormonal balance in women.

Nettle (*Urtica dioica*)
Rich in nutrients, nettle leaf supports the endocrine system by providing essential vitamins and minerals, including iron.

Saw Palmetto (*Serenoa repens*)
Particularly beneficial for men, saw palmetto may support prostate health and balance hormones.

Dong Quai (*Angelica sinensis*)
Commonly used in Traditional Chinese Medicine, dong quai is believed to regulate estrogen levels and support female reproductive health.

Guggul (*Commiphora wightii*)
Known for its potential to support thyroid function and maintain cholesterol levels within the normal range.

Schisandra (*Schisandra chinensis*)
Adaptogenic herb with antioxidant properties, supporting adrenal health and aiding in stress adaptation.

Black Cohosh (Actaea racemosa)
Commonly used by women to alleviate menopausal symptoms and support hormonal balance.

Red Clover (Trifolium pratense)
Contains phytoestrogens that may help balance estrogen levels, particularly beneficial for women during menopause.

Bacopa (Bacopa monnieri)
Adaptogenic herb known for its cognitive-enhancing properties, which can indirectly support the endocrine system by reducing stress.

Turmeric (Curcuma longa)
Anti-inflammatory and antioxidant properties may contribute to overall endocrine health.

Spearmint (Mentha spicata)
Spearmint tea may help reduce elevated androgen levels in women with PCOS, contributing to hormonal balance.

Cinnamon (Cinnamomum verum)
Known for its potential to improve insulin sensitivity, cinnamon may be helpful for managing insulin resistance in PCOS.

Licorice Root (Glycyrrhiza glabra)
May help regulate menstrual cycles and reduce testosterone levels in women with PCOS.

Inositol (Myo-inositol)
While not an herb, inositol, particularly myo-inositol, has shown promise in improving insulin sensitivity and ovarian function in women with PCOS.

Bladderwrack (Fucus vesiculosus)
Rich in iodine, bladderwrack may support thyroid function, making it potentially beneficial for individuals with hypothyroidism.

Ashwagandha (Withania somnifera)
Adaptogenic herb that may support the thyroid gland and help balance hormone levels in cases of hypothyroidism.

Holy Basil (Ocimum sanctum)
Adaptogenic herb with anti-inflammatory properties, supporting overall endocrine health, including the thyroid.

Selenium (Mineral)
While not an herb, selenium is crucial for thyroid function and may be considered as a supplement for individuals with hypothyroidism.

Bugleweed (Lycopus virginicus)
Traditionally used to address hyperthyroidism by reducing the production of thyroid hormones.

Lemon Balm (Melissa officinalis)
Known for its calming properties, lemon balm may help manage symptoms of hyperthyroidism, such as anxiety.

Motherwort (Leonurus cardiaca)
May help regulate heart palpitations and reduce anxiety associated with hyperthyroidism.

L-Carnitine (Amino Acid)
While not an herb, L-carnitine has been studied for its potential to alleviate symptoms of hyperthyroidism.

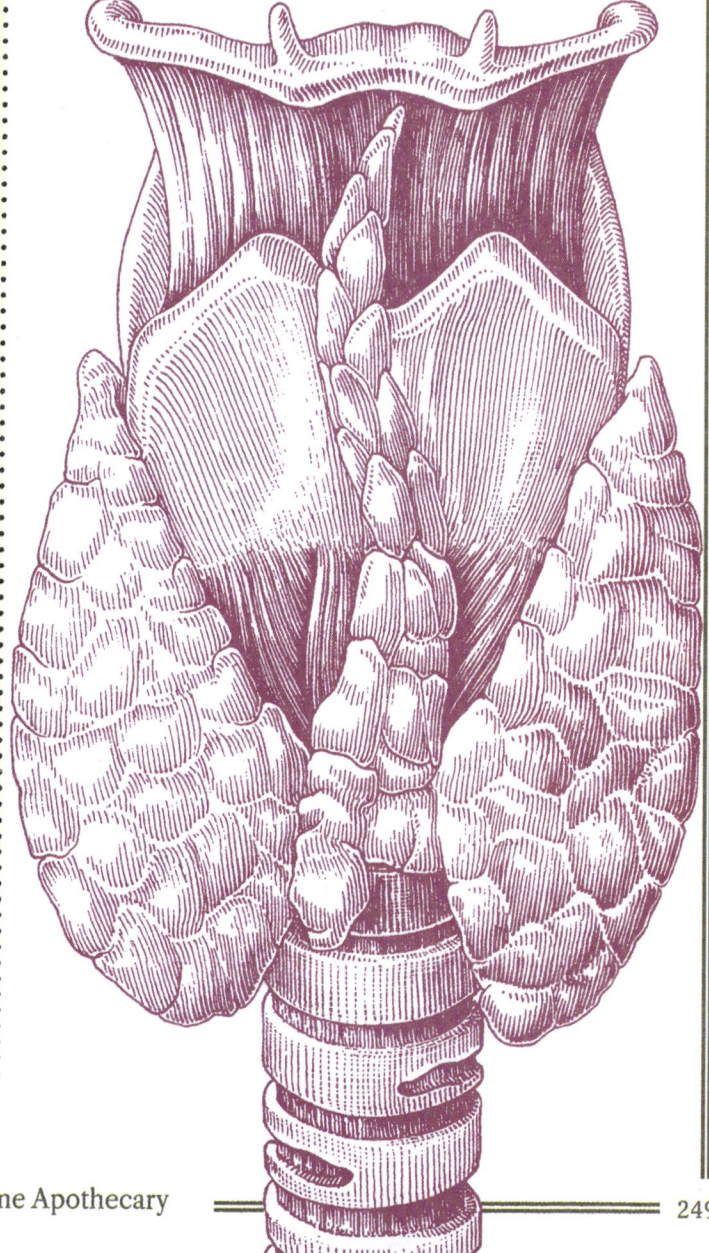

Forgotten Home Apothecary

Bugleweed Gycerite
for Thyroid Balance

Hyperthyroidism, characterized by an overactive thyroid gland, demands careful attention to manage its symptoms effectively. Bugleweed, recognized for its support in thyroid hormone regulation, may provide relief from symptoms associated with hyperthyroidism by potentially inhibiting antibody binding to the thyroid gland. Lemon balm, renowned for its calming properties and effects on anxiety, complements bugleweed to create a synergistic blend that supports the reduction of excessive thyroid activity. Together, these herbs address both the physiological and emotional aspects associated with hyperthyroidism.

INGREDIENTS:

- 1 part bugleweed (*Lycopus virginicus*) leaves, chopped
- 1 part lemon balm (*Melissa officinalis*) leaves, chopped
- 2 parts vegetable glycerin
- 1 part distilled water

NOTES:

Consult with a healthcare professional before starting any herbal regimen, especially if you are pregnant, nursing, or taking medications.

Bugleweed may interact with certain medications, so it's crucial to inform your healthcare provider about all supplements you are taking.

INSTRUCTIONS:

1| **Preparation of Herbs:** Clean the bugleweed and lemon balm leaves thoroughly. Finely chop the leaves to enhance the extraction process.
2| **Combining Ingredients:** In a glass jar, combine the chopped bugleweed and lemon balm leaves. Pour 2 parts vegetable glycerin over the herbs. Add 1 part distilled water to the mixture.
3| **Maceration Process:** Seal the jar tightly and shake well to ensure even distribution. Place the jar in a dark, cool place for 4-6 weeks, shaking it daily to enhance the extraction.
4| **Straining the Glycerite:** After the maceration period, strain the liquid through cheesecloth or a fine mesh strainer into a clean glass container.
5| **Store:** Store the glycerite in a dark glass bottle to protect it from light, preserving its potency.

DOSAGE:

Take 1-2 ml (approximately 20-40 drops) of the bugleweed glycerite up to three times daily. Start with a lower dose and adjust as needed.

Bladderwrack Tincture
for Thyroid Support

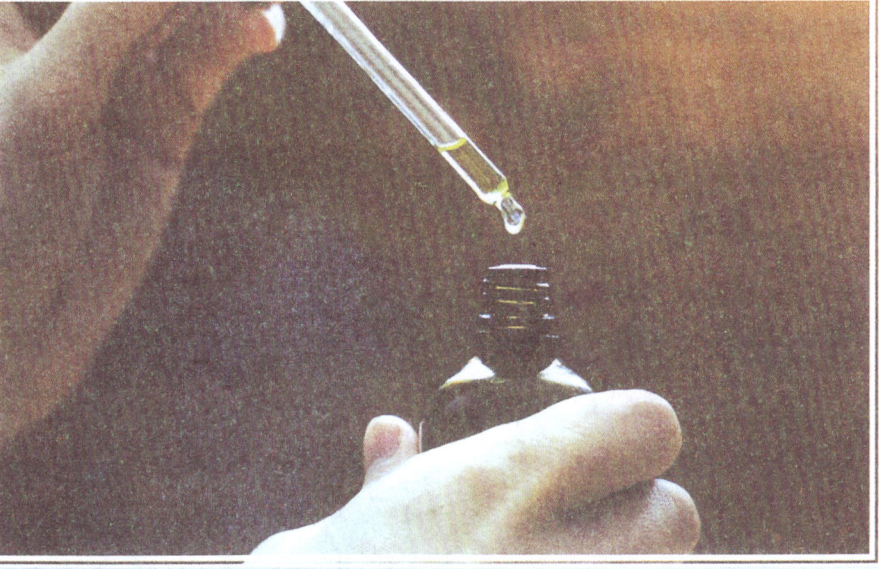

Bladderwrack, scientifically known as *Fucus vesiculosus*, is a brown seaweed rich in iodine, which can be beneficial for individuals with hypothyroidism. Use if you are iodine deficient.

The iodine content in bladderwrack supports the production of thyroid hormones, helping to regulate the thyroid gland. It also contains other essential nutrients like vitamins, minerals, and antioxidants that contribute to overall thyroid health.

INGREDIENTS:

- 1 cup dried bladderwrack (*Fucus vesiculosus*)
- 2 cups high-proof vodka (50% alcohol)

NOTES:

Consult with a healthcare provider before starting any herbal supplement, especially if you have pre-existing medical conditions or are taking medications.

Due to its iodine content, excessive consumption of bladderwrack may lead to thyroid dysfunction.

Strictly adhere to recommended dosages.

It's crucial to consult with a healthcare professional for personalized advice.

INSTRUCTIONS:

1 | **Preparare the Ingredients:** Ensure the bladderwrack is thoroughly dried to prevent the introduction of extra moisture into this tincture.
2 | **Measure the Ingredients:** Measure 1 cup of dried bladderwrack and 2 cups of high-proof vodka.
3 | **Combine the Ingredients:** Place the dried bladderwrack in a clean glass jar and pour the vodka over it, making sure the herb is completely submerged.
4 | **Infusion:** Seal the jar tightly and store it in a cool, dark place for about 4-6 weeks, shaking it every few days to enhance the extraction process.
5 | **Strain:** After the infusion period, strain the tincture through a fine mesh strainer or cheesecloth into a clean glass bottle, separating the liquid from the bladderwrack residue.

DOSAGE:

The typical dosage for bladderwrack tincture is 1-2 ml (approximately 20-40 drops) three times a day.

PCOS Support
Blend

This tea blend incorporates four herbs renowned for their potential benefits in managing PCOS symptoms. Spearmint aids in hormonal balance, particularly by reducing elevated androgen levels. Raspberry leaf has a traditional use in promoting female reproductive health and regulating menstrual cycles. Hibiscus contributes to managing oxidative stress, a common concern in PCOS, owing to its rich antioxidant content. Nettles, known for its anti-inflammatory properties, assists in reducing inflammation associated with PCOS.

INGREDIENTS:

- 1-part dried spearmint (*Mentha spicata*)
- 1-part dried raspberry leaf (*Rubus idaeus*)
- 1-part hibiscus (*Hibiscus sabdariffa*)
- Nettle (*Urtica dioica*)

NOTES:

Store the herbal blend in a cool, dark place to maintain freshness.

Integrate this tea into a balanced lifestyle, including a healthy diet and regular exercise.

If you are pregnant, nursing, or have any medical conditions, consult with a healthcare professional before consuming this tea.

Monitor your body's response and discontinue use if you experience any adverse effects.

INSTRUCTIONS:

1| **Prepare the Herbal Blend:** Mix the equal parts of spearmint, raspberry leaf, hibiscus, and nettle in a bowl.
2| **Individual Tea Serving:** Use 1 teaspoon of the herbal blend per 8 ounces (240 ml) of hot water.
3| **Infusion:** Place 1 teaspoon of the herbal blend in a teapot or infuser. Pour the hot water over the herbs.
4| **Steeping:** Allow the herbs to steep for 5-7 minutes to extract the beneficial compounds.
5| **Strain:** Strain the tea to remove the herbal blend, ensuring a clear infusion.
6| **Optional Sweetening:** Add honey to taste, if desired.

In addition to the herbs mentioned in this tea blend, several other ingredients can be beneficial for individuals managing PCOS. These ingredients contribute to overall well-being and may help address specific symptoms associated with PCOS: Cinnamon (*Cinnamomum verum*), fenugreek (*Trigonella foenum-graecum*), turmeric (*Curcuma longa*), chaste tree berry (*Vitex agnus-castus*), licorice root (*Glycyrrhiza glabra*), maca root (*Lepidium meyenii*), omega-3 fatty acids, vitamin D, Inositol, green tea (*Camellia sinensis*), and berberine. Other good herbs for PCOS include reishi (as a dual-extracted tincture), false unicorn root, and yarrow.

DOSAGE:

Consume one cup of this herbal tea blend per day, preferably in the morning.

Spiced Milk
for Pancreas

Ginger and cinnamon are renowned for their potential benefits in managing diabetes.
Ginger has anti-inflammatory properties and may enhance insulin sensitivity, while cinnamon has been studied for its ability to lower blood sugar levels. This warm spiced ginger and cinnamon milk recipe combines these two powerful herbs to create a delicious and diabetes-friendly beverage.

INGREDIENTS:

- 1 cup unsweetened almond milk
- ½ teaspoon ground Ginger (*Zingiber officinale*)
- ½ teaspoon ground Cinnamon (*Cinnamomum verum*)
- 1 teaspoon raw honey (optional, use in moderation)
- ¼ teaspoon vanilla extract

NOTES:

Consult with your healthcare provider before incorporating this or any new herbal remedy into your routine, especially if you are on medication or have existing health conditions. Monitor your blood sugar levels regularly and adjust the recipe or dosage as needed.

INSTRUCTIONS:

1. **Heat the Almond Milk:** In a small saucepan, warm 1 cup of unsweetened almond milk over low to medium heat. Consider using another milk alternative if almond milk is not your preference.
2. **Add Ginger and Cinnamon:** Once the almond milk is warm, add ½ teaspoon of ground ginger and ½ teaspoon of ground cinnamon to the saucepan. Experiment with the spice levels to suit your taste preferences.
3. **Stir and Simmer:** Stir the mixture well to ensure the even distribution of the spices. Allow the mixture to simmer for 5-7 minutes, but do not bring to a boil.
4. **Sweeten with Honey (Optional):** If desired, add 1 teaspoon of raw honey for sweetness. Keep in mind that honey adds natural sugars, so use it in moderation, especially if managing diabetes.
5. **Add Vanilla Extract:** Stir in ¼ teaspoon of vanilla extract for additional flavor.
6. **Strain and Serve:** For a smoother texture, you can strain the spiced milk before serving. Pour the warm spiced ginger and cinnamon milk into your favorite mug.

DOSAGE:

Consume this beverage once a day, preferably in the evening, to harness the potential benefits of ginger and cinnamon for diabetes management.

Bitter Melon and Green Tea Blend
for Erratic Blood Sugar

Bitter melon (*Momordica charantia*), also known as bitter gourd, and green tea (*Camellia sinensis*) are both renowned for their potential in regulating blood sugar levels. This herbal blend combines the unique properties of these two plants to create a natural remedy for managing blood sugar.

Bitter melon is rich in compounds like charantin, polypeptide-p, and vicine, which are believed to have hypoglycemic effects. It may aid in lowering blood sugar levels and improving glucose tolerance. Green tea is well-known for its high concentration of antioxidants, particularly catechins.

These antioxidants may contribute to improved insulin sensitivity and support the body in utilizing glucose effectively.

INGREDIENTS:

- 1 teaspoon of dried bitter melon slices (*Momordica charantia*)
- 1 teaspoon of green tea leaves (*Camellia sinensis*)
- 1 cup of hot water

NOTES:

Consult with a healthcare professional before incorporating this blend, especially if you are taking medication or have pre-existing health conditions.

Monitor blood sugar levels regularly, especially if you are diabetic, to adjust medication as needed.

Individuals with a sensitive digestive system or a history of gastrointestinal issues should introduce this blend gradually to monitor its effects on digestion.

INSTRUCTIONS:

1. **Preparation:** Start by boiling one cup of water.
2. **Combine Herbs:** In a teapot or infuser, add 1 teaspoon each of dried bitter melon slices and green tea leaves.
3. **Pour Hot Water:** Pour the hot water over the herbs in the teapot or infuser.
4. **Steep:** Let the herbs steep for about 5-7 minutes to extract the beneficial compounds.
5. **Strain:** After steeping, strain the mixture to remove the herbs. Consider adding a slice of lemon or a touch of honey for flavor if desired. For added flavor, you can also consider experimenting with different herbs or spices, keeping in mind their potential impact on blood sugar.

DOSAGE:

Consume one cup of this bitter melon and green tea blend daily, preferably before meals.

Backyard
Pancreas Support

Costus igneus, commonly referred to as the insulin plant or spiral flag, and also called *Chamaecostus cuspidatus*, is a fascinating herb renowned for its potential anti-diabetic properties. The name "insulin plant" derives from its unique characteristic of containing compounds that mimic the action of insulin, the hormone responsible for regulating blood sugar levels in the body. This distinctive feature has garnered significant attention, particularly in traditional medicine systems, where *Costus igneus* has been utilized for centuries in the management of diabetes and related conditions.

INGREDIENTS:

- 5-6 fresh *Costus igneus* leaves (alternatively, 1-2 teaspoons of dried leaves)
- 1 cup of water
- Optional: Honey or stevia for sweetness (if needed)

NOTES:

Consult with a healthcare professional before using *Costus igneus*, especially if you're pregnant, breastfeeding, or have any underlying medical conditions. Monitor your blood sugar levels regularly, especially if you're using *Costus igneus* as a complementary treatment for diabetes. Consider growing *Costus igneus* in your backyard for a fresh and readily available supply of leaves. Insulin plant often contains aristolochic acid, a contaminant that can cause damage to the kidneys and cancer. Use with great care and do not use as a tincture; best as tea if used with caution.

INSTRUCTIONS:

1 | **Prepare the Ingredients:** Wash the *Costus igneus* leaves thoroughly under running water to remove any dirt or impurities. If using dried leaves, skip this step.
2 | **Boil the Water:** In a small saucepan, bring one cup of water to a boil.
3 | **Add *Costus igneus*:** Once the water reaches a rolling boil, add the leaves to the saucepan. Experiment with the strength of the tea by adjusting the number of leaves or steeping time to suit your taste preferences.
4 | **Steep:** Turn off the heat and let the leaves steep in the hot water for about 5-10 minutes. This allows the beneficial compounds from the leaves to infuse into the water.
5 | **Strain:** After steeping, strain the tea to remove the leaves, leaving behind a clear liquid.
6 | **Optional Sweetening:** If desired, add honey or stevia to sweeten the tea. Stir well until the sweetener is dissolved.
7 | **Serve:** Pour the prepared *Costus igneus* tea into a cup and serve it warm.

One of the simplest ways to incorporate *Costus igneus* into your routine is by chewing on the leaves directly. This method allows for the direct ingestion of the plant's bioactive compounds, potentially enhancing its therapeutic effects. However, chewing on *Costus igneus* leaves may not be suitable for everyone, particularly those with dental issues or sensitivities.

DOSAGE:

Drink this tea once or twice a day, preferably before meals, to help regulate blood sugar levels, after checking with your physician.

Rhodiola Capsules
for Cortisol Balance

Rhodiola rosea, commonly known as golden root, is recognized for its adaptogenic qualities, which may help balance cortisol levels, alleviate stress, and promote overall well-being. Rhodiola's adaptogenic properties make it a valuable option for enhancing resilience to diverse stressors. It is reputed for boosting energy, enhancing mental focus, and supporting adrenal gland function. Rhodiola is particularly noted for its role in regulating cortisol levels, crucial in stress management.

INGREDIENTS:

- 5 ounces (150 grams) *Rhodiola rosea* extract powder
- Vegetable-based capsules (size 00)

NOTES:

Keep capsules away from children and pets.

Individuals with autoimmune diseases should consult their healthcare provider before using rhodiola, as it may stimulate the immune system. Dual-extracted reishi tincture is a good alternative.

Rhodiola may interact with certain medications. Consult with a healthcare professional if you are taking medications, especially antidepressants, anticoagulants, or immunosuppressants.

INSTRUCTIONS:

1| **Preparing Rhodiola Extract:** Source a high-quality *Rhodiola rosea* extract powder.
2| **Fill the Capsules:** If using a capsule-filling machine: Follow the machine's instructions to fill each capsule with the measured rhodiola powder. If manually filling: Take one half of an empty size 00 capsule and carefully fill it with the measured rhodiola powder. Use a clean, flat surface to level the powder for consistent dosage.
3| **Close the Capsules:** Place the other half of the size 00 capsule on top, ensuring a secure fit. Press gently until the capsules are closed, creating a seamless seal.
4| **Batch Labeling:** Label the storage container with the content and dosage instructions.
5| **Store:** Store the capsules in a cool, dry place, away from direct sunlight. Ensure the storage container is airtight to maintain the potency of the rhodiola.

DOSAGE:

Take one size capsule daily with a meal. Regularly assess your response and consult with a healthcare professional for any adjustments.

Hormone Harmony
Elixir

The hormone harmony elixir is a purposefully formulated herbal tincture combining red clover (*Trifolium pratense*), black cohosh (*Actaea racemosa*), and chasteberry (*Vitex agnus-castus*).

This blend is crafted to address hormonal imbalances, particularly in menopausal and peri-menopausal women.

Due to its phytoestrogen isoflavonoid levels, red clover is considered a beneficial option for managing menopausal symptoms as an alternative to or in addition to hormone replacement therapy (HRT). It may alleviate symptoms like hot flashes and night sweats, and potentially contribute to preventing osteoporosis and cardiovascular disease. Black cohosh is known for its effectiveness in alleviating menopausal symptoms - reducing the severity of hot flashes and night sweats. It also can help with insomnia and address hormonal fluctuations associated with fibroids and diabetes. Chasteberry contributes to hormonal balance, especially concerning the menstrual cycle, aiding in managing PMS symptoms, supporting fertility, and balancing menopausal hormone fluctuations, especially as they involve mood imbalances.

INGREDIENTS:

- 1-part red clover (*Trifolium pratense*)
- 1-part black cohosh (*Actaea racemosa*)
- 1-part chasteberry (*Vitex agnus-castus*)
- 80 proof alcohol (*e.g.,* vodka) - enough to cover the herbs

NOTES:

Avoid use during pregnancy or breastfeeding due to potential hormonal effects. Consult a healthcare professional if you have hormone-sensitive conditions, as these herbs may influence hormone levels.

Exercise caution if you have liver conditions, as high doses of black cohosh may impact the liver. Check with your naturopath about *Vitex* use if your are on HRT.

Discontinue use if adverse reactions occur.

INSTRUCTIONS:

1 | **Preparation:** Measure equal parts of red clover, black cohosh, and vitex. Coarsely chop or grind the herbs for optimal extraction.
2 | **Combining Ingredients:** Place the prepared herbs in a clean glass jar. Ensure full submersion by pouring enough alcohol over the herbs to fully cover them. You may also fill your jar half-full of your dried herbs and then fill it to the top with your alcohol.
3 | **Extraction:** Seal the jar and store it in a cool, dark place for 4-6 weeks, shaking daily to facilitate extraction.
4 | **Straining:** After the extraction period, strain the liquid through cheesecloth or a fine mesh sieve into a dark glass tincture bottle.
5 | **Store:** Store the tincture in a cool, dark place to maintain potency.

DOSAGE:

Consume 1-2 dropperfuls (approximately 30-60 drops) in a small amount of water, 1-3 times daily.

HERBAL SUPPORT
for the Reproductive System

The reproductive system is a vital component of life, intricately managing various physiological functions and hormonal processes. In women, it governs menstrual cycles and hormonal balance, impacting both physical and emotional well-being. For men, it goes beyond fertility, influencing hormone levels and overall vitality. Recognizing the interdependence of male and female reproductive health is crucial, particularly for couples aiming to conceive. A balanced reproductive system not only supports fertility but also contributes to overall health.

Tips to Maintain a Healthy Reproductive System:

BALANCED DIET:
Consume a well-balanced diet rich in fruits, vegetables, whole grains, and lean proteins to provide essential nutrients for reproductive health.

HYDRATION:
Stay adequately hydrated with water, herbal teas, and infusions.

REGULAR EXERCISE:
Engage in regular physical activity to promote blood circulation and overall well-being. Exercise can also help manage stress, a factor that can impact reproductive health.

STRESS MANAGEMENT:
Practice stress-reducing techniques like meditation, yoga, or deep breathing exercises.

AVOID HARMFUL SUBSTANCES:
Limit the intake of alcohol, tobacco, and recreational drugs, as they can negatively impact reproductive function.

MAINTAIN A HEALTHY WEIGHT:
Achieve and maintain a healthy weight, as being underweight or overweight can affect reproductive hormones.

SLEEP HYGIENE:
Prioritize good sleep hygiene. Adequate and quality sleep is crucial for overall health, including reproductive function.

REGULAR CHECK-UPS:
Schedule regular check-ups with a healthcare provider to monitor reproductive health and address any concerns promptly.

HERBAL SUPPORT

Chaste Tree Berry (*Vitex agnus-castus*)
Consider incorporating Chaste Tree Berry, known for its potential to regulate menstrual cycles and hormonal imbalances in women.

Red Clover (*Trifolium pratense*)
Red Clover contains phytoestrogens, which may help balance estrogen levels.

Maca (*Lepidium meyenii*)
Maca is an adaptogenic herb that may support energy, stamina, and hormonal balance.

Dong Quai (*Angelica sinensis*)
Known as the "female ginseng," Dong Quai may be beneficial for menstrual and reproductive health.

Raspberry Leaf (*Rubus idaeus*)
Raspberry Leaf is often used to tone the uterus and support reproductive health in women.

Saw Palmetto (*Serenoa repens*)
Saw Palmetto is thought to support prostate health in men, promoting overall reproductive well-being.

Nettle (*Urtica dioica*)
Nettle is rich in nutrients, helping support overall reproductive health.

Tribulus (*Tribulus terrestris*)
Tribulus is believed to support male reproductive health by promoting testosterone levels.

Evening Primrose (*Oenothera biennis*)
Contains gamma-linolenic acid (GLA), which may help support hormonal balance.

Moon Tea

"Moon Tea" is a traditional herbal infusion designed to support women's health, particularly during menstruation. This tea combines herbs known for their soothing and balancing properties, offering natural relief from menstrual discomfort.

INGREDIENTS:

- 1 teaspoon dried red raspberry leaf (*Rubus idaeus*)
- 1 teaspoon dried nettle leaf (*Urtica dioica*)
- 1 teaspoon dried chamomile flowers (*Matricaria chamomilla*) 1 teaspoon dried lemon balm (*Melissa officinalis*)
- 1 teaspoon dried peppermint (*Mentha piperita*)
- 2 cups water
- honey (optional, to taste)

NOTES:

Consult a healthcare professional before using this tea if you are pregnant, nursing, or have chronic health conditions. Discontinue use if allergic reactions occur. Check for herb-medication interactions with your healthcare provider.

INSTRUCTIONS:

1. **Combine the Herbs:** In a teapot or a heatproof container, combine the dried red raspberry leaf, nettle leaf, chamomile flowers, lemon balm, and peppermint.
2. **Boil the Water:** Bring 2 cups of water to a boil.
3. **Steep the Tea:** Pour the boiling water over the herbs. Cover and let the tea steep for 10-15 minutes.
4. **Strain the Tea:** After steeping, strain the herbs from the tea using a fine mesh strainer or cheesecloth.
5. **Serve:** Pour the strained tea into a cup. Add honey to taste if desired. You can make a larger batch of the dried herbal blend and store it in an airtight container for convenience.

DOSAGE:

Drink 1-2 cups of "Moon Tea" daily, especially during your menstrual cycle, to help alleviate symptoms such as cramps and mood swings.

Evening Primrose Oil
for Women's Health

Evening primrose oil (*Oenothera biennis*) is a popular herbal remedy known for its potential benefits for women's health. The oil is extracted from the seeds of the evening primrose plant and contains gamma-linolenic acid (GLA), an essential fatty acid with anti-inflammatory properties. Evening primrose oil has been traditionally used to alleviate symptoms associated with hormonal imbalances in women, such as premenstrual syndrome (PMS), breast pain, and menopausal symptoms.

INGREDIENTS:

- Evening primrose seeds
- Carrier oil (such as grapeseed oil or sweet almond oil)

NOTES:

While the cold-press method is preferred for retaining maximum nutrients, you can still make infused evening primrose oil at home using a simpler method.

Begin by harvesting mature evening primrose seeds, allowing them to air-dry before crushing them with a mortar and pestle. Transfer the crushed seeds to a dark glass jar and cover them with a high-quality carrier oil like grapeseed or sweet almond oil. Seal the jar tightly and let the mixture infuse for 4 to 6 weeks in a cool, dark place, shaking it occasionally.

INSTRUCTIONS:

1. **Harvest Seeds:** Collect mature evening primrose seeds during late summer or early fall. Ensure the seeds are fully ripened for optimal oil quality.
2. **Dry the Seeds:** Lay out the harvested seeds in a single layer on a clean, dry surface. Allow them to air-dry for several days until thoroughly dried.
3. **Cold-Pressing:** Use a cold-press extraction method to obtain the oil. You can do this using a cold-press oil extractor or a traditional oil press. Follow the manufacturer's instructions for your specific device.
4. **Infuse with Carrier Oil:** Once you have cold-pressed the evening primrose oil, transfer it to a clean, dark glass jar.
5. **Add Carrier Oil:** Pour a high-quality carrier oil, such as grapeseed oil or sweet almond oil, into the jar with the cold-pressed evening primrose oil. Ensure that the oil covers the seeds completely.
6. **Seal the Jar:** Seal the jar tightly and place it in a cool, dark area for infusion. Allow the mixture to infuse for at least 4 to 6 weeks. Shake the jar gently every few days to enhance the infusion process.
7. **Strain the Oil:** After the infusion period, strain the oil through a fine mesh strainer or cheesecloth into a clean, dark glass bottle. Squeeze out as much oil as possible from the seeds.
8. **Storage:** Store the cold-pressed infused evening primrose oil in a cool, dark place to maintain its freshness and potency.

DOSAGE:

The standard dosage for internal use is 1 gram (¼ tsp) of oil daily, broken into 2 to 3 doses.

Menopause Relief
Elixir

Menopause is a natural phase in a woman's life, often accompanied by various symptoms such as hot flashes. Black cohosh is traditionally used for its estrogen-like effects that may help support hormonal balance, especially during menopause. This can contribute to the relief of hot flashes, night sweats, and other associated symptoms. Red clover contains compounds known as phytoestrogens, which are plant-based compounds that mimic the effects of estrogen in the body. Phytoestrogens in red clover may help reduce the frequency and intensity of hot flashes by providing a natural balance to declining estrogen levels. Red clover is also known for its potential benefits in supporting bone health, which is particularly relevant during menopause when estrogen levels decrease, impacting bone density. Black cohosh's hormonal balancing properties complement red clover's phytoestrogen content, working together to alleviate hot flashes and other associated discomfort.

INGREDIENTS:

- 1 tablespoon dried black cohosh root (*Actaea racemosa*)
- 1 tablespoon dried red clover blossoms (*Trifolium pratense*)
- 2 cups water

NOTES:

Women with a history of estrogen-sensitive conditions, such as breast cancer or uterine cancer, should exercise caution when using these herbs. Consult with a healthcare provider to assess individual risks and benefits.

Black Cohosh has been associated with rare instances of liver toxicity. If you have a history of liver problems or are taking medications that affect the liver, consult with a healthcare professional before using black cohosh.

INSTRUCTIONS:

1 | **Preparation:** Start by bringing 2 cups of water to a gentle boil.
2 | **Herb Infusion:** Add the dried black cohosh root and red clover blossoms to the boiling water.
3 | **Simmer:** Reduce the heat to low, cover the pot, and let the herbs simmer for 15-20 minutes. This allows the medicinal compounds to infuse into the water.
4 | **Strain:** After simmering, strain the infusion to remove the herbal material, leaving you with a concentrated elixir.
5 | **Serve:** Consider adding honey or lemon for taste. Keep a consistent schedule for taking the elixir to maximize its benefits.

Complement the herbal treatment with a healthy lifestyle, including a balanced diet, regular exercise, and stress management, to promote overall well-being during menopause. You may also make a tincture using these herbs; recommended dosage is a dropperful every morning and one every evening.

DOSAGE:

Consume ½ to 1 cup of the elixir daily. Adjust the dosage based on individual needs and response.

Forgotten Home Apothecary

Anise Seed Tea
for Dysmenorrhea (Menstrual Cramping and Pain)

Anise seed (*Pimpinella anisum*), renowned for its aromatic properties, has an extensive history of use in traditional medicine. Beyond its culinary applications, anise seed is valued for its potential therapeutic effects, particularly in alleviating digestive issues and addressing menstrual discomfort. This recipe focuses on harnessing the medicinal properties of anise seed to create a soothing tea for dysmenorrhea, commonly known as menstrual cramping and pain. Cramp bark (*Viburnum opulus*) and motherwort (*Leonurus cardiaca*) pair well with this; simply add a teaspoon to this tea remedy.

INGREDIENTS:

- 1 teaspoon of anise seeds (*Pimpinella anisum*)
- 1 cup of hot water

NOTES:

Individuals with known allergies to anise, fennel, or similar plants in the Apiaceae family should refrain from using this remedy to avoid potential allergic reactions.

Anise seed may interact with certain blood pressure medications; those on such medications should seek medical advice before incorporating this herbal remedy.

INSTRUCTIONS:

1 | **Preparation:** Begin by slightly crushing the anise seeds. This helps to release the essential oils and enhance the infusion process.

2 | **Boiling Water:** In a pot or kettle, bring 1 cup of water to a gentle boil.

3 | **Infusion:** Place the crushed anise seeds in a teapot or heatproof container. Pour the hot water over the anise seeds, ensuring they are fully immersed.

4 | **Steeping:** Allow the mixture to steep for a duration of 5-10 minutes. This allows the volatile compounds, such as anethole, to infuse into the water.

5 | **Strain and Serve:** After steeping, strain the tea to separate the liquid from the anise seeds. This ensures a smooth, seed-free beverage. Enhance the flavor by adding a natural sweetener like honey or agave syrup. For a comprehensive menstrual support blend, consider combining anise seed tea with chamomile or ginger tea.

DOSAGE:

Consume 1 cup of anise seed tea during the onset of menstrual cramps. For sustained relief, repeat the dosage every 4-6 hours as needed.

Fertility Boosting
Tonic

This fertility-boosting tonic is a carefully crafted blend of herbs known for their potential benefits in supporting reproductive health. The combination of red clover, dong quai, maca root, and shatavari aims to address various aspects of fertility, from hormonal balance to improved circulation.

INGREDIENTS:

- 1 tablespoon dried red clover (*Trifolium pratense*) blossoms
- 1 tablespoon dong quai (*Angelica sinensis*) root slices
- 1 teaspoon maca root (*Lepidium meyenii*) powder
- 1 teaspoon shatavari (*Asparagus racemosus*) powder
- 2 cups water

NOTES:

If you are currently taking medications, especially hormonal therapies or blood-thinning medications, consult your healthcare provider before incorporating this tonic. The herbs may interact with medications, potentially affecting their effectiveness. While dong quai is traditionally used to regulate menstrual cycles, excessive use may lead to increased menstrual flow.

- **Red Clover** (*Trifolium pratense*): Rich in phytoestrogens, red clover is believed to help regulate estrogen levels, supporting hormonal balance.
- **Dong Quai** (*Angelica sinensis*): Known as the "female ginseng," dong quai may help regulate menstrual cycles and support overall reproductive health.
- **Maca Root** (*Lepidium meyenii*): Maca is believed to enhance fertility by balancing hormones and improving stamina and energy levels.
- **Shatavari** (*Asparagus racemosus*): Shatavari is known for its adaptogenic properties, supporting hormonal balance and promoting reproductive health.

INSTRUCTIONS:

1 | **Preparation of Herbs:** Combine red clover, ddong quai, maca root, and shatavari in a bowl. Boil 2 cups of water.
2 | **Brewing the Tonic:** Pour the boiling water over the herb mixture. Cover and steep for 15-20 minutes.
3 | **Strain and Serve:** Strain the tonic into a cup. Add honey or sweetener if desired.

Incorporate this tonic into a holistic fertility approach, including a balanced diet, regular exercise, and stress management.

DOSAGE:

Consume 1 cup daily, preferably in the morning, for optimal benefits.

Nature's Aphrodisiac

This herbal elixir combines herbs traditionally known for their aphrodisiac properties to create an elixir for libido enhancement. Damiana (*Turnera diffusa*), is renowned for its historical use as an aphrodisiac, potentially boosting sexual function. Maca root (*Lepidium meyenii*) is an adaptogenic herb with reported benefits for sexual health and libido. Cocoa (*Theobroma cacao*) not only adds a delicious flavor but also contains compounds that may contribute to mood enhancement and overall well-being.

INGREDIENTS:

- 1 tablespoon damiana leaves
- 1 teaspoon maca root powder
- 1 teaspoon cocoa powder
- ½ cup coconut milk
- ½ cup water
- 1 teaspoon honey (optional, for taste)

NOTES:

While this elixir is designed to enhance libido, individual responses may vary. If you have pre-existing health conditions, especially related to the reproductive system, consult with a healthcare professional before incorporating this elixir into your routine.

If you have known allergies to coconut or coconut-derived products, substitute with a non-allergenic alternative like almond or soy milk.

INSTRUCTIONS:

1 | **Prepare the Herbal Infusion:** Boil ½ cup of water. Add 1 tablespoon of Damiana leaves to the boiling water. Simmer for 5-7 minutes to extract the medicinal properties. Strain the infusion into a cup.

2 | **Combine with Creamy Elements:** In a separate container, mix ½ cup of coconut milk with the damiana infusion. Adjust the coconut milk quantity for your desired creaminess. Stir in 1 teaspoon each of maca root powder and cocoa powder. Ensure a smooth blend of all ingredients (a hand frother works well).

3 | **Sweeten with Honey (Optional):** If desired, add 1 teaspoon of honey for sweetness. Stir well.

4 | **Serve Chilled or Warm:** You can enjoy this elixir either chilled or gently warmed based on your preference.

Herbal aphrodisiacs come in a diverse range, each with its unique properties and potential benefits. Exploring this variety allows individuals to find what resonates best with their bodies and preferences. Here are some other herbal aphrodisiacs that you might consider incorporating into your elixirs. Puncture vine or bindii (*Tribulus terrestris*), ginseng (*Panax ginseng*), horny goat weed (*Epimedium sagittatum*), ginkgo biloba (*Ginkgo biloba*), yohimbe (*Pausinystalia yohimbe*), cinnamon (*Cinnamomum verum*), saw palmetto (*Serenoa repens*), ashwagandha (*Withania somnifera*), fenugreek (*Trigonella foenum-graecum*), and vanilla (*Vanilla planifolia*).

DOSAGE:

Consume this herbal elixir once daily for libido enhancement. It's recommended to take it in the evening for its relaxing effects.

Herbal ED Support

INGREDIENTS:

- 2 tbsp yohimbe bark powder
- 2 tbsp *Panax ginseng* powder
- 2 tbsp puncture vine (*Tribulus terrestris*) powder
- 1.5 tbsp horny goat weed powder
- 1.5 tbsp muira puama powder
- 6 tbsp powdered soy protein or gelatin
- Empty gelatin or vegetable capsules

NOTES:

Yohimbe can have significant side effects, including increased heart rate, elevated blood pressure, anxiety, and gastrointestinal distress.

Individuals with a sensitive stomach should take these capsules with food to minimize the risk of gastrointestinal discomfort.

Erectile dysfunction is a common concern, and some herbal remedies may offer support.

- **Yohimbe** (*Pausinystalia yohimbe*) is known for its potential benefits in improving blood flow and addressing certain aspects of sexual dysfunction.
- **Ginseng** (*Panax ginseng*) supports nitric oxide synthesis, promoting better blood flow, which can aid in treating ED.
- **Puncture vine** (*Tribulus terrestris*) may enhance testosterone levels, contributing to improved libido and sexual function.
- **Horny goat weed** (*Epimedium grandiflorum*) is thought to increase blood flow and improve sexual function by supporting nitric oxide levels.
- ***Muira puama*** (*Ptychopetalum olacoides*) is traditionally used to address sexual disorders, including erectile dysfunction, by promoting circulation and supporting libido.
- Possible additions: **Ginkgo biloba** (check with your doctor if you are on blood thinners or cardiovascular drugs) and Garlic are known to increase blood flow, which can help with ED.

INSTRUCTIONS:

1 | **Prepare the Herbal Blend:** In a mixing bowl, combine yohimbe, *Panax ginseng*, *Tribulus terrestris*, horny goat weed, muira puama powders, and powdered soy protein or gelatin.
2 | **Mix Thoroughly:** Blend the powders thoroughly to ensure an even distribution.
3 | **Fill the Capsules:** Using either a capsule-filling device or manually, open the empty capsules and fill them with the herbal blend. You would need approximately 20 "00" capsules to encapsulate the entire herbal blend.
4 | **Seal the Capsules:** Follow the instructions on the capsule-filling device or manually seal the capsules securely.

DOSAGE:

Take 3 capsules daily (preferably after meals) for 10 weeks or add a teaspoon or two to your daily smoothie. It is best to start with a small dose and see how your body reacts.

Forgotten Home Apothecary

Saw Palmetto Infusion
for Prostate Support

Saw Palmetto is renowned for its potential benefits in promoting prostate health. It contains active compounds that are believed to inhibit the enzyme 5-alpha-reductase, responsible for converting testosterone into dihydrotestosterone (DHT). Elevated levels of DHT are associated with prostate enlargement. Note that reishi mushroom works in a similar way on the prostate, and may be used in conjunction with saw palmetto; use as a dual-extracted tincture. Saw palmetto berries also possess anti-inflammatory and anti-androgenic properties, contributing to their effectiveness.

INGREDIENTS:

- 1 teaspoon of dried saw palmetto (*Serenoa repens*) berries
- 1 cup of hot water

NOTES:

Individuals with known allergies to plants in the Arecaceae family should avoid saw palmetto.

Saw palmetto may interact with hormonal medications; consult a healthcare professional if using such medications.

Some individuals may experience mild gastrointestinal discomfort; discontinue use if adverse effects persist.

INSTRUCTIONS:

1 | **Prepare the Infusion:** Measure 1 teaspoon of dried saw palmetto berries.
2 | **Boil the Water:** Boil 1 cup of water and pour it over the berries in a heat-resistant container.
3 | **Steep:** Allow the mixture to steep for 10-15 minutes, ensuring a covered vessel to retain volatile oils.
4 | **Strain and Serve:** After steeping, strain the infusion using a fine mesh strainer to separate the liquid from the berries.
5 | **Optional Ingredients:** Enhance the flavor by adding a touch of honey or a slice of lemon.

Apart from its well-known benefits for prostate health, saw palmetto has also gained attention for its potential positive effects on hair health. You can create a hair oil blend by mixing a few drops of saw palmetto oil or extract with a carrier oil (jojoba or coconut oil). Gently massage it into the scalp, leaving it in for a few hours or overnight before rinsing. Repeat 1-2 times a week.

DOSAGE:

Consume the tea once daily for potential prostate health benefits. The recommended dosage is 1 cup, preferably in the evening. Consistency is crucial; incorporate this herbal remedy into your daily routine for long-term benefits.

"Milk Flow" Tea

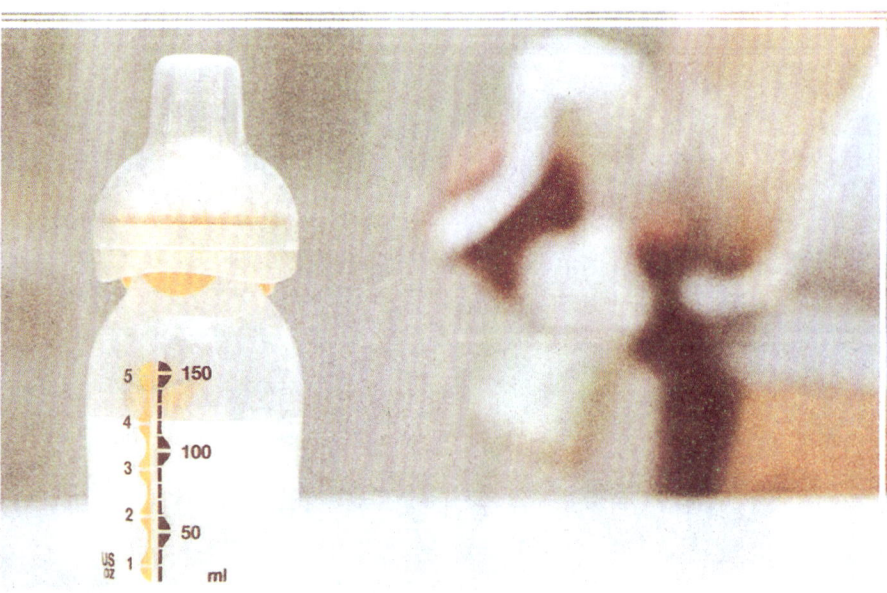

Not all mothers naturally produce enough breast milk.

Fenugreek (*Trigonella foenum-graecum*) and blessed thistle (*Cnicus benedictus*) are two herbs commonly used to support milk production in breastfeeding mothers. Fenugreek is known for its galactagogue properties, which stimulate milk production. It contains compounds that mimic estrogen, contributing to increased lactation. Blessed thistle is also a galactagogue that is believed to enhance the flow of milk by increasing prolactin levels.

If blessed thistle isn't available a blend of fenugreek and fennel (*Foeniculum vulgare*) can be an effective alternative for supporting milk production in breastfeeding mothers.

INGREDIENTS:

- 1 teaspoon fenugreek seeds (*Trigonella foenum-graecum*)
- 1 teaspoon blessed thistle (*Cnicus benedictus*)
- 1 cup water

NOTES:

It's important to note that individual responses to herbs may vary.

Pregnant women and individuals with allergies or medical conditions should consult a healthcare professional before incorporating this herbal remedy.

If you experience any adverse effects, discontinue use.

INSTRUCTIONS:

1| **Herb Preparation:** Measure 1 teaspoon each of fenugreek seeds and blessed thistle. Ensure the herbs are clean and free from contaminants. Fenugreek may have a maple syrup-like smell; this is normal.

2| **Infusion:** Boil 1 cup of water. Add the measured fenugreek seeds and blessed thistle to the boiling water. Let the herbs steep for 10-15 minutes.

3| **Strain and Serve:** After steeping, strain the infusion to remove the herb particles. Stay hydrated while consuming this herbal infusion.

DOSAGE:

Consume the herbal infusion once a day. Start with a lower dosage and monitor your body's response.

Yarrow, Shepherd's Purse, and Cramp Bark
Tincture for Menstrual Health

Yarrow (*Achillea millefolium*), shepherd's purse (*Capsella bursa-pastoris*), and cramp bark (*Viburnum opulus*) are three herbs renowned for their ability to alleviate menstrual cramps.

Yarrow has anti-inflammatory properties and is believed to help regulate menstrual flow. Shepherd's purse and yarrow are known for their hemostatic properties, assisting in reducing excessive bleeding during menstruation. Cramp bark helps ease muscle cramping and muscle spasms, especially helpful during menstruation.

INGREDIENTS:

- 1-part dried yarrow flowers/aerial parts (*Achillea millefolium*)
- 1-part dried shepherd's purse aerial parts (*Capsella bursa-pastoris*)
- 1-part cramp bark (*Viburnum opulus*)
- High-proof alcohol (such as vodka)

NOTES:
Consult with a healthcare professional before using this tincture, especially if pregnant or nursing.

If you experience any adverse reactions, discontinue use and seek medical advice.

INSTRUCTIONS:

1 | **Preparation:** Ensure all equipment is clean and sterilized. Measure the dried yarrow flowers, shepherd's purse aerial parts, and the bark from cramp bark.
2 | **Combine the Herbs:** Combine the measured herbs in a glass jar.
3 | **Add Alcohol:** Pour the high-proof alcohol over the herbs, making sure they are fully submerged. Use a ratio of 1-part herbs to 2 parts alcohol.
4 | **Seal the Jar:** Secure the lid tightly on the jar, ensuring it is airtight.
5 | **Infusion Period:** Place the sealed jar in a cool, dark place for about 4-6 weeks. Shake the jar daily to facilitate the extraction process.
6 | **Strain:** After the infusion period, strain the tincture using cheesecloth or a fine mesh strainer into a clean, dark glass bottle. Label.

DOSAGE:

Take ½ to 1 teaspoon of the tincture in a small amount of water, three times daily, starting a few days before your menstrual cycle and continuing throughout to help alleviate menstrual cramps.

HERBAL SUPPORT
for a Healthy Urinary System

A well-functioning urinary system is essential for overall health, aiding in the elimination of waste and regulating fluid balance. Incorporating healthy habits into your lifestyle can contribute to the optimal functioning of your urinary system.

Tips to Maintain a Healthy Urinary System:

PROPER HYDRATION:

Proper hydration is fundamental for a healthy urinary system. Water helps flush out toxins and maintains the balance of electrolytes in the body. Aim to drink at least 8 cups (64 oz) of water per day. Adjust this based on individual needs, activity levels, and climate. Strenuous exercise can lead to dehydration, impacting urinary function. Proper hydration before, during, and after exercise is crucial. Drink water consistently during physical activity to maintain fluid balance and support kidney function.

INCLUDE FOODS RICH IN POTASSIUM:

Potassium helps regulate fluid balance and supports kidney function. Foods like bananas, oranges, and spinach are excellent sources.

LIMIT SODIUM INTAKE:

High sodium levels can lead to water retention and increased blood pressure, impacting kidney function. Limiting sodium intake is crucial for maintaining a healthy urinary system. Read food labels and choose low-sodium alternatives. Cooking with herbs and spices can add flavor without excess sodium.

LIMIT CAFFEINE AND ALCOHOL:

Excessive caffeine and alcohol consumption can lead to dehydration and irritate the bladder. Moderation is key for maintaining a healthy urinary balance. Opt for herbal teas and water as alternatives.

PRACTICE GOOD BATHROOM HABITS:

Holding in urine for prolonged periods can contribute to urinary issues. Regular and timely bathroom visits promote a healthy urinary flow. Listen to your body's signals and make regular trips to the bathroom. Avoid delaying urination when the urge arises.

MAINTAIN A HEALTHY WEIGHT:

Excess weight can put pressure on the bladder and contribute to urinary incontinence. Achieving and maintaining a healthy weight is beneficial for urinary health.

PRACTICE GOOD HYGIENE:

Maintaining good personal hygiene helps prevent urinary tract infections. Practices such as wiping front to back after using the toilet are crucial.

KEGEL EXERCISES:

Kegel exercises strengthen the pelvic floor muscles, supporting bladder control and preventing urinary incontinence. Incorporate Kegel exercises into your daily routine to enhance pelvic muscle strength. Consistency is key for optimal results.

HERBAL SUPPORT

Uva Ursi (*Arctostaphylos uva-ursi*)
Contains arbutin, which may have diuretic effects, promoting urine flow and helping flush out toxins from the urinary tract.

Horsetail (*Equisetum arvense*)
Rich in silica, it may contribute to tissue repair and support overall urinary tract function.

Dandelion (*Taraxacum officinale*)
Known for its diuretic properties, dandelion can help increase urine production and support kidney function.

Nettle (*Urtica dioica*)
A nutritive herb rich in essential minerals like magnesium and calcium, contributing to the health of the urinary tract.

Cranberry (*Vaccinium macrocarpon*)
Contains compounds that may help prevent urinary tract infections by inhibiting bacteria from adhering to the urinary tract walls.

Parsley (*Petroselinum crispum*)
Contains compounds with diuretic properties, promoting urine production and potentially supporting kidney health.

Goldenrod (*Solidago virgaurea*)
Traditionally used to support urinary tract health and believed to have mild diuretic properties.

Corn Silk (*Zea mays*)
Known for its mild diuretic effects, corn silk may help promote urine flow and support kidney function.

Usnea (*Usnea* spp.)
Its potent antimicrobial effects contribute to fighting off infections.

Juniper Berry (*Juniperus communis*)
Traditionally used for its diuretic properties, juniper berry may help increase urine production.

Marshmallow Root *(Althaea officinalis)*
Contains mucilage, which can have soothing effects on the urinary tract, potentially alleviating irritation.

Couch Grass *(Elymus repens)*
Traditionally used for its diuretic properties, couch grass may help increase urine flow and support overall urinary health.

Lovage *(Levisticum officinale)*
Known for its diuretic effects, lovage may help promote urine production and contribute to a healthy urinary system.

Buchu *(Agathosma betulina)*
Traditionally used for urinary tract infections, buchu is believed to have mild diuretic and antiseptic properties.

Cleavers *(Galium aparine)*
Known for its mild diuretic effects, cleavers may help support the elimination of waste through the urinary system.

Ginger *(Zingiber officinale)*
While commonly known for digestive support, ginger may also have mild diuretic properties, contributing to fluid balance.

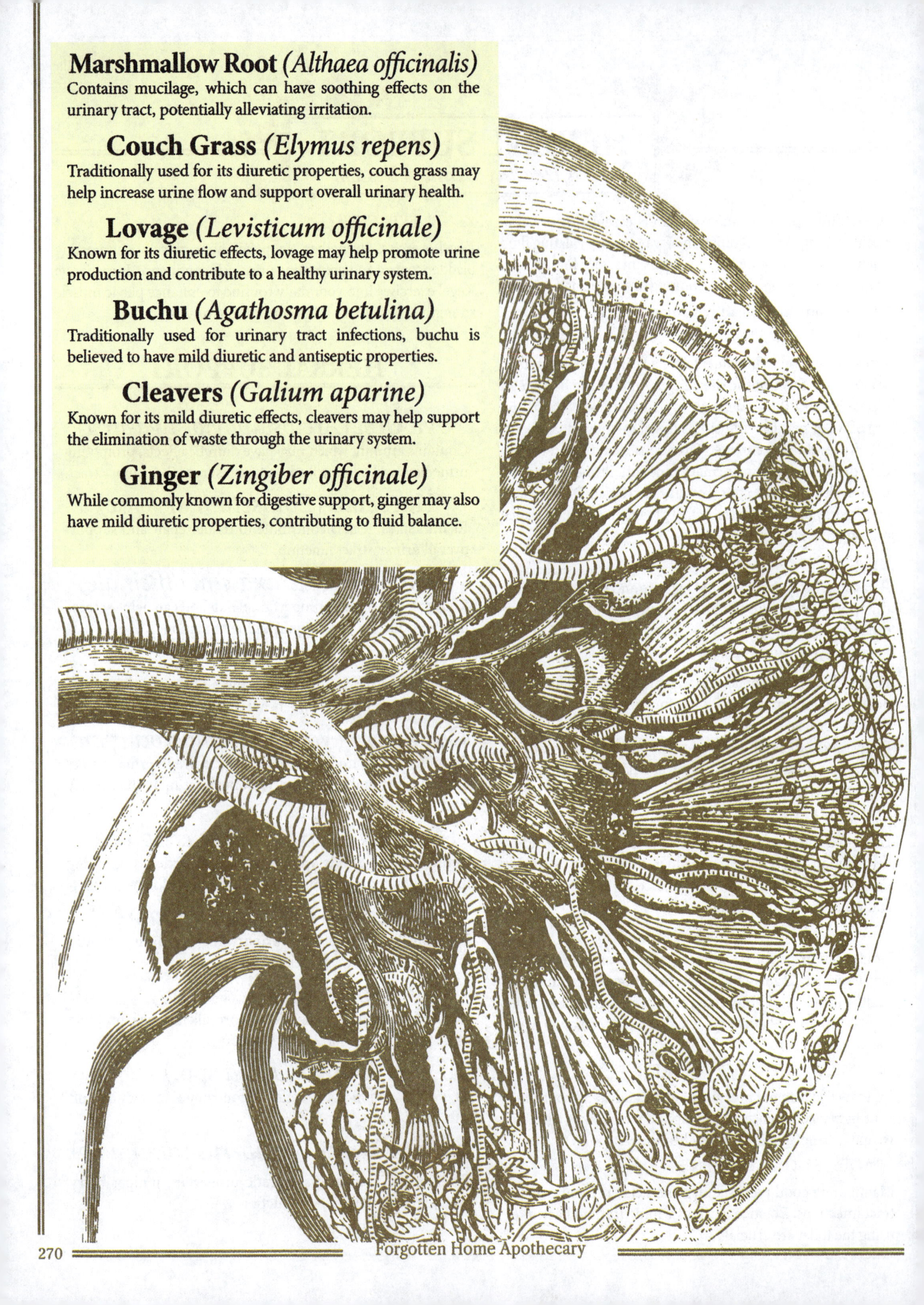

Cranberry and Hibiscus Tea
for Urinary Tract Support

Cranberry (*Vaccinium macrocarpon*) and hibiscus (*Hibiscus sabdariffa*) tea is a delightful herbal infusion that not only offers a refreshing taste but also provides benefits for urinary tract support. Both herbs have been traditionally used for their potential to promote urinary health.

- **Cranberries** are rich in compounds called proanthocyanidins, which have been associated with preventing the adherence of bacteria, particularly E. coli, to the urinary tract walls. This anti-adhesive property may help reduce the risk of urinary tract infections (UTIs).
- **Hibiscus** is known for its diuretic properties, which can support the flushing of toxins from the body. Additionally, it has antioxidant compounds that contribute to overall urinary health.

INGREDIENTS:

- 2 teaspoons of dried cranberry (*Vaccinium macrocarpon*)
- 1 teaspoon of dried hibiscus (*Hibiscus sabdariffa*)
- 8 ounces of hot water
- Optional: honey or lemon for taste

NOTES:

Hydration is essential for urinary health, so drink plenty of water alongside this herbal tea.

Individuals on blood-thinning medications should consult their healthcare provider before consuming cranberry, as it may interact with these medications. Hibiscus may lower blood pressure, so individuals with low blood pressure should monitor their levels closely.

INSTRUCTIONS:

1. **Prepare the Herbs:** Combine the dried cranberry and hibiscus in a teapot or infuser.
2. **Boil the Water:** Bring 8 ounces of water to a near-boil.
3. **Infusion:** Pour the hot water over the herbs in the teapot or infuser.
4. **Steep:** Allow the herbs to steep for 10-15 minutes to extract the beneficial compounds.
5. **Strain:** Strain the tea to remove the herbs, leaving a clear infusion.
6. **Optional Additions:** Add honey or lemon for taste if desired. Hydration is essential for urinary health, so drink plenty of water alongside this herbal tea.

DOSAGE:

Consume 1-2 cups per day for urinary tract support.

Forgotten Home Apothecary

Parsley Tea
for Urinary Tract Inflammation

Parsley is a well-known herb that not only adds flavor to dishes but also offers various health benefits. It contains compounds like apiol and myristicin, known for their diuretic properties and potential anti-inflammatory effects.

Apiol is believed to enhance urine production, facilitating the removal of toxins and waste. This diuretic action may be beneficial for individuals dealing with mild water retention issues and those seeking to support their urinary system. Parsley's potential anti-inflammatory effects can be attributed to its unique blend of flavonoids, carotenoids, and volatile compounds. These constituents may help modulate inflammatory responses in the body, offering relief to conditions associated with inflammation, including certain urinary tract issues.

INGREDIENTS:

- 1-2 teaspoons of dried parsley leaves (*Petroselinum crispum*) or 1-2 tablespoons of fresh parsley leaves
- 1 cup of warm water

NOTES:

Pregnant women should consult a healthcare professional before consuming parsley tea due to its potential to stimulate uterine contractions.

Parsley contains compounds known as oxalates, which can contribute to the formation of kidney stones in susceptible individuals. People with a history of kidney stones or existing kidney issues may want to avoid parsley tea to minimize the risk of exacerbating these conditions.

INSTRUCTIONS:

For maximum vitamin C retention, use the low-heat stovetop method. Directly pouring boiling water over the leaves is quicker but may reduce the vitamin C content.

1 | **Low Heat Method (Stovetop):** Place the measured parsley leaves in a pot on the stovetop. Pour 1 cup of cold water over the leaves.
2 | **Low Heat Steeping:** Heat the water and parsley mixture on low heat. Keep the temperature below 140°F (60°C) to preserve vitamin C. Allow the mixture to steep for 5-10 minutes.
3 | **Strain:** Strain the tea to remove the parsley leaves.
4 | **Serve:** You can customize the flavor by adding a squeeze of lemon or a teaspoon of honey if desired.

DOSAGE:

Drink a cup of parsley tea 3 times a day for at least 2 weeks or until the relief of symptoms. As a preventative, drink a cup of parsley tea 1 – 2 times a week.

Kidney Elixir

Nettle leaf tea is a herbal infusion renowned for its potential to nurture kidney health.

Rich in essential vitamins A and C, iron, and vital minerals, nettle presents a gentle yet effective way to incorporate herbal support into your daily routine. Nettle leaf tea, with its mild diuretic properties, encourages healthy urine flow, aiding in the elimination of toxins.

The anti-inflammatory characteristics of nettle may also contribute to reducing kidney inflammation, making it a comforting choice for those seeking to support renal well-being.

INGREDIENTS:

- 1 tablespoon of dried stinging nettle leaves (*Urtica dioica*)
- 1 cup of hot water

NOTES:

Exercise caution if you have a known allergy to nettle.

Monitor for any signs of allergic reactions, such as itching or swelling.

Consult with a healthcare professional before consuming nettle tea, especially during pregnancy, as it may have uterine-stimulating effects.

INSTRUCTIONS:

1| **Prepare the Tea:** Place 1 tablespoon of dried nettle leaves in a teapot or infuser.
2| **Infusion:** Pour 1 cup of hot water over the nettle leaves, allowing them to steep for 5-7 minutes.
3| **Strain and Enjoy:** Strain the tea into a cup, separating the liquid from the leaves. Sip and savor the comforting essence of nettle. Add a touch of honey or lemon to enhance the flavor of your nettle tea. Consider blending nettle leaves with other herbal teas for a delightful infusion.

DOSAGE:

Enjoy 2-3 cups of nettle leaf tea throughout the day for optimal kidney support. You may also take this as a stinging nettle tincture but remember to also drink plenty of water to stay hydrated.

Kidney Cleanse
Juice

This homemade kidney cleanse juice combines a powerful blend of ingredients, each renowned for its unique benefits in supporting kidney health.

- **Red grapes:** Packed with antioxidants and natural diuretics, red grapes aid in reducing inflammation and eliminating toxins from the kidneys.
- **Parsley:** Known for its diuretic properties, parsley helps increase urine production, flushing out toxins and supporting kidney function.
- **Dandelion** is prized for its diuretic and antioxidant properties, which help cleanse the kidneys and protect against damage.
- **Ginger's** anti-inflammatory properties support kidney health while aiding digestion and circulation.
- **Apple:** Rich in fiber and antioxidants, apples help regulate blood sugar levels and protect against kidney damage.
- **Lemons** contain citric acid, which helps prevent kidney stone formation, and vitamin C, providing antioxidant protection for the kidneys.

INGREDIENTS:

- 8 oz red grapes
- A few sprigs of parsley
- 20-30 drops of dandelion extract/tincture (*Taraxacum officinale*)
- 1 tsp grated ginger (*Zingiber officinale*)
- 1 red apple
- 1 lemon
- ½ cup water (or more for desired consistency)

NOTES:

If you have any pre-existing health conditions or are pregnant or breastfeeding, consult with a healthcare professional before incorporating this juice into your routine. Dandelion extract may interact with certain medications or medical conditions.

Excessive consumption of parsley may have diuretic effects and lead to electrolyte imbalances.

INSTRUCTIONS:

1| **Prepare the Ingredients:** Wash the red apple thoroughly and cut it into small pieces. Wash the red grapes. Wash the parsley sprigs and dice the leaves and stems. Peel and grate a small knob of ginger to obtain approximately 1 teaspoon of grated ginger. Add all the ingredients to the blender or juicer. Squeeze the juice of 1 lemon and add it to the blender. If desired, you can substitute the apple or grapes with other kidney-friendly fruits such as blueberries, raspberries, strawberries, cherries, or watermelon.

2| **Blend:** Add 20-30 drops of dandelion extract and ½ cup of water to the blender. Adjust the water amount to achieve your preferred consistency. Blend all the ingredients until smooth and well combined. For a smoother texture (if desired), strain the juice through a fine-mesh strainer or layers of cheesecloth after blending. Save the pulp from the apple and grapes for other culinary uses, such as topping natural yogurt.

DOSAGE:

Consume this kidney cleanse juice immediately after preparation to enjoy maximum freshness and benefits, preferably in the morning on an empty stomach, for optimal results.

Corn Silk Tea
for Bladder Comfort (and Prostate)

Recognized for generations in traditional herbalism, fresh corn silk is renowned for its potential to nurture and support bladder health. Infused with antioxidants and bioactive compounds, this tea offers a unique and enjoyable way to experience the therapeutic benefits of this natural remedy.

Corn silk works as a diuretic agent, increasing urine secretion. It also promotes urinary health by reducing bladder irritation by soothing and relaxing the lining of the bladder and urinary tubules. Corn silk's biological activity is mainly due to its flavonoid and terpenoid content. The bioactive constituents are phenolic compounds, which are effective antioxidants. Corn silk is also made up of proteins, vitamins, carbohydrates, minerals including calcium, potassium, and magnesium, as well as volatile oils.

INGREDIENTS:

- Corn Silk from 2 ears of corn
- 2 cups water
- 1 teaspoon honey (optional, for sweetness)

NOTES:

If you have allergies to corn, consult with a healthcare professional before incorporating this tea into your routine.

Official dosage recommendations for corn silk are limited due to a lack of human research.

However, corn silk has been tested for safety, and up to 4.5 g per pound of weight is likely safe for most individuals.

INSTRUCTIONS:

1 | **Harvest and Dry Corn Silk:** Extract corn silk from two ears of fresh, organically grown corn. Spread the strands in a cool, dry place to air dry naturally for a few days until fully dried. Due to its fine, thin nature, it dries readily. When collecting corn silk, ensure it is free of debris from the husks and corn cobs.

2 | **Preparing the Tea:** Bring 2 cups of water to a gentle boil in a saucepan. Add the dried cornsilk to the boiling water and let it simmer for 10-15 minutes, allowing the dried strands to rehydrate and infuse the water with their beneficial compounds.

3 | **Strain:** Strain the tea to remove the rehydrated corn silk, leaving a clear and potent infusion.

4 | **Sweeten (Optional):** Enhance the flavor with 1 teaspoon of honey, if desired. Stir until dissolved.

DOSAGE:

Consume 1-2 cups of fresh-to-dried corn silk tea daily for bladder health support.

Herbal Blend
for Urinary Tract Infections

This herbal tincture, crafted with dried goldenrod (*Solidago* spp.), usnea (*Usnea* spp.), uva ursi (*Arctostaphylos uva-ursi*), and oregon grape root (*Mahonia aquifolium*), offers a natural approach to addressing urinary tract infections (UTIs). The combination of these herbs, preserved in alcohol, is designed to extract their medicinal properties effectively.

- **Goldenrod** (*Solidago* spp.): Diuretic properties to aid in toxin elimination from the urinary system.
- **Usnea** (*Usnea* spp.): Potent antimicrobial/antibacterial effects that contribute to fighting off infections.
- **Uva Ursi/Bearberry** (*Arctostaphylos uva-ursi*): Arbutin content shown to have antibacterial properties beneficial for UTI management.
- **Oregon Grape Root** (*Mahonia aquifolium*): Antimicrobial properties in berberine can support the immune system, inhibit bacterial growth, and prevent bacteria from adhering to the bladder wall.

INGREDIENTS:

- 1 part dried goldenrod (aerial parts)
- 1 part dried and cut usnea lichen
- 1 part dried uva ursi
- 1 part dried and sliced oregon grape root
- 80-proof vodka or grain alcohol

NOTES:

Consult with a healthcare professional before using if pregnant, nursing, or on medication.

Individuals with pre-existing kidney or renal conditions should consult a healthcare provider before using uva ursi, as it has diuretic properties and may impact renal function.

Discontinue use if any adverse reactions occur.

INSTRUCTIONS:

1. **Combine Dried Herbs:** Measure equal parts of dried goldenrod, usnea, uva ursi, and oregon grape root. Place the dried cut herbs in a clean, dry glass jar, filling the jar half-full of your dried herbs.
2. **Add Alcohol:** Pour enough 80-proof vodka or grain alcohol over the herbs to completely cover them.
3. **Seal and Shake:** Seal the jar tightly and shake it well to ensure the herbs are fully submerged.
4. **Steep:** Place the jar in a cool, dark place for 6-8 weeks, shaking it daily to promote herbal extraction.
5. **Strain and Bottle:** After steeping, strain the tincture through cheesecloth or a fine mesh strainer into a dark glass bottle

DOSAGE:

Take 1-2 droppers full (approximately 30-60 drops) in a small amount of water or directly in the mouth 3x/day for UTIs. Adding in D-mannose as a supplement is also recommended.

Forgotten Home Apothecary

Pumpkin Seed Tincture
for Overactive Bladder

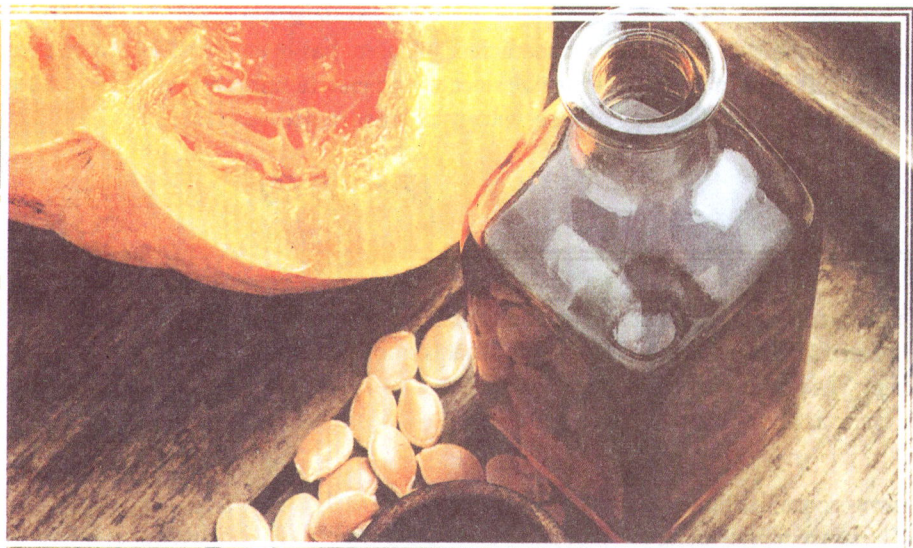

The pumpkin seed oil or extract obtained from *Cucurbita pepo* has been shown to be useful for the treatment of nocturia in patients. Renowned for their nutritional richness, these seeds house an array of antioxidants, essential fatty acids, and other bioactive compounds that may offer relief to those grappling with the challenges of an overactive bladder.

INGREDIENTS AND MATERIALS:

- 2 cups raw, organic pumpkin seeds
- Electric spice or coffee grinder
- Double boiler setup (*e.g.*, a Pyrex bowl over a pot)
- Sheer fabric (*e.g.*, chiffon or cheesecloth, 12 x 12" square)
- Dark glass bottle

NOTES:

If your overactive bladder symptoms are still bothersome or affecting your quality of life, it's recommended to see a healthcare provider who can help determine the underlying cause and recommend appropriate treatments.

They may suggest lifestyle modifications, behavioral therapies, medications, or other interventions depending on your specific situation.

INSTRUCTIONS:

1 | **Prepare Pumpkin Seeds:** Rinse the pumpkin seeds thoroughly to remove any impurities.
2 | **Create Pumpkin Seed Flour:** Using the grinder, grind the pumpkin seeds into a fine powder, about the texture of flour. Work in increments to not overwhelm the grinder.
3 | **Form Pumpkin Seed Paste:** Add 2-3 tablespoons of water to the pumpkin seed flour. Stir until distributed and it reaches the consistency of a paste. Creating a paste will help the oil extract more evenly.
4 | **Double Boil:** Once you have your pumpkin seed paste, place it in a double boiler. You can create your double boiler by placing a Pyrex bowl over a small pot with water. Warming the pumpkin seed paste helps extract the oils from the seeds. To evenly heat the paste, stir consistently. As the paste warms, it will start to look shiny from the oil extraction. This should take about five minutes. Remove from heat. It's critical to not get the paste too hot during this step. Heating the paste above 120°F can damage the medicinal compounds.
5 | **Extract the Oil:** Prepare to extract the oil from the paste using sheer fabric and a clean bowl. Spoon the pumpkin seed paste onto the center of the chiffon cloth or fine mesh fabric (*e.g.* cheesecloth). Wrap the fabric tightly and squeeze it over the bowl. While it may require some effort, you should observe the oil starting to flow from the fabric.
6 | **Bottle the Oil:** Transfer the strained oil into a dark glass bottle for storage.

DOSAGE:

Start with 10-20 drops of the tincture diluted in water, taken one to three times per day. This dosage may be adjusted based on individual response and tolerance.

Forgotten Home Apothecary

SAFETY GUIDELINES
and Precautions

Herbalism, the use of plants for medicinal purposes, has been practiced for centuries. While herbs can offer various health benefits, it's important to use them with caution to ensure safety and effectiveness. This chapter delves into crucial aspects of maintaining the well-being of those who seek herbal remedies.

Proper Usage and Dosage

Understanding the proper usage and dosage of herbal remedies is essential for harnessing their therapeutic benefits while ensuring safety. The guidelines below offer a general overview applicable to various herbs:

CONSULT WITH A PROFESSIONAL:
Always consult with a qualified healthcare professional (*e.g.* ND: naturopathic doctor) or herbalist before using herbs, especially if you are pregnant, nursing, have pre-existing health conditions or are taking medications.

IDENTIFICATION OF PLANTS:
Ensure accurate identification of plants before use. Mistaking one plant for another can lead to harmful effects.

QUALITY OF HERBS
Choose high-quality herbs from reputable sources to ensure purity and avoid contamination.

PRECISION IN MEASUREMENT:
Invest in high-quality measuring instruments. Be meticulous in your measurements

ALLERGIES AND SENSITIVITIES:
Be aware of potential allergies or sensitivities to specific herbs. Start with a small amount to test for adverse reactions.

DOSAGE:
Adhere to recommended dosage guidelines. More is not always better, and excessive doses may lead to adverse effects.

FORM OF ADMINISTRATION:
Pay attention to the recommended form of administration (*e.g.*, tea, tincture, capsule). Different forms may have different concentrations.

CONSISTENCY IS KEY:
Take herbal remedies consistently for the desired effects. For acute conditions, follow the recommended dosage for the specified duration.

CHILDREN AND ELDERLY:
Exercise caution when administering herbs to children or the elderly, as they may be more sensitive to certain compounds.

COMMON SENSE:
Trust your instincts. If you experience unusual or severe side effects, discontinue use and seek medical attention.

START SLOWLY:
Begin with a lower dose and gradually increase if needed. This helps assess your body's response to the herb.

KEEP RECORDS:
Maintain a record of the herbs you're using, dosages, and any effects experienced. This information can be valuable for future reference.

MONITOR EFFECTS:
Pay attention to how your body responds to the herbs. If you notice any adverse effects, adjust the dosage or discontinue use.

INDIVIDUAL VARIATIONS:
Recognize that individual responses to herbs can vary. What works for one person may not work the same way for another.

CUSTOMIZATION:
Work with a qualified herbalist or ND to tailor herbal regimens to your specific health needs and constitution.

EDUCATE YOURSELF:
Stay informed about the herbs you're using. Understand their properties, potential side effects, and contraindications.

DRUG INTERACTIONS:
Research potential interactions between herbs and medications. Some herbs may interact with pharmaceutical drugs, reducing their effectiveness or causing unwanted side effects.

AGE-APPROPRIATE FORMULATIONS:
Recognize that children may require different formulations. Understand the developmental stages and adjust your concoctions accordingly. Consult reputable references for age-specific dosages and formulations.

Here are some age-based rules and weight-based rules commonly used to determine the dosage of medications or herbal remedies for different age groups:

Age-Based Rules

BEST FOR	ages 2-12 years old
FORMULA	(Age in years) / (Age + 12) = Percentage of adult dose
EXAMPLE	For a 6-year-old, the calculation would be 6 / (6 + 12) = 6/18 = ⅓ or approximately 33% of the adult dose

BEST FOR	infants and up to 2 years old
FORMULA	(Age in months) / 150 = Percentage of adult dose
EXAMPLE	For a 12-month-old, the calculation would be 12 / 150 = 0.08 or 8% of the adult dose.

Weight-Based Rules

FORMULA	(Weight in lbs.) / 150 = Percentage of adult dose
EXAMPLE	For a child weighing 60 lbs., the calculation would be 60 / 150 = 0.4 or 40% of the adult dose.

Reflects the faster metabolism of children.

FORMULA	(Weight in kg x 1.5) + 10 = Percentage of adult dose
EXAMPLE	For a child weighing 30 kg, the calculation would be (30 x 1.5) + 10 = 55% of the adult dose.

Considered a close approximation to body surface area (BSA) calculations.

FORMULA	(Weight in kg x 2) if weight ≤ 30 kg, or (Weight in kg + 30) if weight > 30 kg = Percentage of adult dose
EXAMPLE	For a child weighing 40 kg, the calculation would be (40 + 30) = 70% of the adult dose.

Side Effects
and Allergies

Incorporating herbs into healthcare routines can provide various benefits, but it's essential to approach herbalism with a thorough understanding of potential side effects and allergies. If in doubt or if adverse effects occur, promptly seek the advice of a healthcare professional

PLANT ALLERGIES

Individuals with known allergies to specific plant families (*e.g.*, Asteraceae) should exercise caution. Symptoms of an allergic reaction may include skin rash, itching, swelling, or difficulty breathing. Discontinue use immediately if any signs of an allergy appear and seek medical attention.

CROSS-REACTIVITY

Cross-reactivity between herbs and common allergens is possible. Individuals allergic to specific plants (*e.g.*, ragweed) may also react to herbs from the same botanical family. Consider this possibility, especially in cases of known allergies.

PRE-EXISTING CONDITIONS

Individuals with pre-existing health conditions, such as liver or kidney disorders, may be more susceptible to side effects. Exercise caution and seek professional guidance when using herbal remedies in such cases.

HERBS AND PREGNANCY

Pregnant or breastfeeding individuals should exercise particular caution. Some herbs can be contraindicated during pregnancy, potentially causing harm to the fetus. Always consult with a healthcare professional before using herbs in these situations.

GASTROINTESTINAL DISTRESS

Some individuals may experience upset stomach, bloating, or diarrhea with certain herbal remedies. Adjusting the dosage or taking remedies with meals can help mitigate these effects.

SENSITIVITY TO SUNLIGHT

Certain herbs, like St. John's Wort, may increase sensitivity to sunlight. Caution is advised, and sun exposure should be limited during use.

SKIN REACTIONS

External application of herbal preparations may cause skin irritation in sensitive individuals. Perform a patch test before using topically, especially with essential oils.

RESPIRATORY ALLERGIES

Inhaling certain herbal powders or extracts may trigger respiratory allergies. Use caution, especially in those prone to respiratory issues.

REPORTING ADVERSE EFFECTS

Report any unexpected or severe side effects to healthcare professionals. This information contributes to the overall understanding of herbal safety.

Interactions
with Medications

As a general rule of thumb, you should avoid taking natural remedies with drugs that are meant to do the same thing. For example, don't take a natural blood thinner when you are already taking blood thinners. This can result in some serious health issues. When you visit your healthcare providers, it's important to tell them about all the medicines and supplements you take. Bring a written list of everything you take, how often you take them, and the doses you take.

Let's dive into the specifics, fostering a clear understanding of how herbs and conventional medications may interact, and empowering you with knowledge for informed decision-making:

Level of Evidence to Support Use

CT = Controlled trial	CS = Case series
CR = Case report	AS = Animal study
TU = Traditional use	P = Pharmacology
TH = Theoretical	

DRUG CATEGORY	HERBS	HERB EFFECT	MECHANISM (EVIDENCE TYPE)
Alkaloids	High tannin-containing (*e.g.*, caffeine-containing herbs, cat's claw, tea, *uva ursi*)	Decreased plasma levels	Precipitation of alkaloids by tannins (TU)
Anesthetics	Kava, valerian	Prolongation of sedation time	Additive effect (CR)
Antihypertensives	Licorice	Decreased therapeutic effect	Increased salt and water retention (CR)
Antiarrhythmics	Cathartic laxatives (*e.g.*, aloe, cascara, senna, yellow dock), diuretics (*e.g.*, celery seed, corn silk, horsetail, juniper), licorice	Increased side effects (arrhythmia)	Increased potassium loss (P)
Antiarrhythmics	Anticholinergic herbs (not generally used clinically, *e.g.*, belladonna)	Decreased therapeutic effect	Decreased absorption (P, TH)
Anticoagulants	Antiplatelet-aggregating (*e.g.*, *Panax ginseng*, feverfew, garlic, ginkgo)	Increased side effect (bleeding)	Inhibition of platelet aggregation through inhibition of thromboxane synthetase (ginger) (P); arachadonic acid production (feverfew) (P); inhibition of epinephrine induced in vitro (garlic) (P); platelet thromboxane synthetase aggregation (garlic) (P, CR); inhibition of platelet activating factor (ginkgo) (CR)
Anticoagulants: Warfarin	*Panax ginseng*, St. John's wort	Opposition of therapeutic effect; decreased enzyme bioavailability	Unknown (CR); hepatic induction (CS)
Anticoagulants: Warfarin	Coumarin-rich herbs, (*e.g.*, sweet clover, danshen), white clover	Increased therapeutic effect	Only danshen has been observed to do this clinically. Increased maximum concentration and decreased volume of distribution (CR, P)
Anticoagulants: Warfarin	Vitamin K-rich herbs (*e.g.*, collard, kale, spinach)	Decreased therapeutic effect	Opposes activity (CR, P)
Anticonvulsants	GLA-rich herbs Thujone-containing herbs (*e.g.*, cedar, tansy, sage)	Decreased therapeutic effect	GLA (CR) and thujone may decrease seizure threshold; mechanism unknown
Anticonvulsants	Salicylate-rich herbs (*e.g.*, cramp bark, willow, wintergreen)	Increased therapeutic effect	Transient; unknown mechanism (CR)
Anticonvulsants: Phenytoin	Shankapulshpi (Ayurvedic preparation with multiple herbs)	Opposition of therapeutic action	Decreased effectiveness of drug; decreased drug levels (CR)
Antiplatelet-aggregating	Antiplatelet-aggregating (*e.g.*, *Panax ginseng*, feverfew, garlic, ginkgo)	Increased side effect (bleeding)	Similar therapeutic action (P, CR)
Barbiturates	Valerian	Increased therapeutic effect; increased side effects	Shown to prolong barbiturate-induced sleep (AS)
Benzodiazepines	St. John's wort, kava	Decreased therapeutic efficacy; may increase side effects; increased sedation	Herb binds to GABA receptor site (AS, P)
Cardiac glycosides	Cardiac glycoside-containing herbs (*e.g.*, foxglove, lily of the valley)	a. Enhanced therapeutic effect b. Increased side effects (arrhythmia)	Same active constituents (TH)
Cardiac glycosides	Cathartic laxative herbs (*e.g.*, aloe, cascara, senna, yellow dock), licorice, diuretic herbs (*e.g.*, celery seed, corn silk, horsetail, juniper)	Increased side effects (arrhythmia)	Increased potassium loss (TH)
Cardiac glycosides	Quinine-containing herb (*e.g.*, cinchona bark)	Increased plasma levels	(TH)

DRUG CATEGORY	HERBS	HERB EFFECT	MECHANISM (EVIDENCE TYPE)
Cholesterol-lowering drugs	Garlic, artichoke, ginger, fenugreek	Increased therapeutic effect	Similar clinical effect via different mechanism (TH)
Corticosteroids	Licorice	Increased plasma levels	Increased half-life (increased bioavailability) (CR); inhibition of ll-ß-dehydrogenase (P)
Corticosteroids	*Panax ginseng*	Increased side effects	Similar side effects of CNS stimulation and insomnia (CR)
Digoxin	Siberian ginseng	Increased plasma level	Mechanism unknown; validated by rechallenge (CR)
Digoxin	a. Kyushin (Chinese remedy containing the venom of the Chinese toad) b. *Panax ginseng*	Increased serum levels	Interferes with assay (P, CR) without toxic effects
Diuretic: Lasix	*Panax ginseng*	Decreased therapeutic effect	Diuretic resistance with ginseng; unknown mechanism (CR)
Diuretic: Potassium sparing	Licorice	Decreased therapeutic effect	Interferes with potassium-sparing effects by wasting K+
Estrogen replacement therapy	a. Herbs high in phytoestrogens (*e.g.*, soy, fenugreek, licorice, black cohosh) b. *Panax ginseng*	a. Increased therapeutic b. Increased side effect (estrogen excess)	a. Never reported (TH) effect to excess b. Reported in few cases to produce postmenopausal bleeding or mastalgia (CR)
General medication	High-fiber herbs (*e.g.*, flax, psyllium, acacia, slippery elm, marshmallow)	Decreased absorption	(P)
General medication	"Hot" remedies (*e.g.*, ginger, garlic, black pepper, red pepper)	Increased absorption	Taken internally, "hot" remedies lead to vasodilatation of gut wall and increased absorption (TU)
GI motility drugs	Anticholinergic herbs (not generally used clinically, *e.g.*, belladonna)	Decreased activity	Opposition of therapeutic activity
Hepatotoxic drugs	Hepatotoxic herbs (*e.g.*, borage, coltsfoot, comfrey, rue, tansy)	Increased side effect (hepatotoxicity)	Additive toxicity from similar side effects (CR)
Hypoglycemic agents: Oral and insulin	Hypoglycemic (*e.g.*, *Panax ginseng*, garlic, fenugreek, bitter melon, aloe, gymnema)	Enhanced therapeutic effect	a. Direct hypoglycemic activity (CR, AS, P) b. Decreased glucose absorption
Hypoglycemic agents: Oral and insulin	Hyperglycemic (*e.g.*, cocoa, rosemary, stinging nettle)	Decreased therapeutic effect	Direct opposition of therapeutic action (CS)
Immune suppressants	Echinacea, astragalus	Opposition of therapeutic action	General immune stimulation by these herbs may interfere with ability of immunosuppressive drugs to prevent tissue rejection; never reported (TH)
Iron	Tannin-rich herbs (*e.g.*, caffeine-containing herbs, cat's claw, tea, *uva ursi*)	Decreased therapeutic	Tannin binds with iron, effect decreasing absorption (TH, P)
Lithium	Diuretic herbs (*e.g.*, celery seed, corn silk, horsetail, juniper)	Increased side effects	Decreased sodium leads to increased lithium toxicity
Lower seizure threshold	GLA-rich herbs (*e.g.*, evening primrose, borage, black currant)	Increased side effect to additive side effect	Decreased seizure threshold (CR)
Methotrexate and similar cytotoxic drugs	Salicylate herbs (*e.g.*, cramp bark, willow, wintergreen)	Increased plasma levels (toxicity)	Decreased excretion (TH)
Minerals	Fiber-containing herbs (*e.g.*, flax, psyllium, acacia, slippery elm, marshmallow)	Decreased bioavailability	Psyllium has been reported to decrease the absorption of Ca, Mg, Cu, Zn (CR)

DRUG CATEGORY	HERBS	HERB EFFECT	MECHANISM (EVIDENCE TYPE)
Monoamine oxidase inhibitors (MAOIs)	*Panax ginseng*, bioactive amines, licorice	Increased side effects	Additive side effects may lead to toxicity; glycyrrhizin is reported to be a very potent MAOI (TH, CR)
Monoamine oxidase inhibitors (MAOIs)	Ginkgo	Increased therapeutic effect; increased side effects	Inhibition of monoamine oxidase (P)
Nonsteroidal anti-inflammatory drugs (NSAIDs)	Gastric irritant herbs (*e.g.*, caffeine, rue, *uva ursi*)	Increased side effects	Similar side effects may increase risk of gastric erosion and bleeding (TH)
Nonsteroidal anti-inflammatory drugs (NSAIDs)	Nettles	Increased therapeutic effect	Potentiation of the anti-inflammatory activity of NSAIDs (CT)
Opioids	*Panax ginseng*	Decreased therapeutic effects	Animal model demonstrated the blunting of the analgesic effects of morphine via a non-opioid receptor-mediated mechanism (AS)
Photosensitizing drugs	Photosensitizing herbs (*e.g.*, St. John's wort, angelica, rue, fennel)	Increased side effects	Furanocoumarins found often in umbelliferae resemble pso-ralens (P, AS, CR)
Salicylates	Herbs that alkalinize urine (*e.g.*, *uva ursi*)	Decreased plasma levels	Increased urinary excretion (P)
Sedative hypnotics	Opioid herbs (*e.g.*, opium poppy, California poppy)	Increased side effects (CNS depression)	Additive side effects
Sedative hypnotics including alcohol	Sedative herbs (*e.g.*, hops, kava, valerian)	Increased therapeutic action; increased side effects (CNS depression)	Additive effects lead to CNS depression except valerian does not potentiate the effects of alcohol (AS, P)
SSRIs	St. John's wort	Increased therapeutic activity; increased side effects	May contribute to serotonin syndrome—similar action (TH)
Statin drugs	Red yeast (Cholestin®)	Increased therapeutic effect	Similar active compounds; not known if taking both products simultaneously increases side effects of statin drugs (TH)
Thyroid hormone	a. Horseradish b. Kelp	a. Decreased therapeutic effect b. Increased therapeutic effect	Depressed thyroid function

Herb-Drug Interactions: An Evidence-Based Table
By Mary L. Hardy, MD

In conclusion, using herbs for health benefits requires a careful approach. This chapter outlines essential guidelines for safe and effective herbal use, emphasizing consultation with healthcare professionals, accurate plant identification, and choosing high-quality herbs. It discusses age-based formulations and the importance of customization under herbalists' guidance. The chapter also highlights the need to watch for potential side effects and allergies and be cautious about interactions with medications, as detailed in the provided herb-drug interaction table. Adhering to these practical principles enables individuals to navigate herbalism responsibly, ensuring both well-being and safety in herbal practices.

In wrapping up this book, we sincerely hope you found it informative and valuable in your exploration of herbalism. The provided guidelines aim to empower you with the knowledge needed for safe and effective herbal practices. Whether you're a novice or experienced in herbal remedies, our wish is that this information enhances your understanding and contributes to your well-being. If you have any questions or feedback, remember that learning about herbs is a continual journey, and we encourage you to seek further insights from us or other professionals in the field. Thank you for joining us on this exploration of herbalism, and we hope it brings positive contributions to your health and lifestyle.

REFERENCES:

1 | Apelian N. The Holistic Guide to Wellness. Claude Davis; 2023

2 | The Lost Herbs, The Healing Power of Backyard Plants at Your Fingertips [Internet]. The Lost Herbs. 2024 Available from: https://thelostherbs.com

3 | World Health Organization. WHO Monographs On Selected Medicinal Plants. Vol. 3. Geneva: World Health Organization; 2007

4 | McGarey WA. The Oil That Heals. ARE Press; 1993

5 | Chevallier A. Encyclopedia of Herbal Medicine. Penguin; 2016

6 | Valerie Ann Worwood. The Complete Book Of Essential Oils And Aromatherapy : Over 800 Natural, Nontoxic, And Fragrant Recipes To Create Health, Beauty, And Safe Home And Work Environments. Novato, California: New World Library; 2016

7 | Gladstar R. Rosemary Gladstar's Medicinal Herbs: A Beginner's Guide. Storey Publishing, LLC; 2012

8 | Duke JA. Handbook of Medicinal Herbs. Hoboken: CRC Press; 2002

9 | Hoffmann D. Medical Herbalism - The Science And Practice Of Herbal Medicine. Healing Arts Press; 2003

10 | Benzie IFF, Wachtel-Galor S, Packer L. Herbal Medicine: Biomolecular and Clinical Aspects. Hoboken: CRC Press; 2011

11 | Natural Medicines - Databases [Internet]. naturalmedicines.therapeuticresearch.com. Available from: https://naturalmedicines.therapeuticresearch.com/databases.aspx

12 | Kolen R. How to make herbal tinctures [Internet]. Mountain Rose Herbs. 2017. Available from: https://blog.mountainroseherbs.com/guide-tinctures-extracts

13 | Noveille A. Art of the Alcohol-Free Apothecary [Internet]. Herbal Academy. 2015 [cited 2024 Mar 12]. Available from: https://theherbalacademy.com/art-of-the-alcohol-free-apothecary/

14 | 93 Types of Tea: Complete List of Tea Names [Internet]. Steeped Dreams. Available from: https://steepeddreams.com/blog/different-types-of-tea

15 | Cinnamon Tea: Are There Health Benefits? [Internet]. WebMD. Available from: https://www.webmd.com/diet/health-benefits-cinnamon-tea

16 | Leech J. 10 Evidence-Based Health Benefits of Cinnamon [Internet]. Healthline. 2018. Available from: https://www.healthline.com/nutrition/10-proven-benefits-of-cinnamon

17 | Hawthorn Information | Mount Sinai - New York [Internet]. Mount Sinai Health System. Available from: https://www.mountsinai.org/health-library/herb/hawthorn

18 | Mahdi JG, Mahdi AJ, Mahdi AJ, Bowen ID. The Historical Analysis Of Aspirin Discovery, Its Relation To The Willow Tree, And Antiproliferative And Anticancer Potential. Cell Proliferation. 2006 Apr;39(2):147–55.

19 | Entezari M, Aslani N, Askari G, Maghsoudi Z, Maracy M. Effect Of Garlic And Lemon Juice Mixture On Lipid Profile And Some Cardiovascular Risk Factors In People 30-60 Years Old With Moderate Hyperlipidemia: A Randomized Clinical Trial. International Journal of Preventive Medicine. 2016;7(1):95

20 | Kasprzak-Drozd K, Oniszczuk T, Soja J, Gancarz M, Wojtunik-Kulesza K, Markut-Miotła E, et al. The Efficacy of Black Chokeberry Fruits against Cardiovascular Diseases. International Journal of Molecular Sciences. 2021 Jun 18;22(12):6541.

21 | Zheng J, Zhou Y, Li S, Zhang P, Zhou T, Xu DP, et al. Effects and Mechanisms of Fruit and Vegetable Juices on Cardiovascular Diseases. International Journal of Molecular Sciences [Internet]. 2017 Mar 4;18(3). Available from: https://pubmed.ncbi.nlm.nih.gov/28273863/

22 | Raposo A, Saraiva A, Ramos F, Carrascosa C, Raheem D, Bárbara R, et al. The Role of Food Supplementation in Microcirculation—A Comprehensive Review. Biology. 2021 Jul 2;10(7):616.

23 | Vaneková Z, Rollinger JM. Bilberries: Curative and Miraculous – A Review on Bioactive Constituents and Clinical Research. Frontiers in Pharmacology. 2022 Jun 29;13.

24 | Horse Chestnut: Uses, Side Effects, Interactions, Dosage, and Warning [Internet]. www.webmd.com. Available from: https://www.webmd.com/vitamins/ai/ingredientmono-1055/horse-chestnut

Kharlamenko A. 7 Health Benefits of Horse Chestnut Extract [Internet]. Healthline. Healthline Media; 2019. Available from: https://www.healthline.com/nutrition/horse-chestnut-benefits

25 | Owczarek A, Kołodziejczyk-Czepas J, Marczuk P, Siwek J, Wąsowicz K, Olszewska MA. Bioactivity Potential of Aesculus hippocastanum L. Flower: Phytochemical Profile, Antiradical Capacity and Protective Effects on Human Plasma Components under Oxidative/Nitrative Stress In Vitro. Pharmaceuticals [Internet]. 2021 Dec 14 [cited 2023 Dec 7];14(12):1301. Available from: https://www.ncbi.nlm.nih.gov/pmc/articles/PMC8706066/

26 | El-Saadony MT, Yang T, Korma SA, Sitohy M, Abd El-Mageed TA, Selim S, et al. Impacts Of Turmeric And Its Principal Bioactive Curcumin On Human Health: Pharmaceutical, Medicinal, And Food Applications: A Comprehensive Review. Frontiers in Nutrition. 2023 Jan 10;9.

27 | Yuandani, Jantan I, Rohani AS, Sumantri IB. Immunomodulatory Effects and Mechanisms of Curcuma Species and Their Bioactive Compounds: A Review. Frontiers in Pharmacology. 2021 Apr 30;12.

28 | Prasad S, Aggarwal BB. Turmeric, the Golden Spice [Internet]. Nih.gov. CRC Press/Taylor & Francis; 2011. Available from: https://www.ncbi.nlm.nih.gov/books/NBK92752/

29 | Health Benefits of Fennel [Internet]. WebMD. Available from: https://www.webmd.com/food-recipes/health-benefits-fennel

30 | Peppermint oil benefits: Properties and uses [Internet]. www.medicalnewstoday.com. 2020. Available from: https://www.medicalnewstoday.com/articles/peppermint-oil-benefits#benefits

31 | Esimone CO, Akah PA, Nworu CS. Efficacy and Safety Assessment of T. Angelica Herbal Tonic, a Phytomedicinal Product Popularly Used in Nigeria. Evidence-Based Complementary and Alternative Medicine. 2011;2011:1–6.

32 | Gupta S. Chamomile: A Herbal Medicine Of The Past With A Bright Future. Molecular Medicine Reports [Internet]. 2010 Sep 28;3(6). Available from: https://www.ncbi.nlm.nih.gov/pmc/articles/PMC2995283/

33 | Nikkhah Bodagh M, Maleki I, Hekmatdoost A. Ginger in Gastrointestinal Disorders: a Systematic Review of Clinical Trials. Food Science & Nutrition [Internet]. 2018 Nov 5;7(1):96–108. Available from: https://www.ncbi.nlm.nih.gov/pmc/articles/PMC6341159/

34 | Bijak M. Silybin, a Major Bioactive Component of Milk Thistle (Silybum marianum L. Gaernt.)—Chemistry, Bioavailability, and Metabolism. Molecules. 2017 Nov 10;22(11):1942.

35 | Chiu HF, Chen TY, Tzeng YT, Wang CK. Improvement Of Liver Function In Humans Using A Mixture Of Schisandra Fruit Extract And Sesamin. Phytotherapy research: PTR [Internet]. 2013 Mar 1 [cited 2021 Oct 13];27(3):368–73. Available from: https://pubmed.ncbi.nlm.nih.gov/22610748/

36 | Park HJ, Lee SJ, Song Y, Jang SH, Ko YG, Kang SN, et al. Schisandra chinensis Prevents Alcohol-Induced Fatty Liver Disease. Journal of Medicinal Food. 2014 Jan;17(1):103–10.

37 | Nur Shazwani Muhammad, Kasimu Ghandi Ibrahim, Ndhlala AR, Erlwanger KH. Moringa Oleifera Lam. Prevents The Development Of High Fructose Diet-Induced Fatty Liver. South African Journal of Botany. 2020 Mar 1;129:32–9.

38 | Peppermint Oil: A Medicine To Treat To Treat Stomach Cramps And Bloating [Internet]. nhs.uk. 2021. Available from: https://www.nhs.uk/medicines/peppermint-oil/

39 | L M, M N, R H, A H. Peppermint and Its Functionality: A Review. Archives of Clinical Microbiology [Internet]. 2017;08(04). Available from: http://www.acmicrob.com/microbiology/peppermint-and-its-functionality-a-review.php?aid=19955

40 | A Guide to Bitters: How to Use, Benefits, Flavors, and Recipes [Internet]. Healthline. 2019. Available from: https://www.healthline.com/health/food-nutrition/how-to-use-bitters#what-are-they-good-for

41 | Pfingstgraf IO, Taulescu M, Pop RM, Orăsan R, Vlase L, Uifalean A, et al. Protective Effects of Taraxacum officinale L. (Dandelion) Root Extract in Experimental Acute on Chronic Liver Failure. Antioxidants (Basel, Switzerland) [Internet]. 2021 Mar 24;10(4). Available from: https://pubmed.ncbi.nlm.nih.gov/33804908/

42 | Raak C, Ostermann T, Boehm K, Molsberger F. Regular Consumption of Sauerkraut and Its Effect on Human Health: A Bibliometric Analysis. Global Advances in Health and Medicine [Internet]. 2014 Nov;3(6):12–8. Available from: https://www.ncbi.nlm.nih.gov/pmc/articles/PMC4268643/

43 | Contributors WE. Health Benefits of Sauerkraut [Internet]. WebMD. Available from: https://www.webmd.com/diet/health-benefits-sauerkraut

44 | Yu M, Jin X, Liang C, Bu F, Pan D, He Q, et al. Berberine For Diarrhea In Children And Adults: A Systematic Review And Meta-Analysis. Therapeutic Advances in Gastroenterology [Internet]. 2020 Oct 23 [cited 2022 Nov 6];13:1756284820961299. Available from: https://www.ncbi.nlm.nih.gov/pmc/articles/PMC7586028/

45 | Selvaraj S, Gurumurthy K. An overview of probiotic health booster-kombucha tea. Chinese Herbal Medicines. 2022 Dec; https://www.sciencedirect.com/science/article/pii/S1674638422001289

46 | Sandor Ellix Katz. The Art of Fermentation: An In-Depth Exploration Of Essential Concepts And Processes From Around The World. White River Junction, Vt.: Chelsea Green Pub; 2012.

47 | Kelber O, Bauer R, Kubelka W. Phytotherapy in Functional Gastrointestinal Disorders. Digestive Diseases. 2017;35(1):36–42

48 | Psyllium Information | Mount Sinai - New York [Internet]. Mount Sinai Health System. Available from: https://www.mountsinai.org/health-library/supplement/psyllium

49 | Hawrelak JA, Myers SP. Effects of Two Natural Medicine Formulations on Irritable Bowel Syndrome Symptoms: A Pilot Study. The Journal of Alternative and Complementary Medicine. 2010 Oct;16(10):1065–71

50 | 10 Natural Appetite Suppressants That Help You Lose Weight [Internet]. Healthline. 2020. Available from: https://www.healthline.com/nutrition/10-natural-appetite-suppressants#garcinia-cambogia

51 | Contributors WE. Health Benefits of Beetroot [Internet]. WebMD. 2020. Available from: https://www.webmd.com/diet/health-benefits-beetroot

52 | Contributors WE. Bay Leaf: Health Benefits, Nutrition, and Uses [Internet]. WebMD. 2022. Available from: https://www.webmd.com/diet/bay-leaf-health-benefits

53 | Dube P. Bay Leaf - Benefits, Nutrition Value, Uses, and Recipes [Internet]. Blog - HealthifyMe. 2022. Available from: https://www.healthifyme.com/blog/benefits-of-bay-leaf/

54 | Khan A, Zaman G, Anderson RA. Bay Leaves Improve Glucose and Lipid Profile of People with Type 2 Diabetes. Journal of Clinical Biochemistry and Nutrition [Internet]. 2009 [cited 2019 Dec 11];44(1):52–6. Available from: https://www.ncbi.nlm.nih.gov/pmc/articles/PMC2613499/

55 | Does Forskolin Actually Work? An Evidence-Based Review [Internet]. Healthline. 2017 [cited 2024 Mar 12]. Available from: https://www.healthline.com/nutrition/forskolin-review#Frequently-asked-questions-about-forskolin

56 | Salehi B, Staniak M, Czopek K, Stępień A, Dua K, Wadhwa R, et al. The Therapeutic Potential of the Labdane Diterpenoid Forskolin. Applied Sciences. 2019 Sep 30;9(19):4089

57 | Lose Weight More Easily With a Bowl of Nettle Soup [Internet]. Men's Health. 2020 [cited 2024 Mar 12]. Available from: https://www.menshealth.com/uk/nutrition/food-drink/a34685756/lose-weight-nettle-soup/

58 | 6 Benefits of Stinging Nettle (Plus Side Effects) [Internet]. Healthline. 2018. Available from: https://www.healthline.com/nutrition/stinging-nettle

59 | Mahalapbutr P, Sangkhawasi M, Kammarabutr J, Chamni S, Rungrotmongkol T. Rosmarinic Acid as a Potent Influenza Neuraminidase Inhibitor: In Vitro and In Silico Study. Current Topics in Medicinal Chemistry [Internet]. 2020 [cited 2024 Mar 12];20(23):2046–55. Available from: https://pubmed.ncbi.nlm.nih.gov/31738149/

60 | Klein AH, Carstens MI, Carstens E. Eugenol and carvacrol induce temporally desensitizing patterns of oral irritation and enhance innocuous warmth and noxious heat sensation on the tongue. Pain. 2013 Oct;154(10):2078–87

61 | Bang S, Li W, Ha TKQ, Lee C, Oh WK, Shim SH. Anti-Influenza Effect Of The Major Flavonoids From Salvia Plebeia R.Br. Via Inhibition Of Influenza H1N1 Virus Neuraminidase. Natural Product Research [Internet]. 2018 May 1 [cited 2024 Mar 12];32(10):1224–8. Available from: https://pubmed.ncbi.nlm.nih.gov/28504013/

62 | Wijesundara NM, Rupasinghe HPVasantha. Essential Oils From Origanum Vulgare And Salvia Officinalis Exhibit Antibacterial And Anti-Biofilm Activities Against Streptococcus pyogenes. Microbial Pathogenesis. 2018 Apr;117:118–27

63 | How to Use Essential Oils for Sinus Congestion [Internet]. Healthline. 2016 [cited 2024 Mar 12]. Available from: https://www.healthline.com/health/essential-oils-for-sinus-congestion

64 | Yadav N, Chandra H. Suppression Of Inflammatory And Infection Responses In Lung Macrophages By Eucalyptus Oil And Its Constituent 1,8-cineole: Role of pattern recognition receptors TREM-1 and NLRP3, the MAP kinase regulator MKP-1, and NFκB. Khan MF, 2017 Nov 15;12(11):e0188232

65 | Mustard Plaster [Internet]. Wikipedia. 2021. Available from: https://en.wikipedia.org/wiki/Mustard_plaster

66 | Camphor Oil: Uses, Benefits, And Precautions [Internet]. www.medicalnewstoday.com. 2020. Available from: https://www.medicalnewstoday.com/articles/camphor-oil

67 | 10 Potential Uses for Vicks VapoRub [Internet]. Healthline. 2020. Available from: https://www.healthline.com/health/vicks-vaporub-benefits

68 | Cohen HA, Rozen J, Kristal H, Laks Y, Berkovitch M, Uziel Y, et al. Effect of Honey on Nocturnal Cough and Sleep Quality: A Double-blind, Randomized, Placebo-Controlled Study. PEDIATRICS. 2012 Aug 6;130(3):465–71

69 | Cough Information | Mount Sinai - New York [Internet]. Mount Sinai Health System. [cited 2024 Mar 12]. Available from: https://www.mountsinai.org/health-library/condition/cough

70 | Kemmerich B, Eberhardt R, Stammer H. Efficacy And Tolerability Of A Fluid Extract Combination Of Thyme Herb And Ivy Leaves And Matched Placebo In Adults Suffering From Acute Bronchitis With Productive Cough. A Prospective, Double-Blind, Placebo-Controlled Clinical Trial. Arzneimittel-Forschung [Internet]. 2006;56(9):652–60. Available from: https://www.ncbi.nlm.nih.gov/pubmed/17063641

71 | Krzyzanowska-Kowalczyk J, Kowalczyk M, Ponczek MB, Pecio Ł, Nowak P, Kolodziejczyk-Czepas J. Pulmonaria obscura and Pulmonaria officinalis Extracts as Mitigators of Peroxynitrite-Induced Oxidative Stress and Cyclooxygenase-2 Inhibitors–In Vitro and In Silico Studies. Molecules. 2021 Jan 26;26(3):631

72 | Lungmoss Potential Benefits, Side Effects, Uses, and Where to Get It [Internet]. Healthline. 2020 [cited 2024 Mar 14]. Available from: https://www.healthline.com/health/lungmoss

73 | 4 Ways Mullein Benefits Your Lungs [Internet]. Cleveland Clinic. Available from: https://health.clevelandclinic.org/mullein-benefits

74 | Nagata K, Sakagami H, Harada H, Nonoyama M, Ishihama A, Konno K. Inhibition Of Influenza Virus Infection By Pine Cone Antitumor Substances. Antiviral Research [Internet]. 1990 Jan 1 [cited 2024 Mar 14];13(1):.1–21. Available from: https://www.sciencedirect.com/science/article/abs/pii/0166354290900415

75 | What to Know About Natural Expectorants [Internet]. WebMD. Available from: https://www.webmd.com/cold-and-flu/what-to-know-about-natural-expectorants

76 | Roschek B, Fink RC, McMichael M, Alberte RS. Nettle extract (Urtica dioica) Affects Key Receptors And Enzymes Associated With Allergic Rhinitis. Phytotherapy Research. 2009 Jul;23(7):920–6

77 | Rahbardar M, Hosseinzadeh H. Therapeutic Effects Of Rosemary (Rosmarinus Officinalis L.) And Its Active Constituents On Nervous System Disorders. Therapeutic Effects Of Rosemary (Rosmarinus Officinalis L) And Its Active Constituents On Nervous System Disorders [Internet]. 2020 Sep 23;23(9). Available from: https://ijbms.mums.ac.ir/article_15705_a9abf2c1cf4e9cf81095f88315336f4c.pdf

78 | Scholey A, Gibbs A, Neale C, Perry N, Ossoukhova A, Bilog V, et al. Anti-Stress Effects of Lemon Balm-Containing Foods. Nutrients [Internet]. 2014 Oct 30;6(11):4805–21. Available from: https://www.mdpi.com/2072-6643/6/11/4805/html

79 | Mahalapbutr P, Sangkhawasi M, Kammarabutr J, Chamni S, Rungrotmongkol T. Rosmarinic Acid as a Potent Influenza

Neuraminidase Inhibitor: In Vitro and In Silico Study. Current Topics in Medicinal Chemistry [Internet]. 2020;20(23):2046–55. Available from: https://pubmed.ncbi.nlm.nih.gov/31738149/

80 | Health Benefits Of Lion's Mane [Internet]. Forbes Health. 2023. Available from: https://www.forbes.com/health/supplements/health-benefits-of-lions-mane/

81 | Wijesundara NM, Rupasinghe HPVasantha. Essential oils from Origanum vulgare and Salvia officinalis exhibit antibacterial and anti-biofilm activities against Streptococcus pyogenes. Microbial Pathogenesis. 2018 Apr;117:118–27.

82 | Jurenka, J. S. (2009). Anti-Inflammatory Properties Of Curcumin, A Major Constituent of Curcuma longa: A review of preclinical and clinical research. Alternative Medicine Review, 14(2), 141-153.

83 | Aggarwal, B. B., & Harikumar, K. B. (2009). Potential Therapeutic Effects Of Curcumin, The Anti-Inflammatory Agent, Against Neurodegenerative, Cardiovascular, Pulmonary, Metabolic, Autoimmune, And Neoplastic Diseases. The International Journal of Biochemistry & Cell Biology, 41(1), 40-59.

84 | Hewlings S, Kalman D. Curcumin: A Review of Its' Effects on Human Health. Foods [Internet]. 2017 Oct 22;6(10):92. Available from: https://www.ncbi.nlm.nih.gov/pmc/articles/PMC5664031/

85 | Klein AH, Carstens MI, Carstens E. Eugenol And Carvacrol Induce Temporally Desensitizing Patterns Of Oral Irritation And Enhance Innocuous Warmth And Noxious Heat Sensation On The Tongue. Pain. 2013 Oct;154(10):2078–87

86 | Ghorbani A, Esmaeilizadeh M. Pharmacological Properties of Salvia officinalis and its Components. Journal of Traditional and Complementary Medicine [Internet]. 2017 Jan 13;7(4):433–40. Available from: https://www.ncbi.nlm.nih.gov/pmc/articles/PMC5634728/

87 | C. S, P. N, J. L, J. C, C. H, L. D, et al. The Chronic Effects of an extract of Bacopa monniera (Brahmi) on Cognitive Function in Healthy Human Subjects. Psychopharmacology [Internet]. 2001 Aug 1;156(4):481–4. Available from: https://www.gwern.net/docs/nootropics/2001-stough-2.pdf

88 | Cheng H, Lin L, Wang S, Zhang Y, Liu T, Yuan Y, et al. Aromatherapy With Single Essential Oils Can Significantly Improve The Sleep Quality Of Cancer Patients: A Meta-Analysis. BMC Complementary Medicine and Therapies. 2022 Jul 14;22(1)

89 | Perry NSL, Bollen C, Perry EK, Ballard C. Salvia for Dementia Therapy: Review Of Pharmacological Activity And Pilot Tolerability Clinical Trial. Pharmacology Biochemistry and Behavior. 2003 Jun;75(3):651–9

90 | Heck CI, de Mejia EG. Yerba Mate Tea (Ilex paraguariensis): A Comprehensive Review On Chemistry, Health Implications, And Technological Considerations. Journal of food science [Internet]. 2007;72(9):R138-51. Available from: https://www.ncbi.nlm.nih.gov/pubmed/18034743/

91 | Perry NSL, Bollen C, Perry EK, Ballard C. Salvia for Dementia Therapy: Review Of Pharmacological Activity And Pilot Tolerability Clinical Trial. Pharmacology Biochemistry and Behavior. 2003 Jun;75(3):651–9

92 | Garlic in Ear: Benefits and Risks for Earaches [Internet]. Healthline. 2018. Available from: https://www.healthline.com/health/garlic-in-ear

93 | Winston D, Maimes S. Adaptogens : Herbs for Strength, Stamina, And Stress Relief. Rochester, Vt: Healing Arts Press; 2007

94 | St. John's Wort Information | Mount Sinai - New York [Internet]. Mount Sinai Health System. Available from: https://www.mountsinai.org/health-library/herb/st-johns-wort

95 | Szaro M. How to Use Mugwort for Dreams, Sleep, and More [Internet]. Herbal Academy. 2020 [cited 2024 Jan 14]. Available from: https://theherbalacademy.com/blog/how-to-use-mugwort/

96 | Edwards D, Heufelder A, Zimmermann A. Therapeutic Effects And Safety of Rhodiola rosea Extract WS® 1375 In Subjects With Life-Stress Symptoms--Results Of An Open-Label Study. Phytotherapy research: PTR [Internet]. 2012 Aug 1;26(8):1220–5. Available from: https://pubmed.ncbi.nlm.nih.gov/22228617

97 | Oken BS. Complementary Therapies In Neurology : An Evidence-Based Approach. Boca Raton, Fl: Parthenon Pub. Group; 2004

98 | Valerian Information | Mount Sinai - New York [Internet]. Mount Sinai Health System. Available from: https://www.mountsinai.org/health-library/herb/valerian

99 | Kubala J. How Valerian Root Helps You Relax and Sleep Better [Internet]. Healthline. 2021. Available from: https://www.healthline.com/nutrition/valerian-root

100 | Van De Walle G. Kava Kava: Benefits, Side Effects and Dosage [Internet]. Healthline. 2018. Available from: https://www.healthline.com/nutrition/kava-kava

101 | Neroli Oil Overview, Benefits, Uses, Side Effects, and Precautions [Internet]. Healthline. 2019. Available from: https://www.healthline.com/health/neroli-oil

102 | Scandurra C, Mezzalira S, Cutillo S, Zapparella R, Statti G, Maldonato NM, et al. The Effectiveness of Neroli Essential Oil in Relieving Anxiety and Perceived Pain in Women during Labor: A Randomized Controlled Trial. Healthcare. 2022 Feb 14;10(2):366

103 | Panossian A, Wikman G. Effects of Adaptogens on the Central Nervous System and the Molecular Mechanisms Associated with Their Stress—Protective Activity. Pharmaceuticals [Internet]. 2010 Jan 19 [cited 2019 Jul 21];3(1):188–224. Available from: https://www.ncbi.nlm.nih.gov/pmc/articles/PMC3991026/

104 | Tahereh Eteraf-Oskouei, Najafi M. Traditional And Modern Uses Of Natural Honey In Human Diseases: A Review. PubMed. 2013 Jun 1;

105 | Schmid B, Lüdtke R, Selbmann H-K, Kötter I, Tschirdewahn B, Schaffner W, et al. Efficacy And Tolerability Of A Standardized Willow Bark Extract In Patients With Osteoarthritis: Randomized Placebo-Controlled, Double-Blind Clinical Trial. Phytotherapy Research. 2001 Jun;15(4):344–50

106 | Gupta S. Chamomile: A herbal medicine of the past with a bright future. Molecular Medicine Reports [Internet]. 2010 Sep 28;3(6). Available from: https://www.ncbi.nlm.nih.gov/pmc/articles/PMC2995283/

107 | Hale LP, Greer PK, Trinh CT, James CL. Proteinase Activity And Stability Of Natural Bromelain Preparations. International Immunopharmacology [Internet]. 2005 Apr;5(4):783–93. Available from: https://www.sciencedirect.com/science/article/pii/S156757690400400X

108 | Magnesium for Leg Cramps: Does It Work? What to Do If It Doesn't [Internet]. Healthline. 2019. Available from: https://www.healthline.com/health/magnesium-for-leg-cramps

109 | Ravikumar ini. Therapeutic Potential of Brassica oleracea (Broccoli) - A Review. International Journal of Drug Development and Research. 2015 Jan 1;7(2)

110 | Cheung PCK. The Nutritional And Health Benefits Of Mushrooms. Nutrition Bulletin. 2010 Nov 19;35(4):292–9.

111 | Wasser SP. Medicinal Mushrooms in Human Clinical Studies. Part I. Anticancer, Oncoimmunological, and Immunomodulatory Activities: A Review. International Journal of Medicinal Mushrooms. 2017;19(4):279–317

112 | Zhang Y. Ganoderma lucidum (Reishi) Suppresses Proliferation And Migration Of Breast Cancer Cells Via Inhibiting Wnt/β-catenin Signaling. Biochemical and Biophysical Research Communications. 2017 Jul;488(4):679–84

113 | Dai X, Stanilka JM, Rowe CA, Esteves EA, Nieves C, Spaiser SJ, et al. Consuming Lentinula edodes (Shiitake) Mushrooms Daily Improves Human Immunity: A Randomized Dietary Intervention in Healthy Young Adults. Journal of the American College of Nutrition [Internet]. 2015;34(6):478–87. Available from: https://www.ncbi.nlm.nih.gov/pubmed/25866155

114 | Lindequist U, Niedermeyer THJ, Jülich WD. The Pharmacological Potential of Mushrooms. Evidence-Based Complementary and Alternative Medicine [Internet]. 2005 [cited 2019 Oct 30];2(3):285–99. Available from: https://www.hindawi.com/journals/ecam/2005/906016/citations/jul/

115 | Chang Y, Zhang M, Jiang Y, Liu Y, Luo H, Hao C, et al. Preclinical And Clinical Studies of Coriolus versicolor polysaccharopeptide as an immunotherapeutic in China. Discovery Medicine [Internet]. 2017 Apr 1 [cited 2023 Jan 13];23(127):207–19. Available from: https://pubmed.ncbi.nlm.nih.gov/28595034/

116 | Rokos T, Pribulova T, Kozubik E, Biringer K, Holubekova V, Kudela E. Exploring the Bioactive Mycocompounds (Fungal Compounds) of Selected Medicinal Mushrooms and Their Potentials against HPV Infection and Associated Cancer in Humans. Life [Internet]. 2023 Jan 1 [cited 2023 Feb 6];13(1):244. Available from: https://www.mdpi.com/2075-1729/13/1/244

117 | Vetvicka V, Vetvickova J. Immune Enhancing Effects of WB365, a Novel Combination of Ashwagandha (Withania somnifera) and Maitake (Grifola frondosa) Extracts. North American Journal of Medical Sciences. 2011;320–4.

118 | Wasser S. Medicinal Mushroom Science: Current Perspectives, Advances, Evidences, And Challenges. Biomedical Journal. 2014;37(6):345

119 | Joseph R, Pulimood SA, Abraham P, John GT. Successful Treatment of verruca vulgaris with Thuja occidentalis in a Renal Allograft Recipient. Indian Journal of Nephrology [Internet]. 2013;23(5):362–4. Available from: https://www.ncbi.nlm.nih.gov/pmc/articles/PMC3764712/

120 | Repajić M, Cegledi E, Zorić Z, Pedisić S, Elez Garofulić I, Radman S, et al. Bioactive Compounds in Wild Nettle (Urtica dioica L.) Leaves and Stalks: Polyphenols and Pigments upon Seasonal and Habitat Variations. Foods. 2021 Jan 18;10(1):190

121 | Kumar, A., Shukla, R., Singh, P., & Dubey, N. K. (2008). Chemical Composition, Antifungal And Antiaflatoxigenic Activities of Ocimum sanctum L. essential oil and its safety assessment as plant-based antimicrobial. Food and Chemical Toxicology, 46(7), 2725-2731.

122 | Toloza, A. C., Zygadlo, J., & Biurrun, F. (2006). Effects of Mentha piperita and Mentha × piperita Essential Oils On Survival And Behavior of Acanthoscelides obtectus (Coleoptera: Chrysomelidae). Journal of Economic Entomology, 99(1), 173-179.

123 | De Almeida, L. F. R., Frei, F., Mancini, E., De Martino, L., De Feo, V., & De Almeida, L. F. R. (2010). Phytotoxic activities of Mediterranean essential oils. Molecules, 15(6), 4309-4323

124 | Joubert E, de Beer D. Rooibos (Aspalathus linearis) beyond the farm gate: From herbal tea to potential phytopharmaceutical. South African Journal of Botany. 2011 Oct;77(4):869–86

125 | Edgar J. Bilberry Extract for Vision: What the Research Says [Internet]. WebMD. [cited 2022 Dec 20]. Available from: https://www.webmd.com/eye-health/features/bilberry-extract-and-vision

126 | Nomi Y, Iwasaki-Kurashige K, Matsumoto H. Therapeutic Effects of Anthocyanins for Vision and Eye Health. Molecules [Internet]. 2019 Sep 11;24(18):3311. Available from: https://www.ncbi.nlm.nih.gov/pmc/articles/PMC6767261/

127 | Kosehira M, Machida N, Kitaichi N. A 12-Week-Long Intake of Bilberry Extract (Vaccinium myrtillus L.) Improved Objective Findings of Ciliary Muscle Contraction of the Eye: A Randomized, Double-Blind, Placebo-Controlled, Parallel-Group Comparison Trial. Nutrients. 2020 Feb 25;12(3):600

128 | Labkovich M, Jacobs EB, Bhargava S, Pasquale LR, Ritch R. Ginkgo Biloba Extract in Ophthalmic and Systemic Disease, With a Focus on Normal-Tension Glaucoma. Asia-Pacific Journal of Ophthalmology. 2020 Apr 10;9(3):215–25

129 | Radomska-Leśniewska DM, Osiecka-Iwan A, Hyc A, Góźdź A, Dąbrowska AM, Skopiński P. Therapeutic potential of curcumin in eye diseases. Central European Journal of Immunology [Internet]. 2019 [cited 2019 Dec 1];44(2):181–9. Available from: https://www.termedia.pl/Therapeutic-potential-of-curcumin-in-eye-diseases,10,37377,1,1.html

130 | Understanding Varicose Veins -- the Basics [Internet]. WebMD. WebMD; 2001. Available from: https://www.webmd.com/skin-problems-and-treatments/understanding-varicose-veins-basics

131 | Kubala J. 10 Science-Based Benefits of Fennel and Fennel Seeds [Internet]. Healthline. 2019. Available from: https://www.healthline.com/nutrition/fennel-and-fennel-seed-benefits

132 | Eyebright: Benefits, Dosage, and Side Effects [Internet]. Healthline. 2019 [cited 2024 Mar 18]. Available from: https://www.healthline.com/nutrition/eyebright#eye-health

133 | Yu M, Jin X, Liang C, Bu F, Pan D, He Q, et al. Berberine for diarrhea in children and adults: a systematic review and meta-analysis. Therapeutic Advances in Gastroenterology [Internet]. 2020 Oct 23;13:1756284820961299. Available from: https://www.ncbi.nlm.nih.gov/pmc/articles/PMC7586028/

134 | Ajmera R. 13 potential health benefits of dandelion [Internet]. Healthline. 2018. Available from: https://www.healthline.com/nutrition/dandelion-benefits

135 | Lambert MNT, Hu LM, Jeppesen PB. A systematic review and meta-analysis of the effects of isoflavone formulations against estrogen-deficient bone resorption in peri- and postmenopausal women. The American Journal of Clinical Nutrition. 2017 Aug

136 | Watercress: Health benefits and nutritional breakdown [Internet]. www.medicalnewstoday.com. 2019. Available from: https://www.medicalnewstoday.com/articles/285412

137 | Kasarello K, Köhling I, Kosowska A, Pucia K, Lukasik A, Cudnoch-Jedrzejewska A, et al. The Anti-Inflammatory Effect of Cabbage Leaves Explained by the Influence of bol-miRNA172a on FAN Expression. Frontiers in Pharmacology. 2022 Mar 24;13.

138 | Zakay-Rones Z, Varsano N, Zlotnik M, Manor O, Regev L, Schlesinger M, et al. Inhibition of Several Strains of Influenza Virus in Vitro and Reduction of Symptoms by an Elderberry Extract (Sambucus nigra L.) during an Outbreak of Influenza B Panama. The Journal of Alternative and Complementary Medicine. 1995 Dec;1(4):361–9

139 | Apple Cider Vinegar For Eczema: How It Works And Uses [Internet]. www.medicalnewstoday.com. 2018 [cited 2023 Dec 20]. Available from: https://www.medicalnewstoday.com/articles/323160

140 | Apple Cider Vinegar Baths: Do They Have Any Benefits? [Internet]. www.medicalnewstoday.com. 2019 [cited 2023 Dec 20]. Available from: https://www.medicalnewstoday.com/articles/326876

141 | Yagnik D, Ward M, Shah AJ. Antibacterial Apple Cider Vinegar Eradicates Methicillin Resistant Staphylococcus aureus and resistant Escherichia coli. Scientific Reports [Internet]. 2021 Jan 20;11(1):1854. Available from: https://www.nature.com/articles/s41598-020-78407-x

142 | Armanini D, Mattarello MJ, Fiore C, Bonanni G, Scaroni C, Sartorato P, Et Al. Licorice Reduces Serum Testosterone In Healthy Women. Steroids. 2004 Oct;69(11-12):763–6

143 | Manach C, Williamson G, Morand C, Scalbert A, Rémésy C. Bioavailability and Bioefficacy of Polyphenols in Humans. I. Review of 97 Bioavailability Sudies. The American Journal of Clinical Nutrition. 2005 Jan 1;81(1):230S242S.

144 | BOCA AN, TATARU A, BUZOIANU AD, PINCELLI C, SOCACIU C. Pharmacological Benefits of Herbal Formulations in the Management of Psoriasis vulgaris. Notulae Botanicae Horti Agrobotanici Cluj-Napoca. 2014 Jun 3;42(1)

145 | Rice Water for Skin: Uses, Benefits and Efficacy [Internet]. Healthline. 2019. Available from: https://www.healthline.com/health/rice-water-for-skin#benefits

146 | Rice Water for Hair: Benefits and How to Use it [Internet]. www.medicalnewstoday.com. 2018. Available from: https://www.medicalnewstoday.com/articles/321353

147 | Malik I, Zarnigar. Aloe Vera: A Review Of Its Clinical Effectiveness. International Research Journal Of Pharmacy. 2013 Sep 9;4(8):75–9

148 | Ferreira EDS, Rosalen PL, Benso B, de Cássia Orlandi Sardi J, Denny C, Alves de Sousa S, et al. The Use of Essential Oils and Their Isolated Compounds for the Treatment of Oral Candidiasis: A Literature Review. Evidence-Based Complementary and Alternative Medicine: eCAM [Internet]. 2021 [cited 2022 Mar 17];2021:1059274. Available from: https://pubmed.ncbi.nlm.nih.gov/33505486/

149 | Prusinowska R, Śmigielski KB. Composition, biological properties and therapeutic effects of lavender (Lavandula angustifolia L). A review. Herba Polonica. 2014 Oct 2;60(2):56–66

150 | Chaudhuri RK, Bojanowski K. Bakuchiol: A Retinol-Like Functional Compound Revealed by Gene Expression Profiling and Clinically Proven to Have Anti-Aging Effects. International Journal of Cosmetic Science [Internet]. 2014 Jun 1;36(3):221–30. Available from: https://pubmed.ncbi.nlm.nih.gov/24471735/

151 | Kaplan D, Dosiou C. Two Cases of Graves' Hyperthyroidism Treated With Homeopathic Remedies Containing Herbal Extracts from Lycopus spp. and Melissa officinalis. Journal of the Endocrine Society. 2021 May 1;5(Supplement_1):A971–1

152 | Grant P. Spearmint Herbal Tea has Significant Anti-Androgen Efects in Polycystic Ovarian Syndrome. A Randomized Controlled Trial. Phytotherapy Research : PTR [Internet]. 2010;24(2):186–8. Available from: https://www.ncbi.nlm.nih.gov/pubmed/19585478

153 | Esmaeil Bandariyan, Asghar Mogheiseh, Ahmadi A. The Effect of Lutein And Urtica Dioica Extract on in Vitro Production of Embryo and Oxidative Status in Polycystic Ovary

Syndrome BMC Complementary Medicine And Therapies. 2021 Feb 8;21(1)

154 | Arablou T, Aryaeian N, Valizadeh M, Sharifi F, Hosseini A, Djalali M. The Effect of Ginger Consumption on Glycemic Status, Lipid Profile and Some Inflammatory Markers in Patients with Type 2 Diabetes Mellitus. International Journal of Food Sciences and Nutrition. 2014 Feb 4;65(4):515–20

155 | Cerqueira RO, Frey BN, Leclerc E, Brietzke E. Vitex agnus castus for Premenstrual Syndrome and Premenstrual Dysphoric Disorder: A Systematic Review. Archives of Women's Mental Health. 2017 Oct 23;20(6):713–9

156 | Verkaik S, Kamperman AM, van Westrhenen R, Schulte PFJ. The Treatment of Premenstrual Syndrome with Preparations of Vitex agnus castus: A Systematic Review and Meta-analysis. American Journal of Obstetrics and Gynecology. 2017 Aug;217(2):150–66

157 | Vitex Agnus-Castus - an overview | ScienceDirect Topics [Internet]. www.sciencedirect.com. Available from: https://www.sciencedirect.com/topics/medicine-and-dentistry/vitex-agnus-castus

158 | What Is Chasteberry, and What Can It Do? [Internet]. Cleveland Clinic. Available from: https://health.clevelandclinic.org/chasteberry-benefits-and-risks

159 | Geller SE, Studee L. Botanical and Dietary Supplements for Menopausal Symptoms: What Works, What Does Not. Journal of Women's Health [Internet]. 2005 Sep;14(7):634–49. Available from: https://www.ncbi.nlm.nih.gov/pmc/articles/PMC1764641/

160 | van de Weijer PHM, Barentsen R. Isoflavones from Red Clover (Promensil®) Significantly Reduce Menopausal Hot Flush Symptoms Compared with Placebo. Maturitas. 2002 Jul;42(3):187–93

161 | Sun W, Shahrajabian MH, Cheng Q. Anise (pimpinella anisum l.), a Dominant Spice and Traditional Medicinal Herb for Both Food and Medicinal Purposes. Sabatini S, editor. Cogent Biology. 2019 Sep 30;0(0)

162 | Estrada-Reyes R, Ortiz-López P, Gutiérrez-Ortíz J, Martínez-Mota L. Turnera diffusa Wild (Turneraceae) Recovers Sexual Behavior in Sexually Exhausted Males. Journal of Ethnopharmacology [Internet]. 2009 Jun 25 [cited 2021 Jun 30];123(3):423–9. Available from: http://www.ncbi.nlm.nih.gov/pubmed/19501274

163 | Gonzales GF. Ethnobiology and Ethnopharmacology of Lepidium meyenii(Maca), a Plant from the Peruvian Highlands. Evidence-Based Complementary and Alternative Medicine [Internet]. 2012;2012:1–10. Available from: https://www.ncbi.nlm.nih.gov/pmc/articles/PMC3184420/

164 | Manouchehri A, Abbaszadeh S, Ahmadi M, Nejad FK, Bahmani M, Dastyar N. Polycystic Ovaries and Herbal Remedies: A Systematic Review. JBRA Assisted Reproduction. 2022

165 | Haroon Elrasheid Tahir, Gustav Komla Mahunu, Abdalbasit Adam Mariod, Zou X, Newlove Akowuah Afoakwah. Biological Activities of Evening Primrose Oil. 2022 Jan 1;317–32.

166 | Wilt, T. J., et al. (1998). Saw Palmetto Extracts for Treatment of Benign Prostatic Hyperplasia: A Systematic Review. JAMA, 280(18), 1604-1609

167 | Rossi A, Mari E, Scarnò M, Garelli V, Maxia C, Scali E, et al. Comparitive Effectiveness and Finasteride Vs Serenoa Repens in Male Androgenetic Alopecia: A Two-Year Study. International Journal of Immunopathology and Pharmacology. 2012 Oct;25(4):1167–73

168 | Lin HH, Chen JH, Wang CJ. Chemopreventive Properties and Molecular Mechanisms of the Bioactive Compounds in Hibiscus Sabdariffa Linne. Current Medicinal Chemistry. 2011 Mar 1;18(8):1245–54

169 | Kreydiyyeh SI, Usta J. Diuretic Effect and Mechanism of Action of Parsley. Journal of Ethnopharmacology [Internet]. 2002 Mar 1 [cited 2020 Aug 31];79(3):353–7. Available from: https://pubmed.ncbi.nlm.nih.gov/11849841/

170 | Koetter U, Schrader E, Käufeler R, Brattström A. A Randomized, Double Blind, Placebo-Controlled, Prospective Clinical Study To Demonstrate Clinical Efficacy of A Fixed Valerian Hops Extract Combination (Ze 91019) in Patients Suffering From Non-Organic Sleep Disorder. Phytotherapy Research. 2007;21(9):847–51

171 | Shams. Efficacy of Black Cohosh-Containing Preparations on Menopausal Symptoms: A Meta-Analysis. Alternative Therapies in Health and Medicine [Internet]. 2015;16(1). Available from: https://pubmed.ncbi.nlm.nih.gov/20085176/

172 | Bazzano AN, Hofer R, Thibeau S, Gillispie V, Jacobs M, Theall KP. A Review of Herbal and Pharmaceutical Galactagogues for Breast-Feeding. The Ochsner Journal [Internet]. 2016;16(4):511–24. Available from: https://www.ncbi.nlm.nih.gov/pmc/articles/PMC5158159/

173 | Chrubasik S, Eisenberg E, Balan E, Weinberger T, Luzzati R, Conradt C. Treatment of Low Back Pain Exacerbations With Willow Bark Extract: a Randomized Double-Blind Study. The American Journal of Medicine [Internet]. 2000 Jul 28;109(1):9–14. Available from: https://www.amjmed.com/article/S0002-9343(00)00442-3/abstract

174 | Khan, M. F., & Abul Kalam Azad, M. (2019). Mosquito Repellent Activity of Essential Oils of Lemongrass (Cymbopogon citratus), Mint (Mentha piperita), and Basil (Ocimum basilicum) in a Vegetable-Based Repellent. Journal of Arthropod-Borne Diseases, 13(3), 258–273. PMID: 31934461

175 | Maia, M. F., & Moore, S. J. (2011). Plant-Based Insect Repellents: a Review of Their Efficacy, Development and Testing. Malaria Journal, 10(Suppl 1), S11. DOI: 10.1186/1475-2875-10-S1-S11

176 | Pazyar N, Yaghoobi R, Bagherani N, Kazerouni A. A Review of Applications of Tea Tree Oil in Dermatology. International Journal of Dermatology. 2012 Sep 24;52(7):784–90

177 | Vaughn AR, Clark AK, Sivamani RK, Shi VY. Natural Oils for Skin-Barrier Repair: Ancient Compounds Now Backed by Modern Science. American Journal of Clinical Dermatology. 2017 Jul 13;19(1):103–17

178 | Kshirsagar MM, Dodamani AS, Karibasappa GN, Vishwakarma PK, Vathar JB, Sonawane KR, et al. Antibacterial Activity of Garlic Extract on Cariogenic Bacteria: An in Vitro Study. AYU (An international quarterly journal of research in Ayurveda) [Internet]. 2018;39(3):165. Available from: https://www.ncbi.nlm.nih.gov/pmc/articles/PMC6454914/

179 | Lopresti AL. Salvia (Sage): A Review of its Potential Cognitive-Enhancing and Protective Effects. Drugs in R&D [Internet]. 2016 Nov 25;17(1):53–64. Available from: https://www.ncbi.nlm.nih.gov/pmc/articles/PMC5318325/

180 | Agar: Uses, Side Effects, Interactions, Dosage, and Warning [Internet]. www.webmd.com. Available from: https://www.webmd.com/vitamins/ai/ingredientmono-80/agar

181 | Healthy LB. Unlocking Thyroid Health: Discover the Best Castor Oil for Thyroid [Internet]. Medium. 2023 [cited 2024 Mar 19]. Available from: https://medium.com/(LivingBeautifullyHealthy/unlocking-thyroid-health-discover-the-best-castor-oil-for-thyroid-6fe99ad442e0

182 | NHS. Herbal Medicines [Internet]. NHS. 2022. Available from: https://www.nhs.uk/conditions/herbal-medicines/

183 | Aronson JK, Leopold Meyler. Meyler's Side Effects of Drugs: The International Encyclopedia of Adverse Drug Reactions And Interactions. Amsterdam: Elsevier Science; 2016

184 | Risk of Drug Interactions With St John's Wort. JAMA. 2000 Apr 5;283(13):1679

185 | Bove M. An Encyclopedia of Natural Healing for Children And Infants. Chicago: Keats Pub; 2001

186 | Balch PA. Prescription For Nutritional Healing : A Practical A-To-Z Reference To Drug-Free Remedies Using Vitamins, Minerals, Herbs & Food Supplements. London: Penguin; 2011

187 | Brinker FJ. Herbal Contraindications And Drug Interactions Plus Herbal Adjuncts With Medicines. Sandy, Or: Eclectic Medical Publications; 2010.

188 | Foster S, Johnson RL, National Geographic Society (U.S. Desk reference to nature's medicine. Washington, D.C.: National Geographic; 2008

189 | WholisticMatters. Herbs for Children - Safe Dosing and Indications [Internet]. WholisticMatters. 2020 [cited 2024 Jan 19]. Available from: https://wholisticmatters.com/herbs-for-children/